THE FONTANA ECONOMIC HISTORY OF EUROPE

General Editor: Carlo M. Cipolla

There is at present no satisfactory economic history of
Europe – covering Europe both as a whole and with
particular relation to the individual countries – that is
both concise enough for convenient use and yet full
enough to include the results of individual and detailed
scholarship. This series is designed to fill that gap.

Unlike most current works in this field the *Fontana
Economic History of Europe* does not end at the outbreak
of the First World War. More than half a century has
elapsed since 1914, a half-century that has transformed
the economic background of Europe. In recognition
of this the present work has set its terminal date at
1970 and provides for sixty contributions each written
by a specialist.

The Fontana
Economic History of Europe
Volume 4

The Emergence of Industrial Societies PART ONE

Editor Carlo M. Cipolla

Harvester Press/Barnes & Noble
In association with Fontana Books

This edition first published in 1976 by
THE HARVESTER PRESS LIMITED
Publisher: John Spiers
2 Stanford Terrace
Hassocks, Nr Brighton
Sussex, England
and published in the U.S.A. 1976 by
HARPER & ROW PUBLISHERS, INC.
BARNES & NOBLE IMPORT DIVISION
10 East 53rd Street, New York 10022

The Emergence of Industrial Societies — Part One
This edition first published in 1976
by The Harvester Press Limited
and by Barnes & Noble
in association with Fontana

First published in paperback in 1973
by Fontana Books

The Harvester Press Limited
ISBN 0 85527 274 0

Barnes & Noble
ISBN 0-06-492179-4

Typesetting by Wm. Collins Sons & Co. Ltd.
London and Glasgow
Printed in Great Britain by Redwood Burn Limited
Trowbridge, Wiltshire
Bound by Cedric Chivers Limited, Portway, Bath

Contents

1. The Industrial Revolution in France 1700–1914

Claude Fohlen

THE SCOPE OF THE PROBLEM

The expression 'Industrial Revolution', which made its appearance in the first third of the nineteenth century and has since then been widely used by economists and historians, covers without discrimination, in all countries, the phase of economic development in which the period of agricultural predominance gives way to industrial predominance. The habit has arisen of speaking of an industrial revolution in England, which was imitated, in the course of the nineteenth century, in the great countries of the European continent, France, Prussia, Piedmont, Austria-Hungary and Russia, before being exported to other continents, to the United States and Japan. The same expression is used nowadays to describe the transition from what is now called under-development, characteristic of former colonial territories, to the economic independence which should go together with political independence. Finally, Marxist terminology has ensured the success of the expression by making it, implicitly or otherwise, the criterion of transition from a society described as 'feudal' to a 'bourgeois' or even a 'proletarian' classless society. This is equivalent to saying that bourgeois society can only exist insofar as it is industrialised, a theory disproved by the history of medieval urban societies or even of certain societies based on landed property.

The problem is further complicated by certain contemporary transformations. Historians, often working backwards from the *fait accompli*, have allowed themselves to be dominated by the idea of a phenomenon which is finalised and limited in time. At the present time, we can better realise the incorrectness of such a preconceived idea, because the industrial revolution is in fact a continuing phenomenon which is going on in front of our eyes in countries which have already in the past experienced a profound industrial mutation. The industrial revolution is basically a revolution of coal, steel and cotton. But it is also the revolution of electricity and of the internal combustion engine, of the atomic reactor and of the interplanetary rockets. Does not the conquest of the moon seem as important as the invention of the steam-engine? Is it not the generating force behind industrial transformations even more profound than those we have hitherto experienced? We must recognise that the process once launched knows no limits and that the revolution is rather a series of revolutions, even if the phrase thereby runs the risk of losing its original meaning. And we may well ask which in this series of revolutions is the proper one.

If there is a certain ambiguity about the phrase 'Industrial Revolution', this is particularly true of France. First of all because this revolution was not original, being in large part imported from England and imitated from there, in accordance with a process general to western Europe. This is not to underestimate the originality of French inventions such as Jacquard's loom, Thimonnier's sewing-machine, Berthollet's chlorine-bleacher or Philippe de Girard's flax-spinner. But it must be admitted that the basic technique is of English inspiration, for example, Watt's steam-engine, spindles, the iron forges exactly described as 'in the English style', puddling. The spontaneity associated with a revolution cannot be found in France, because the prototype was derived from abroad. France was very largely inspired by what had been achieved across the Channel as is proved, at the end of the eighteenth century, by the efforts of the French monarchy to attract English specialists such as Milne, Holker, Wilkinson and others or by the missions of French businessmen to England to try to penetrate the industrial secrets of the neighbouring country. The founder of the Belgian, and to some extent of the French, textile industry, Liévin Bauwens, went to England, under the protection of the Directory, in 1798 to bring back both machines and workers, and he was not the only person to do this. This explains why the first study devoted to the Industrial Revolution in France adopted a more modest title: 'The introduction of the machine system into French industry'.[1] Written, it is true, by an historian killed before the publication of his work, it was limited to the technical aspect of things, leaving on one side the financial, banking and demographic transformations which Paul Mantoux had emphasised in his study on England.

The only work devoted to the overall study of the problem, that of the American historian Louis Dunham, took as its title 'The Industrial Revolution' and limited it to the period 1815–1848. The change in chronology is characteristic: whilst in England the industrial revolution was considered a creation of the eighteenth century, the American historian fixed its limits in France as the first half of the following century with a certain number of restrictions, moreover, since he wrote: 'France in 1848 had developed far beyond the France of 1815, although few of the changes were sudden or dramatic.' And he adds, on the following page, 'The period from 1815 to 1848 marks in France the infancy and the beginning of the adolescence of the Industrial Revolution, but not its maturity, which was not attained until after 1860. In 1848 France was still largely agricultural. Mills were more numerous and larger and were coming to play a decisive part in most of the processes of the textile industry . . . But France in the Industrial Revolution, as in other things, retained her individuality and remained shrewdly realistic. She continued to use much wood because she had it, and she continued to use water power in preference to steam because she had it in abundance and could use it at far lower cost . . .'[2]

According to Dunham, the Industrial Revolution should be considered a late phenomenon — the middle of the nineteenth century — and of long duration — because not

1. Charles Ballot, *L'introduction du machinisme dans l'industrie française*, Paris, 1923.

2. Arthur Louis Dunham, *The Industrial Revolution in France (1815–1848)*, New York, 1955, pp. 432–433.

finally achieved until after 1848. Why, then, speak of an Industrial Revolution? It must be recognised, however, that in the light of contemporary developments, historians have a tendency to make the Industrial Revolution younger, that is to say, to bring it closer to the present time.

Dunham's uncertainties show the ambiguity of the question. That is why a younger generation has proposed to substitute the concept of a 'take-off' for that of industrial revolution. This is the theory put forward by Rostow in his 'Stages of Economic Growth'. His search for an overall explanation leads him to apply an identical scheme to every country: after a long period of agricultural preponderance the conditions favourable to a take-off are assembled, before the take-off itself, which is an essential phase of the transition to an industrial economy. For France, Rostow places this take-off between 1830 and 1860, thus reaching, by a different route, the same conclusions as Dunham. But this is as far as the two authors, whose methods and objects differ, go together. In Rostow's opinion a quantitative analysis enables, or should enable, us to isolate the take-off phase while Dunham's approach is exclusively qualitative: an analysis of production, of investments, of capital formation and, if possible, of the national revenue takes the place of an analysis of technical transformations, whose sum alone is not sufficient to explain economic changes. On the other hand, as Maurice Lévy-Leboyer has emphasised, 'the idea of industrial revolution pre-supposes that the historian is more interested in long-term problems, while a study of the take-off leads in general to the isolation of a period of twenty or thirty years in which production begins to grow in a decisive fashion'.[3] The idea of a medium-term analysis takes the place of a long-term analysis, without, however, making chronological delimitation any easier.

Rostow's attractive hypothesis has also led to studies intended to examine the merits of his claim. These have been

3. Maurice Lévy-Leboyer, La croissance économique en France au XIXe siècle. Resultats préliminaires, *Annales* (Economies, Sociétés, Civilisations), July-August, p. 788

undertaken by the I.S.E.A. (Institute of Applied Economic Sciences — *Institut des Sciences Economiques Appliquées*), inspired by Jean Marczewski, who had resumed in 1956 the work begun by François Perroux in the wake of Simon Kuznets. The initial object of the enterprise consisted of establishing, for France, a continuous series of statistics since the eighteenth century in the fields of production, exchanges and incomes. This work is far from being finished[4] but, as things are at present, there are sufficient statistics to draw conclusions with regard to the take-off hypothesis. A first group of conclusions was presented in 1961 in *Economic Development and Cultural Change*,[5] by Jean Marczewski:

'. . . Since the beginning of the eighteenth century, the economic growth of France has been following a continuously rising curve, with some alternative periods of acceleration and deceleration. The years 1830–60, which were recently designed as a "take-off" period, are by no means unique from this point of view. It may also be shown that several epochs of brilliant expansion and severe decline were necessary during the earlier period to forge the particular set of conditions that prepared the industrial revolution of the last two centuries. As for some other old countries of western Europe, the economic growth of France is determined by a succession of progressive and declining forces, whose effects have been building up for many centuries without any discernible "beginning".'

According to Marczewski's reckoning, the rate of industrial growth is on an appreciably lower level than that of other countries where it has attained or often exceeded 8 per cent per annum. In the peak industrial sectors a first maximum is reached, between 1830 and 1840, with a growth rate of 5.6 per cent, and a second between 1890 and 1900 with a rate of 6.9 per cent, which in conjunction with

4. Histoire quantitative de l'Economie française, dans *Cahiers de l'I.S.E.A.* 9 vol.

5. Jean Marczewski, Some aspects of the economic growth of France, 1660–1958, in *Economic Development and Cultural Change*, Vol. 9, Part II, 1961, pp. 369–386.

the rest of the industrial sector gives a rate of 3.5 per cent for the first period and an approximately similar rate for the second. Furthermore, Marczewski emphasises that there has not been one dominant sector, but a succession of sectors depending on the different periods: cotton at the beginning of the nineteenth century, wool at the end of the same century, silk between 1800 and 1850, coal between 1786 and 1810, metals between 1830 and 1910, chemicals in the last forty years of the nineteenth century. Of these sectors, whose influences often overlap, it is difficult to say which has provided an overall impulse to the economy as a whole.

In these circumstances Marczewski recognises that nothing in the gradual development of the French economy either validates or invalidates Rostow's hypothesis.

'Rostow says that the take-off in France began in 1830 and was essentially due to railway construction. My answer is that there was no true take-off in France at all; the growth of the French economy was very gradual and its origins lie far in the past. In any case, even if one insists on giving the name of take-off to the acceleration characteristic of the period of industrialisation, this take-off began as early as 1800 or thereabouts — or even . . . around 1750.'[6]

And at the end of the same essay:

'. . . If (a) precise phase of economic development is to be called take-off, then the take-off in France occurred around the middle of the eighteenth century or, at the latest, towards 1799. Personally, I am inclined to choose the earlier date, because the share of industry in physical product actually began to increase steadily from 1715–20 onwards. The French take-off would thus have come very soon after the English take-off. But, for a number of historical reasons, the most important of which no doubt resides in the two countries' different agricultural structure, industrialisation proceeded much more slowly in France and within narrower limits than was the case in England.'[7]

6. Jean Marczewski, The take-off hypothesis and French Experience, in W. W. Rostow, *The Economics of take-off into sustained growth*, New York, 1963, p. 129.
7. *Id. ibid.*, p. 138.

To the different reasons put forward to explain the specific way in which industrial growth occurred in France, Marczewski could simply have added political development: as we shall see later, the revolutionary wars, a factor of expansion in England, because England possessed mastery of the sea, imposed a brake on France, deprived of sources of supply and deprived of the opportunity of following the technical advances of its powerful neighbour.

What is clear is that the hypothesis of the take-off in no way casts light on the phenomenon of the Industrial Revolution in France and that the ambiguity of this historical phrase appears more clearly than before. We can, of course, use the lack of adequate statistics and tables derived from them to explain these difficulties. But these two questions should definitely be separated. The first statisticians worthy of the name appeared in France in the eighteenth century, with Messance and Boulainvilliers, their research going hand-in-hand with the rationalist spirit of their age. The French Revolution encouraged this type of research by the creation of the Commission of Agriculture and Arts. François de Neufchâteau provided a stimulant under the Directory. In the Year VIII, Chaptal created the Statistical Office of the Republic, attached to the Ministry of the Interior. This office was closed down in 1811, but industrial statistics were made the responsibility of the Ministry of Manufactures created in the same year. Meanwhile, drawing the lessons of the first attempts made under the Revolution, the Government had decided to institute five-yearly censuses. The first took place in 1801 and the five-yearly interval has been maintained except during wars and as a result of very recent modifications. The Restoration dismantled the statistical services as a legacy of the hated Empire and their re-establishment was only decided on in 1833, under various names, as a result of a decision by Thiers, at that time Minister of the Interior. Finally, in 1840, the General Statistical Office of France was created which, under different names, has continued the census work right up to the present time. The tables worked out by this administration go back to different dates, depending on different sectors. The oldest are, of course, those for the population, although their accuracy is only approximate, at least for the first censuses which were made very unmethodically. Next to appear were statistics of bill-receipts, monetary circulation and current accounts recorded by the Bank of France since 1807. The figures for production, the most important in our field, have been put together at different times: coal and combustible minerals since 1811 (following the law governing mines of 1810 thanks to the work of the 'Ingénieurs des Mines', a state body), corn and potatoes since 1815, cast-iron and iron since 1824, iron and salt mines since 1835, steam-engines since 1839, fodder, flax, hemp and sugar since 1840. For overseas trade the first precise figures are available from 1827. Finally, the French statistical office set up a national index of wholesale and retail prices from 1820 onwards.

Thus the economic historian is relatively well provided for with respect to the nineteenth century, though comparisons are sometimes made difficult by the divergences between different tables. In general, there are no difficulties in the way of statistical analysis after 1848, but prior to this we are in the realm of conjecture and hypothesis. In a series of publications the Institute of Applied Economic Studies has attempted to work backwards by drawing up tables for the eighteenth century based on isolated figures of private statisticians. In this way in particular series have been reconstructed both for agricultural and textile production. These efforts are certainly praiseworthy but, at best, they are only conjectures which must be used with caution, solidly based though they may be. Furthermore, the Institute of Applied Economic Studies tables are based on a five-yearly average, the only method compatible with the extent of the work undertaken, which covers more than two centuries of economic evolution. This method has the disadvantage of diminishing the way in which the tables can reflect small movements and of making more difficult the discovery of breaks in the rate growth, whether they be accelerations or checks. The overwhelming advantage is that the eighteenth century is brought in again despite the reserves just expressed.

Very recently, two other historians have undertaken the construction of statistical tables, doubtless less long and complete, but more responsive to significant detail. One set is by Maurice Lévy-Leboyer,[8] the other by François Crouzet.[9] Both make use, in general, of the same sources as Marczewski-Markovitch, that is to say, the publications of the French statistical office, with additional material for tables poorly represented in the latter, such as home production of wool or raw flax. Both present their results year by year, starting from an almost identical date, 1809 in the first case, 1815 in the second, and ending together at 1913. This pre-supposes that the phenomena studied, in this case the industrial revolution, took place in the nineteenth century.

What differentiates the endeavours of Lévy-Leboyer and of Crouzet is the number of tables and their balance. The first has collected a small number of tables: three for agriculture, five for industry, together with one for building and two for foreign commerce. In each of these tables the elements have been weighted according to a very flexible system varying according to the period dealt with. The figures worked out by Crouzet exclude agriculture but present a large number of tables for industry: mines, primary smelting, transformation of metals, chemicals, food production, the textile industry (with several tables, dealing with a different range of manufactures). Here again the figures given are based on a very flexible system of weighting. The author recognises that a wide range of manufactures are not represented for lack of sufficiently reliable data: glass and ceramics, industrial fats, paper and publishing, clothing and clothing manufacture, timber. Some of the sectors omitted are without doubt important, although all the basic sectors are represented.

8. Maurice Lévy-Leboyer, *art. cit. passim.*

9. François Crouzet Essai de construction d'un indice annuel de la production industrielle française au XIXe siècle. *Annales*, E.S.C., 1970, 1, pp. 56-99.

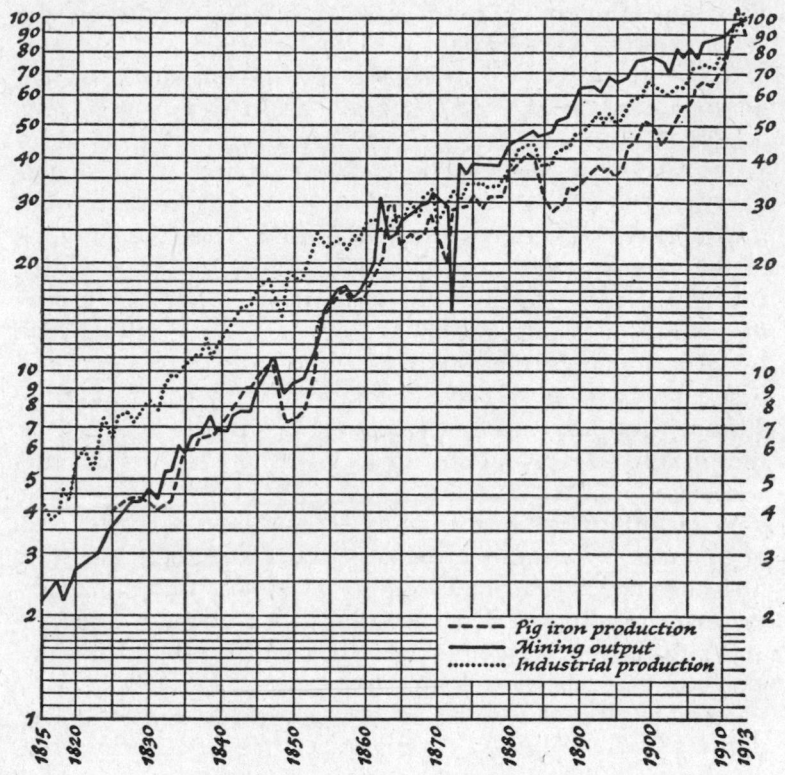

Economic Growth 1815-1913 showing Pig Iron Production, Mining Output and Industrial Production after F. Crouzet.

The economic historian now has an impressive battery of tables covering a long period of time. The enormous progress made in France in the last decade and the new possibilities thereby opened up, as well as the overall conclusions which can be drawn, must be recognised with some satisfaction.

Both historians share a common lack of certainty about the exact date of the take-off and of an industrial revolution. In Lévy-Leboyer's view, 'the French economy in the nineteenth century is dominated by the progress of industry, which finishes by carrying with it the whole range of activities. The relative decline of agriculture did not handicap the economy, but at the end of the century a new market was created in the towns to such an extent that "urbanisation gave the economy its second wind".' He shares Marczewski's conclusions about the absence of a take-off which he says he cannot find in France, 'because industrialisation was based on two opposing structures: at first the traditional rural markets, brought together by the railway system, but after 1880 the urban markets attracting towards themselves the population of the countryside'. A relatively well-balanced expansion characterised the evolution of the French economy in the nineteenth century. In Crouzet's view, it is difficult to lay down the law about the period before the thirties because of the very approximate nature of the figures available. Industrial growth appears to be relatively slow, varying between 1.6 per cent and 3 per cent per annum according to the figures made use of (these in turn depending both on the industries included and their weighting). In his view, the most intensive period of industrialisation is achieved under the authoritarian Empire (1850–1860), but it overlaps the period of the end of the July Monarchy and the beginning of the Third Republic. In general, it is a question of the period 1845–1875, which coincides with Dunham's conclusions and confirms the inexactitude of the title given to his work by the latter. A tendency towards stagnation can be seen in the last quarter of the nineteenth century, with a vigorous revival at the beginning of the twentieth century, although this revival can in no way be considered as an industrial revolution.

The three authors who have studied the problem have given three different answers. The most cautious, Lévy-Leboyer, recognises nothing which can be compared to a take-off. Marczewski, after having emphasised the regularity of growth, has a tendency to place the take-off back in the eighteenth century. This view is opposed to the results obtained by Crouzet who, without using the word take-off, puts the critical period in the middle of the nineteenth century. He had, moreover, answered Marczewski in a previous article in which he compared the economic evolution of France and England in the eighteenth century.[10] While recognising the very real progress accomplished during this century, he recognised that favourable conditions for the birth of an industrial revolution were not fulfilled in France despite a resemblance between the two countries. 'In England conditions were more favourable to technical progress than in France.' In the former the critical point, that is to say, the overall conditions necessary for the phenomenon to occur, was reached by the middle of the eighteenth century, which was not the case for France, 'and that is why she did not achieve her industrial revolution spontaneously'. At that period the gap between the two neighbours was limited to only a few things, but it was seriously worsened by the troubles of the revolutionary and imperial period. Once these had ended the gap had become unbridgeable.

This long discussion has shown the difficulties of a precise definition and dating of the industrial revolution. If recent research has made it possible to enumerate and quantify economic phenomena, it has nevertheless not shed light on the phenomenon at the centre of this discussion. Side by side with quantative data, we must look at qualitative elements and the national environment.

The historical environment of the Industrial Revolution in France appears to be dominated by three non-economic factors: political evolution, the level of education, demographic changes.

The political evolution worked against the full development of a phenomenon which had shown itself in the eighteenth century with the adoption of machines which had come from England and the interest shown by the monarchy in the industrialisation of the country. It is worth recalling that the imitators of the Industrial Revolution, like Holker, Milne and Wilkinson, were attracted and protected by the Controllers-General and that only a short

10. François Crouzet, Angleterre et France au XVIIIe siècle: essai d'analyse comparée de deux croissances économiques, *Annales* (Economies, Sociétés, Civilisations), March-April 1966, pp. 254–291.

time before the Revolution Calonne took a personal interest in the foundation of Creusot's foundries, while following closely Wilkinson's experiments at Indret. During the last years of the Ancien Régime, a French-style variation of Enlightened Despotism developed, paying special attention to the economy. At that time the government sought to develop the country by all possible means with a dual method, state aid and the suppression of every obstacle to individual activities. From this preoccupation follow on the measures undertaken by Turgot in favour, on the one hand, of the suppression of guilds and corporations, and on the other, of free circulation of grain. Thus, for a short while, could be found the clearly-defined outline of a liberal economic régime animated by state-impulse. But the Turgot experiment lasted only a short time and Calonne's, which resembled it, encountered a more active opposition. These successive checks did not prevent very active efforts in favour of industrialisation, in particular, for textiles, under the double impulse of English competition in foreign markets and the importance of colonial commerce in particular in the 'isles', that is to say, the Antilles. The Anglo-French Commercial Treaty of 1786 should, according to the idea of its promoters, have further stimulated this competition and incited the French producers to follow the industrial pattern of England.

There was indeed, in the second half of the eighteenth century, as Marczewski asserts, a very widespread industrial transformation, though this is hard to measure.

The outbreak of the Revolution interrupted the first phase of industrialisation, in spite of the fact that its supporters were business people, industrialists, large property-owners, all of whom favoured a liberal economic régime. In fact, the Revolution and the Empire were caught in a dilemma which they never succeeded in surmounting. The liberalisation of individual activities was legally favoured by a series of well-known measures like Allarde's decree which suppressed the vestiges of the old corporate system, the Le Chapelier law which prohibited commercial groupings, and later on the Civil Code, which protected the

initiative of the individual, strengthened the rights of
property and legalised the advances made by the bourgeoisie. The Imperial Codes were aimed in the same direction,
whether it is a question of the Penal Code or the Commercial
Code. But as against this positive side, important though it
is, of which historians have been very aware the negative
side greatly predominates. First of all, there was the loss of
overseas markets, colonies like Santo Domingo, or commercial outlets which France had patiently secured in the
course of the eighteenth century (the United States, among
others) as well as the cutting-off of sources of supply, as a
result of the blockade, which was more or less effective after
1793, and of the elimination of the French ocean-going
fleet. British superiority was thereby reinforced and our
competitors were able to develop all their advantages while
France's position weakened. What was fatal and irreversible
was the total loss of her colonial empire. Cut off from the
world outside, France also lost contact with technical progress. The encouragements given by a François de Neufchâteau or a Napoleon could not compensate for the
enormous losses stemming from the break with other
countries and the creation of a continental market could not
compensate for the coastal blockade. The shortages caused
by this blockade doubtless provided the search for replacements, but here again the negative outweighed the positive,
as in all periods of war. Finally, the priority given to the
external struggle relegated to second place the more pacific
problems of the economy where these were not closely tied
in with the struggle. And so, if France developed institutions
which were going to allow the spread of modern industrial capitalism, she also developed backwardness at the
same time. 'The "national catastrophe" for the French economy represented by the Revolution and twenty years of
war increased this backwardness and made it irremediable.'[11]

It is true that after 1815 France had a long period of
peace, beneficial to economic growth. The effects of

11. François Crouzet, *op. cit.*, p. 291.

revolutionary and imperial legislation beneficial to individualism, to the unification of the internal market and the development of private property could, in fact, be felt during these years. The State, for its part, favoured the development of means of transport, first roads and canals and then railways. What previous governments had not been able to accomplish because of war expenditure, the Restoration government and its successors gradually achieved. But the handicaps remained numerous and preoccupying. First of all, the recession which had piled up in previous years. Then the loss of continental markets, without any overseas compensation, because the colonial empire had been irretrievably lost. Finally, the rigorous protectionist régime introduced in 1816 could help the expansion of industry, provided that the producers did not take things too easily, as in fact they did. The absence of an external stimulant, in the form of English competition, too often led them to cling to out-of-date plant, to maintain high prices in a very protected market and to content themselves with the profits of the national market without taking the risks of commercial adventure. The stagnation of prices made industrial expansion less exciting and also less remunerative than before 1789. These general conditions changed only after 1850, as a result of the general improvement of circumstances in every country and the coming to power of the government of Napoleon III, more favourable than its predecessors to the 'business community'. From 1850 to 1870 was the golden age of the businessmen who were disciples of Saint-Simon, such as the Péreires, ArlèsDufour, Talabot, F. de Lesseps . . . This explains why numerous authors have attributed to the Second Empire a determining role in the economic transformation of France.

Even under a liberal economic régime account must be taken of the political circumstances. However favourable the governments of the Revolution and the Empire may have shown themselves to be towards industrialists, they had to give priority to more urgent tasks, on which the safety of the country depended. The best conditions only prevailed after 1815, with slight variations according to the governments in power.

Anglo-Saxon economic historians have recently underlined the importance of educational expansion in the evolution of their countries. We can then ask what the position was in regard to France. This subject has been very little touched on by historians who have, moreover, often preferred an administrative history of education to the more delicate problem of the expansion of education among the masses.

The problem of education arises on two different levels: on the one hand, that of the masses for whom the essential is to read, write and add (the three R's — reading, writing, arithmetic), and on the other that of those in charge of undertakings who needed, in addition, technical knowledge.

Our knowledge about the end of the Ancien Régime is very shadowy. According to certain studies carried out in the last century by Louis Maggiolo[12] and some more recent research, the educational effort was greater in the eastern provinces (Lorraine, Franche-Comté, Burgundy, Alsace) than elsewhere and was carried further with men than with women, as is shown by the disparity among spouses of those able to sign their marriage certificates. For obvious reasons the towns had a more favourable record than the countryside. For lack of financial resources the Revolution could do nothing for primary education despite very novel plans like that of Lakanal. Napoleon's government paid no attention to this problem and limited itself to the training of future officers and state officials. At the end of the Restoration, Baron Dupin asserted that in this field France was far behind its neighbours, England, Switzerland, Holland, Prussia and Tuscany, and put it on the same level as back-

---

12. Cf. R. P. de Dainville, Effectifs des collèges et scolarité aux XVIIe et XVIIIe siècles dans le Nord-Est de la France, *Population*, 1955, No. 3, pp. 455–488.

Michel Fleury et Pierre Valmary, Le Progrès de l'instruction élémentaire de Louis XIV à Napoléon III, d'après l'enquête de Louis Maggiolo (1877–1879), *Population*, 1957, No. 1, pp. 71–92, with a discussion of the method used by Maggiolo.

ward countries like Russia, Spain and the Kingdom of Naples.[13] Out of about 40,000 communes more than 15,000 had absolutely no schoolmasters. Above all, he deplored the absence of elementary technical schools where future workers could learn the rudiments of arithmetic, geometry, mechanics and the 'whole range of arts of which human industry is composed'. At the same period, again according to Dupin, out of twenty-five million adults only ten million could read and write. Recruiting documents show that at that time 58 per cent of recruits were illiterate,[14] but these figures, of course, only cover a minority of the male population.

After 1835 the situation steadily got better, that is to say, that the number of illiterates steadily declined. It still represented 36 per cent of army recruits in 1847, 23 per cent in 1867 and 15 per cent in 1877. But the distribution of education remained very unequal between the regions, the most favoured being the north-east within a triangle whose points were situated at Geneva, Mézières (Ardennes) and a little to the east of Paris. And it was not necessarily the most urbanised provinces that were the most favoured: Doubs, Meuse, Jura, Bas-Rhin, Haut-Rhin, Haute-Marne, Vosges within the old provinces of Lorraine, Champagne, Alsace and Franche-Comté. The regions with the lowest rate of school attendance were Brittany, Berry, Limousin and Bourbonnais. Was this just a coincidence? The regions with the best educational record were also those which contributed most to industrialisation, and it is symbolic to count Britanny as the most 'ignorant'. The question remains: does lack of education explain the non-industrialisation of these regions or is it the result?

At the level of those in charge of undertaking, the spread of technical education took place earlier, as an excellent

13. Baron Charles Dupin, *Forces productives et commerciales de la France*, Paris, 1827, v. I, pp. 51–53.
14. *Id. ibid*, p. 55. On the whole of this question it is worth consulting
(i) the various reports and statistics of the Ministry of Public Education and, in particular, the statistics for primary education;
(ii) the statistics drawn up by the War Ministry, referring to the educational level of Army recruits.

work by Frederick B. Artz has shown.[15] From the middle of
the eighteenth century onwards the royal government felt
it necessary to train specialists for its own purposes, the
Highways Department and the mines. The great technical
schools were, however, a creation of the Revolution, the
École polytechnique (which was soon diverted from its
original aim to provide the cadres of Napoleon's army), the
Conservatoire des Arts et Métiers, the Écoles d'Arts et
Métiers, which Baron Dupin thought the most useful in the
training of cadres for industry. The institution most in line
with his needs was the École Centrale des Arts et Manufactures, a private and belated (1829) foundation. These
different schools gave a technical education of high quality
and served as a model in other countries until the beginning
of the twentieth century, when they were eclipsed by the
German Technical High Schools.

It seems probable that the weak and slow spread of
elementary education was a handicap to industrialisation,
provided we can establish the link between this phenomenon
and the rural predominance of illiterates. It is more difficult
to say anything definite about the technical competence of
contractors for lack of studies on this subject. In the big
undertakings the higher cadres had received a training
adapted to their jobs, but given the family character of
French enterprises in the nineteenth century any generalisa-
tion would be rash. It is not even certain that the training
received was really adapted to the future jobs of the pupils
as Baron Dupin had already pointed out. 'In these schools
(Écoles d'Arts et Métiers) they should have given a preference to those skills which create and make perfect, in all
fields, motorised machinery and measuring instruments.
Pupils who would come out of these establishments, whether
they were to found their own workshops or whether they
worked in workshops already founded, would work together
powerfully for the increase of motorised machinery.
Instead of which, even in those schools intended to be most
practical, the teaching was too theoretical and formed a

15. Frederick B. Artz, *The Development of Technical Education in
France*, 1500–1850, Cambridge, Mass., 1966.

poor preparation for the handling of machinery.'[16]

All the authors who have studied the industrial revolution assign to the pressure of population a decisive role in the opening out of the secondary sector. They are, moreover, encouraged to do this by what is actually happening today in the so-called under-developed countries where investments are made with the object of finding work for the excess population driven out of the rural areas and without resources. In eighteenth-century England, which we always use as a back cloth, the increase in population from about five to eight million was considerable.

In the eighteenth century France had by far the largest population in Europe with the exception of Russia. It consisted of 18 million inhabitants at the beginning of the century and probably 25 million on the eve of the Revolution, an increase of about 40 per cent. The first official census, that of 1801, gives a population of 27 million, after which there is a noticeable increase in the first half of the nineteenth century, because there are 38 million inhabitants on the eve of the Franco-German war. Between 1865 and 1914, on the other hand, the population remained more or less constant in the region of 38/39 million, while that of other industrial countries continued to grow. In short, there are three stages: a rapid growth (but still little known about except on the local level) up to 1800, a more gradual increase from 1800 to 1850 and a long stagnation afterwards.

Overall figures are not enough to explain the reasons for the industrial revolution; we must consider the division between the rural and urban sectors. At the beginning of the nineteenth century only three cities, Paris, Lyons and Marseilles, had more than 100,000 inhabitants, while in 1851 two more, Bordeaux and Rouen, had reached these figures. Of these five cities only one, Lyons, could be called industrial, three others being ports with mercantile activities and some industrial manufactures, and Paris being the capital of an ultra-centralised state. The first census to draw a distinction between rural and urban population (on

16. Baron Ch. Dupin *op. cit. passim.*

a debatable basis since these communes considered urban were those in which the chief town had more than 2,000 inhabitants) was that of 1846. On this basis the urban population represented 25 per cent of the total against 75 per cent for the rural population. The decrease in rural population was slow and steady: 69 per cent in 1872, 59 per cent in 1901, 50 per cent in 1931. As against this the rate of growth of the urban population averaged 3 per cent over each period of five years, which is a small rate of increase. It follows that, all through the nineteenth century, France remained a rural country in contrast to Germany and England.

Was the fact that the bulk of the population lived in the country a handicap to industrialisation? Yes, to the extent that industrial entrepreneurs had only a limited labour market, as was frequently the case: the workers of Mulhouse often came from Baden or were Swiss, and those of Roubaix-Tourcoing were often Flemish. It seems that in the nineteenth century the urban labour force was scarcer than in certain foreign countries. As against this the same entrepreneurs had at their disposal a very numerous and far from demanding rural labour force. From this derived the idea of spreading manufactures into country districts, of putting work out on commission which was more flexible than work in large factories. A manufacturer or commission agent distributed the primary material for the work to homes, for example, the thread for weaving, and took the pieces of material when completed. This 'domestic system' was very largely followed in the French countryside all through the nineteenth century, and its vitality was a sign of the industrial revolution: the uneven technical development between successive stages of the same product, from raw material to finished product, created gaps, 'mechanical gaps', which had to be bridged by manual work. The way in which the French population was spread out favoured this way of working, so that the distinction between industrial and agricultural work is often artificial. This domestic system, related to the Koustarni of Russia, was practised in Flanders, in Picardy, in Normandy, in the Lyons region (silk) and in Brittany (making veils), to name only some of the best known.

After 1840–1850 this system of work at home declined and was limited to the most delicate operations which a machine could not accomplish. There were many reasons for this. First of all technical advances, in particular in connection with spinning which thenceforth made it possible to produce mechanically figured material and not simply plain material. This was true of the printed cotton material with check patterns which was a speciality of Normandy. The machine gradually took over and manual skill was used only for luxury articles like silks and materials of very high quality, and not for those intended for general use. Furthermore, as businessmen invested in factories they more and more wanted to amortise their equipment and for this reason gave work to their own workmen rather than to casual labour. Finally, a succession of economic crises in 1827, in 1831, in 1837 and in 1846–47 gradually wore away the system of work at home and led the rural labour force to seek more stable sources of income. This point has been well taken by Ch-H. Pouthas, who writes: 'The maintenance of rural prosperity was only possible because of the variety of sources and horizons of work represented by agricultural labour and rural industry . . . The crisis of 1848 resulted in the destruction of this rural industry and hence of the foundations of the countryman's prosperity.'[17]

But, as against this, the continued existence of a large rural population constituted, in the long run, a very severe handicap to the industrial revolution in France. Rural society provides a limited consumer market, since it has a tendency to live drawn in upon itself, especially when lack of communications do not afford outlets and sources of supply of sufficient extent. This seems to have been the case with France in the first half of the nineteenth century: there were roads, there were canals, but apart from the main highways the countryside remained shut off. It was the combination of railways and roads, after 1850, and perhaps

17. Charles-H. Pouthas, *La population française dans la première moitié du XIXe siècle*, Paris, 1956, p. 224.

only after 1870, which opened up those regions which the habits of centuries had obliged to live drawn in upon themselves. In the majority of cases, rural crafts sufficed for local needs, whether it was a case of tool-making, clothing, building and, to an even greater extent, food. The poverty of education in these remote areas further reduced curiosity and therefore needs. This allowed M. Lévy-Leboyer to write: 'Internal demand was never as great in France as in England. *Per capita* income has always been lower and inequality of income more marked. The unification of the French market took place late and was certainly not completed till the 1860s. As for the increase in the general mass of consumers, this remained moderate.'[18] Thus, despite a large population, the French market remained narrow and did not stimulate production as much as it might have done.

The state of agriculture largely explained why there was a substantial rural population up to the dawn of the twentieth century. In this respect France evolved in a quite different way to the other countries of western Europe.

In contrast to England, Germany, Italy and the Iberian peninsula, rural land was split up from the eighteenth century onwards between a large number of tenants who were in the process of becoming owners of the soil. The anti-aristocratic policy of the Monarchy had gradually led to the weakening of the dominant class and to their being held in check both politically and economically. Feudal rights had been undermined until the moment, on the eve of the Revolution, when the aristocracy had tried to react by reviving them. It was then too late, as the tenants of the soil considered themselves as *de facto* owners. The French Revolution, by suppressing these feudal rights, without compensation, transformed these *de facto* owners into *de jure* owners. Naturally there was a tendency in France, in the course of the eighteenth century, for large estates to be

18. Maurice Lévy-Leboyer, Les processus d'industrialisation: le cas de l'Angleterre et de la France, *Revue Historique*, fasc. 486, April-June 1968, p. 285.

joined together in the hand either of particularly enterprising aristocrats or of bourgeois who had made their
fortunes in commerce. But, as Marc Bloch has already
shown, this never happened in France on the scale that it
did in England because capital was more limited and
because of some resistance by the peasants who were
opposed to the edicts of enclosure issued in certain
districts. We can doubtless observe in Normandy, Picardy,
Flanders and the Ile-de-France the development of large
estates of the capitalist type, using a wage-earning labour
force. There was also, without any doubt, on the eve of the
Revolution, an aristocratic reaction whose object was to
revive old and abandoned usages advantageous to the land-
owner. It remains true, nevertheless, that the peasantry
were solidly established in the countryside although still
subject to many so-called feudal rights.

The French Revolution freed the peasants from the
burdens which weighed on them and made them pro-
prietors of the land which they were already cultivating as
tenants. Once feudal rights were abolished without compensation, these peasants found themselves in possession of
the land, a bond, if anything, stronger, since it was a
conquest they had long been working for. There remained
the problem of country people without land, what one may
call the proletariat of the countryside. Before the Revolution
there had existed a group of country people without land,
who lived either by earning wages from landowners employing labour or by the advantages derived in the French
countryside from collective rights such as common land
and pasturage and the right to cut firewood. This proletariat
did not gain from the changes of the French Revolution
since it did not receive lands because it did not occupy
them. Certain collective rights were suppressed and it was
too poor to buy the land put up for sale after the nationalisation of the Church lands and the dispossession of the
émigrés. Did they have to leave the countryside for the
towns, as in England, where they could have provided the
labour force for new industries? Nothing is less certain
since this exodus, if it happened, has left no trace in the

records of the past and because, above all, the need for a wage-earning force increased in the countryside: those who bought state lands were often 'bourgeois' who wanted it cultivated by farm labourers.

Thus the French Revolution and the legislation it established, especially the different Napoleonic codes, strengthened and stabilised a peasantry more firmly attached than ever to the land it had coveted for centuries. We can understand why the rural exodus happened on so small a scale in the nineteenth century, why there was no reserve labour force on which employers could draw to satisfy the needs of their new-born industries, and finally why French society in the nineteenth century was so remarkably conservative despite political revolutions which were more frequent than anywhere else.

This rigidity of rural society was intensified by the economic conditions of French agriculture in the course of the nineteenth century. Almost entirely sheltered from foreign competition by very high tariff barriers, it existed in a vacuum, preserving out-of-date methods of production and an anachronistic society. This situation developed during the years 1815 to 1845, during which landowners succeeded in imposing a sliding scale which safeguarded the growth of cereals and from 1875 to 1895, when a wave of protectionism (the Meline tariffs) saved the peasantry from the competition of overseas markets. Thanks to these artificial conditions, the rural world was able to keep its structure and numbers right up to the end of the nineteenth century, but at the same time it deprived industry of outlets and manpower. The only palliative was the preservation of rural industries, of the 'home industry' type, to give some support to a population too numerous for its resources. The French countryside has known periods of congestion and difficulties as, for example, in the period around 1840, but the balance then existing between the primary and secondary sectors put a brake on the exodus of the population towards the towns.

Finally, French rural society throughout the nineteenth century was prosperous, doubtless relatively so in certain regions and certain periods, in contrast with other western countries. Why should it have given way to an industrialisation which was in no way forced on it from the moment that there was no external pressure or necessity? Agricultural prosperity largely explains the weak and late industrial development as well as the brutal awakening of the twentieth century. The French Revolution fixed society and the economy in such a way as to do the greatest damage to industrialisation.

Thus we can define the factors imposing a brake on the French economy and explain the way in which the industrial revolution got out of step.

The accumulation of capital and its injection into the economy is one of the conditions necessary to the blossoming of an industrial revolution. Thus it must be certain that the profit derived will equal or surpass that from other sources such as agriculture.

Capital can be derived from the yield of land, but much more from commerce and, in particular, from large-scale international commerce which, at every period, has produced considerable profits. In this respect France was well placed in the eighteenth century, a period of commercial expansion. According to Arnould's calculations, France's trade passed from 215 million livres in 1716–1720 to a little more than 1,000 million on the eve of the Revolution, that is to say, it increased five times.[19] According to other calculations the increase was greater,[20] but in any case we must allow for the increase in prices which would reduce the expansion to a proportion of one to three or one to four. Nevertheless, the increase of trade through the great sea ports Bordeaux, Nantes, Rouen, Marseilles exceeds these figures. This expansion can be explained both by the development of colonial commerce, in particular with

19. A. M. Arnould, De la balance du commerce et des relations commerciales extérieures de la France . . . ,t. III, Table 10, cited by Fr. Crouzet, *art. cit.*, p. 261.

20. Calculs de Ruggiero Romano, ds Studi in onore di Armando Sapori, t. II, p. 1274, cited by Fr. Crouzet, *art. cit.*, pp. 261–262.

Santo Domingo, responsible for three-quarters of the trade with the French colonies, and by continental trade which we know little about. Nantes, Bordeaux and Rouen took the lead as innovators in material for industry, providing textiles, partly produced in the neighbouring countryside, refining sugar and oils coming from the colonies and making the shoddy goods necessary for the purchase of slaves. For these towns the eighteenth century was a period of enrichment, as the town-planning carried out at that time testifies even today.

At the end of the century, banking establishments such as the Caisse d'Escompte were created which testify both to the way in which the country was getting richer and to the new needs which individuals could no longer meet. Capital began to be directed towards industrial enterprises, such as the Société des Mines d'Anzin, founded at the beginning of the eighteenth century and reorganised in 1757 by nobility, among whom were the Prince de Croy, with the participation of bourgeois capitalists, and the foundries of Creusot and Indret. The very large majority of enterprises, however, were still financed on a family basis. In addition, none of the financial institutions of the Ancien Régime withstood the revolutionary shock.

The Revolution and the Empire threw international commerce into confusion and ruined what had been achieved in the course of the preceding century. This was an irremediable loss and we again find the influence of political factors because, despite territory lost for ever, such as Santo Domingo, other markets, such as the United States, for example, passed to our competitors and, at all events, could not be recovered until the return of peace, in 1815 and after. As a result of monetary difficulties and inflation, possessors of capital sought security which, at this period of political instability, could only take the form of real estate and property. This explains the ease with which Church property was sold after 1789 and later the property of the émigrés. In any case, the movement of investment into industry, noticeable after 1775, ceased from 1790 to the first years of the Empire. The Napoleonic government tried to revive this enthusiasm by creating a stable currency, based on gold, and by founding a central bank, the Bank of France, which also gave discount facilities, by giving prizes to inventors and by encouraging industrial exhibitions. But even then general circumstances were scarcely favourable (the continuation of wars, the cutting-off of overseas markets and the lack of raw materials as the result of the blockade).

In short, certain beneficient effects of previous governments, especially the juridicial changes in the structure of industrial companies, had to await the return of peace in 1815. The 1808 Code of Commerce had created three types of company: the joint company, the limited company and the company with shares (or joint-stock company). The first kind were like family companies in which those who put up the capital at the same time looked after the company's management: only two individuals were necessary to found such a company, which was subject to no regulations other than its registration with a notary. With the limited companies a distinction was made between the shareholders who provided the capital and those responsible for management. Such a combination encouraged the creation of industrial businesses provided that the shareholders had confidence in the management and that the capital lent was well remunerated. It should be noted that the formula limited the bringing in of capital to a limited family or business circle while still giving more flexibility than for the joint company. Finally, the legislation had foreseen joint-stock companies by surrounding them with many precautions to safeguard the rights of the shareholders against sharp practice: the authorisation of the Conseil d'Etat for their creation and the six-monthly submission of a balance sheet to the authorities. These precautions made the creation of joint-stock companies more difficult so that they remained uncommon up to the middle of the nineteenth century, more precisely till 1867, when it was decided to do away with all the restrictions which had hindered them.[21]

21. Claude Fohlen, Sociétés anonymes et développement capital-

The legislative attitude which was scarcely favourable to the concentration of capital in large companies resulted in restraining investment in industrial enterprises which, in France, remained essentially family affairs. Between 1815 and 1848 the foundation of 342 joint-stock companies was authorised, with a capital of about 2,000 million francs. We do not know the number of companies of other types founded during the same period, but we can make an interesting comparison at least for one year, 1847, in the course of which 2,615 companies were founded, divided up as follows:

1,952 joint companies;
   647 limited companies of which 408 were simple limited partnerships and 239 partnerships limited by shares;
    14 joint-stock companies of which 8 were mutual assurance companies.

In fact, joint-stock companies constituted the exception, as Jean Lhomme has noted: 'capitalists divided their favours between two types of companies: joint companies, provided that the size of the business made family capital sufficient, and partnerships limited by shares if it did not'.[22] This explains the way in which the family system was so prominent in French industry.

French industrial enterprises are, in fact, for the greater part family businesses. Of the 342 joint-stock companies counted above scarcely 100 deal with industrial production with only 6.5 per cent of the capital (as against 83 per cent for transport businesses). Among these we notice mining companies (above all, coal-mining), metallurgical factories, chemical companies (Cie de Saint Gobain), a few textile and provision businesses (sugar-mills and sugar beet refineries). All this adds up to very little in comparison with family businesses, which form the vast majority of industrial enterprises at this period. Very large businesses, like the foundries and steel-works of Creusot (Schneider brothers), the spinning and weaving factories of Haussmann at Logelbach (near Colmar), and the Perenchies Company (near Lille) took the form of limited companies.

The first result of this preference for the family organisation was the modest, not to say small size of French industrial enterprises from the eighteenth century to our own time, and especially at the time of the Industrial Revolution. Even the very large textile enterprises had very few workers in the middle of the nineteenth century: 3,000 to be precise at Dollfus-Mieg and Co., the largest cotton factory at Mulhouse, under the Second Empire, and 1,000 at Motte-Bossut, the most important cotton-thread maker at Roubaix. In the mining and metallurgical industries, the units of production were often bigger and the labour force larger: 3,250 workers at the Creusot foundries in 1850, 6,000 in 1860. But this was an exceptional business far surpassing the average. The capital is not often known but, where it is, one is struck by the low figures: eight million francs for Saint-Gobain in 1830, four million for the Imphy Foundry and Smelting Works (1828). Industrial enterprises never attracted such massive capital as railways or canals, and industrial wage-owners formed only a small part of the working population. Why should we be surprised, moreover, knowing the preponderance of agriculture and the crafts?

The second consequence is the very great independence of industrial enterprises with regard to banking institutions. The companies got the funds they needed from members of the family or had recourse to self-financing by using part of the profits to reinvest in the business. When Motte-Bossut decided to build a new and vast spinning factory in 1843, he was able to do so without recourse to outside capital. An establishment as important as de Wendel, in Lorraine, was able to finance from its own resources its

increases in size and radical alterations right up to 1908, although metallurgy eats up more capital than textiles.

We can choose, as an example, the process of financing the metallurgical industry, well known thanks to the work of Bertrand Gille. In creating enterprises, family funds provided the basis, with occasionally some help from bankers. Thus when the Schneiders bought Creusot in 1836, the Seilliere Bank took part in the financing operation. Bankers can be found in several metallurgical companies. But the chief resource of companies continued to be self-financing: from 1832 to 1845 the Decazeville Company succeeded in doubling its capital by turning interest and dividends into capital. Banking advances were so exceptional that two bankers who were administrators of this Decazeville Company refused a loan in 1833. On the other hand, some banks were interested in metallurgy like the already mentioned Seilliere Bank, which advanced money to Creusot, to the Bazeille foundry and to Wendel. A revealing case is that of Fourchambault, who received the deposits of the local population and paid interest on them. If direct increases in capital were rare, firms, on the other hand, often got into debt through issuing bonds like the Decazeville Company in 1842. These bond issues were numerous at a time of major technical changes when new machinery had to be installed. We can therefore support the conclusions of Bertrand Gille, who distinguishes between three financing techniques: increase in capital (rare), the issue of bonds and, above all, financing from own resources.

In these circumstances, as recent research shows, the banks played a minor role in industrial financing. Up to the middle of the nineteenth century, France had no business bank helping industrial enterprises: the Haute-Banque dealt particularly with state loans and international commerce (Rothschilds, Mallet, Vernes, Mirabaud), and local banks dealt in discounts of commercial goods, which were later rediscounted with the Banque de France. Some bankers, like Jacques Laffitte, tried to set up a credit establishment for industry. Two of these projects in succession failed, before the setting up in 1837 of the Caisse

Générale du Commerce et de l'Industrie, inspired by the example, a few years before, of the Société Générale de Belgique. The 1837 project, moreover, was a long way from meeting the hopes and plans of its author, who wrote: 'I shall in no way conceal my thoughts: at first I am only setting up an ordinary banking establishment with the object of converting it by the careful choice of associates and their co-operation into a real bank for commerce and industry.' The Caisse Générale failed in its purpose, as did several similar institutions founded around 1840. Even the Crédit Mobilier of the Péreire brothers provided little capital for industry, helping as first priority transport and public utility companies. The researches of Jean Bouvier into the Crédit Lyonnais have shown how this bank gave up industrial investments after several losses in the Lyons chemical industry between 1863 and 1870. In its beginnings French industry only rarely and exceptionally called on bank credits.[23]

Did the small size of businesses and the narrow sources of finance hinder the industrial development of France? Several American historians have drawn the conclusion from these facts that French industrialists lacked a spirit of enterprise and have said that this explains France's economic backwardness.[24] Thus David Landes points out that family businesses are of necessity cautious, cutting out risks to the maximum extent, including the risk of launching new inventions whose commercial success is not assured. The

23. Jean Bouvier, *Le Crédit Lyonnais de 1863 à 1882, les années de formation d'une banque de dépôts*, Paris, 1961, 2 vol., especially pp. 371–381.

24. David Landes, French Entrepreneurship and Industrial Growth in the Nineteenth Century, *Journal of Economic History*, 1949, pp. 45–61.

ID — French Business and the businessman: A social and cultural Analysis, ds. E. M. Earle, *Modern France, Problems of the Third and Fourth Republic*, Princeton, 1951, pp. 334–353.

John E. Sawyer, *Strains in the social structure of Modern France*, ibid., pp. 293–312.

Shepard B. Clough, Retardative factors in French Economic Development in the 19th and 20th centuries, *Journal of Economic History*, supplement, 1946, pp. 91–102.

businessman prefers the safe profits of a small-scale business to the uncertainties of an increase in size which present certain momentary dangers but offers very favourable prospects for the future. This line of argument calls for certain comments. First of all, the idea of a spirit of enterprise is subjective and can only be defined by comparison with businessmen highly endowed with this spirit. It is obvious that France has had no McCormick, no Vanderbilt, no Carnegie and no Rockefeller, to confine oneself to certain great figures of the nineteenth century. It must be recognised, however, that Schneider and de Wendel did not lack a spirit of enterprise, as the development of their businesses shows, and that the great Alsatian industrialists, Dollfus, Schlumberger, Koechlin, showed proof of an aggressive audacity which paid off, not only in terms of industrial organisation, but in getting hold of markets. France had an élite of manufacturers, few in numbers, no doubt, but endowed with a spirit of enterprise, in contrast to an overwhelming majority of routine and conservative manufacturers. But does not history preserve the name of the boldest to leave the mass of run-of-the-mill in the shadows? Moreover, one must not lose sight of the narrowness of the internal French market, which made mass American-style production impossible. It is by no means certain that lack of access to the capital market was satisfactory to industrialists: the withdrawal by the Crédit Lyonnais from the fuchsine dye business, mentioned earlier on, shows that the initiative came from the bank. Some industrialists tried to make arrangements with banks, but met with a refusal or had to decline the conditions proposed to them because they were too difficult. Industrial investment is a long-term affair, while banks seek a rapid and sure profit: the two requirements are contradictory and no reconciliation between them has yet been found.

In fact, French industrialists were divided into two groups, one open to progress, the other more conservative, in the sense in which conservative means maintaining what has been acquired. The conflict between these two tendencies has had an echo in literature with J-R. Bloch's novel

Et Compagnie. Two industrialists, one Hippolyte Simler, a refugee from Alsace after the war of 1870, the other, M. Lorilleux, who has been established for a long time in the imaginary town of Vendoeuvre, discuss the investment of available money. 'I find that I have a few sous in my safe,' M. Lorilleux confided one day to M. Hippolyte. 'They tell me of a nice piece of property in the Melle direction. If you know of any investments you can recommend, you must know all about that sort of thing. I would rather that you ... yes, I should prefer to hear you ...' M. Hippolyte could not contain himself. 'Infestments? A broberty? And you a spinner? Buy new macheenz, buy varping-plant, buy new cards, there is your broberty, there are your infestments!' Nonetheless, M. Lorilleux resigned himself to seeking unaided a profitable use for his savings, and finally entrusted them, like a wise man, to the enlightened care of the Union Générale, which very soon went bankrupt.[25] A contrast between two different entrepreneurial outlooks and attitudes which are not confined to France. The fact remains that the possession of real estate and property has always been considered a kind of guarantee by industrialists, no doubt in memory of difficulties in the past.

One final question remains: to what extent did the communications network and policy help the industrial revolution? What distinguishes an industrial from an agricultural economy is the way in which products are more widely distributed, whether they be raw materials or manufactured products. In pre-industrial France each region was virtually self-sufficient and lived almost as an autarky. With industrialisation, markets became much wider, provided that there were good communications.

The France of the Ancien Régime had a good network of roads, which Arthur Young had admired on his tours on the eve of the Revolution. They reflected, however, the political centralisation going out from Paris and Versailles towards the ports or frontiers. Cross-country communications were difficult, especially when the roads crossed mountainous districts like the Massif Central or the Alps,

25. Jean-Richard Bloch, *Et Compagnie* . . . p. 318.

which at that time were almost impenetrable. These roads were often unreliable, either because of the difficult lie of the road or, more frequently, because the surface was not sufficiently resistant. Thus, 'the highway between Troyes and Paris consisted, between Coubert and Brie, only of a ballast-bed of stones so soft that they are immediately crushed and flattened out . . . it is simply mud in winter and dust in summer'.[26] Nevertheless, a big effort was made to improve the roads, thanks above all to the engineers of the Ponts et Chaussées (Highways Department), trained in the school of the same name founded in 1747 and thus the oldest of the technical schools in France. This precious heritage was well maintained in the nineteenth century, after the negligences of the Revolution and the Empire. Napoleon gave the roads their administrative organisation, dividing the expenses of construction and maintenance between the state and the local communities (departments or communes). New roads were constructed towards the frontiers, in the Pyrenees, in the Alps, often for strategic rather than economic purposes. However excellent the road might be, it could not carry the heavy materials necessary for industry.

This was what had been understood in England by the Duke of Bridgewater and the other canal builders: only waterways could satisfy the needs of industry. The French rivers most used under the Ancien Régime were the Loire and the Garonne, serving respectively Nantes and Bordeaux. The Seine was little used, because the excessive number of bends in the river made it difficult for navigation by sail. At the same period there were still few canals: that of the Midi, joining Toulouse to Sète, constructed by the engineer Riquet, under the reign of Louis XIV, those of Briare, Loing and Orleans, all dating from before the industrial revolution, and these latter in different ways joining the Seine to the Loire. In all, a few hundred kilometres of canals in agricultural regions and of old-fashioned construction. In the twenty years preceding the French Revolution, a

26. Extract from Cahier de doléances de Paris-hors-les-murs, cited by Henri Cavailles, *la Route française*, Paris, 1946, p. 163.

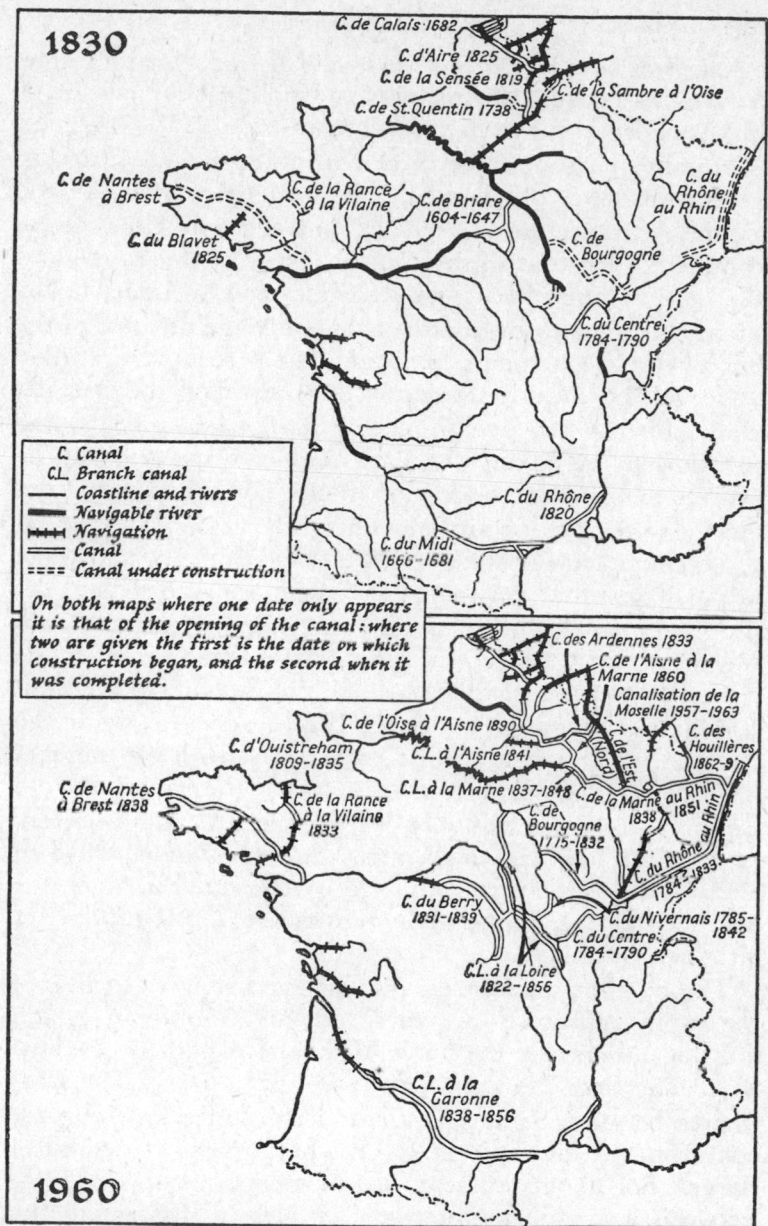

The Canal System in France in 1830 and 1960

canal fever swept France as it had England, but produced few results because of financial and political difficulties. A link was begun between the Seine and the Saone (through Burgundy), between the Saone and the Rhine (through Franche-Comté and Alsace), between the Loire and the Yonne (through the Nivernais), but the only canal to be completed was that of the Centre, between the Saone and the Loire through Montceau les Mines and Le Creusot. The situation only improved after 1815, once the director of the Highways Department, Becquet, had secured in 1820 approval for an ambitious programme called the Becquet plan which aimed at completing that interrupted by the Revolution, by linking the Paris region to the areas in the process of being industrialised in the north and east, thus favouring the mining and metallurgical sectors. Thus about 2,500 kilometres of canals were dug between 1820 and 1850, in particular that between the Rhone and the Rhine, the Burgundy canal, the Nivernais canal, the Berry canal, from Nantes to Brest, the lateral canal of the Loire, which made it possible to transport the coal of Saint-Etienne to the Paris region, and the canals from the Somme and the Oise to the Sambre, which joined up the Paris region with the mines of the north. The work was completed under the Second Empire, with the bringing into service of an important canal, that between the Marne and the Rhine, between Vitry and Strasbourg, completed by the canal between the Marne and the Saone. The results are most impressive, although belated.

The opening-up of railways was even slower because of the strong resistance they met from public opinion, which did not understand the value of this new method of transport. The first line was opened in 1827, over a few kilometres between Saint-Etienne and the Loire, to transport coal from the mines to the river, where it was loaded on to barges. For about ten years the only sections opened were between coal mines and rivers or canals (Epinac to the Canal du Centre, Alès to Beaucaire), or between industrial towns (Thann to Mulhouse). A different experiment, the

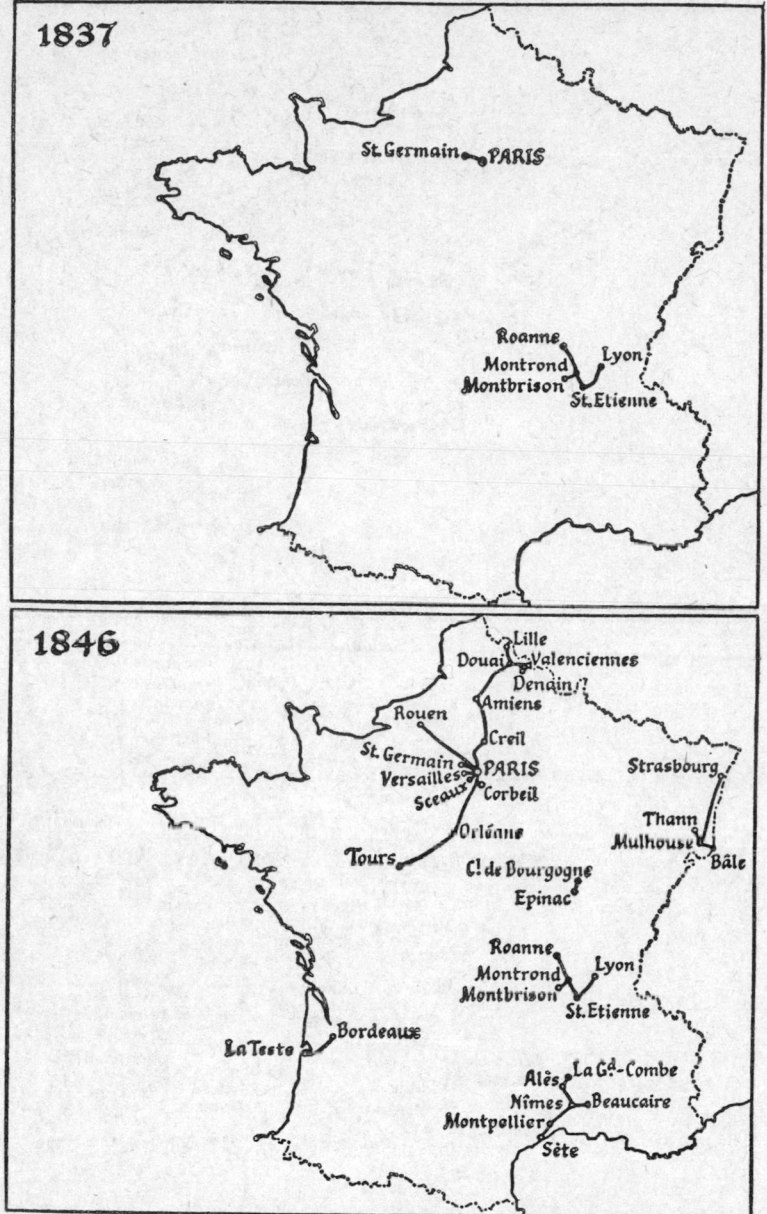

The Spread of the Railways in France over Less than Forty Years

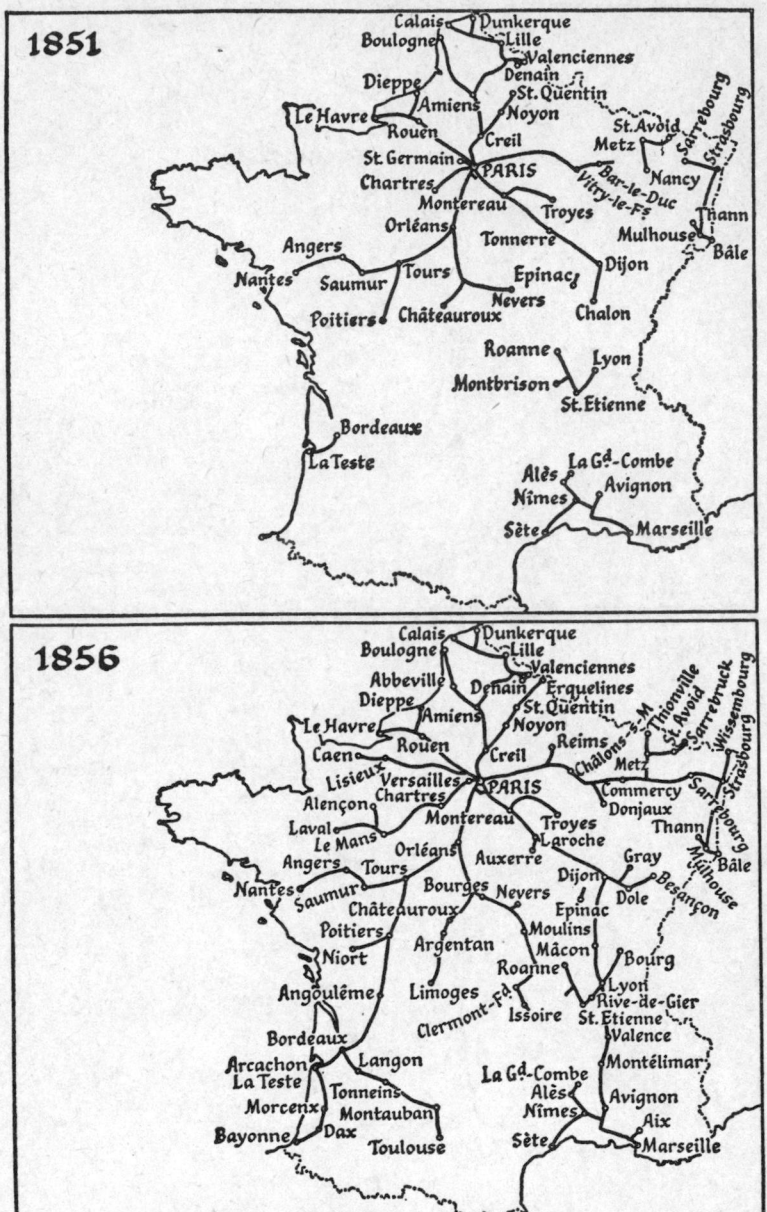

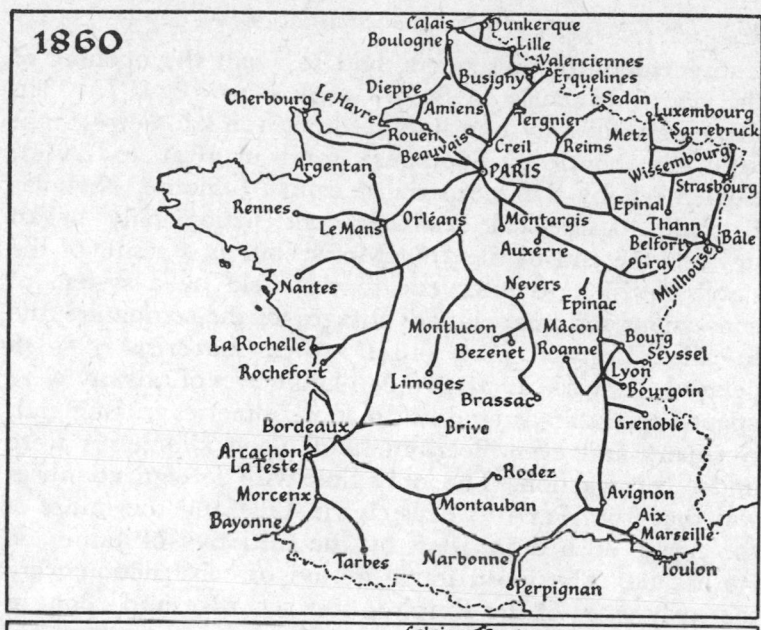

1860

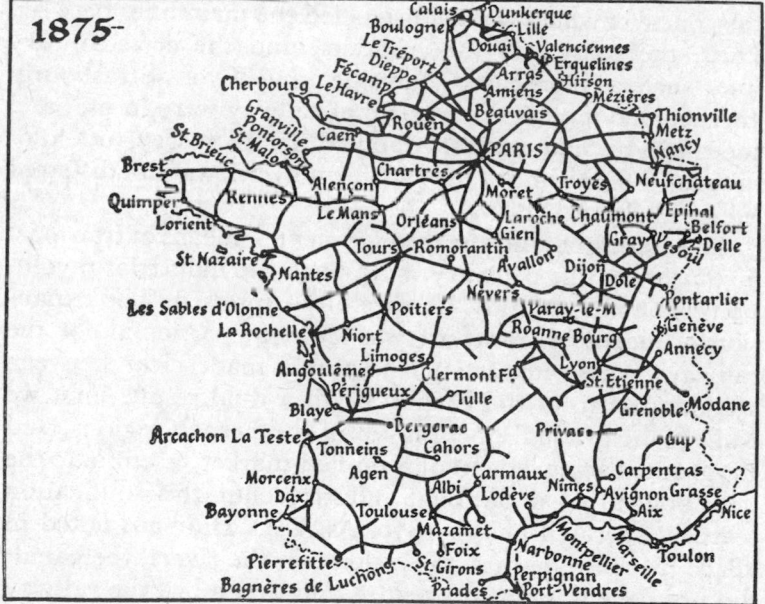

1875

transportation of passengers, had to await the opening of the line from Paris to Saint-Germain in 1837. In 1840 there was still only one line of about 100 kilometres, that from Strasbourg to Mulhouse (and in 1841 to Basle), carried out by the industrialist from Mulhouse, Nicholas Koechlin. Large-scale railway construction only began towards the end of the July Monarchy, as a result of the state's decision to intervene in this field by a system of concessions and financial advantages for the companies, the so-called Legraud plan (1841); then the crisis of 1846 delayed the work. In 1848 1,800 kilometres of railway were opened to traffic as against 10,000 kilometres in England, Germany and even Belgium, and 2,900 kilometres were under construction. The only link with foreign countries was that from Paris to Brussels via Lille and the mines of the north, opened in 1846 by the initiative of James de Rothschild. The most active period of construction were the early years of the Empire, between 1852 and 1860, in the course of which were constructed the main lines between Paris, the coast and the frontiers, and the cross-country lines such as Bordeaux-Marseilles and Lyons-Strasbourg. In 1860 about 9,000 kilometres of railway were in use, and their length had almost doubled in 1870 (17,500 kilometres). The outline of the railway network was not different then to what it is now.

To what extent did the development of means of transport favour or, on the contrary, hold back the industrial revolution? The answer must be carefully expressed. The expansion of means of transport was slow, in particular for the railways, whose importance was only made clear between 1845 and 1850 at the earliest, with a dual result. First we can see the gradual opening-up of the French regions, and the gradual achievement of a unified market, essential to the development of a national industry. But this unification scarcely operated before 1870. As A. L. Dunham noted in 1848: 'Much remained to be done on the rivers, the canals did not have a uniform breadth and depth . . . the railway had been well planned, but very few lines had been finished, and these had only been so in the last five years before

1848.'[27] Here we rejoin Maurice Lévy-Leboyer's views on the belated unification of the French market, without doubt not before the 1860s.[28] Nevertheless, despite the belatedness of France in comparison with its neighbours, the development of railways and canals had, from 1850, put the centres of consumption like the Paris district in communication with the zones of mining and industrial production, the north, on the one hand, and the centre on the other, both rich in coal. Moreover, the cost of transport had noticeably decreased, from about two-thirds for heavy products to more than a half for primary textile materials, which caused a decrease in the cost price.

The originality of the industrial revolution consists in the use made of mechanical forms of energy and, in particular, of the steam-engine. Its use posed two different problems: on the one hand that of its mechanical possibilities and, on the other, that of keeping it supplied with coal.

Watt's engine was known in France very shortly after its invention in England, thanks to the brothers Périer, who imported one and made it work at their foundry at Chaillot in 1781. They got from Watt a fifteen-year concession to make steam-engines in France. Their rate of production remained modest because the latest of machinery often came directly from England. Nevertheless, they supplied one to Creusot at the time of the firing of the new foundries.

The use of the steam-engine before the French Revolution remained an exception. At that time they had begun to install them in the coal mines, to operate the water-pumps and to bring the coal up to the surface, in flour-mills (in 1790 at the Ile des Cygnes in Paris) and in cotton-mills (in 1787 at Orleans). In 1810 there were only about 200 steam-engines in France, of which some came from the workshops at Chaillot, closed under the Revolution for lack of outlet. Most of the engines were out-of-date, some still single action. The break with England and the primacy of

27. Arthur Louis Dunham, *La Révolution Industrielle en France*, p. 388.
28. Maurice Lévy-Leboyer, *Les processus d'industrialisation art.* cit., p. 285.

strategic objectives had relegated technical improvements to second place.

After 1815 English engine-builders came to set themselves up in France, bringing with them technical improvements and opening workshops of mechanical engine building. At the same time the French re-established contact with English technology and drew their inspiration from methods across the Channel. At one stroke the number of engines, their power and efficiency increased:

Number of machines		Horse-power
1830	625	10,000
1839	2,450	33,000
1845	4,114	50,000
1848	5,200	60,000
1852	16,080	75,500
1862	17,000	205,000
1875	32,000	401,000

As one can see, progress was slow during the first half of the nineteenth century and the steam-engine only really asserted itself from the time of the Second Empire. Why? Because a large number of industries had already previously installed themselves in regions well provided with water-power and it was easier to use waterfalls. Clapham estimates the power of hydraulic installations at 150,000 horsepower in about 1845, which is three times the power of steam-engines.[29] The latter first played a leading part in the mines and in very flat districts. Thus it is not surprising to see two departments in the lead in 1850, Le Nord (878 engines, 12,500 H.P.) and the Seine (748 engines, 5,400 H.P.). In numerous industries, the supremacy of hydraulic power was very clear: in cotton, 462 hydraulic engines against 243 steam-engines in 1845, and in silk 435 against 143 at the same date. It is sometimes forgotten that, if the steam-engine was steadily improved in the course of this period, the same thing also happened to hydraulic machines, thanks, amongst others, to the turbine of Fourneyron,

29. John H. Clapham, *The Economic Development of France and Germany, 1815–1914,* Cambridge, 1948, p. 63.

whose efficiency was in the region of 75 per cent. Between 1833 and 1845, 129 factories in France and abroad worked with a turbine put in by Fourneyron, and one of them attained a power of 220 H.P.[30] France went on with improvements in hydraulic turbines later than other countries, as is shown in exhibition reports after 1850. This persistence is indicative of the opposition met by the steam-engine.[31]

It imposed itself more easily in the field of land and river transport, where it represented an undeniable improvement, especially after Marc Seguin's improvements to the boiler. His system of tubes placed in the boiler increased the heating surface and the output of the locomotives. But here again, steam only really asserted itself after 1850.

One of the arguments put forward by historians or economists to explain the slow expansion of the steam-engine is the lack of coal and its high price. By comparison with England and Germany, France had less combustible minerals and its consumption has always exceeded production, imports representing from between 25 per cent to 45 per cent of its needs. Overall, for an average year, they represent one-third of the national requirements, coming above all from England, but also from Belgium and Prussia along the canals of the north. More important in this con-

30. L'expansion du Machinisme, in *Histoire Générale des Techniques,* published under the direction of Maurice Daumas, pp. 23–25.

31. The distribution of steam engines in different sectors in 1852, from *Statistique de l'Industrie minerale, 1847–1852,* Paris, 1854, p. CV:

Speciality	No. of establishments	No. of machines	Power HP
Spinning factories	1,438	1,179	16,494
Foundries and machine workshops	431	539	3,791
Sugar-mills	406	515	5,192
Fuel mines	289	453	12,306
Dye and finishing works	270	192	1,325
Blast furnaces and iron works	161	368	12,354
Flour mills	152	151	1,933
Metal and sheet iron rolling	64	94	1,354

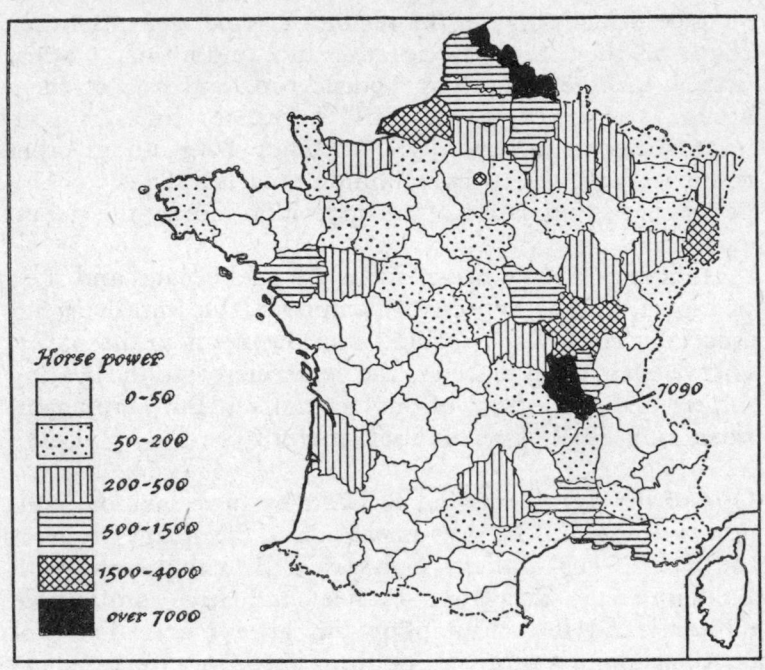

Steam Engines in France in 1841

nection is the localisation of the coal mines, divided between two main groups, that of the north, also called the Valenciennes Basin, and that of the Centre, divided between about ten workings, Le Creusot, Saint-Etienne, Blanzy,

STEAM-ENGINE AND MEANS OF TRANSPORT

	No. of locomotives	No. of vessels	Steam vessels Steam-engines	HP of steam-engine
1833		75	90	2,635
1835		100	118	3,863
1840	405	211	263	11,422
1845	903	259	446	18,050
1850	3,056	252	501	22,025
1852	3,907	304	552	29,193

Epinac, Decazeville. Up to the middle of the nineteenth
century, the production of this latter group exceeded that
of the north. A reversal of the balance came about after
the discovery, in 1846, of the mines of the Pas de Calais,
which continue to the west the deposits of Valenciennes
and Douai. Other deposits of small importance were dispersed in the east, the south, and even in the west of the
country.[32]

The higher prices of coal in France are explained by the
cost of extraction and carriage. The coal mines, according to
those concerned, were difficult to exploit because of their
depth, because the seams were thin and because of pockets
of gas. It is certain that in this respect, France was less well
endowed than her neighbours. Moreover, the belated
development of means of transport for a long time imposed
high prices because of the large amount of handling
required. Up to 1844 almost all the coal consumed in the
Paris region came from the Saint-Etienne coalfield after a
very complicated and costly journey. After this date, thanks
to the opening of canals between the Oise and the north,
coal from the north finally took the place of that from the
central region and its price declined, though still remaining
affected by the length of the journey. A large number of
French industrial centres, in Alsace, in Normandy and in

32. Production and consumption of coal (thousands of tons):

Year	Production	Consumption	Imports	Imports as % of consumption
1789	230	450		
1815	882			
1820	1,094			
1827	1,691	2,226	540	26
1830	1,863	2,494	631	25.5
1840	3,000	4,257	1,257	30.3
1850	4,434	7,225	2,791	39
1860	8,300	14,270	5,970	43
1870		21,432	8,304	38
1880	19,362	28,846	9,484	33
1890	26,083	36,653	10,520	31
1900	33,404	48,803	15,399	32

Source: *Annuaire statistique*, 1910, Partie rétrospective.

the Paris region, had begun to develop by hydraulic energy and found themselves at a disadvantage when they reconverted to the steam-engine. In Normandy it was more advantageous to import coal from England, despite the customs' duties. In Alsace they had to use either coal from Epinac or Blanzy (the central coalfield), despite a long journey by canals, or that of the Saar (the Prussian bank of the Rhine), about 200 kilometres distant. The question was less that of the cost-price at the pit-heads than of the cost of transport. At all events, France was less well placed in this respect than England or Germany because the cost of transport doubled or tripled the cost of the coal. Thus at Mulhouse, in about 1830, coal from the Loire, which cost 15 francs a ton on the spot, came to 45–55 francs, while coal from the Saar rose from 9 francs to 50–60 francs. These prices declined after the opening of canals, but give nonetheless an idea of the rise in prices due to transport costs. Coal, of Belgian origin, consumed in Paris in about 1840 to make gas came to 44 francs a ton, of which 30 were for transport costs.[33]

A final factor: France lacked certain qualities of coal for which it had to resort to imports. Neither the coal from the north nor from the central region could easily be made into coke, essential both for the making of gas for lighting and for metallurgical purposes. If Paris imported the coal necessary for its lighting from Belgium, it was above all because the French mines did not produce the required quality. The metallurgical industry ran into severe difficulties, in the first half of the nineteenth century, because of the high cost of coke, always imported, which was used by the blast-furnaces. This partly explains their long attachment to wood.

It remains to determine the importance of the 'coal factor' in the economic fortunes of France. In 1819 Chaptal pointed out: 'If we have not made as extensive use of machinery (as in England) it is because manual labour

33. Rondo Cameron, Profit, Croissance et Stagnation en France au XIXe siècle, *Economie Appliquée*, Archives de l'I.S.E.A., vol. 10, April-September 1957, pp. 433–434.

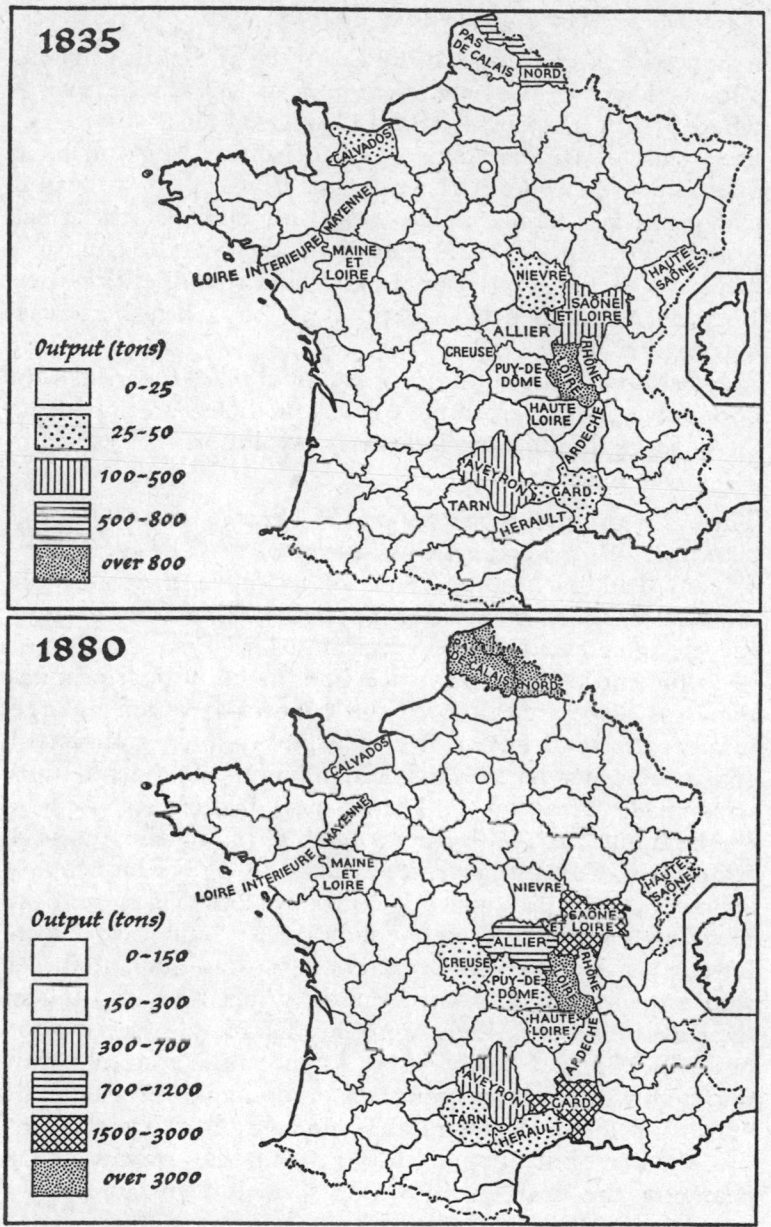

Coal Output in 1835 and 1880

here costs less and because the low price of fuel in England allows them to use steam-engines to advantage everywhere.'[34] On his part, Richard Cobden noted:

'. . . whilst the indigenous coal and iron in England have attracted to her shores the raw materials of her industry, and given her almost a European monopoly of the great primary elements of steam power, France on the contrary, relying on her ingenuity only to sustain a competition with England, is compelled to purchase a portion of hers from her great rival.'

The shortage, both in quantity and quality, of fuel resources does not explain everything, but is nonetheless an important factor in explaining the industrial revolution in France.

The coal-producing situation of France explains the character of its metallurgical development. The high price of coal held back some forms of technical progress, but original solutions were often applied, taking into account the specific conditions of French industry.

At the end of the Ancien Régime, metallurgical production was dispersed all over the country between a large number of small enterprises of a family and estate-based character using local wood and minerals. Some attempts were made to adopt in France new techniques used in England, in particular the coke-smelter, in the recently established Creusot factories where, in 1785, four blast-furnaces were producing 5,000 tons per year, and at Hayange, where the de Wendels had built two blast-furnaces with an annual capacity of 900 tons. Such attempts were exceptional, and with the delay accumulated under the Revolution and the Empire, French metallurgy was not radically changed before 1815. At that time contacts were resumed with foreign countries, and above all England, which put forward new models, not only in the making of the smelter, but also puddling, and the processes for changing the castings into iron, which were known as foundries 'in the English style'.

34. Chaptal, *De l'Industrie française*, Paris, 1819, v. 2, p. 31.

The essential question was that of the use of coal instead of wood in the different smelting operations. France's rich forest resources and the fact that blast-furnaces and foundries had been installed near forests and mineral deposits led to serious difficulties in the adoption of new techniques as a foundry-master from Berry emphasised at that time. 'Those people who so readily suggest the substitution of coal for charcoal do not appear to realise that this leads to changing practically everything in the foundries, the refining works, the machinery and the workshops. The foundry has to be near coal pits that yield a suitable kind of coal, the ore has to be within range of the fuel, and workmen have to be trained for this new kind of work.' Moreover, he did not hide the superiority of the English. 'Favoured by nature with regard to the fuel and ore which they find together in the same pit, they convert this into coke and, by means of steam and rotary engines, they impart enormous power to their cylinders sufficient to draw out this raw material into bars. A large number of canals take these iron bars and help to bring them down to the sea. All these advantages, which we are far from possessing, are for them immense sources of economy.'[35] That is why the adoption of coke in the making of cast-iron was especially slow. In 1850 cast-iron made with wood largely exceeded cast-iron made with coal. Foundry-masters maintained tenaciously the prejudice that cast-iron made from wood was of superior quality to that made from coke, that it was more malleable and easier to make into iron. Even enlightened foundry-masters, like Boigues, the creator of Fourchambault, declared in 1829 that iron of really good quality would always be made with wood. Audincourt, in Franche-Comté, kept until the end of the nineteenth century a blast-furnace using wood to make iron of high quality. Moreover, the change-over to coke called for capital which most of the foundry-masters did not possess. Only companies or bold businessmen could take such a risk. In

35. Bertrand Gille, L'expansion du Machines, v. 3 of *l'Histoire Générale des Techniques*, sous la direction de M. Daumas, pp. 602–603.

the long run, large-scale businesses found themselves favoured and concentration was stimulated.[36]

The transformation of foundries took place more rapidly after the model set by England and the expression 'foundries in the English style' often appears at this period. They included two innovations: on the one hand, the refining of the cast-iron by a reverberatory furnace, heated with coal, and on the other, the treatment of the iron thus obtained by mechanically operated rolling-mills. Several foundry-masters after 1815 flung themselves with enthusiasm into these new procedures. Thus Marshal Marmont in the Chatillon district (Burgundy): 'The English way of manufacture began to be known; its results having struck me, I resolved to make my province benefit from it. Some English people, making machines at Charenton, persuaded me that for a modest outlay I could undertake it while prompt and considerable rewards would soon recompense me.'[37] The investment made was fairly modest (700,000 francs), and Marmont counted on the numerous furnaces of the region to maintain a supply of cast-iron, but the establishment thus set up ended in bankruptcy in 1827. In the same way, the Boigues set up English-style foundries at Fourchambault in 1821, at a cost of putting up 800,000 francs between the cast-iron producing centres of the Nivernais and Berry. Some English people set themselves up near Nantes, in the Basse-Indre, counting on the importation of English coal

36. Foundries using wood and using coke:

| Year | Number of blast-furnaces | | Production of cast-iron | |
	Wood	Coke	Wood	Coke
1819	?	?	110,500 tons	2,000 tons
1825	379	14	194,166	4,000
1830	379	29	239,257	27,300
1835	410	28	241,484	48,314
1840	421	41	270,710	70,063
1845	353	79	246,400	137,000
1850	?	?	229,400	176,000
1860	282	113	316,000	582,000
1870	91	142	1,178,000	

37. Cited by Bertrand Gille, *La Sidérurgie française au XIXe siècle*, Paris, 1968, p. 47.

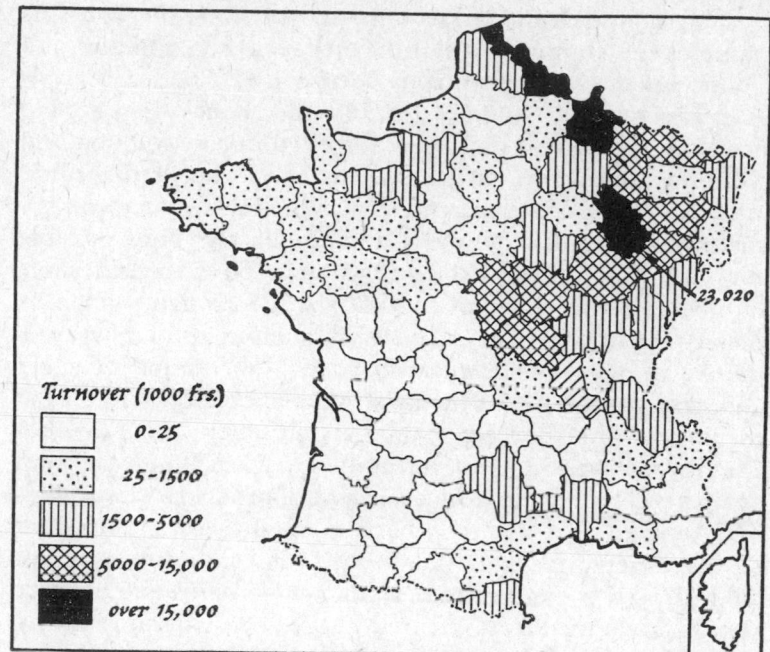

Turnover (1000 frs.)

☐ 0-25

▫ 25-1500

▥ 1500-5000

▨ 5000-15,000

■ over 15,000

The Iron Industry in France about 1840

and the use of cast-iron from Brittany. The English-style foundries had a great success from 1830 to 1860 and noticeably encouraged the increase in production of iron (44 per cent increase between 1844 and 1860). But these enterprises ran into two difficulties, lack of coal and insufficient sources of cast-iron.

That is why, after 1820, several engineers and foundry-masters thought of an overall solution which, starting with ore and coal, made them go through the whole range of metallurgical operations. That was the solution already reached by François de Wendel, when he had bought back the Hayange (Lorraine) foundries in 1802. It was the solution adopted in 1820 and 1821 by the Saint-Etienne mines company and the Terrenoire company, both in the Saint-Etienne coalfields, the Creusot company taken up again by Manby and Wilson in 1826, the Collieries,

Foundries and Iron-Works company of Alais in 1829 (the name of the company is significant) and the Collieries and Foundries of the Aveyron at Decazeville. There were few enterprises which could withstand the shocks of the 1830 crisis: all the capital had been absorbed in construction and working capital ran out just when the market had shrunk.

If this first thrust had ended in a set-back, it had nevertheless propounded a model and shown the only possible way for the future. From 1830 to 1860 a considerable number of enterprises of modest size continued, which at the cost of improvements in detail, such as the recovery of the warm gases of the blast-furnaces, the mixing of wood and coal in the blast-furnaces and the adoption of the turbine of Fourneyron (Pont sur l'Ognon, in Franche-Comté) survived in a not yet unified market. They came up against difficulties because their cost of production was high and kept going only on a basis of quality in a more and more restricted market. The needs of the railways, as much for rails as for engines and rolling-stock, stimulated, after 1840, a new up-thrust in metallurgy, helped this time by rising demand. The reorganisation of Creusot, just after 1836, under the direction of the Schneider brothers, is well known, and one can mention the prosperity of Decazeville, which was at that time the largest French rail-producer (12,000 tons in 1842), and the foundation of the Châtillon-Commentry company in 1845. In response to the demand, several of these metallurgical companies took up the making of engines, which rounded off their integration: Schneiders opened in 1837 a factory to make locomotives and, in 1841, naval construction yards at Châlon sur Sâone.

After 1850, in the wake of a crisis which had exceeded in scope that of 1830, two features characterise French metallurgy. First, the rate of concentration grew more rapid: in 1854 a large number of foundries and iron-works of a traditional type in Franche-Comté came together into one company, the 'Compagnie de Forges de Franche-Comté', whose existence was difficult as the combination of backward enterprises did not make for one competitive enterprise. The marrying-up in 1854 of the collieries of Commentry, the blast-furnaces of Montlucon and the factories of Fourchambault into the Compagnie de Commentry-Fourchambault was happier. The same year brought together the foundries and steel-works of the Loire basin into the new Naval and Railway Foundries and Steel-works Company. In 1849 the Denain and d'Anzin factories, both adjacent to their coal supply, came together and surmounted, not without difficulty, the lack of ore. What characterises metallurgical enterprises created at this period are the not always successful search for integration and also a diversification in production, in order to avoid the harmful effects of previous crises. As well as rails they made steel-plate and girders, and rolling-stock as well as engines.

The second transforming factor was technical: the making of steel. Up till then this had been a rare and expensive metal, produced in very small quantities in France by the puddling process used by the Jacksons in their Loire works. This was why Bessemer's discovery in 1855 aroused great interest in France, despite initial scepticism. 'At this moment the iron and steel industry is rather keenly preoccupied with a new and strange process, which is already six or seven years old, in whose future no one believed and which was even looked down on by scientists as well as practical men: Bessemer's invention.'[38] In fact, the foundry-masters were attracted by the new process which had a rapid success in France. In 1858 a converter was installed by the Jackson brothers at the Saint-Seurin works, in 1862 at the Imphy, Assailly and Terrenoire works, and in 1870 at the Creusot foundries. The adoption of the Bessemer process obliged enterprises to modify their organisation again and to increase their production of cast-iron, in return for often heavy investments. In 1870 about twenty Bessemer ovens were working in France and rather more Martin ovens, perfected in 1867 in the Firminy works and adopted by businesses which had less pure castings.[39]

Towards 1870 metallurgy underwent a complete change

38. *Id. ibid.*, p. 242.   39. *Id. ibid.*, p. 105.

which gave it all the characteristics of a great modern industry: financial concentration, integration of production and the employment of a large labour force. There were, of course, still a large number of small businesses in Franche-Comté, in Champagne, in the Pyrenees, but they played a very marginal role in the overall production. More typical were the Creusot foundries which, in 1870, employed 12,500 workers, that is to say, more than half the population of Creusot (23,000 inhabitants), producing 13,000 tons of cast-iron in their 15 blast-furnaces, fed with coke by 160 ovens, and 120,000 tons of iron which fed 130 puddling ovens, 41 rolling-mills and 30 power hammers. Their engineering workshops produced, taking one year with another, about 100 locomotives. And the whole process was operated by 85 steam-engines developing a power of 5,500 H.P. The Creusot works was not, of course, of average size, but at the same period there were seven businesses whose production of cast-iron equalled or surpassed 50,000 tons and five whose production of iron or steel exceeded this figure. Ten businesses were responsible for 55 per cent of the national production of iron and steel, and one of them, Wendel, produced 11.2 per cent (134,000 tons of cast-iron, 112,500 tons of iron and steel). One cannot, of course, talk of a monopoly, but of a domination of the market by a few large firms which, in 1864, had decided to work together in what became the Comité des Forges, the instrument of a well-established and solidly organised industry.

The same thing cannot be said of the chemical industry, which was only beginning to move out of the artisan period in its methods and organisation. Up to 1870 it remained in strict dependence on other sectors and, in particular, on textiles.

The evolution of chemical manufacture was at that time dominated by the problems of bleaching and dyeing, specifically as they affected the makers of woven materials. 'The bleaching of textile products was done at the time by repeated washing, soaping and rinsing, between which processes the pieces of linen were exposed for a long time to the fresh air by spreading them out over the meadows which surrounded the factories.'[40] About six months of constant human effort were needed to bleach linens. The first advance achieved was the discovery of the bleaching properties of chlorine by Berthollet in 1785, but chlorine could still only be made in small quantities. The first decisive advance was the discovery by Nicholas Leblanc of how to make artificial soda industrially, by the action of sulphuric acid on a common and cheap product, salt. From 1791 the factory of Saint-Denis was producing between 200 and 300 kgs. of crude soda per day. But the manufacture was soon stopped for financial reasons and, moreover, depended on the production of sulphuric acid, at that time restricted, which in turn depended on Sicilian pyrites.

The Leblanc process, however, attracted capital and gave birth to a new industry, that of chemical products. In 1806 the Cie de Saint-Gobain, which had specialised since the seventeenth century in the making of glass, set up at Charlefontaine, in the Saint-Gobain forest, a soda-works, transferred in 1823 to the banks of the Oise, at Chauny, on the route of the coal coming from the north. In 1834 the company used 3,000 tons of salt and delivered soda produced industrially. In the north, Kuhlmann, starting with colouring products for the local textile industry, went on to take up mass-production of sulphuric acid. Thus it was that salt became the basis of the chemical industry, handicapped by the lack of sulphuric acid up to the moment when Solvay perfected his process with ammonia (1863). But what is important, even more than the detail of chemical reactions, is the mass-production, the call for capital and the geographic concentration, all of which became apparent in this field in the middle of the nineteenth century.

The range of chemical industries was enriched by other manufactures which brought into play chemical as well as mechanical skill. The ever-increasing need for paper, for the Press among others, led to the mechanical manufacture of wood-pulp, instead of in a vat in the way traditional

40. Maurice Daumas, l'Exposition du Machinisme, *op. cit.*, p. 618.

since the twelfth century. From 1830 onwards systems of continuous manufacture were used which, starting with the pulp and thanks to a system of metal sheets and cylinders made to work by an engine, produced a continuous ribbon of paper which rolled itself automatically on to a roller. The small paper-mills, set up on river banks, survived by specialising in luxury papers, while the machines with continuous action often worked by steam gave a cheap product for large-scale consumption. The problem remained of finding a raw material, first rags, then straw, both later than 1870.

One other manufacture owing as much to chemistry as to the progress of mechanical industry is that of sugar-beet, which was very successful in the first half of the nineteenth century. It was, in fact, based on a crop to which the loss of the colonial empire provided a vigorous stimulus. This manufacture made use of the latest technical improvements, the hydraulic press to extract the juice, lamp-black to bleach the sugar, the blowing-engine to dry out the sugar loaves. These techniques needed capital, so that the sugar-mills were, from the first, one of the large-scale industries.

But it was above all the use of coal, not just as a fuel, but as a raw material which opened the way to new manufactures. At the end of the eighteenth century, the experiments of Murdoch in England had led to the manufacture of gas-lighting and the first company had been founded in 1812. The process crossed the Channel and aroused great interest because it provided a solution to not very fruitful research carried out by Lebon. Paris had a factory making gas-lighting in 1822, and was followed by Bordeaux and Nantes. Altogether about ten limited companies were founded in this field between 1822 and 1846, so that the majority of large towns were lit in this way. In Paris the production of gas which was 41 million cubic metres in 1855 reached 300 million forty years later. Coal was also the basis of another branch of the chemical industry, that of synthetic colouring agents. Up to the middle of the nineteenth century natural colouring agents, derived from indigo, madder or animal black, were used in the dyeing of textiles. Since the beginning of the nineteenth century factories making dyes and colouring agents had appeared near textile centres, in the region of Lyons, in Alsace, in the north. The difficulty was to get hold of a raw material that was expensive because produced in limited quantities. That was why experiments were undertaken to derive colouring agents from coal tar: this was the origin of the success of aniline. The process known in France in about 1860 was at once exploited industrially, so great was the need for colouring agents. A company called La Fuchsine, founded in Lyons in 1863, had as its object, 'the making and sale of all industrial products derived from coal, and especially of colouring materials extracted from these products'.[41] For many reasons this company failed and had to be rapidly liquidated. The making of synthetic colouring agents became the speciality of Germany, richer in coal and better endowed with laboratories, and France had to have recourse to imports.

Was it lack of coal which explains the check in France to the great organic chemical industry? Or should we look for the explanation elsewhere, for example, in the lack of sufficient capital? Both factors certainly played a part so that France was less well endowed in the chemical industry than the neighbouring countries.

Of all the products consumed on a large scale those most profoundly transformed by the industrial revolution were textiles. It was, moreover, in this sector that England had begun her transformation in the eighteenth century.

It was certainly in the textile industry that the solutions, both technical and financial, were most inspired by English models which were greatly imitated.

As Michelet has noted, 'The great revolution of capital importance was that of printed calico. The combined effort of science and art was needed to force a difficult and un-promising material, cotton, to bear every day so many brilliant transformations and then, when it was thus trans-formed, to distribute it everywhere and to put it within

41. Jean Bouvier, *op. cit.*, p. 376.

range of the poor. Before, every woman wore a blue or grey dress, which she kept ten years without washing for fear that it would go into rags. To-day, her husband, at the cost of one day's work, covers her with a cloth of flowers.' This text summarises very well the revolutionary character of the cotton industry, which was the real force behind the transformation that followed in the textile industry.

Cotton-spinning was the first branch to organise itself in about fifty years, from 1780 to 1830. The technical innovations, the jenny, the mule and the water-frame, were known in France before the Revolution, thanks to Englishmen like Milne and Holker, who had settled in the country and set up spinning-mills which served as models. By about 1790 there were several large spinning-mills, each with about 10,000 spindles, of which the most remarkable was that of the Duke of Orleans in the town of Orleans. We can assume that the Revolution held back the movement of industrialisation, but, despite serious problems of getting supplies, the construction of new spinning-mills was actively pursued under the Empire, thanks to the energy of businessmen like Richard-Lenoir and Bauwens from Ghent, who had studied the new manufacturing processes in England. From the technical point of view, all the new elements were largely known and used in 1815, but many of these enterprises had suffered financially from the instability of prices and fluctuations in sales. Cotton-spinning took on its new image, which it was to keep for nearly a century, between 1815 and 1830. Thanks to the steam-engine and hydraulic motors the number of spindles increased; about 50,000 for the largest mills in Alsace, about 30,000 in Normandy. The northern region, which had taken up cotton later, soon had some large mills (one of 40,000 spindles at Roubaix in 1843). After 1830/40, the major changes in the spinning of cotton resulted above all from market conditions and, to a lesser extent, from technical improvements. As far as markets go, the two determining factors were the end of customs protectionism after 1860 and the cotton famine following the American Civil War. A number of small businesses, poorly equipped and not really able to stand on their own feet financially, disappeared. Technically, the only innovation was the mechanisation of the combing, perfected simultaneously in France and England between 1849 and 1850 and adopted after 1850. The adoption of this process added to the installation of more and more powerful engines, increased the demand for capital and thus led to the elimination of small enterprises.

For other textile fibres, mechanisation took place later, either because the demand was less strong, as cotton had to some extent replaced flax and wool, or because it was less expensive to have them spun by hand in the countryside (where labour was never lacking and the domestic system had many advantages), or finally because there were technical difficulties. The mechanical spinning of wool and silk had scarcely begun by 1815 and progressed slowly between that date and 1850. The units of production remained on a small scale in relation to cotton-mills: between 5,000 and 6,000 spindles to each establishment. The last branch of the industry to adopt mechanical processes was flax. As it was a native fibre, it was traditionally worked on in the farm-houses. The first successful attempt at the mechanical spinning of flax was carried out at Lille in 1837, as a result of which active propaganda was made to spread this example, without great results it seems until about 1860. Here again, for financial and technical reasons, the units of production were on a small scale, only about 3,000 spindles.

The mechanisation of weaving was even slower because its advantages were not decisive in a country with a large trained and (most important of all) cheap labour force. In addition, the very modest price of hand-looms made this work at home better value. The need for a radical change only made itself felt slowly because of the pressure of the owners of spinning-mills who, as a result of the mechanisation of their plant, found that they had a surplus of yarn and because of the consumers, who with the reduction in the price of the product, were consuming more. In this changeover in weaving two different aspects must be distinguished. First, the adoption of the Jacquard loom, which thanks to a system of pasteboards pierced with holes, ensures the automatic carrying-out of often complicated designs. This loom includes a most ingenious mechanism, but it is not a mechanical loom since its working continues to be carried out by hand. The Jacquard loom had a big success for figured materials, in particular in the silk factories of the Lyons district, where it was used without any change throughout the nineteenth century. In 1870 there were about 10,000 in the Isère, and this number was maintained right up to 1888–1890. Secondly, a loom worked by water or by a steam-engine using a belt, a real mechanical loom, appeared towards 1820, at first in the cotton industry, where production of thread had been swollen by the mechanisation of the spinning-mill. The mechanical loom, known in Alsace since 1803, was effectively used in the valleys of the Vosges towards 1820, but even in this region open to progress made a slow advance: 2,000 in 1830, 3,000 in 1834, 20,000 in 1846. Elsewhere, the rate of progress was even slower, because as a Normandy industrialist said in 1860: 'Up to now, the labour-force available in the Normandy countryside has not obliged the makers of coloured textiles to use the mechanical loom, but labour has become expensive and scarce and the employers are trying to find ways of evading its demands.'[42] It is from the moment when the productivity of the mechanical loom prevailed over the cost of labour inherent n hand weaving that mechanical weaving took over. The date varies according to the regions: towards 1840–50 in Alsace, towards 1860–70 in Normandy, after 1870 in the Lyons region.

The bleaching, finishing and printing of fabrics, on the other hand, changed radically and more rapidly. Two technical innovations, bleaching by chlorine instead of laying out the fabric on a meadow, and printing by rollers instead of on a block, profoundly modified the final stages

42. Pouyer-Quertier, *Enquête de 1860 sur le Traité de commerce avec l'Angleterre*, v. IV, p. 22. Cf. Claude Fohlen, La concentration dans l'industrie textile française au milieu du XIXe siècle, *Revue d' Histoire moderne et contemporaine*, 1955, pp. 46–58.

in the making of fabrics. The advantages of these new techniques as against tradition were so great that they were rapidly adopted. But they required a big capital investment, at least for the printing, because improvements followed each other rapidly. The first printing machines, with two colours, had worked at Oberkampf's in 1802, and then came machines with four, eight and finally twelve colours towards 1860. At the same time the techniques of colouring were modified, artificial colouring agents taking the place of natural. Printing on fabrics ate up a great deal of capital and greatly contributed to concentration in the textile industry.

By its nature a textile business is less capitalised than foundries, mines or mechanical construction firms: the machinery costs less and can be bought unit by unit without the structure of the business being modified. Mechanical wool-carders can be interpolated into the manufacturing cycle, carding-brushes or roving frames be renewed, looms bought or changed. For this reason textile businesses are particularly family affairs. Of the five hundred limited companies authorised from 1815 to 1867 there are only nineteen textile businesses and their capital represents less than 1 per cent of that of all these companies. These textile businesses are, moreover, very diverse: some do only spinning, others weaving, others only the complete cycle of manufacturing. For the latter, the tendency was to work backwards, that is to say, starting with the printing and finishing, to ensure supplies of fabrics and then of the yarn necessary for these fabrics. Thus the Mulhouse print-makers became successively weavers, then spinners, integrating the whole range of manufacturing, from raw cotton to coloured prints. Such cases are not very numerous and become rarer in the middle of the nineteenth century: the typical textile business at that time combines spinning and weaving, leaving to other more specialised businesses the bleaching, dyeing or printing. The textile business, after having been integrated, tended to break up again.

The industrial revolution began to make its effects felt

in France in about 1770–1780 and continued its manifestations up to about the 1870s. It was an abnormally long period for a so-called revolution, and this length of time shows how inadequate is the expression 'industrial revolution', which has to be used in default of anything more appropriate. More than a revolution, it is a transformation one sees because France had already previously had crafts and even industries, when one thinks, among other things, of the industries stimulated by Colbert. The transformation was more gradual than in other countries precisely because everything did not have to start from scratch. It only took on a revolutionary character in the sectors where it was starting from nothing, as with the cotton industry, for example. Where there were already traditions and a production — wool and flax, metallurgy — we can see a gradual adaptation to new conditions, either by the adoption of new methods of power, or by a renovation of the manufacturing industry. Thus very different techniques existed side by side, some archaic, others more progressive, sometimes even within the same enterprise. There is nothing surprising about this because the changes took place at different dates as a result of inventions and financial needs and what one can call the linking principle, that is to say, the discovery by series of new techniques. We can see noticeable gaps within the same sector of production, and even from one region to another. In a market which, up to 1870, was far from being unified, very varying methods of production exist side by side, some traditional (the charcoal foundry, for example), others more up-to-date (the Bessemer steel converter). This shows the difficulty of drawing general conclusions valid for the whole country and for every sphere of production. One must above all keep a sense of subtle differences.

Taking this for granted, it is however possible to divide the industrial revolution in France into periods. Four periods followed each other:

1. From about 1760 to about 1790: *a rapid and brilliant beginning*, as a result of new techniques (imported from England) exploited thanks to the country's prosperity,

derived from the accumulation of capital and the strength of its foreign trade. This is what has enabled some economic historians like Fr. Crouzet to claim that England and France were not, basically, so far apart at this period, even if certain factors allowed a technical 'breakthrough' across the Channel.

2. From about 1790 to about 1815: *a noticeable slowing-down* in the industrial development of France, for essentially political reasons, with their monetary sequels. The war, disorder, inflation slowed down, sometimes even halted industrial progress. The only sector to have made progress was cotton-spinning, and that in artificial conditions because of the blockade. Investments turned away from the productive sector in favour of real estate and property.[43]

3. From about 1815 to about 1850: *a resumption of industrialisation* made easier by the return of peace and the prospect of profits, stimulated by the policy of the governments of the time. The spirit of the period can be found in Guizot's famous slogan, 'Make yourselves rich'. Other factors worked in favour of industrialisation, especially the development of canals and railways, with the direct participation of the state, in the form of subsidies, monopolies or the guaranteeing of interest on loans.

4. From 1850 to 1870/75 we can see the *spread* of industrial effort thanks to the conjunction of several factors: unification of the home market by railways, use of new techniques (in metallurgy, among other sectors) and the development of foreign competition. Nor should we forget the openly favourable attitude of the state to industrialists and businessmen.

This attempt to place things within periods is only meant

43. On this point cf. François Crouzet, Les conséquences économiques de la Révolution, à propos d'un inédit de Sir Francis d'Ivernois, *Annales Historiques de la Révolution française*, 34e année, No. 168 and 169, 1962, pp. 182–217 and 336–362. On page 212 one can find good examples of the preference of contemporaries for investments in property rather than industry. All the very tendencious assertions of Sir Francis d'Ivernois need certainly not be accepted, because of his systematic hostility to the Revolution, but some of his ideas can be retained after examination.

to provide a framework without in any way being intended to be rigid. With regard to the length of each period, it is better to go back to the idea of economic growth, in this case industrial growth, which corresponds more closely to the reality in France, which is based more on continuity over a century than on decisive breaks. This interpretation, moreover, fits in with the calculations made by Marczewski and Crouzet. The former says that the average annual rate of growth of industrial products is as follows:

from 1815–1824 to 1845–1854   2.5%
     1835–1844 to 1865–1874   1.9%
     1845–1854 to 1875–1884   1.8% [44]

Crouzet says that the average annual rate of growth between 1815 and 1913 is 1.61 per cent if one takes the whole range of industries, 3 per cent if one takes the 'dynamic' industries, that is to say, those affected by the industrial revolution.[45]

None of these figures takes account, and this is quite natural, of the division into periods which we have used. The former, Marczewski's, tends to show a slowing-up after 1860. The second, calculated in a continuous way over a long period, cannot take note of these divisions. But in fact the two rates are not so very far apart from each other, and show a very modest, if not mediocre, growth in comparison to England or Germany.

The reasons for this slowness having been explained, we must now look at its consequences. On the one hand, and this is the most marked consequence, France developed a noticeable backwardness in comparison with other economic powers, and this backwardness became striking in the middle of the twentieth century. Starting the race almost level with England, she has allowed herself to be outdistanced first by her, then by Germany, America, Japan and Russia. She has steadily slipped back in this race, for lack of sufficiently solid bases, and the accumulated delay cannot be made up. On the other hand, this incompletely

44. Jean Marczewski, Introduction à l'Histoire Quantitative, v. 41, p. 171.
45. Cf. above, note 9, p. 15.

achieved industrialisation has had serious social consequences. It has allowed the survival of a peasantry, if not powerful, at least numerous and politically influential. It has created a world of workers unsatisfied, because ill-paid, ill-housed and looked down on in a society which bases its values other than on production and pride in technical skill — at any rate up to a recent period. In France the framework of society and the state, within which this 'industrial revolution' was accomplished, favoured traditional values, the state, religion, authority, submission, rather than new values. Industrialisation, because it was slow, because it was not accompanied by a large-scale movement from the countryside to the towns, because it allowed men to go on believing in the superiority of landed property, has not succeeded in achieving either the technical or the mental breakthrough which would have led to a revision of these values and to a more homogeneous and harmonious society.

BIBLIOGRAPHY

I — Sources

Only some of the printed sources are mentioned here. For the manuscript sources, there is a huge amount deposited in the public Archives (National, Departmental, Local), as well as in the Chambers of Commerce, the Tribunaux de Commerce . . . There are also private sources, many of them not yet available, deposited, in the offices of the Notaires or in the industrial plants themselves. After World War II, some of these private papers were deposited in the National Archives or the Departmental Archives, where they may be consulted.

The main statistical material is the *Annuaire statistique de la France*, published yearly since 1878 by various Government agencies. Some of the volumes contain recapitulative data, going back to the early nineteenth century. It may be completed by other publications of the Statistique générale de la France, such as the Census (Résultats du dénombrement de la population en . . . title varies), the industrial census (title varies) . . .

These statistical sources may be completed by the various *Enquêtes*, inquiries which were made during the nineteenth century, especially the one of 1860 on the Treaty of Commerce with Great Britain, and the one of 1870.

For further details on these official sources, there is a good description in: Gille (Bertrand), Les sources statistiques de l'Histoire de France, des Enquêtes du XVIIe siècle à 1870, Genève-Paris, 1964, 288 pp. See also the information provided by David S. Landes, in The Cambridge Economic History of Europe, Vol. VI, The Industrial Revolutions and after, pp. 967–970.

II — General Works

As already stated, there is no satisfactory book covering the industrial revolution in France. Ballot (Charles), L'introduction du machinisme dans l'industrie française, Paris,

1923, is well-informed but outdated. Dunham (Arthur Louis), The Industrial Revolution in France, 1815–1848, New York, 1955 (there is also a French edition, Paris, 1953), covers only a part of the story and is rather boring.

One should not neglect the old classics of French Economic History, such as Emile Levasseur, whose books are still valuable and contain a core of precious data. Among the ones of special value here, his *Histoire de la Population française* (3 vol.), and his *Histoire des classes ouvrières et de l'industrie en France*, divided into two sets (before 1789, between 1789 and 1870), with a supplement on the Third Republic.

Among recent contributions to the Industrial Revolution in France, see The Cambridge Economic History of Europe, vol. VI, already mentioned, and especially the outstanding contribution of David S. Landes, *Technological Change and Development in Western Europe*, 1750–1914, pp. 274–601, and his more recent *Unbound Prometheus*, Cambridge, 1969. See also Claude Fohlen, *La rivoluzione industriale in Francia*, in Studi Storici, 1961, pp. 517–547.

Of special interest for the economic historian is the research being undertaken by the Institut de Science Economique Appliquée (isea), under the direction of Jean Marczewski. The first results have been published under the general title of *Histoire Quantitative de l'Economie française*, since 1961. In this series, four volumes have been devoted by T. J. Markovitch to industry, under the title *L'Industrie française de 1789 à 1964* (AF 4 to 7), Paris, 1965–66. The last volume presents the general conclusions of the whole study. The purpose and the methods of this study have been explained by Jean Marczewski in his *Introduction à l'Histoire Quantitative*, Genève, 1965.

In contrast with these scholarly works, it may be added that French literature is especially rich in economic as well as social information, e.g. in the many novels from Balzac to Philippe Hériat, with special emphasis on Zola. Anyone interested in French economic history has first to read some of these novels in order to get acquainted with France from the inside.

III — Specialised Works

For most of the industrial branches and the geographical regions there are some specialised studies.

For the *iron and steel industries* the best book is Gille (Bertrand), *La sidérurgie française au XIXe siècle*, Genève, 1968, which is a collection of articles previously published in various reviews. For *textile industries*, see Fohlen (Claude), *L'industrie textile au temps du Second Empire*, Paris, 1956.

There is no adequate book on *mining*, apart from the already old book of Rouff (Marcel), *Les mines de charbon en France au XVIIIe siècle*, Paris, 1922. Some new views are expressed in *Charbon et Sciences humaines*, Actes du colloque organisé par la Faculté des Lettres de l'Université de Lille, Paris, 1966. On *chemical industries*, the only valuable book is Baud (Paul), *L'industrie chimique en France*, Paris, 1931. Some new research is under way in this field, but not yet published.

During the last fifteen years there has been an emphasis on banks and banking institutions. The two leaders in this field are Cameron (Rondo E.), *France and the Economic Development of Europe, 1800–1914*, Princeton, 1961, and Gille (Bertrand), *La Banque et le Crédit en France de 1815 à 1848*, Paris, 1959. It should be read in conjunction with Bouvier (Jean), *Le Crédit Lyonnais de 1863 à 1882: les années de formation d'une banque de dépôts*, Paris, 1961, 2 vol.

There is no adequate book on *transportation*, and especially on the railroads and their impact on the industrial revolution. One may consult Girard (Louis), *La politique des travaux publics du Second Empire*, Paris, 1952. François Caron is publishing shortly his book on the Northern Railways. The navigation on the Rhône has been reviewed by Rivet (Félix), *La navigation à vapeur sur la Saône et le Rhône (1783–1863)*, Paris, 1962.

There is a long tradition in France of local and regional works, which are of great interest for the economic historian. Among the best ones published in recent years, Leon (Pierre), *La naissance de la grande industrie en Dauphiné* (fin du XVII siècle, 1869), Paris, 1954, 2 vol., which is a superb piece of scholarship, and Leuilliot (Paul), *L'Alsace au début du XIXe siècle: essais d'histoire politique, économique et religieuse* (1815–1830), Paris, 1959, 3 vol., which is full of fascinating information on one of the leading industrial districts. One may add Thuillier (Guy), *Aspects de l'Economie nivernaise au XIXe siècle*, Paris, 1966.

IV — Discussions on the Industrial Revolution in France

On the general problem of the Industrial Revolution, one may refer to Bairoca (Paul), *Révolution industrielle et sous-développement*, Paris, 1963.

The main discussion on the industrial revolution in France has been conducted in the United States and was started by the article of Clough (Sheperd B.), Retardative factors in French Economic Development in the 19th and 20th centuries, *Journal of Economic History*, supplement, III, 1946, pp. 91–102. Other views have been expressed by Landes (David S.), French Entrepreneurship and Industrial Growth in the Nineteenth Century, *Journal of Economic History*, IX, 1949, pp. 45–61. The discussion has been summarised in some of the articles published in the collective book edited by Earle (Edward Mead), *Modern France*, Problems of the Third and Fourth Republics, Princeton, 1951.

Different views on the *economic growth* of France have been expressed in the following articles:

Leon (Pierre), L'industrialisation en France en tant que facteur de croissance économique du XVIIIe siècle à nos jours, *Première conférence internationale d'histoire économique, Stockholm, 1960*, Paris-La Haye, 1960, pp. 163–197.

Marczewski (Jean), Some aspects of the Economic Growth of France, 1660–1958, *Economic Development and Cultural Change*, Vol. 9, Part II, 1961, pp. 369–386.

Marczewski (Jean), The Take-off Hypothesis and French Experience, in W. W. Rostow, *The Economics of take-off into sustained Growth*, New York, 1963, pp. 119–138.

A synthesis has been presented by Kindleberger (Charles P.), *Economic Growth in France and Britain, 1851–1950*, Cambridge (Mass.), 1964.

2. The Industrial Revolution in Germany 1700–1914

Knut Borchardt

INTRODUCTION

We cannot expect to establish for the Industrial Revolution in Germany a more precise set of dates than has been possible in other countries whose historians are engaged in vigorous debates about this problem. Unlike W. W. Rostow with his period of 'take off' we are not here attempting to propose simultaneously a concept and an enveloping hypothesis: the term industrial revolution will demand rather less precision in the determination of chronological limits.

In Germany intimations of industrialisation may be discerned towards the end of the eighteenth century: a mechanised cotton spinning mill was set up at Ratingen near Düsseldorf in 1784; a coke blastfurnace began to operate in Upper Silesia in 1792 and several copies of Newcomen and of Watt steam engines were constructed. Any account of the industrial revolution in Germany must begin with these events. But the transformation of these early beginnings into a solid advance, a 'forward leap' for modern eyes, took much longer here than in Britain. Experts still disagree whether this spurt started about 1834, 1842–3 or even 1850. For reasons which should be made evident below I have decided to place the break in my account of industrialisation in 1850 and to describe as 'preliminary' the first period from the end of the eighteenth century to the middle of the nineteenth. This leaves open the question as to the end of the industrial revolution in Germany. It may well be true that the institutions thrown up by economic growth between 1850 and 1873 more or less guaranteed its continuation: nevertheless this cannot be regarded as terminating the German industrial revolution. Indeed there is much to be said for directing attention to the subsequent period of expansion, especially from 1896 to 1913, when Germany was no longer overshadowed by its erstwhile exemplars.

A few tables may demonstrate the development which will be described and explained in more detail below. Unfortunately sufficiently accurate data do not exist for the period before 1850. Figure 1 shows that since 1850 agriculture has employed a declining, mining and industry (including crafts) an increasing share of the working population. It makes evident too that some parts of the tertiary sector grew even more rapidly than the producing industries. For the growth of industrial production including crafts we possess some data which are probably fairly

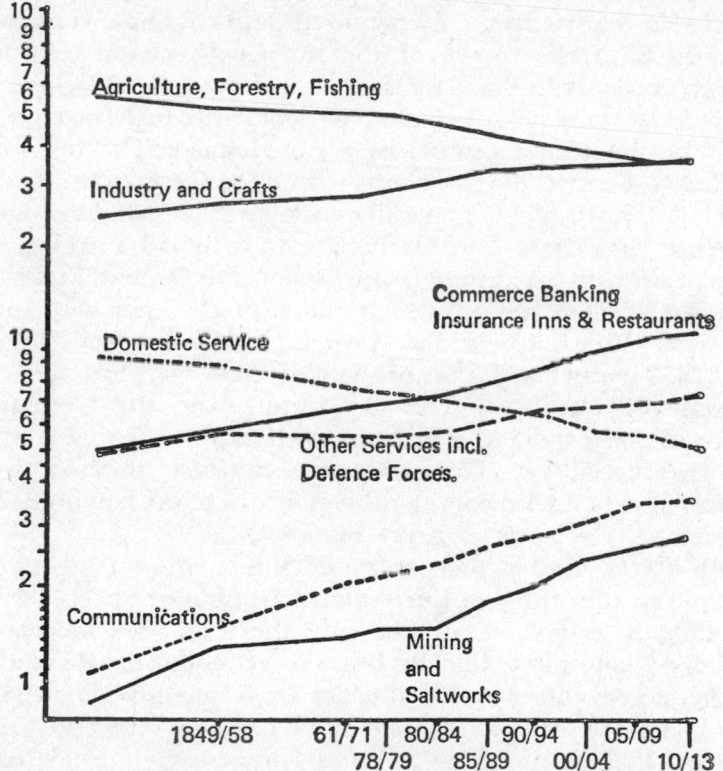

FIGURE 1 *Numbers employed in each sector of the Economy, 1849-1913*

unreliable. Figure 2 displays the indices of industrial production and simultaneously the consumption of iron and steel per head of the German population as important indications of industrial development.

Unfortunately there are no data for the development of the national product before 1850. But Figure 3 at least shows the trends from then on. The tables reflect a basically steady growth, apart from the period 1873–83.

It remains highly problematical whether such very long run series of macro-economic data may be used in support of any statement at all. Their value as evidence is limited by numerous insoluble enigmas, concerning contents and statistical method. Germany presents an additional difficulty in that its area only acquired political and economic cohesion in the course of the nineteenth century. It is even necessary to elucidate the political concept of Germany as here employed because its constitutional meaning in the nineteenth century was not defined. The present treatise discusses developments within the German frontiers of 1871 although it generally disregards Alsace-Lorraine before that date. The German empire of 1871 was not identical with the ancient realm of the 'Holy Roman Empire of the German Nation' which ended in 1806 nor with the territory controlled by the German Federation from 1815 to 1866 neither with that of the North-German Federation from 1867 to 1871. The old empire and the German Federation extended well beyond the later imperial frontiers, especially in the south and south-east; they on the other hand omitted considerable portions of the kingdom of Prussia in the north-east (see Figure 4).

Is it permissible then to make statements intended to apply to the whole of this region? In many respects conditions in each part differed and the total area long remained not only politically but also economically divided. Therefore comprehensive statistics are frequently somewhat unhistorical: occasionally we shall have to revert to this point. For the time being we must crave some latitude for any failure to pay due regard to local features in every region and for the too frequent employment of comprehen-

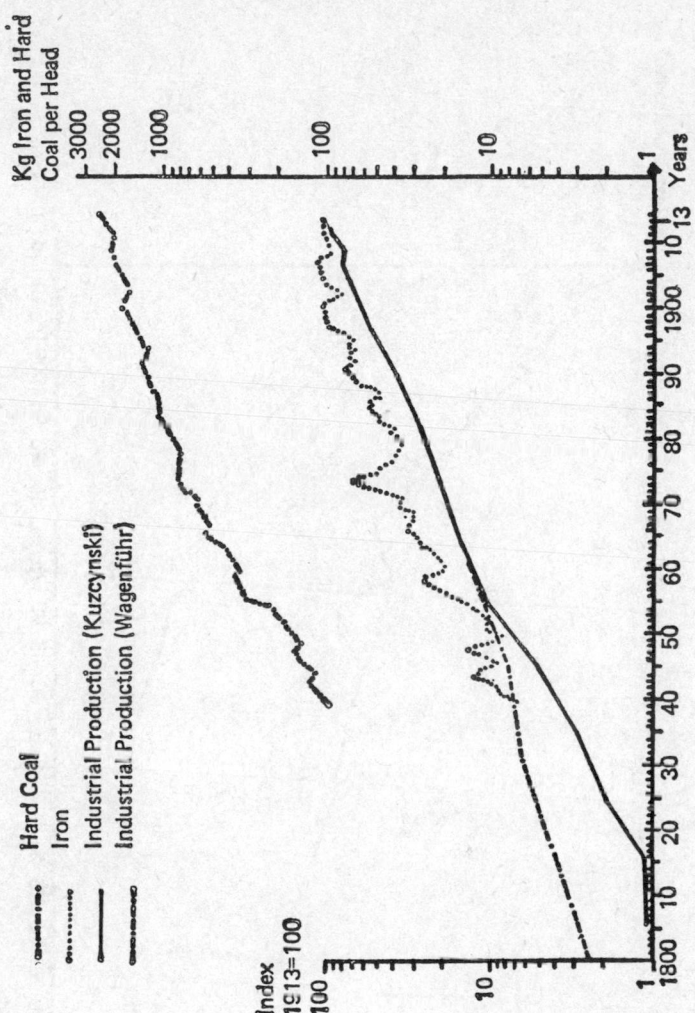

FIGURE 2 *Indicators of Industrialisation 1800-1913. Index of Industrial Production, Consumption of Iron and Hard Coal*

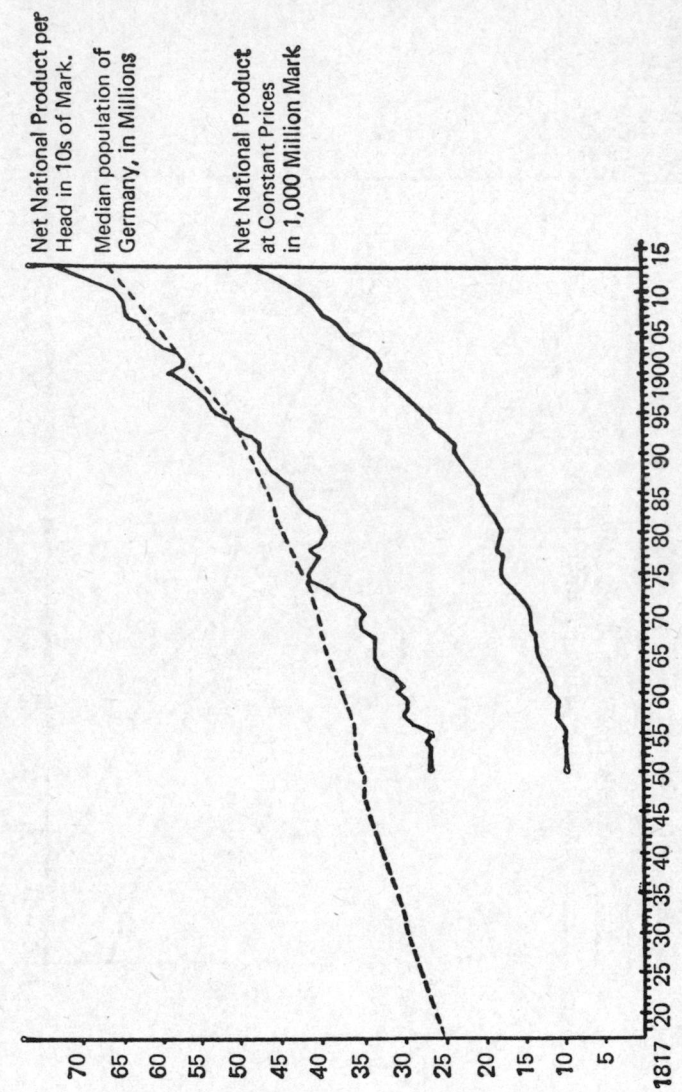

FIGURE 3 *Net National Product at Constant Prices 1850-1913.*
Net National Product at Constant Prices per Head
1850-1913. Population 1816-1913

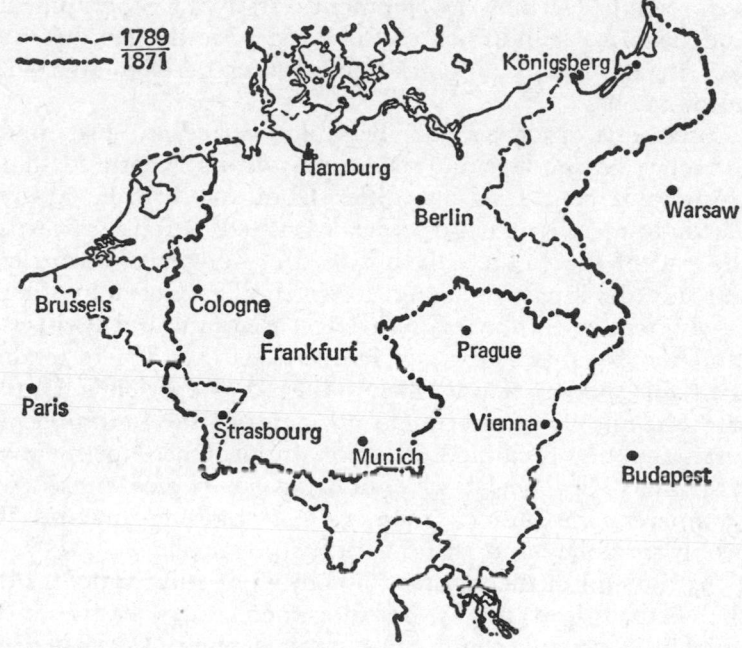

FIGURE 4 *Map of Germany showing the changes in boundaries between 1789 and 1871*

sive totals and averages, without precise indication of the regional scatter of values.

THE SPECIAL CONDITIONS FOR THE INDUSTRIAL REVOLUTION IN GERMANY

Many events which have been characterised as elements of the industrial revolution recur in several countries. Thus in Germany too industrialisation is accompanied by a demographic revolution, an agrarian revolution and a transport revolution. But the German timing differs from that of its western and eastern neighbours; and socio-economic structures, however similar, were far from identical.

Two factors were primarily responsible for the special

nature of the German development. Firstly the geographical and historical conditions of the country and secondly the fact that German industrialisation was derived and not autonomous.

Economic progress in Britain exerted a profound influence on the German evolution and itself ensured that Germany's course should differ from the British. Many German merchants and officials visited Britain towards the end of the eighteenth and in the nineteenth centuries to study the innovations and to transmit to Germany their newly acquired knowledge. France, Belgium and Switzerland too became sources of innovations. Foreigners made their fortunes by selling their—alleged—experience. Until after the middle of the nineteenth century the imitation of foreign models remained of major importance. Not merely machinery but 'social inventions' were copied, i.e. new commercial institutions, mercantile techniques, maxims of economic policy and administrative postures.

At the end of the eighteenth century it still seemed as if the British lead might be shortened fairly easily and quickly. Germany could draw upon a body of experience which had been built up meanwhile and it might avoid some of the consequences of experiment and spontaneity which had afflicted the leading countries. In reality, for reasons which will be discussed below, it took several decades. By then both public administrations and other central decision making bodies, such as the banks, could make themselves felt effectively. The technology which was taken over in the second third of the nineteenth century was by then fairly advanced. Some industries were introduced at once as large scale enterprises without having to wait upon slow growth and thus immediately benefited from economies of scale.

Viewed from the end of the nineteenth century, Germany's slow start proved to be of real benefit for its later development. Not too much capital had been tied up earlier on in the 'old industries' nor had the excess of rural population been tied up in the traditional trades. From mid century it was thus easier than in Britain, for instance, to shift labour and capital into new industries such as mining, engineering, chemicals and electrics and to equip them with the latest technology. Real wages too were relatively low and this helped to nullify the former competitive advantage of western neighbours.

Last but not least German producers and consumers benefited directly from the efficiency of the British and other west-European sellers. In 1849 German cotton-weavers bought 62 per cent of their yarn from abroad. British capital goods were especially important in the establishment of German industry. The first German railways from 1835 on, for instance, were largely equipped with British engines, wagons and rails.

Superior British competiton though could hamper the evolution of native industries too; indeed it might help to explain the sluggish progress of industrialisation in the first third of the century. The German cotton industry could not affect industrialisation in this country as it had affected it in the first industrial nation. Neither did the German cotton industry have access to export markets as lucrative nor did the domestic market, depressed by the competition of British productive capacity after 1815, offer a rate of return like the British until 1802. These matters will be discussed in more detail below.

More detailed attention will have to be devoted to the second factor which determined the special nature of German development. As Germany was neither one of the first to emulate the British experience nor yet as far behind as the countries of southern and eastern Europe it must have been subject to a rough balance of fairly negative and fairly positive impulses. One of the favourable factors in the long run was certainly the wealth of coal and iron, once they had been discovered and developed. But we will have to begin further back.

Until the nineteenth century Germany did not possess an integrated territory with an economic and administrative centre. Mountains and rivers delimited its divisions which frequently developed closer links with non-German regions than with each other. For all its own cultural and economic achievements, as for instance in the mining, printing and metal working industries, Germany had never been a genuine centre of European economic progress until well into the nineteenth century. Northern Italy, the Netherlands, France and England had been the foci, one after the other, from which the secondary German centres took their cues. The eastern parts of Europe on the other hand remained normally even more backward than Germany. For centuries thus the German lands had served as intermediary on the gradient between west and east and this has done something to determine the regional organisation of her economy until to-day. Since the sixteenth century indeed the west–east gradient had become steeper: its western neighbours had received multiple stimuli from their colonial expansion whose effect on Germany was much attenuated. None of the German seaports managed to break the trading monopoly of the colonial powers or to acquire a notable share of direct overseas trade for any length of time. The organisation of German foreign and domestic trade was left without the creative stimulus for change because it was virtually excluded from independent colonial trade and had to rely on the colonial powers as intermediaries for overseas exports and imports. Except for a few coastal towns, industrial centres lay generally well into the interior and agriculture dominated around the coasts.

Germany's situation in the centre of Europe and its lack of political unity involved it more frequently in political conflicts than the peripheral countries. Often it became the scene of destructive wars. The Thirty Years' War had devastated the country politically and economically. In the eighteenth century too, warfare in some part of the empire was the rule rather than the exception. Rulers and their subjects remained fully alive to the risk of war and this delayed the growth of economic interdependence between the regions. In addition there were the deleterious effects of diverting a major share of the national product into military expenditure.

In 1789 Germany remained politically divided into 314 independent territories and more than 1,400 imperial knight's fees. Germany's internal traffic was, as is well known, obstructed by innumerable customs barriers, currencies and trading monopolies. Their effect may indeed have been exaggerated. But the fact that since the sixteenth century the vitality of the old towns and of their burgesses had been sapped in their conflict with the more powerful secular and spiritual principalities needs greater emphasis. The city as princely residence did not substitute for the free metropolitan centre of industry and trade as the nucleus of bourgeois autonomy.

While in seventeenth-century England the power of the crown became restricted, the growing absolutism of the German princes succeeded in largely by-passing the control of their traditional estates. The contradiction between this and the observable revival of the nobility in eighteenth-century Germany is only apparent: its demotion from one kind of political power was balanced by the immediate creation of privilege to posts at Court, in the officer corps and in the higher ranks of the administration.

The local sway of the nobility was founded on the economic system of landlords' dominion which remained inviolate in any case. In north-eastern Germany indeed the system of Gutsherrschaft had emerged since the fifteenth century; where this prevailed, villeins by inheritance had sunk into a position tantamount to slavery, in fact although not in law. To the challenge of profitable long-range trade in grain with western markets the east German nobility responded by accentuating feudal dependence rather than adapting the organisation of their enterprises to 'capitalist conditions'. That accounts for an important peculiarity of the pre-industrial period in Germany; it also contributed to a persistent rupture in the framework of German society between east and west, characterised by the east German 'Junkerdom'.

There was little mobility in pre-industrial German society: rigid lines of demarcation between the estates were not just retained but frequently emphatically reinforced. Many traditional rules of status still dominated village and urban life in the eighteenth century, cocooning the individual in social security: they rigidly pressed his economic activity into a political and social mould, thus curbing individual initiative and innovations. It was generally assumed that individual riches resulted from the mere redistribution of wealth rather than from achievements of general utility. Restrictions on marriage and migration helped to safeguard the utilisation of the common property. True, the urban gilds had lost some of their hold over industry and commerce, as rural crafts and manufactures evolved in Germany as well: at an estimate, rural industry accounted for a third of all artisans in 1800. But rural artisans were often just assimilated into the rural hierarchy and therefore not free either.

The mutual estrangement of classes and estates was in Germany accentuated by the cultural division between rulers and subjects. Courts, courtiers and anyone who wielded power at Court took France, its courtly manners and its civilisation as the guiding light. Its general adoption of the French language alone set the political élite apart from the people. This was the time when the intellectuals, albeit somewhat furtively, developed the notion of a national German culture which became synonymous with the rejection of feudalism. For this, English poetry and philosophy became models worthy of the most direct emulation. Since 1517 Germany's divisions had not been solely political but also religious. It is therefore of great importance for the history of Germany that it first found its national identity in the cultural sphere of literature and philosophy, that this was secondly followed by economic unification in the customs union of 1834, while its political unification had to wait until 1871. Among the ideas common to the economically active bourgeoisie, the lack of German unity was well to the fore. Thus the aspirations for unity in the end eclipsed the bourgeois appetite for democracy. This appreciation followed inexorably from German conditions: national divisions more seriously obstructed the full play of bourgeois economic capabilities, whether at home or abroad, than exclusion from political participation in government.

Families engaged in agriculture or industry during the eighteenth century were heavily burdened with feudal dues and public taxation. This further depressed the purchasing power of the population at large, well below the meagre level appropriate to the inadequately developed methods of production. As a corollary, probably a large part of the dues and taxes was spent on high grade consumption. German culture too flourished in the eighteenth century, at many secular and spiritual courts. Mercantilist writers had long pointed out that a high rate of expenditure on luxuries and military supplies tended to promote growth. Of known Prussian public expenditure between 1740 and 1786 from 70 to 80 per cent was devoted to military purposes. Because the records are not full enough, neither the effects of such expenditures nor of the corresponding revenue collections can be properly assessed; hitherto all suggestions have at best been backed by persuasive examples but none has been properly tested. The pressure of taxation on the subject probably extended the circulation of money and contributed to speculative innovations in the manufacture of arms and of luxuries. In view of the simultaneous destruction and waste, the immediate effect of such expenditures on net growth may well have amounted to less than has long been taken for granted.

From the seventeenth century on, it is true, princely entrepreneurs and their officials had promoted manufactures outside the gilds, at least in some export industries and in those of importance for the court or the armed forces. Thus Germany too had many manufactories in the eighteenth century. On the whole however they had a short life and most of them collapsed with the *ancien régime*, either because now there was no demand or even because competing traditional crafts turned out to be superior to them. Too often success or failure of the 'proto factories' (Freudenberger) did not depend primarily on their technical performance but on the skill of the entrepreneur in procuring courtly extravagance or the compulsory recruitment of labour. The industrialists depended on the whims of a few people and their privileges were akin to monopoly: this was not the kind of economic activity which would readily serve as an example for the rest of the entrepreneurial economy.

Domestic self-sufficiency still played a much greater part in Germany than it did in Britain. When the peasant had payed his feudal rent and taxes, the return from his marketable produce left him with little freely disposable cash. Of course there was interchange between the economic sectors. But it is generally estimated that in 1800 something like 80 per cent of the population was employed in agriculture. These figures undoubtedly understate the significance of other employments of the rural population, for instance in spinning and weaving. Nevertheless four out of every five people around 1800 lived in households which, as a matter of course, attached great importance to their involvement in agricultural production.

There were then a number of reasons why Germany, at the end of the eighteenth century, lagged behind some western parts of Europe. Compared to eastern or southern Europe though, to say nothing of countries outside Europe, Germany was relatively advanced. Conditions certainly differed a great deal in different parts of the country. There is every justification for calling Germany, on the whole, a predominantly agrarian country, yet in 1800 only 20 per cent of the population of Saxony was employed exclusively in agriculture. In the valleys south of the Ruhr, engaged in the textile and iron industries, population density had reached 150 to 250 people per square kilometre. The export industries which had grown up on the Lower Rhine, in Westphalia, Lusatia and Lower Saxony benefited from the conflict between Britain and France at the end of the eighteenth century and from the American achievement of independence in 1783. Evidently then there existed a reasonably trained labour force, in some trades, it is true, incompetent to meet the most exacting standards but mostly on a par with contemporary attainment. Some parts of Germany had introduced compulsory education; state and church helped to promote work discipline and even economic ambition was by no means lacking. Venturesome entrepreneurs existed, perhaps as yet only in small numbers; presumably the impediments to their multiplication were structural rather than mental or psychological. Even in Germany a noticeable trend towards greater objectivity in the bureaucratic decisions of government checked the personal arbitrariness of princely régimes. If it were possible to imagine the course of history with Britain's contribution cut out, it does not become inconceivable that an autonomous industrial revolution might some day have occurred in Germany.

Apart from a few sectors the difference in technical accomplishment between the two countries was probably less than the difference in the standards of living. In some trades, such as cutlery, silver wares, paper and printing, German craft manufacture enjoyed an international reputation. Why should this have been limited to them alone?

If the German economy was retarded despite this, as is generally accepted, there must have been some other explanation. Perhaps the explanation must be sought primarily in terms consonant with the theories of Adam Smith which apply admirably to the eighteenth century. Unlike the more advanced countries, most of Germany during the seventeenth and eighteenth centuries had hardly participated in the continuing development of the 'market economy' which owed a vital impetus to the activities of the merchants. A social organisation and a political structure as outlined above, communications virtually unaltered until the end of the eighteenth century and persistent discrimination against free commerce had combined to inhibit the increasing division of labour or a rational selection of sites and hence the efficient exploitation of resources. Everything pointed to the existence of a great deal of spare capacity. Factors of production were nowhere near being fully employed. The seasonal employment of the rural labour force was of course very uneven but industrial labour did not work regularly either. This was caused not only by the many holidays but by considerable fluctuations in demand and by the irregular delivery of materials. Much industrial capacity was only employed by way of a side-line. As late as 1831 no more than 74 per cent of Prussian linen looms were attended by workers whose sole occupation was weaving. Many other indications likewise suggest a relatively high degree of capital intensiveness for the pre-industrial period as well. There does not appear to be any justification for the assumption that capital intensiveness had always been as low as in 1850 if not even lower. True, it did rise continuously after 1850. Could it not have declined in the preliminary period? (In this calculation, it should be remembered, it is the quantity of labour actually employed in a year and not the number of workers, which must form the denominator in the proportion of capital to labour.) Uncertainties of production and supplies and protracted transport were responsible for tying up large amounts of capital in stocks as a matter of course. The seasonal rhythm of the harvest in a predominantly agrarian society ensured anyhow that a high proportion of annual production had to be stored for long periods.

One of the peculiarities of the great leap forward in nineteenth-century Germany would appear to be the simultaneous advance in manufacturing technology and in the speed of conversion to the market economy, the 'revolution in organisation'.

THE PRELIMINARY PERIOD

One of the most striking phenomena is the growth of population. Between 1816 and 1850 the number of inhabitants increased from 24·8 to 35·5 millions; in Saxony, the Prussian Rhineland and eastern Prussia growth was exceptionally rapid, in southern Germany, Hesse and Hanover less so. Nuptiality and in consequence the birth rate immediately after the war were extremely high and mortality simultaneously remained fairly low. After 1830 birth rate tended to remain at 3·6 per hundred and mortality at about 2·7 per hundred until the end of the sixties

(Figure 5). But the population did not increase regularly by the excess of births (0·9 per hundred), as even then the balance of international migration markedly affected the result. In the 1820s there was slight net emigration but in the thirties the balance became positive as eastern Germany gained from immigration, while south Germany experienced considerable emigration. In the forties emigration was responsible for major losses, especially during the period of political reaction from 1847 to 1849 when excess emigration absorbed almost half the excess of births.

Unfortunately there is no series of population statistics for the period before 1816. Hence it cannot be determined with certainty, when and why the rapid growth of population started in Germany. It is claimed that people, released from the clutches of landlords, estate owners and compulsory gilds, married more frequently and earlier. (So afraid were some German principalities of over-population that they re-introduced legal restrictions on marriage after 1828 which some of them did not formally abolish until the end of the nineteenth century.) But not enough is yet known of reproductive habits in the eighteenth and early nineteenth centuries to accept the significance of emancipating legislation without reservation. The population of Brandenburg-Prussia presumably increased by more than 1 per cent per annum as early as the period from 1750 to 1800; this however includes net gains by immigration. Altogether the rate of population growth in the German principalities from 1740 to 1800 has been estimated at about half a per cent yearly. Probably it would not have been lower before then, when recovery from the loss of population during the Thirty Years' War, estimated at approximately a third, had been the order of the day.

With the growth of population, industry and agriculture expanded in the eighteenth century too. Demand and the supply of labour increased simultaneously. How did production respond to the changed requirements? In Germany too we can find a number of minor technical innovations which helped to improve the productivity of

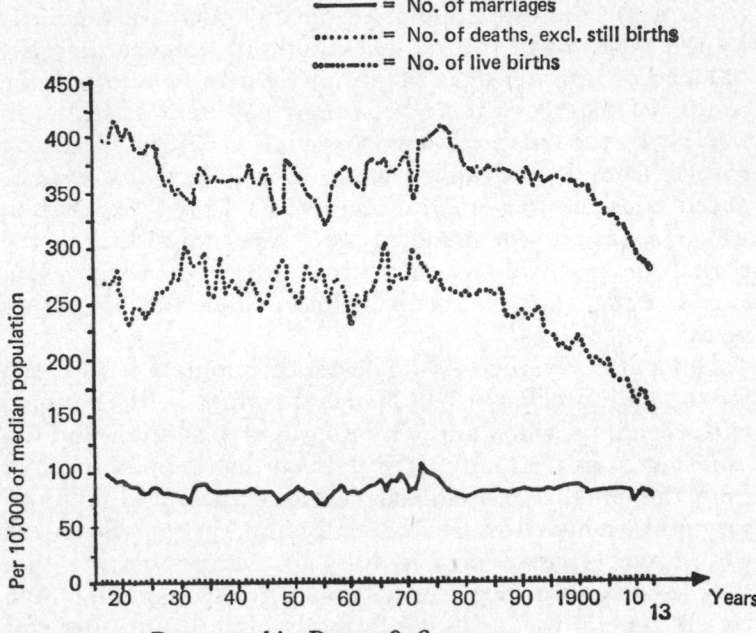

FIGURE 5 *Demographic Data 1816-1913*

land and labour. Primarily though it was by extension of the arable and by harder work that people responded to increased demand in the eighteenth century. Towards the end of the eighteenth century German agriculture was seized by an 'arable mania' as buoyant export conditions reinforced growing domestic demand. Mainly from 1780 onwards the prices of rye and of landed estates rose: the previous longstanding average was doubled within twenty years. The real wages of urban labour simultaneously fell to the lowest level for a century.

The sources do not tell us whether national product per head increased during the period of economic growth in the eighteenth century. If it occurred at all its effect must have been minimal, for the accounts of increasing hunger and misery bear the stamp of conviction. But the organisation of production was evidently elastic enough to ensure the physical survival of a growing population.

Ricardo's law though may well apply fairly closely to the condition of the German economy: as greater yields were forced from the soil, this came to be largely dominated by the law of diminishing returns.

Innovations in industry which can be found, do nothing to contradict that judgment. Naturally industrial production grew in the eighteenth century as population growth augmented both the labour force and demand. In addition a boom in exports towards the end of the century accentuated expansion, benefiting in particular the linen industry. In craft or domestic industries however growth relied primarily on existing techniques. Mechanised spinning, steam engines and coke blast furnaces remained isolated ventures.

The confusions of wartime between 1792 and 1815 at first inhibited the progressive international diffusion of innovations. In the course of a few years different industries in each German territory experienced radical reversals in their economic prospects. When western German territories were incorporated into the French state after 1794 this stimulated some trades but also deprived industries east of the Rhine of an important market. When Amsterdam was occupied, Hamburg, its substitute, flourished unexpectedly, as a centre for the colonial trade and for finance, until 1806. Most of the vanquished states though suffered under the exactions of contributions and the imposition of manifold political burdens. The Continental Blockade from 1806 to 1813 stimulated the cotton industry by excluding British competition and promoted the processing of native sugar beet but it depressed the linen, woollen and silk industries which had hitherto depended on export markets. The political burdens tended on the whole to diminish the capacity of individuals or governments to accumulate capital; simultaneously though it remained possible for the Rothschilds and others to acquire large private fortunes. A massive redistribution of wealth resulted from the decree of 1803 which secularised church property.

Developments until 1815 need not be described here in too much detail. After the lifting of the Continental Blockade and the disappearance of wartime demand, a series of years which were on the whole very poor, put paid to many hothouse plants. Several disastrous harvests between 1816 and 1818 once more raised agricultural prices to the levels of 1805 but this only helped that group of rural producers who had significant marketing outlets. There followed years of over-abundant harvests and a complete collapse of prices until 1825 (see Figure 6) which diminished the cash revenues from farming; the agricultural crisis then infected the whole economy. Some of the factors which had favoured expansion before 1800 had disappeared by the post-war period. Export demand and government orders had much diminished since the eighteenth century. Some German principalities, Prussia among them, deliberately operated deflationary policies to stabilise their currencies. Such a period of depression would obviously not conduce to the rapid deployment of novel techniques. There was little propensity to invest. Although technical progress had advanced visibly still further in Britain, emulation remained sluggish.

It would be mistaken however to disregard the opportunities for progress beyond all the difficulties. The rapid reversals of fortune, the alternation of prosperity and disaster, helped to shake and loosen the traditional structure of the economy. Few remained unaffected by the redistribution of economic opportunities and of real and monetary property to which this contributed: all this reduced the weight of tradition and custom. Most of the minor German principalities and the old German empire had collapsed under the blows of the French armies; more than anything this shook up the traditional political system and created some pressure for modernisation. As a cordial for economic development though this could take effect only in the long run.

Much of the western territory of the empire was incorporated in France after 1794 and adopted the results of the French revolution. One of the last constitutional acts of the old German empire, procured by the grace of Napoleon in 1803, formally permitted the greater German principalities to share out the surviving remnants of the empire among themselves. This concerned primarily the ecclesiastical properties which were being secularised. All this was bound to affect the internal political stability of the German states as it amounted to major interference with accepted standards of legality. It forms the proper context too for those promises of constitutions which were meant to establish the monarchies on fresh foundations; they were honoured after 1814, though by Prussia only in 1850. The re-allocations of territory similarly underlay the famed 'liberalism' of German civil servants during the period of reform. The officials found that they could not administer their newly acquired territories effectively, unless they were prepared to discard a great many traditions on which authority in each of their parts had long been based. Even politicians with conservative principles were compelled to adopt a reforming rationalism.

The failure of the traditional ruling élite enabled a more forward looking political élite, most of whom were still noble, to interfere with the traditional liberties of the ruling caste itself. Thus originated the promises of peasant emancipation and of industrial freedom. As these measures were ordered by the public administration, they have been called 'a revolution from above': neither their extent nor their effects justify that. Firstly emancipation was not altogether a new idea but had antecedents in the eighteenth century; secondly many of the promises were not honoured for several generations; thirdly emancipation was frequently hedged around with conditions which imposed heavy economic burdens upon those emancipated as a corollary of their new liberties. The so-called emancipation laws can, with some justice, be described as a major victory of the centralising authority of the state in its 200 years of conflict with the rival authority of the estates. It was only now that everyone came to be equally a subject of the state and that the immediate authority of the state applied to every person; simultaneously, as an intentional by-product of political reform, the power to raise compulsory levies became a public monopoly.

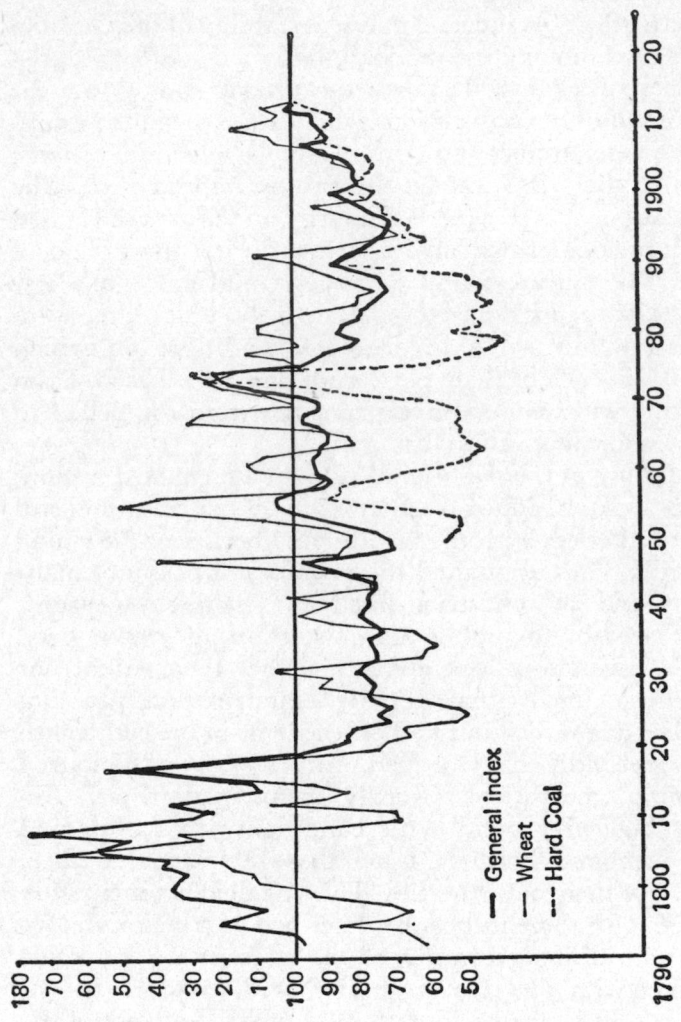

FIGURE 6 *Indexes of Wholesale Prices 1792-1913*

First of all we shall examine the measures which have been called 'abolition of serfdom'. Merely personal bondage (Leibeigenschaft) had become fairly unimportant before then and could be abolished without difficulty. Much the greatest proportion of the relationships between lord and peasant however were closely linked with control of the land, either by the manorial lords or by the east German 'estate lords'. More was involved here than the mere legal freedom of the individual or especially his freedom of movement: it concerned rights of property in the land worked by the peasant.

In Germany neither manorial nor estate lords were expropriated without compensation as this would have spelt economic ruin for the nobility: no reformer wanted to go as far as that. Provision was rather made for the redemption of rights of lordship. Manorial peasants who acquired outright the land they farmed, were to compound with a fixed multiple of their former annual dues, e.g. twentyfold, either in a lump sum or in instalments. In the majority of German principalities the transition was eased by setting up so-called 'Rentenbanken' which rapidly provided capital for the claimants while arranging for more gradual repayment by the debtors. Several hundred million Taler or Gulden were transferred in this manner. The time taken over the completion of this procedure differed from one principality to another. Most of the erstwhile manorial peasants were not properly freed until 1850; at a later stage the remaining instalments of compensation payments were converted into ordinary commercial obligations and some of these were still outstanding in 1913.

The ordinary manorial restraints had not been the chief object of the Prussian reforms of 1807 but the peculiar system under which the eastern 'estate lords' operated. This did not merely hold the peasants in heritable bondage but prevented the lords from freely alienating their estates. Stein's decree of 1807 was intended to secure mobility in principle for all the parties. The estate had formed an administrative district but was now stripped of some, though by no means all, of the more substantial features which made it into a territorial political institution. Administrative schedules to the decree, mainly those of 1811, 1816 and 1850, established the conditions under which a peasant might acquire land outright. Only the more substantial peasants who had farmed viable holdings in any case, obtained the ownership of their land. For this they had to compensate their lords, sometimes in cash, more often in land which came to as much as a third to one half of their former holdings. On the face of it that should have implied a massive redistribution of land in favour of the noble landed estate and all the textbooks so describe the outcome. But redistribution in the east did not, for a number of reasons, directly affect much more than 3 per cent of all peasant land, whether on manor or estate. The real victims were those who did not acquire any claim to land and who now lost in addition their erstwhile share in the communal property, with the abolition of rights of common, of pasture and of wood gathering. They simply replenished the pool of agricultural labour. In practice they continued to be looked after but legally they had become free labour without any visible productive resources. In the following decades it was this class which multiplied with more than common rapidity in the east.

The emancipation of the peasantry did not rapidly set free a rural proletariat for urban industry, as is sometimes mistakenly assumed. Indeed in most German states local communities could obstruct the immigration of poor persons with the help of a reinforced law of settlement. Moreover industries based on the factory could not provide employment for the excess of rural population until after mid-century. Until then domestic industry, organised on a putting-out basis, took on large numbers of this cheap agrarian labour which could be flexibly employed.

It is difficult to say how far peasant emancipation contributed to an increase in agricultural productivity, especially as the reforms stretched over fifty years. Emancipation is generally regarded as a significant prerequisite for this. Yet despite the progress of agricultural science and the dissolution of the old rural order, agricultural production in the first half of the nineteenth century was expanded mostly by increasing the area under cultivation (Figure 7). There was little improvement in the ratio of yield to seed until the last third of the nineteenth century. Between 1816 and 1852 the area under corn in Prussia expanded by more than a third, part by the cultivation of former waste, part at the expense of meadow and pasture. Fallow too was reduced and, most significantly, root vegetables of high calorific value were introduced. Roots accounted for only 3 per cent of Prussian crops produced in 1800 but forty years later their share had risen as high as 24 per cent. It was very largely due to the roots that the output of vegetable produce in Germany during the first half of the nineteenth century could keep in step with population growth. They also helped to stabilise the supply of food by reducing its dependence on the corn harvest with its fluctuations which had still been so extreme in the eighteenth century. Nevertheless general famine recurred when the potato blight reached Germany too in 1845–6, to be followed in 1846 and 1847 by grain harvests almost one third below previous years. This however was the last manifestation of the age old cycle of famine and plenty in agrarian society.

The production of animal produce increased more rapidly after 1815 than that of vegetable. The preceding wars had entailed severe losses for animal husbandry particularly: Prussia for instance had lost as much as a third of its stock. Moreover horned cattle were at that time produced mainly for haulage, as a form of capital goods. Thus until beyond mid-century the meat supply for the population was no better than before 1800.

On the whole labour in agriculture must have become more productive. But this development was far from being revolutionary. The land carried a particularly heavy surplus of labour until well past mid-century. In his 'Niveaux de dévelopment économique de 1810 à 1910' (*Annales*, XX (1965), 1091 ff.), Bairoch estimated the productivity of a male German agricultural worker in 1870 as at 75 per cent of a Belgian, 65 per cent of a French,

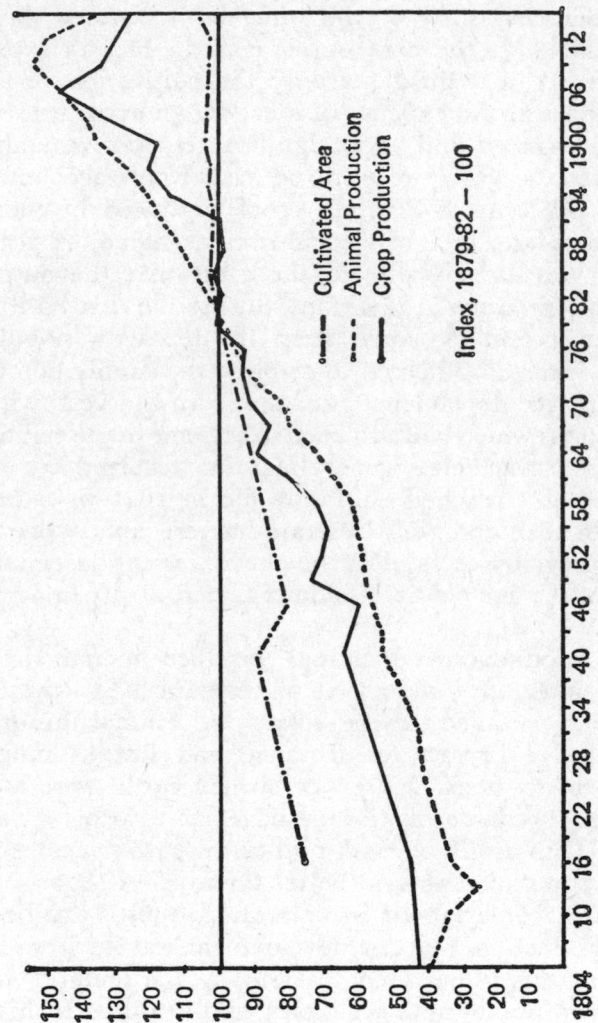

FIGURE 7 *Agricultural Production*

43 per cent of a British and 35 per cent of an American agricultural worker. Despite the rise in population however, Germany in the first half of the century remained almost entirely self-sufficient for its food supplies and in addition raised a considerable export trade in agrarian produce, such as grain, wool and timber. It was surely important for the early phase of its industrialisation that this largely compensated for the growing need for industrial raw materials, colonial produce, semi-manufactured goods and manufactures, thus avoiding a more pronounced deterioration in the balance of trade.

The emancipation of industry may be regarded as another effect of the revolutionary wars and of the subsequent reforming movements. Here too we may properly ask how far this contributed to growth. The dissolution of the gild régime had indeed made some progress in the eighteenth century. But outside the western territories under French administration, the decisive impetus towards a change in legal status was given by Prussia between 1807 and 1811, with a procedure which was once again neither consistently nor thoroughly revolutionary. When a trade tax was introduced in 1810 the exercise of selected important trades in the eastern provinces of Prussia was thrown open. Evidently though the question of industrial freedom of trades was not regarded as pressing so that other states did not feel compelled to adopt this innovation immediately: on the contrary some limitation of the number of workshops was widely accepted as desirable on grounds of social policy. Thus even Prussia reverted to some restriction later on, in 1845–9. Industrial Saxony and the agrarian states of south Germany did not in fact revoke their gild privileges until the 1860s. The middle classes as a body did not champion this sort of freedom; in Germany it continued to be regarded as a contentious subject, even after the North German Federation in 1869 and the whole empire in 1871 had become committed to the principle of free enterprise.

The thorough enforcement of gild privileges had never been easy: they were confined to traditional handicrafts so that their abolition mattered much less than other changes in policy. After 1815 the public administrations used more liberally their power to license industrial firms; they almost abandoned the mercantilist habit of granting monopoly privileges to individual manufacturers. Joint stock companies, it is true, still had to apply for a special licence in Prussia until 1870. But, apart from joint stock banking in Prussia, governments did not face them with any systematic opposition. Perhaps the co-operation of governments in issuing such grants may even be seen as a kind of warranty of reliability which ensured for this new kind of association more rapid dissemination than might have been expected without such a claim to public participation.

It is sometimes suggested that German governments pursued a policy of systematic industrialisation. Silesia aside, that is at best an exaggeration for the period prior to 1850. The authorities were inclined rather to tolerate the evolution of industry; they took an interest in fostering the workers, diligence and in safeguarding 'the nourishment of the people', but their support for the tendency towards concentration was lukewarm. Of course the administration occasionally assisted the import of machinery with subsidies or donations. It concerned itself with technological education too, as in the Prussian Gewerbeschule in Berlin, the Polytechnical School in Karlsruhe, etc. Factories were kept going with loans and reductions of interest; credits helped to tide over the occasional liquidity crisis. Prussia even expanded its holdings in mines, smelters and factories, employing its influential 'Seehandlung' as a kind of holding company until 1855. But there is much evidence showing that public enterprises suppressed nascent private competition and thus obstructed the dissemination of technical progress. On the other hand reforms in the system of school and university education under Humboldt (1810) and similar measures made a significant contribution to modernisation. Yet they were not really aimed at the promotion of industrialisation itself. Frequently so-called policies of industrialisation turn out to amount to no more than the belated creation of conditions which had existed in other western countries long before their industrialisation.

The budgetary resources which governments earmarked exclusively for the promotion of industry were on the whole quite small. More considerable were the funds generally allocated to the construction and maintenance of transport facilities. The investment in the infra-structure improved communications and thus benefited commerce and industry in the result. The tax system too may possibly have favoured industry to some degree, for the bulk of the public tax revenue came from assessments on real property and from indirect taxes. Commercial and industrial wealth and profits made in such businesses were taxed fairly lightly in comparison. The 'class tax' introduced by Prussia in 1820 was still to be based on the 'objective' criteria of stratification of wealth by degree and station; until 1851 it did not take the new sources of wealth adequately into account.

The abolition of compulsory gild membership did not in any way initiate the rapid advance of capitalist enterprise at the expense of the crafts. The number of master craftsmen continued to grow faster than the population and faster too than the number of journeymen. Until the middle of the century the factory system developed but slowly. Heavy industry which became of such importance later on, showed hardly an indication of its prospects before 1840. Between 1820 and 1840 the German output of coal and pig iron did not increase either relatively or absolutely as fast as the British; the smelters remained small and fuel wood remained their most important source of energy. Mining increased its output between 1800 and 1837 by only 70 per cent.

Craft production and domestic industry continued to expand in the majority of textile trades until the middle of the century. Cotton spinning however was transferred almost entirely into factories. Notoriously cotton spinning was comparatively easily mechanised and in addition its relative efficiency was especially high so that its rationalisation had a more pronounced effect on prices than in any other branch of textile production. But German cotton factories did not in reality compete with old crafts but mainly with British imports and hand-made linen.

It is a peculiar feature of German industrialisation that the spinning of flax and the weaving of linen occupied most of the textile manufacturing capacity available in the pre-industrial period. In 1787 linen products made up over 40 per cent of the output of textiles in Prussia and accounted for 60 per cent of the total exports. Of course after 1813 they were exposed to more severe international competition from Irish and Belgian suppliers as well as from the substitute, cotton. During the early phase of industrialisation the structure of German industry was 'flawed'. In the middle of the nineteenth century the cost of its re-alignment turned out to be high. About 1850 the consumption of 'modern' cotton cloth was already three times greater than that of linen.

The miseries of the linen weavers were mistakenly taken as symbolic of the catastrophic consequences of mechanisation *per se*. But in Germany machinery was only adopted slowly, even where it was technically feasible and where an obvious demand existed. In 1840 Saxony, the most highly industrialised German state, possessed no more than fifty steam engines of altogether only 900 horse power. At the same time the Rhine province of Prussia had 211 engines, eighty-six of them for mines. In the whole of Germany about 40,000 horse power of steam had been installed, or about 6 per cent of the available British capacity. Germany's ample woods and reserves of accessible water power sufficed to delay the revolution in the technology of motive power. The sites occupied by the coal deposits in the Saar basin, Upper Silesia and the Ruhr, were too peripheral to promote the ready employment of large quantities in industrialisation. In the mid 1830s however some changes began to appear. In manufacturing industry there were some sensational foundations of large scale enterprises, amongst others on the Lower Rhine, in Augsburg and in northern Baden. Two occasions are held mainly responsible for their success and for the con-

sequent boom of the late 1830s and the 1840s: the foundation of the German Customs Union and the beginnings of
railway construction.

By agreement at the Congress of Vienna in 1815 the
number of German states had been reduced to thirty-nine
with only four free cities. On its own each state did promote
traffic in its interior by equalising indirect taxes and by
removing internal customs barriers. As the customs posts
were transferred to the frontiers though, for Bavaria in 1807
and for Prussia in 1818, this tended, if anything, to aggra-
vate the economic separation of territories, especially when
transit duties were newly imposed. This is not the place
to deal with the special conditions responsible for the creation of the German Customs Union. A nice mixture of
economic motives, dynastic considerations and power
politics, primarily to serve Prussia's turn against Austria
which had been excluded, made up its antecedents. At
any rate when the customs barriers between Prussia and
some central and south German states were removed on
1 January 1834, this was celebrated as the opening of a new
era. However the union was without an associate on the
shores of the North Sea because the Hanseatic Cities and
the other coastal states valued their links with Britain more
highly than those inland. Baden similarly looked towards
Switzerland and France. The other German states joined
the Union between 1835 and 1867, excepting only Bremen
and Hamburg which were not included in the imperial
customs frontiers until 1885 and 1888.

As the result of much debate the Customs Union pursued
a commercial policy of moderate protection for industry.
The Prussian bureaucracy, in agreement with the interests
of agricultural exporters, cherished a considerable preference for the notion of free trade, while other European
countries continued to regard protection as the norm. One
of the immediately tangible results of the Customs Union
was the transfer of Swiss, Belgian and Alsatian enterprises
into the German customs territory to profit from the larger
market.

In this new free trade area every member still reserved

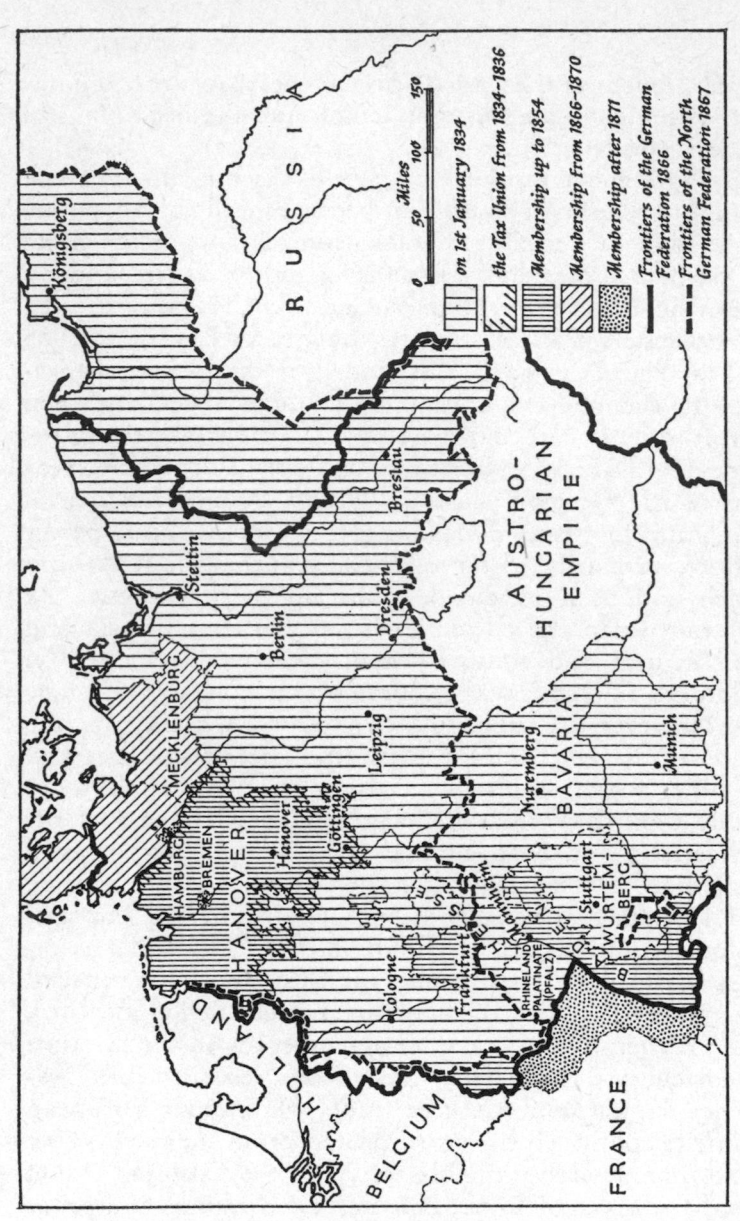

The Zollverein from 1834–1888

the independence of his internal economic policy. Whether its creation really helped to liberate dormant powers of production cannot be determined, because simultaneously an unusually strong cyclical boom began in Britain and in its course relieved the pressure of competition on both international and national markets. Moreover a second event must not be forgotten which, in the long run, turned out to be a significant portent: it was the start of railway building in Germany. The first German railway ran on the short line from Nürnberg to Fürth in 1835. In 1839 the longer line from Leipzig to Dresden was opened. Five hundred and forty-nine kilometres of railway line had been built by 1840, mainly linking towns, to take advantage of the existing demand for passenger transport. The 1840s were a period of very heavy investment in railway construction. In Prussia alone shares and debentures valued at 107 million Taler were issued; the lines which were being completed now were potentially attractive for future freight traffic too, such as Cologne–Aachen in 1843, Berlin–Hamburg in 1846, Cologne–Minden in 1847 and the Berg–Mark line in 1849, as well as south German lines like Munich–Augsburg in 1840 and Nürnberg–Bamberg in 1844. Land and labour were fairly cheap. By 1850 east and west and north and south had been linked. The total network was then about 6,000 kilometres of which approximately 2,000 kilometres were state railways, in Brunswick, Baden, Bavaria and Saxony. At first the Prussian government could take no active part in the building of railways: the loan required for this would have needed the sanction of the diet of estates and the king did not wish to summon a session. The Prussian government intervened nevertheless: the law of 1838 regulated construction, operations and conditions for the eventual purchase of the railways. By 1850 Prussia had in addition spent about fifteen million Taler on planning, subsidies and participation; it supported several projects by guaranteeing their rates of interest. Altogether the German governments until 1850 provided one half of the total investment in railways, about 150 million Taler.

During the 1840s and by 1850 the railways emerged as the most important carrier of long distance bulk traffic. If coal were to be made available at any distance from the rivers Rhine or Oder or merely to compete successfully with British imports, important mainly for Berlin, it had necessarily to rely on the railways. As the long overland haul became possible for coal, so industry could emerge from a phase when temporarily the use of water power had been intensified. Until then the mechanisation of industry had invariably meant the introduction of implements which could either be moved by men, like the jenny or which required animal or water power. The mountains of central Germany with their springs and streams offered a useful reserve of power practically inviting industrial workshops to disperse widely. As a result of the dissolution of 1803 the mountainous regions contained many vacant monasteries; there was a free labour force and, with the availability of buildings, decentralised industrial settlement became even more attractive. The deployment of the railway system however deprived these locations of their industrial value; as a result the Eifel, the Siegerland, the Black Forest, the Thuringian Forest and the Harz lost both their traditional industries and recently acquired new ones. The new industrial centres expanded in regions easy of access, principally around the Ruhr and in Berlin.

This of course could only result from cheaper transport: it did not happen in the 1830s and its first signs could only be felt tentatively in the 1840s. Cheap transport depended on the proper utilisation of the railways' new capabilities; these in turn depended on the length of line and on the volume of industrial and agricultural traffic employing their services. In the event the costs of bulk transport fell by about 80 or 85 per cent and the growth of traffic far exceeded any technical capacity of the traditional forms of transport. As railway construction proceeded, the decline in regional price differentials can be clearly demonstrated. In the short run railway construction stimulated demand and encouraged the spirit of risk-taking enterprise: this was probably more important for the economy in the 1830s and 1840s than the growth of railway transport in these years.

The traditional forms of transport too experienced major improvements up to 1850 and these played their part in the transport revolution of the 1830s and 1840s. By 1800 Germany possessed 490 kilometres of canals and approximately 670 kilometres of river had been made navigable with locks and similar improvements. Eighty per cent of these routes were situated in Prussia's north German lowlands. In 1830 began a new phase of canal building which made available by 1850 some 730 kilometres of canals and 1,400 kilometres of rivers, improved to a similar standard. With the lakes which this had opened up there existed by mid-century 2,380 kilometres of artificial waterways, not counting the rectified stretches of major rivers. Unfortunately we do not have enough reliable information about the volume of traffic. But there is no doubt at all that inland navigation expanded buoyantly until mid-century.

After 1800 the construction of roads too received some attention; here again responsibility devolved almost entirely upon central and regional administrations and upon the communes. Like private companies elsewhere they charged tolls, in Mecklenburg–Strelitz indeed until 1915. In the Prussian territory of Berg the roads were built around 1800 to link the coal mines with their customers or at least with the river banks. The French armies too promoted road building for their own purposes but Prussia continued this work after 1815 while many other German governments, especially the smaller ones, did not begin to build metalled roads until after 1830. On the whole the foundation of the customs union acted as a spur. With its larger territory Prussia had not needed this stimulus: it had doubled its network of roads in the preceding fifteen years. By 1850 Germany had approximately 50,000 kilometres of metalled roads, mainly in the west. This had much improved cost, reliability and speed of freight and passenger transport even before the introduction of railways and may offer some explanation for increased productivity in the total economy before the period of industrialisation.

The first major effect of these innovations was not due to the realisation of their own potential but to effective demand, supported by the creation of very extensive credit. The first cyclical movements in Germany made themselves felt in the 1830s and, more strongly, in the 1840s. Their timing coincided fairly closely with the course of the British economy. A ' "founders" period' from 1834 to 1837 was succeeded by a temporary halt. The boom from 1842 to 1846, under the sign of railway construction, was thus all the more marked. The iron industry and the machine building industry quickened in its train. The capacity of German production was entirely inadequate to meet the demand so that between 1837 and 1844 imports of steel and iron products into the customs union multiplied tenfold. But by 1839 the first German railway engine was being built, indicating the attainment of technical sophistication at a time opportune for the foundation of a heavy machinery industry, during the first great boom. The boom broke a few years later. The expansion of industry did not merely stop from 1847 to 1849: output declined to the level of several years ago. The revolution of 1848 was at once effect and cause of this severe reverse. There is evidence for large scale urban unemployment and for distress in all industries. Some of the newly founded large scale enterprises in textiles and in machinery ran into liquidity troubles and had to be salvaged with government support. The collapse of the great private bank Abraham Schaaffhausen in Cologne could only be averted in 1848 with government assistance in converting a major portion of its liabilities into proprietorial parts, i.e. shares.

Because its rate of innovation in transport and industry had accelerated noticeably between 1835 and 1849, Germany now entered the crucial stage in which its indigenous powers of growth became active. Puddling had been introduced in Germany in 1822 and now asserted itself successfully; the capacity of coke blast furnaces grew. True, in Prussia in 1849 only thirty-two blast furnaces of 247 as yet operated with coke. Nevertheless these already produced a third of all the pig iron in the Saar and in Upper Silesia. Steam engines in large numbers now came into their own as power sources, outside their application to mining.

Many other signs of progress could be enumerated but it would not be proper to disregard the surviving powers of inertia. In 1850 Germany was still predominantly agricultural. The official Prussian enumeration of 1816 showed a rural population of 73·5 per cent: in 1872 it was still 71·5 per cent. Peasant emancipation had not been completed by 1850 and the process of urbanisation was yet to come. New methods of production were mostly confined to new equipment, installed by way of expansion; there had as yet been no thoroughgoing re-equipment. Indeed the output of the older forms of production was still expanding. Nor had the industrial proletariat yet emerged as a distinctive large scale phenomenon. In Prussia of all those occupied and over the age of fourteen no more than 5·44 per cent were described as 'factory workers' in 1849 and this category included workmen in some enterprises employing fewer than five people. The great majority of employees still worked in agriculture. Of those enumerated as gainfully occupied in agriculture in mid-century, only 26 per cent were working on their own account, as against 41 per cent in mining and in manufacturing industry and 70 per cent in commerce. Pig iron production in the 1840s grew more slowly than it had done in the 1830s. Greater speed of expansion could not be expected from an industry based on old sites and old techniques. German iron and steel production was not set free until its centre shifted to the Ruhr after 1850.

The first capitalist boom in Germany terminated still quite in the 'traditional' manner, i.e. with an agricultural depression: when the harvests failed in 1846–7, the terms of trade for industry worsened radically as against agriculture. The prices of rye and potatoes increased respectively by 100 and 135 per cent, while industrial prices generally remained unaltered.

There are no tolerably reliable estimates of German

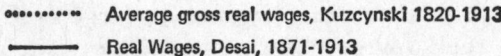

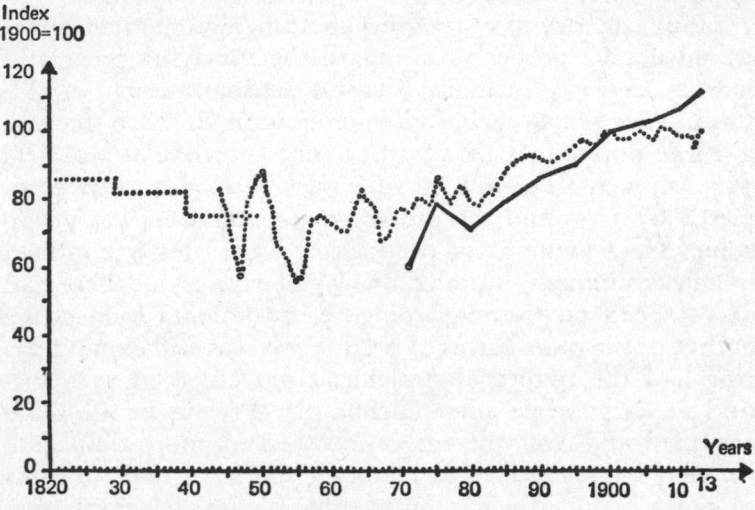

FIGURE 8 *Real Wages 1829-1913*

national product, investment or consumption before 1850. Changes in real wages according to Kuczynski are shown in Figure 8; his detailed figures have been much criticised but nobody has yet produced any better ones. If the growth in industrial and agricultural output can serve as a guide, we may perhaps assume a growth in national product per head for the period 1830–50. But this can hardly have exceeded one half of 1 per cent per annum. The figure could be justified by comparison with estimates for the period after 1850. Contemporary sources, if acceptable, would rather suggest the pauperisation of craftsmen and peasants as a consequence of population growth. In districts remote from industry an increase in cases of destitution becomes evident.

The quickening of international involvement which began in 1835 was not sustained up to 1850 either. Imports certainly increased but between 1840 and 1850 the volume of foreign trade per head probably shrank again. While

Britain, France and the United States became more firmly integrated into the international economy in this decade, Germany lagged behind. In exports, developments before 1850 especially gave little cause for satisfaction, not least because of the crisis in the linen industry. It was unprocessed foodstuffs and agricultural produce which retained their significance among exports. The price of wheat in Germany remained below British prices until mid-century. Fully manufactured items formed only 18 per cent of all exports: this analysis of foreign trade shows up the fairly severe degree of backwardness in German development. After 1850 this was made good in a sudden rush. The volume of foreign trade per head doubled between 1851 and 1857 and again from 1865 to 1868 (Figure 9).

How adverse the situation was between 1800 and 1850 is indicated by the trend in prices. Apart from the rise in the price of foodstuffs caused by the harvest failures of 1846–7, wholesale prices remained at a virtually stable level from 1825 to 1850. Such periods of growth do not encourage enterprises to finance themselves from their profits in the same way as periods of mild inflation. However there is no need to blame the slow development on a general shortage of capital. At 3·5 per cent rates of interest on the public debt were particularly low in the 1830s and early 1840s. The railways too obtained their very large capital fairly easily. There can have been no shortage of freely available funds but only a small proportion of them were attracted into industry which did not offer a return commensurate with the clearly predictable risks. Violent cyclical fluctuations and frequent tightness of liquidity underlined the insecurity of such investments. Agitation grew more urgent for the financial relief made accessible by banks of issue and some were even established but the assistance they could provide before 1850 was very slight.

In a modern expanding economy an inadequate rate of personal saving is known to be no absolute bar to investment, provided that the entrepreneurs' initial capital is adequate and that consumers' demand is sufficient to return

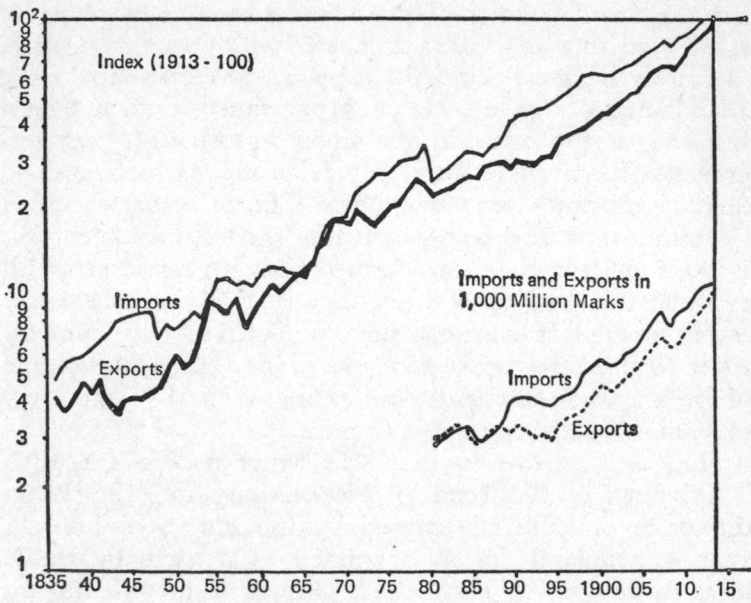

FIGURE 9 *Foreign Trade. Quantity 1869–1913. Value 1880–1913*

their invested capital to them. These two conditions had not been established before 1850. The economy could not release itself from stagnation by its own bootstraps because of sluggish growth rates and excessive cyclical fluctuations. Thus the organisation of a credit system was all the more important for German development. But the monetary and credit systems long remained underdeveloped and the vital innovations in this field were only introduced after 1850. In 1846 financial and credit institutions employed only 1,100 persons in Prussia. Germany did not have a unified currency in 1850 and the large variety of coinages offered multiple opportunities of gain to experienced money changers. The bulk of credit transactions consisted either of supplier and customer credits or of loans among friends and relations. The private bankers of Frankfurt and Berlin catered above all for the financial requirements of governments and of the aristocracy, beyond German frontiers as well as within them.

The balance between capital imports and exports changed quickly in the thirties and forties. Any surplus on average of capital imports before 1850 must have been small. It was the presence of French, Belgian, Swiss and British enterprises in Germany which created the impression that foreign capital had been a principal agent in German industrialisation. This may be an exaggeration. Capital imports indeed were extensively channelled into the establishment of industry in contrast to the capital made available for export. The latter flowed into the international market for government loans. The average German investor was much less inclined to chance a risky investment than were the foreign entrepreneurs.

THE DEVELOPMENT OF THE INDUSTRIAL ECONOMY

(A) THE MACRO-ECONOMIC PERSPECTIVE

In Germany there was no close correspondence between economic growth and democratisation. It may even be justifiable to attribute economic advance at least partly to political retardation. The Prussian bourgeoisie remained to a large extent excluded from direct participation in policy making and the proletariat almost completely so. But this must not be seen as an obstacle to growth; on the contrary it may have encouraged concentration on business matters, especially as the public administration, for a variety of reasons, adequately upheld the principal economic desiderata of the entrepreneurs. Thus in some industries the inflow might have provided a significant initial stimulus to growth.

Political unification in 1871 contributed to economic progress as did the foundation of the North German Federation in 1867. But unification was not, contrary to the tenor of much German historical writing, a 'necessary condition' of economic success. Politically and economically Prussia on her own had been strong enough since 1866 for sustained growth: the foundation of the empire may rather be seen as a result of Prussian growth than as a condition of growth in Germany.

Many more statistical data are available after 1850 and they are much better: they permit us to perceive the process of growth. In particular the works of W. G. Hoffmann have much increased our knowledge. Nevertheless the series reflecting the growth of the national product and of its constituents can still not be accepted without many critical reservations which we must suppress here for lack of space.

With the available data and within the limits set by assumptions underlying the calculations, the process of growth can be expressed in a few figures. Net domestic product at 1913 prices increased approximately fivefold from 1850 to 1913 at a mean annual rate of 2·6 per cent; simultaneously net domestic product per head rose two and a half fold. As between property and the working population distribution of income may have shifted somewhat in favour of the recipients of unearned incomes; as between householders, distribution of personal income may have favoured the recipients of large incomes. But these were fairly small changes: it is thus a reasonable assumption that the majority of the population experienced a direct and perceptible increase in its standard of living. This is borne out by movement in the available series for real industrial wages: according to the most recent estimates, they doubled between 1871 and 1913 (Desai; Figure 8 page 112). As measuring devices such data will always be highly debatable: there can nevertheless be no doubt that, by the end of this period of growth, hunger had ceased to be the large scale phenomenon which it had been sixty years before.

On a highly abstract level, growth in the national product may be attributed to two constituents, 1. an addition to the factors of production labour and capital (including land) and 2. increased productivity of these factors, subsumed under the clumsy title of 'technical progress' which is here interpreted to encompass not merely change in techniques of production proper but all advances in organisation.

Technical progress in this sense was the most important element in German growth. Without technical progress the decline in the marginal efficiency of capital would probably have put a stop to capital accumulation. Capital stocks in Germany however grew from 1850 to 1913 more or less in step with the net domestic product, i.e. fivefold in just over sixty years, with a trend towards acceleration. The mean rate of growth in the stock of capital was 2·3 per cent from 1850 to 1875, 2·7 per cent from 1876 to 1895 and 3·4 per cent from 1896 to 1913. As by and large the labour force no more than doubled (see below), the proportion of stock of capital to labour force, so-called capital intensity, increased two and a half fold or approximately by 1·6 per cent per annum. Because capital stock and national product grew hand in hand, the so-called capital coefficient $(\frac{O}{O})$ and its reciprocal, productivity of capital $(\frac{O}{C})$, showed no general tendency towards change. On the other hand productivity of labour increased at an average rate of 1·5 per cent.

This is substantially the source of the growth in real wages although productivity and wages did not rise in the same fashion during all the different phases of the trade cycle, least of all in 1873–8, when unemployment became an important factor in improving efficiency. The negotiating strength of the trade unions did not affect the level of wages until the end of the century: they had no more than 330,000 members in 1891 and until 1895 their freedom of industrial action was circumscribed, owing to persecution by the government and to the attitude of employers. Until 1913 the number of trade union members increased to about 3,300,000, about 11 per cent of all workers and 30 per cent of industrial workers. Despite such a high level of organisation among German employees and the growing number of wage agreements, the trade union movement probably exerted less influence on wages than did market forces, especially as labour grew relatively scarce.

From 1850 to 1913 three periods may be distinguished,

1850–73, 1874–95 and 1896–1913. From 1850 to 1873 changes in technology and organisation apparently did far more to determine the growth in national product than in later periods. True, that from 1896 to 1913 the mean rate of growth in domestic product at 3·12 per cent was much greater than for 1850–70 but simultaneously capital stocks and the labour force too increased much faster than in mid-century. A decline in the capital coefficient seems evident in mid-century: thus one might well single out the two decades after 1850 as a period of especially intensive growth, although their mean rate of growth at 2·4 per cent was lower than in the following periods. This was still a time of that conversion to the market economy which has been referred to above.

The above-mentioned periods differ too in the character of their trade cycles. Kondratieff viewed them as part of a long cycle in several capitalist countries. With or without the theory of long cycles no doubt remains that the periods 1850 to 1873 and 1874 to 1895 differed markedly from each other and that 1896 to 1913 was different again. The first and last periods are so-called 'growth phases', the central period a 'stagnating phase'. In both the growth phases most years were dominated by a cyclical upswing which was more persistent and intensive than the cyclical downswing. During both growth periods prices followed a rising trend (Figure 6); as is well known, this must be seen too in the context of the discovery of gold, in 1848 in California and in 1890 in South Africa. Expanding demand in these periods sufficiently reinforced the monetary system to warrant, on the whole, the lusty growth in productive capacity. High risk investments found ready support despite high rates of interest and they produced profits. This stimulated the entrepreneurs' propensity to invest; simultaneously their gains provided them with much of the money required for this. Both in the 1850s as well as in 1896–1913 the share of exports in the German economy increased too.

In between lie the years 1874–95 which, in contrast, have been dramatically described as 'the great depression'

(Rosenberg): this term may be more appropriate for Britain than for Germany. In Germany too prices fell under the impact of international competition; the cyclical upswings were shorter and the downswings always longer, but in this country growth was only briefly retarded. The expansion of German heavy industry in particular proceeded apace between 1880 and 1890 and did not come to a stop.

The phase of stagnation was set off by the great crash ('Gründerkrise') which erupted towards the end of 1873: that was indeed a phenomenon of century-wide significance. It affected production more powerfully than the commercial and financial crisis of 1857 had done and contributed to large scale unemployment in some regions of Germany. The boom in investment which had begun in 1869 had not been confined to Germany but had here been reinforced by the successful conclusion of the war and, not least, by the French indemnity payment of 5,000 million gold Francs. The share capital of joint stock companies had doubled in three years from 1870 to 1873. This boom ended in a series of business failures without precedent which exposed major structural defects in the preceding expansion. Growth in capacity had run far ahead of potential growth in demand. The rate of investment had stood at 8·7 per cent in the 1850s; it had risen to 17·2 per cent in 1874. A rapid decline followed. But when the rate of investment touched its cyclical minimum at 7·3 per cent in 1880, this remained above the cyclical minima of previous trade cycles, such as the 3·3 per cent of 1855. Stagnation in coal mining did not last long after 1873 and the output of textiles was only slightly reduced. Growth continued during the 'great depression' and the rate of investment in the German empire recovered to a respectable 13–14 per cent long before the start of the next period of sustained boom in 1896, after which it rose once more beyond 17 per cent.

Figure 10 shows the rate of completion of the German railway network. The growth of railways slackened off a little in the 1850s but then it accelerated again. Eight

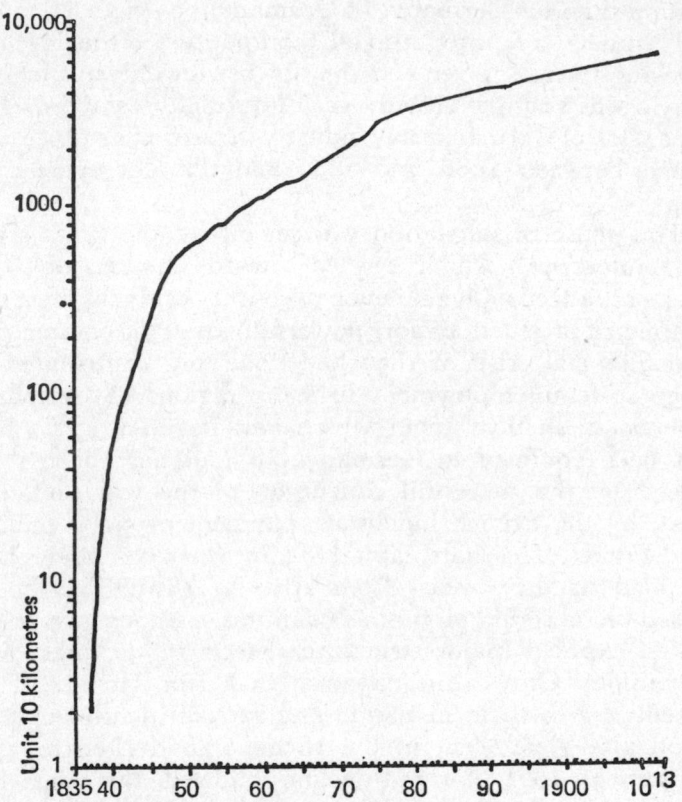

FIGURE 10 *Extent of German Railways*

thousand kilometres of line was constructed between 1850 and 1875. In this period almost a quarter of all net investment was allotted to the railways. Railway building continued after the 1870s: mileage indeed was doubled but the railway ceased to supply the principal impetus for German economic growth. It was not unreasonable to call the boom period between the 1840s and 1873 the 'railway-Kondratieff'.

After 1874 industrial investment unquestionably took the lead. The share of total net investment in every kind of industry rose from 14 per cent in the early 1850s to more than 50 per cent during the great boom at the end of the nineteenth century, though it declined again afterwards. This is admittedly based on data referring to 'trades' which comprehended handicrafts but it was undoubtedly modern industry which received the lion's share.

The building of non-agricultural houses was another centre of investment activity. Until 1871 the proportion of the population living in communities of fewer than 2,000 inhabitants was almost constant at 71·5 per cent. Barely 5 per cent of the population lived in cities of over 100,000 inhabitants. But from then on the absolute number of the rural population remained unchanged and the towns absorbed the increase. By 1910 only 40 per cent lived in small communities but more than a fifth in cities above 100,000, fifteen times as many people as sixty years earlier. Many new towns had grown to the status of big cities, especially in the industrial districts. It is therefore not surprising if in most years non-agricultural housing absorbed from a quarter to a third of the total volume of net investment. The building of towns was a 'leading sector' which stimulated not merely the building industry but industries dealing with stone, bricks, sand and gravel, real estate finance, the glass industry, gas and water works and, after 1880, the electricity industry, the local transport system including tramways and the wholesale and retail trades.

This discussion of macro-economic trends must be concluded with an analysis of the labour supply and of demographic factors which simultaneously offer some pointers to the growth of consumer demand. The population multiplied two and a half fold from 1850 to 1913. The number of employed persons increased rather more quickly than this, mainly with the statistically attested growth in female employment and not because of any change in the balance of age groups: the population structure remained virtually constant. The proportion of those gainfully employed rose from 43 per cent to 46 per cent. Nevertheless the annual quantity of labour performed grew no faster than the population because from mid-century on the working year had been shortened at least in industry, mining and handicrafts. Information about this is rather vague but it may be suggested that in mining and industry the working year was reduced by about 30 per cent, for everyone employed in the economy by about 15 per cent. From 1850 to 1913 population growth remained by far the most important cause of increase in the quantity of labour. That indeed accelerated towards the end of the century. The rate of increase stood at 0·8 per cent in the 1850s, attained 1·1 per cent in 1900 and mounted to 1·4 per cent per annum just before the first world war. This was the global result of an excess of births and of migrations whose separate contributions differed from time to time. The excess of births remained fairly constant until 1870, because the trends in either birth rate or death rate did not change (Figure 5. p. 21). Besides the very high number of births in the prosperous years from 1872 on, the beginnings of a decline in death rates now deserve attention: they had dropped as far as 1·5 per cent by 1913. Birth rate on the other hand maintained for another thirty years the average level which it had held since 1830 and only declined to 2·7 per cent from 1900 to 1913. The excess of births therefore amounted to about 0·9 per cent until 1870, rose to 1·5 per cent until 1900 and declined to 1·2 per cent until 1913.

Simultaneously the expectation of life increased from only thirty-six years for a male at birth in 1870 to forty-five years by 1913. There is no acceptable proof that the introduction of statutory medical insurance in 1883 contributed to the reduction in mortality. At any rate the insurance included a very considerable part of the population; in 1890 insured persons, without their families, amounted to 10 per cent of the population, in 1913 to 39 per cent.

A satisfactory interpretation of German population history would have to concentrate to some extent on the considerable differences in regional population movements. Prussia and the Saxon kingdom had a greater excess of births than the south German states or the north German states outside Prussia. In addition the south German states lost proportionately more inhabitants by emigration before 1870. So great was their loss that Württemberg, Baden and the Palatinate experienced an absolute decline in population during the 1850s. This was due in equal measure to political conditions after the failed revolution of 1848 and to their low level of economic development; most of their emigration went overseas. Later on the centres of emigration moved to eastern Prussia which had hardly been affected by it before 1870. About this time too long range internal migration began in Germany. Until 1870 the new industrial districts tended to rely for recruitment on their environment which produced short range migrations. After 1870 eastern Germany parted with almost the whole of its natural population increase to other regions. Most of these migrants moved as a matter of course into adjacent provinces in the centre of the empire. But the surplus of eastern population decisively affected the rise of the Ruhr district too, especially around 1900.

The statistics for German emigration do not become reasonably reliable until 1871; until then only estimates can provide some guidance.

German emigration overseas

1821–30	8,500
1831–40	167,700
1841–50	469,300
1851–60	1,075,000
1861–70	832,700
1871–80	626,000
1881–90	1,342,400
1891–1900	529,900
1901–10	279,600

The peaks of annual emigration generally coincided with years of prosperity. Since the 1850s movements in the international economy had attained sufficient homogeneity for good years to correspond in Germany and in the U.S.A.;

it was essential for anyone hoping to make a fresh start in the new home to arrive in a period of prosperity. Emigration reached its peak in the year 1881 : 4·9 per thousand inhabitants left imperial Germany. In the three years after 1893 emigration diminished so far that henceforth it comprehended less than 1 per thousand of the population, the average until 1913 being 0·43 per thousand. On the other hand immigration into Germany now acquired some importance, originating mainly in Russian Poland, Austria-Hungary and Italy. This immigration had started some time ago; the gain from immigration during the 1830s has been mentioned above. Overall it did not acquire major significance though until the end of the nineteenth century. Around 1910 an average of 880,000 migrant workers was recorded in Germany: a considerable reinforcement of the labour force, especially for seasonal farm work in the eastern parts of the country.

(B) CHANGES IN THE STRUCTURE AND DEVELOPMENT OF DIFFERENT SECTORS

The industrial revolution is a process of industrialisation, i.e. a shift in the balance between different sectors of the economy, particularly in favour of industry. Figure 1, p. 6 offers a first impression of this development for the period 1815–1913. Figure 11 complements this by showing changes in the contribution of each sector to the value added, i.e. the net domestic product. The structure of employment on the whole changed less radically than did the contribution of each sector to net domestic product due to the different trends in productivity. As the population had doubled and real net domestic product had increased fivefold, the economy changed its structure merely by virtue of diversified rates of growth in employment and production; there was no decline in any major sector.

Domestic service came off worst of all in this. It is a well-known feature of an underdeveloped economy that large numbers of people are available for service in the home. Not surprisingly then this sector almost stagnated in absolute terms and its proportion in the whole declined steeply. The experience of agriculture was rather different: employment in it increased a little, pronouncedly so in the 1860s and again after 1900 and on average over the period by 0·4 per cent per annum, while the value of its output rose more sharply at 1·6 per cent per annum; in either case expansion moved rather more feebly than in the other sectors. Employment in crafts and industry almost trebled with an annual rate of 1·9 per cent and the value of their output increased tenfold at 3·8 per cent per annum: hence the major structural change in their favour. Industry and crafts however by no means led this movement. Numbers in mining increased more than eightfold at 3·2 per cent per annum and the value of their output twentyfold at 5·1 per cent per annum. Even higher was the rate of increase in employment and value in transport, at respectively 3·3 per cent and 6·4 per cent yearly. The modern economy after all depends on a multitude of transport arrangements. These must grow disproportionately as enterprises and regions become more specialised, to promote the continuous increase of total economic activity. A similar reason explains the growth of numbers employed in commerce, banking and insurance by almost fivefold, at an annual 2·6 per cent. Value produced however rose 'only' a little more than sixfold at an annual 3·2 per cent. Unlike industry and transport these services owed little to increased productivity of labour, so that output increased approximately in line with employment.

A detailed account covering the evolution of all the branches of the economy cannot be given in the allotted framework. We will have to concentrate on only some of them and their principal problems.

Agriculture continued to expand its production in the second half of the nineteenth century (Figure 7). Admittedly until the 1860s much of this expansion resulted from an increase in the cultivated area, especially as arable. Some reserves of land were then still available in eastern Germany; there was only a relatively minor increase in

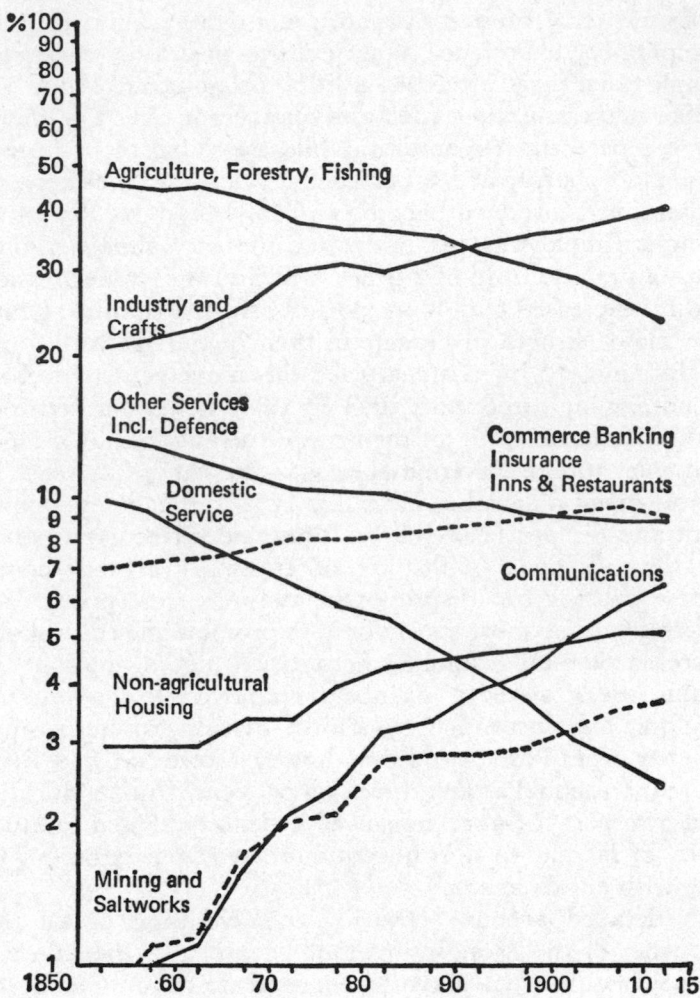

FIGURE 11 *Percentage Contributions of Economic Sectors to Net Domestic Production at Constant Prices 1850-1913*

yields per acre. Crop production kept in step with the rise of population in this period only with the increasing cultivation of root crops. Between 1865 and 1890 almost all useful agricultural land had been taken up and technical progress accelerated; this however did not suffice to expand output in step with population growth. The former export surplus of agricultural produce changed into an import surplus. Against the growing competition of American and Russian grain imports, German farming was protected by customs duties from 1879 but agricultural supply was at first fairly inelastic and could not fully respond to the continuing growth in demand. About 1890 the trend changed again: agriculture entered a period of notable technical advance and, while the area of farmland remained constant, the productivity of labour and of the soil rose quickly. The output of crops again increased faster than the population and Germany once more became a considerable exporter of some agricultural produce towards the end of the period. This was primarily due to the introduction of artificial fertilisers. Germany had acquired an international monopoly in the production of phosphate fertiliser with the discovery of the deposits near Stassfurt in 1860. After 1886 large additional amounts of phosphate became available as a by-product of the Gilchrist Thomas process of iron smelting. For the essential nitrates farmers continued to rely on organic manure, the by-products of coking ovens and the import of Chilean saltpetre.

Mechanisation of agriculture in Germany too only began to progress notably around 1900. The mechanisation of threshing and the increased cultivation of root crops aggravated the seasonal irregularities in the demand for rural labour. In consequence much of the permanent labour left, especially from the east: the large estates were 'defeudalised'. Farms in peasant ownership however remained predominant in central and western Germany. The pattern of ownership hardly altered at all (Figure 12). Reapers, drillers and improved ploughs could often be found on medium-sized farms too. From 1882 to 1907 the number of threshing machines increased by 385 per cent, that of drills by 450 per cent and of reapers by 1,500 per cent. Until the 1860s almost all the new implements were imported from Britain and America; the nascent German farm machine industry did not begin to supplement these sources until the last third of the century.

The output of animal produce expanded more rapidly than that of crops, both before 1850 and after. With prices which rose steadily the production of pork grew rapidly; as wool prices fell on the other hand, the output of wool declined quickly after 1860. In 1850 Germany marketed one tenth of the international output of wool but it could not compete when overseas supplies reached Europe after 1850. Among other food crops the potato acquired increasing importance, not only as the basic food of the poorer people but as pig feed and a base for the distillation of spirits. From mid-century until 1910 potato yields increased approximately fivefold. In 1910 Germany produced a third of the world's output of potatoes. Sugar production, based on the domestic cultivation of sugar beet, expanded even more rapidly. Between 1890 and 1900 sugar made up 6 per cent of the total value of German exports, much exceeding the value of coal, iron or machinery exports.

Until well into the 1870s German farmers stood to gain from the rising trend in prices; notoriously the arrival in Europe of supplies from overseas reversed the trend. As will be shown below, Germany introduced protective duties for corn in 1879. This could not exempt German prices from the force of the falling trend on the world market altogether but did ensure a higher price level for domestic producers. The first moderate import duties on corn were increased in 1885 and again in 1887 which brought them to about 30 per cent *ad valorem*. Between 1891 and 1906 Caprivi's commercial policies lowered protection a little. Certainly protection slowed down the contraction of agriculture and of its revenues but it also delayed possible structural changes in and the upgrading of agricultural output. As the first great war made evident, even this degree of protection for agriculture failed to ensure that it could provide adequately for the population in an emergency. In 1910 about 40 per cent of all wheat and 15 per cent of all grain had to be imported. In 1913 Germany was 95 per cent self-sufficient purely in terms of calories and

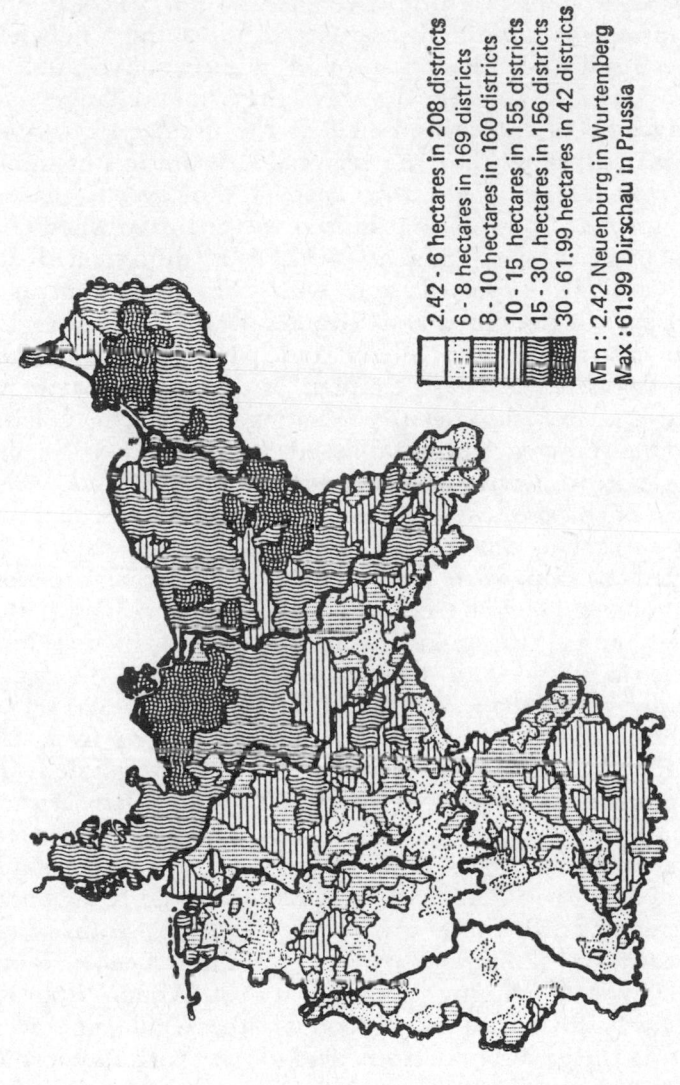

FIGURE 12 *Map giving Average Size of Agrarian Enterprises in Germany 1895*

The map legend reads:

- 2.42 - 6 hectares in 208 districts
- 6 - 8 hectares in 169 districts
- 8 - 10 hectares in 160 districts
- 10 - 15 hectares in 155 districts
- 15 - 30 hectares in 156 districts
- 30 - 61.99 hectares in 42 districts

Min : 2.42 Neuenburg in Wurtemberg
Max : 61.99 Dirschau in Prussia

vegetable foodstuffs but covered only 57 per cent of its requirements in animal products, thus leaving a deficiency in essential foods like fats, proteins and carbohydrates.

In German mining the most important changes were delayed until the second half of the nineteenth century. It was only now that the regional distribution of mining centres changed. Until 1860 coal had not overtaken wood as a source of power; that indeed was the time when charcoal production reached its peak. Iron mining had once been widely dispersed but, with the improvements in transport, it remained worthwhile on only a few sites. The Saar district, Upper Silesia and particularly the Ruhr and Lorraine, the last German after 1871, became new centres of iron mining and smelting. When the Gilchrist Thomas process had established itself, the highly phosphoric ores of Lorraine met three quarters of German needs. Some of this ore was smelted on site with Ruhr coke, some was carried to the coal in the Ruhr. French capital had played an important part in developing the zinc deposits of Stolberg in west Germany and of Upper Silesia; these had assumed a significant role in the early decades of industrialisation and their output continued to expand rapidly until 1878. At that time Upper Silesia was responsible for half the world's output of zinc; from 1880 on however this branch of the economy stagnated. The production of hard coal increased by 5·3 per cent per annum on average between 1815 and 1913; the rate accelerated between 1850 and 1873 when deep mining opened up the Ruhr field. Little by little the Ruhr district extended northwards until 1913. As the seams sloped downwards the mines became continuously deeper. Therefore in coal mining productivity of labour improved relatively little and after 1890 on the whole not at all. During the great boom from 1896 to 1913 with its enormous consumption of coal the number of Ruhr miners grew from about 100,000 to 400,000. The formidable problems of recruitment were solved by resort to east German and Polish labour. But the increase in production was not solely due to the introduction of more labour. Mining absorbed large amounts of capital to counteract the increasingly awkward lie of the seams which accentuated the law of diminishing returns.

Prices fluctuated greatly (Figure 6, p. 25). From 1852 to 1856 demand was high and in its wake prices in the Ruhr rose by 45 per cent, encouraging many owners to sink new shafts. From 1857 to 1863 prices fell below their former level; from 1869 to 1874 they more than doubled and there was a coal 'famine' in the Ruhr. New mines were opened but during the crisis of 1873–4 demand slumped again and prices therefore dropped well below their level in the 1860s. On a very large fixed investment returns seemed utterly unpredictable: this provides one of the fundamental reasons for the efforts to form a cartel of coal producers. These efforts became notable in the 1860s; the foundation of the Rhenish-Westphalian coal syndicate in 1893 crowned them with success. Similar cartels existed in Upper Silesia, Saxony and the Saar as well as for the lignite of western and central Germany.

Government control over German mining had remained extensive in the first half of the nineteenth century still, in direct succession of the older princely mining privileges. The mining authorities concerned themselves with the internal affairs of firms, the conditions of work, financial problems and marketing. This 'supervisory principle' offered advantages in the eighteenth and early nineteenth centuries but it increasingly obstructed the rapid development of private mining. Between 1851 and 1865 a number of Prussian laws released the management of private enterprises from government interference, reduced mining dues and granted the miners free choice of employment. Nevertheless a supervisory mining authority remained in existence. The Prussian government too remained the greatest mine owner in the German empire, with the Saar mines and major parts of the mines of Upper Silesia. The Ruhr however was mainly developed by an outstanding group of entrepreneurs who quickly expanded the scale of their business, with the assistance of west German banking capital. The number of mining firms only grew until 1860 when concentration took over. The Irishman Mulvany was one of the outstanding organisers in the Ruhr and others like Haniel, Grillo and, later on, Stinnes and Kierdorf, were of the same calibre. Iron smelters and iron manufacturers looked more and more for their own supplies of coal: thus originated the giant combines, from coal to manufacture, especially in the Ruhr and in Upper Silesia.

German statistics do not admit a clear distinction between the development of industry or of crafts. Additional defects in the data further mar any attempt to describe unequivocally the fate of the traditional crafts. It is at least certain that industrialisation by no means led to the extinction of the crafts: here, too, employment expanded. Urbanisation and the decline in the practice of making up domestic supplies at home meant a growing demand for many craftsmen, especially in the local food trade. The building and construction industries too remained the province mainly of the small business and the craftsman. But even this kind of enterprise changed its character; its buying and selling was drawn into the new market system and this altered its attitude and its internal organisation.

Textiles had always been the greatest of the specialised industries and here the elimination of craft and domestic industry by factories went farthest. In cotton spinning factories were perhaps predominant even before 1850. The old craft and domestic industry in the spinning of flax and wool was effectively eliminated during the great boom period from 1850 to 1873. In cotton weaving factory production did not become the norm until 1873 and for wool it was later still. Domestic silk weaving in Krefeld and Elberfeld did not yield to the factory until after 1890. Mechanisation in the German textile industry was thus much delayed. In 1882 almost a third of all employees in the textile industry was still working for a putting-out system. After 1840 the centre of the cotton industry shifted to south Germany. The annexation of Alsace-Lorraine in 1871 increased the industry's capacity but this proved a dubious gain. The Alsatian industry obtained a special status and was reduced to serious straits. Cotton printing alone could continue to prosper there.

The manufacture of apparel absorbed almost a quarter of all persons employed in industry in the 1850s: here conditions varied. After shoemaking machinery was introduced about 1870, factories quickly took over this manufacture. The craft of shoe making did not die out but turned mainly to repair work. The large scale demand for standardised masculine and feminine garments continued to be met, as everywhere else, by dispersed manufacture. Bespoke making of clothing by craftsmen and households had been the norm for centuries; they were now replaced by the putting-out-system of the garment industry which established itself in Berlin, Stettin, Frankfurt on Main, Aschaffenburg, Bielefeld, Breslau and other towns. The sewing machine had become familiar in Germany since 1854 but this needed little power and therefore did not affect the organisation of manufacture in dispersed workshops.

The production of food and drink was the third old established trade and in the 1850s this had employed one man in seven of the industrial personnel. Its finishing trades, like butcher and baker, were not exposed to any serious competition from factories. This did not hold for trades which could employ steam-power to advantage and which were linked less closely with the final consumer. The increased flow of beer, sugar, tinned milk, flour and chocolate came mainly from large enterprises. Large mills arose in river and sea ports to grind imported corn while the home product still mostly went to the small local mill, often operated as a sideline.

Even in 1870 the leading British enterprises were much bigger than their largest German competitors; this had changed by 1900. For instance German works in the new steel industry towered above the British by an average of 300 per cent, largely because they exploited the benefits of vertical integration. On the whole there exists in every industry a close connection between the growing size of plant and the amount of power specifically required in its processes. Mining and smelting needed the most power per worker and they most strongly favoured larger enterprises. Far behind them followed the paper industry, machine building, chemicals and the textile industry.

In Germany, as in any country which had passed a certain stage of development in the nineteenth century, the capital goods industry grew much faster than the consumer goods industry, on average more than twice as fast. According to Hoffmann and Wagenführ all manufacturing industry expanded from 1850 to 1913 by about 3·8 per cent per annum but textiles, food and drink, building, apparel including leather processing and leather production remained below this average. In contrast metal production —especially iron and steel, metallic manufactures, paper making, the chemical industry and gas, water and electricity supplies grew a great deal faster. In 1850 these employed about 12 per cent of all those engaged in manufacturing industry, in 1911–13 this had become 27 per cent (Figure 13).

Within these broad classifications significant changes occurred in the leading and lower ranking placings of different industries. The linen industry, as mentioned above, continued its decline. The silk and cotton industries developed fairly steadily from 1850 to 1914, leaving aside cyclical fluctuations and the break, when the American civil war temporarily interrupted cotton supplies. About 1870 the German domestic output of wool still supplied three quarters of the domestic market; its subsequent decline set something like a limit on the expansion of the woollen and worsted industries by 1895. By 1900 domestic sources supplied less than a tenth of the wool required. Yarn was being imported instead of raw wool and imports even of cloth were becoming more frequent; domestic production had almost ceased to grow. On the other hand expansion in the garment industry accelerated precisely at this time.

Steel had become by far the fastest grower around the turn of the century; backed by the Gilchrist Thomas process the output of steel rose tenfold from 1880 to 1900 and British production was left far behind. The cost of steel-making dropped to 10 per cent of the level of the sixties. In 1913 Germany smelted almost twice as much pig iron as Britain.

Statistics of industrial production unfortunately yield no information about the 'science based industries', machine building, chemical, optical, precision instrument and electrical industries which were of outstanding importance for German development. In this situation use can sometimes be made of employment statistics. These indicate for instance that machine building employed 51,000 workers in 1861, 356,000 in 1882 and 1,120,000 in 1907. But this is no adequate substitute for data on output. Werner von Siemens founded his electrical works in 1847 and it quickly gained an international reputation for telegraphic equipment, yet in 1882 the electrical industry employed only 1,690 persons. That industry only really began to expand after 1880 with the exploitation of the newly invented telephone and of high voltage technology for lighting and power; the first cable for cross-country transmission linked Laufen on Neckar to Frankfurt on Main in 1891. 26,000 persons were employed by the electrical industries in 1895, by 1907 that had become 142,000. In 1913 over half of the international trade in electrical products was of German origin.

That the chemical industry played a very prominent role in Germany is a commonplace. In mid-century though it employed barely more than 30,000 people and was inferior to the British and French industries. It began to accelerate in the 1860s and by 1911–13 the chemical industries employed 270,000 people. The detailed growth of production though cannot be shown with any useful degree of precision. Indications exist only for the output of heavy chemicals and these fail to do justice to the special nature of German chemical industry; this owed its international fame mainly to the manufacture of aniline dyes, with 15 per cent of the total turnover in 1915, pharmaceutical products and fertilisers. As early as 1900 Germany supplied 90 per cent of the world production of dyes. The German manufactures of optical products and of precision instruments occupied a special position among industries by virtue of their intimate association with institutions of scientific research and with military requirements. The 'optical workshops' of C. Zeiss and E. Abbé in Jena with their 5,280 employees in 1913, are merely an example of this. The manufacture of clocks and watches for the general consumer, the forces and industry, established itself in the Black Forest; scales came to be made in Württemberg. The manufacture of surgical instruments was concentrated mainly on the Upper Danube, that of spectacles in Rathenow in Brandenburg.

These innovating industries in Germany undoubtedly benefited from foreign inventions, British mainly for the chemical and American for the electrical industries. However Germany developed a system of technological schools and colleges and this, with the cultivation of the natural sciences at the German universities, did much to promote independence. Even in 1850 foreigners praised the standards of German technical schools; machine building especially owed to them successive generations of its leading engineers. The chemical industries maintained a variety of contacts with university laboratories. The electrical industry of course owed much to Werner von Siemens's systematic concentration on invention and to its adoption of Edison's patents but its progress was in no small measure due to the activities of a large number of scientifically trained inventor-managers.

It has been widely accepted that German industry before the first great war had developed monopoly by contractual agreement to a greater extent than industries elsewhere. A large number of arrangements to restrict competition did in fact exist; their legality was confirmed by a decision of the supreme court of the empire in 1897 and thus the terms of such contracts could be enforced in the courts. In some industries such as rails, iron, wire, pig iron, salt and coal, attempts to conclude marketing agreements had been made even in mid-century. But during a period of rapid expansion and with a large number of competitors involved, these rarely lasted any length of time and never

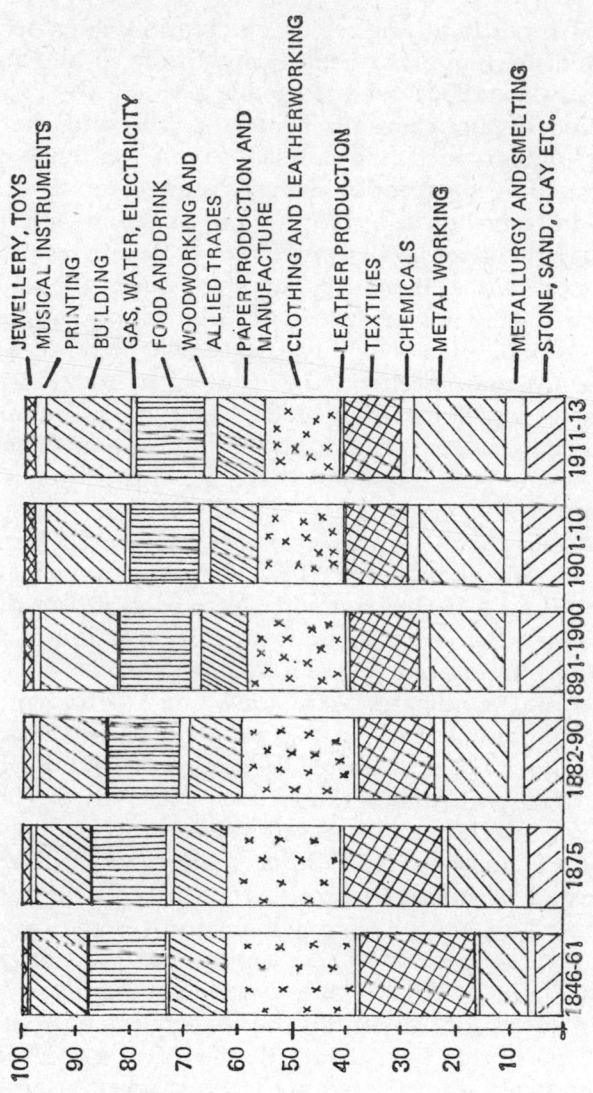

FIGURE 13 *Distribution of Employees by Industries and Crafts 1846-1913*

embraced more than one region. Increasing concentration and diminished international competition in the inland market between 1880 and 1910 made possible the creation of effective organisations to control prices and markets. The big banks which had now come into existence made their distinctive contribution as organising agencies. Cartels in each industry in 1907 controlled the following share of the market: paper 90 per cent, mining 74 per cent, crude steel 50 per cent, cement 48 per cent, glass 36 per cent and railway carriages 23 per cent. The highly important Rhenish-Westphalian coal syndicate was established in 1893, the German steelworks association in 1904. A phosphate cartel was founded in 1881 but the continuous expansion of capacity frustrated this until it was made compulsory by an imperial law in 1910. In this instance the monopoly in the exploitation of the German phosphate deposits was meant to raise export prices. In general, though, the German cartels held domestic above export prices, especially if they were protected by import duties. Quite frequently too the initiative for the creation of international cartels originated in Germany.

Cartels and syndicates were only one method of centralising marketing decisions. Concentration proceeded in almost every kind of industry as well as in banking, insurance, transport undertakings etc. This did not mean the end of all competition but often it was now just competition among the giants. Enormous enterprises were created by amalgamations, frequently in the form of a combine, i.e. enterprises which were separate legal bodies but arranged for linked capital and joint organisation. The joint stock company offered a highly suitable legal framework for this, as did the 'association with limited liability' (G.m.b.H.), created in 1892. In the electrical industries two groups dominated the market after 1901, Siemens and the AEG. In the chemical field the setting up of dyestuff cartels was followed in 1904 by an association with pooled profits of two groups of firms (I.G.).

Industry began in 1850, assisted by the transport system, to remodel the geographical distribution of the German economy and the regional distribution of wealth. Some centres of industrialisation developed in regions with older economic activity, e.g. the Wupper Valley and the kingdom of Saxony where the traditional manufactures of textiles and metal wares continued. The pattern of manufacturing changed in other centres. Thus Berlin, the capital, lost its textile industries and replaced them with the ready made clothing industry, machine building, the electrical industry, banking and insurance. The differences in wealth between industrial and agricultural regions became more accentuated; the Rhineland in particular considerably improved its position as a result of industrialisation, while the formerly wealthy Prussian province of Silesia clearly failed to keep up because of its peripheral situation.

Apart from the concentration of industry near raw materials which was the most prominent feature of the Ruhr, German industry was fairly widely dispersed over the country. The division into small principalities may have contributed to this. Railway engines for instance were built in almost all the larger states; machine building occupied locations far from coal and iron, e.g. in Württemberg, Munich and Nürnberg.

The east however was left far behind. Wage rates sloped steeply down from west to east, reflecting the stage of industrialisation: this explains internal German long range migrations. Calculations by the central statistical office in 1913 of income per head in Marks for the Prussian provinces and the German states show Hamburg in the lead with 1,313, followed by Berlin with 1,254 and Brandenburg with 962. The Prussian provinces of Hessen-Nassau and Rheinprovinz and the Saxon kingdom were on approximately the same level at 899, 897 and 832 respectively. Next came Prussian Schleswig-Holstein with 763, Westphalia with 735 and the first south German state, Baden, with 710. Hanover, another Prussian province, had 697 then came Württemberg with 672 and Bavaria with 629. The tail consisted of the provinces of eastern Prussia, Silesia with 603, Pomerania with 576, East Prussia with 486, West Prussia with 480 and Posen with 465 Marks.

The development of the gradient between German internal incomes was intimately connected with changes in international economic relationships during the nineteenth century. As has been pointed out above, exports rose more rapidly than the national product in the two periods of Kondratieff-upswings, 1850–73 and 1896–1913. Information about the extent of German foreign trade is woefully inadequate but this statement may still be made with some assurance. Official statistics of turnover in foreign trade begin in 1872/1880 but until 1905 they relied only on estimated instead of real prices. Figure 9, p. 114, extracts exports and imports from 1880 to 1913 from this source; it also shows W. G. Hoffmann's figures for volume of exports at 1913 prices. Both sets of data indicate the periods of rapid growth in exports. The balance of trade was usually adverse; at least after 1880 this was made good by invisible exports such as services and investment income.

During industrialisation the physical composition of exports and imports changed considerably, more so after 1880. Foodstuffs, drink and tobacco still accounted for an important share of export commodities in 1850 but declined continuously to 10·2 per cent in 1910-13; this would have been even more severe without sugar which was a major export commodity. Raw material exports retained their place with 15·5 per cent even in 1913. Semi-manufactured and manufactured commodities gained, with 21 per cent and 53·3 per cent respectively in 1910–13. The imports of these two items however expanded at less than average rates and their share in the total fell to respectively 14·7 per cent and 8·8 per cent by 1910–13. As could be expected, raw material imports grew faster than average to 43·1 per cent of all imports. At about 33 per cent the share of food and drink imports remained approximately constant from 1860 on. This can be summed up as follows: until 1870 both industrial and primary commodities were exported and imported in roughly equal quantities; after 1870 a large favourable balance in industrial commodities emerged simultaneously with a large deficit in primary products.

Unfortunately it is not possible to give a precise historical account of the destinations of German exports or the origins of German imports for the more important groups of commodities. Consideration of only the major partners in foreign trade demonstrates for the period after 1890 an unmistakable decline in the share of German imports coming from European countries. This is particularly noticeable for Great Britain, Belgium, the Netherlands, Austria-Hungary and Switzerland. Imports from Russia rose in step with total imports; the Scandinavian countries and Turkey became more important among the European suppliers. The most significant increases though occurred in the position of overseas suppliers, above all the U.S.A. No similar tendency to 'de-Europeanisation' made itself felt where exports were concerned: Europe's share remained practically constant. Here too Great Britain's significance declined relatively but other western and eastern neighbours bought all the more. In the twenty years before the first world war more than three quarters of German exports went to European countries. Increased demand from South American countries in this period partially compensated for falling purchases by the U.S.A.

It was no mere chance which caused the direction of the German export offensive to coincide with the activities of specialised German banks, such as the Deutsche Überseebank founded in 1886, the Deutsch-Asiatische Bank of 1889, the Deutsch-Südamerikanische Bank of 1906 and the Deutsche Orientbank of 1906. The length of the credit terms which German exporters could offer their foreign customers was observed with astonishment by their international competitors.

It has remained a contentious question whether and to what extent the development of the German economy was furthered by the deliberate policy of industrial protection. When Bismarck was engaged in the revision of commercial policy in 1879, industrial duties were introduced or raised, alongside the agricultural ones. It does not seem likely that, at this stage, they could have been a precondition for the development of German industry. Long before then, between 1836–40 and 1867–9 the dependence of cotton weavers on imports of foreign yarn had declined from 70 to 22 per cent. For the finishing industries many of the duties on semi-manufactured imports were, if anything, disadvantageous. The withdrawal of duties on iron in 1873 acknowledged the industrial position prior to the collapse of the boom.

Agitation for colonial possessions emanated mainly from the north German maritime cities and Bismarck in the 1870s maintained his opposition to this. The internal political realignment of 1878–80 also meant that the empire after all joined the race for domination over the last few unclaimed spots, in Africa in 1884–5 and in Asia in 1900. For the German economy these colonies remained by and large without significance. Neither as partners in trade nor for settlement nor yet as fields for investment were they irreplaceable.

Information regarding the extent of German exports of capital is most inadequate. The sum total of German investments abroad has been estimated for 1913 at over 30,000 million Marks of which perhaps 20,000 million was in securities. The role of capital exports in the formation of German wealth was much smaller than for either Britain or France, not least because the level of German interest rates was higher than those of its western neighbours. Domestic capital was in much demand for the enlargement of capacity and for technical improvement, thus tempting the investing public with attractive possibilities. Seventy-eight per cent of securities newly issued in France between 1906 and 1911 had foreign debtors: in Germany it was a mere 11 per cent.

An attempt to characterise the nineteenth century without mentioning the term 'industrialisation' might celebrate it as the 'century of the revolution in communications'. The growth in the output of material commodities was surely impressive but the efficiency of the transmission of freight, persons, news, means of payment and capital, improved even more. Markets extended their range and people who had never before been within reach of one another now entered into specific economic relationships. This is not merely incidental to the great advance in productivity of the nineteenth century: it can equally well be described as one of its prerequisites. In reality they mutually depend upon each other. Without progress in the production of material goods there could have been no railway, steamships, telephones, etc. but without these neither large-scale production nor a mass market can be envisaged. From 1850 to 1913 the railways increased their activity in ton/kilometres twentyfold; the greatest increase, namely sevenfold, fell in the period before 1860, as might be expected. Until 1870 the railway cut into the freight traffic of inland shipping and set off a crisis in long distance freight traffic on the roads. By 1870 though the substitution of rail for road and waterways was ending. Long haul freight, it is true, did not return to the roads until the middle of the twentieth century but on the roads short haul traffic expanded all the more rapidly, especially in urban districts, as did the delivery traffic to railheads. Larger vessels and the use of tugs on inland waterways helped them to retain their share of the growing volume of transport, mainly with the rapid growth of traffic on the Rhine. The volume of freight on inland waterways and on the railways increased from 1880 to 1913 at approximately the same rate, about five per cent per annum. Cheap and bulky commodities which did not require rapid movement, could be carried much more cheaply by water transport, wherever this was feasible; the government indeed did not impose on it the full costs of improving and enlarging rivers and canals—and new canals were being built around 1900.

Until 1875 most of the German railway network, especially in Prussia, was constructed by independent companies with occasional government assistance. But from then on the German states bought up these independent companies piecemeal for military or fiscal reasons or as a matter of economic policy and after 1873 new lines were mostly built to government order. Only 6 per cent of all lines and no important main line remained in private hands by 1910. The most important railway employees were government officials and thus subject to quasi-military discipline. Rail freight and passenger rates were not only further reduced after 1850 but were also called on for special schemes of promotion by setting exceptional or specific rates for exports, for coal, for carriage of grain to Berlin etc. Nevertheless the railways were mostly very profitable and yielded a considerable surplus for the public exchequer. The empire and the individual states together procured in 1910 more than 20 per cent of ordinary public expenditure from the surplus of revenues over and above working expenses in posts, telegraphs, railways, land in the public domain, forests etc. It was partly for fiscal reasons that Bismarck attempted, unsuccessfully, to place the railways under unified imperial administration, on the analogy of the post office.

The transmission of news is a vital condition of flexibility in a system of production based on the division of labour; in the nineteenth century it underwent a large number of changes in techniques and organisation. The telegraph arrived in the late 1840s and the telephone about 1880: these were radically novel means of communication and therefore their dissemination and utilisation expanded at a high rate. The number of telephone conversations rose between 1890 and 1913 at a regular annual rate of about 12 per cent. Even the dispatch of letters increased considerably faster than the production of goods, from 1850 to 1913 regularly by about 7 to 8 per cent per annum.

Germany's merchant shipping at sea had long been minute although the fleet had begun to pick up again after 1825, at an average of 3·6 per cent yearly. The German states in 1870 still owned less tonnage than Britain, the U.S.A., France, Norway and Italy. The number of sailing vessels continued to grow until 1867 and their tonnage did not reach its maximum until 1880. In the meantime shipowning had advanced far towards establishing its independence as a business. In 1847 the Hamburg Amerikanische Paketfahrt A.G. and in 1856 the Norddeutsche Lloyd of Bremen were founded and gradually most of the parts in ships held in these two towns gravitated towards them. After 1885, at least in its home ports, the turnover of the German merchant navy surpassed the British. In the 1890s steam tonnage overtook sail and in 1913 steamships accounted for 85 per cent of German tonnage, about three million tons; in contrast to twenty years earlier, these had mostly been built by German yards, in Stettin, Danzig, Kiel, Hamburg and Elbing. The programme of naval construction and the empire's own colonial activities incidentally helped merchant shipping too; so did mail subsidies. Until 1854 traffic in the Baltic ports had been greater than in the North Sea ports. In the following decades the latter grew incomparably faster because they became centres of passenger traffic, e.g. for emigrants, and staging posts for the import of raw materials such as cotton, wool, tobacco and coal and for exports. In the second half of the century the North Sea ports served the more dynamic part of the German hinterland, as for instance the Berlin region and Saxony, via the railways and the Elbe.

It is inopportune here to describe in detail the organisation of domestic and foreign commerce in the nineteenth century or to demonstrate detailed developments in the business of specific commercial enterprises. Compared to western countries in the early nineteenth century, handicapped as it was by appalling transport conditions, the organisation of German wholesale and retail commerce was severely retarded. There were only a few hundred wholesalers in Prussia and business was often still conducted at periodic fairs and markets. Incisive change started only in mid-century, with the transport revolution. Apart from some specialised exceptions, such as the Leipzig fair for furs and the cattle markets, the old wholesaling fairs disappeared. They were replaced partly by produce exchanges for standardised products and partly by the arrangement of deals through travellers and the mails. Major industrial enterprises created their own sales organisations and eliminated the trade in industrial products. For a different set of purposes however industry relied on the organised intervention of commerce for the disposal of its mass production. With the expansion of business, the wholesalers on their part hived off the transactions connected with the movement of their wares from their own firms to specialised carriers and shipping firms. Even storage could now be handed over to specialised undertakings, at last refining down the central function of the wholesaler to the mere disposal of commodities. The Leipzig fair, after 1894 the first one to concentrate purely on the displaying of samples, became important for the sale of industrial products.

Retail trade too changed its character considerably, partly impelled by growing urbanisation which widened the economic gap between producer and consumer. The local weekly market and direct access to agricultural producers catered less and less effectively for the total supply of food. Industrial commodities too required distribution more efficiently organised than through pedlars and the weekly market. The number of small retailers continued to grow, until Prussia in 1900 had three times as many retailers per thousand of the population as fifty years earlier. The change from itinerant trader or pedlar to the fixed shop was particularly striking in the last quarter of the century. Large scale retail enterprise adopted the form of department stores in imitation of the Parisian model, e.g. Tietz in 1879, Karstadt in 1881 and Althoff in 1885; they disseminated the practice of trading with fixed prices. These were essential in large enterprises employing mere assistants. Towards the end of the century the middle classes mounted an embittered opposition to large scale enterprise in retailing. Hence from 1899 most German governments introduced special taxes on department stores. Outside a few towns though these undertakings plus chain stores and mail order houses obtained only a small fraction of the total retail turnover. Similarly consumers' co-operatives had just 100,000 members in 1885; in 1910 their membership was 1·3 million, barely half the British total. Since 1849 co-operatives had been established in Germany mainly as purchasing agencies for craftsmen and farmers;

they only later on began to cater for working class consumption.

Insufficient information about the financing of investment in Germany prevents us unfortunately from assessing accurately how much financial intermediaries contributed to growth. Governments and the aristocracy remained the chief debtors in the first half of the nineteenth century; for credit they relied on the great private bankers, especially of Frankfurt but of Augsburg and even Berlin too. Private bankers did not refrain from industrial business altogether, least of all in Cologne but they did not really regard this as the core of their activities. Speculation with real estate, and the handling of public loans were more to their taste. In the 1830s and 1840s joint stock banks were under some discussion but this generally revolved around the problem of improving the supply of means of payment for the economy. For this purpose several private banks of issue were founded but their significance for capital formation remained limited.

A few years in mid-century saw a complete change in this picture. The railways still raised most of their finance in a manner analogous to the creation of the public debt; this was supplemented to some extent by the public issue of shares and by the borrower's directly soliciting loans from the public. However this was not a general rule and the private banks were often needed as intermediaries. Various industries too needed assistance in raising their capital but could not obtain this in the customary manner, because great financial backers had few opportunities to refinance themselves. The first joint stock bank in Prussia came into existence accidentally, in order to salvage by this conversion the private bank Abraham Schaaffhausen of Cologne, which had had to put up its shutters in 1848. But the hidden potential of such banks had already been revealed through the example of the brothers Pereire in Paris and perhaps of the older Belgian Banque Générale too. From 1853 to 1856 some joint stock banks and limited companies of considerable size were established, with the express object of providing finance for industry. They were the Darmstädter Bank für Handel und Industrie in 1853, the Berliner Handelsgesellschaft in 1856 and, after a smaller start in 1853, the re-foundation of the Discontogesellschaft in 1856. For lending to their customers they employed mainly their own capital but they met their own obligations by acting as agents for the issue of their clients' shares.

Capital then was raised for the foundation and extension of industrial enterprises in ways reminiscent of the procedures employed in launching the old government loans; the methods of the great German banks thus differed sharply from British practice. However they were faced by a materially different situation. The financial strength of the British merchant class was long established so that it could finance the purchases and sales of the gradually expanding industrial enterprises while obtaining its own finance in the market for short term credits. This worked particularly well in disposing of the products of the consumer goods industries. As has been explained above, Germany lacked a merchant class of comparable financial potency. Besides industrialisation in Germany was mainly carried forward by industries which offered little scope for the financial techniques of the merchants. The mining and capital goods industries needed too much fixed and working capital to be able to rely on suppliers' and customers' credits, without the possibility of adequate internal reinvestment. Anyhow in Germany too industry was to a significant extent financed by bill with banker's rediscount. This however was overshadowed by the more sensational operation of procuring long term capital. The emergence of cartels and of vertical combines in Germany moreover reinforced the influence of the banks and still further weakened the financial role of the merchants.

Even in the 1850s and 1860s banks were of some strategic importance for the evolution of major industrial enterprises. As the focal point of the process of industrial development though they did not emerge until the 1870s: then they began to take over the financing of foreign trade by acceptances in competition with British firms; simultaneously they reformed their erstwhile methods of providing capital. Giant joint stock banks arose, incidentally with the assistance of major private bankers like Bleichröder, Delbrück and others, the Deutsche Bank and the Commerz- und Discontobank both in 1870, the Dresdener Bank in 1872 and the Nationalbank in 1881. Until 1914 the share capital of each of these big German banks far exceeded that of the great industrial enterprises. In the banks' annual balances their own capital plus reserves accounted for more than 50 per cent of the total until 1890. That was the result of defective liaison between the individual banks and of the absence of an effective German money market where financial surpluses could have been cleared easily.

Towards the end of the century some of the big banks promoted short term deposits and discovered that some capital for long term disposal is also made available during the transmission of payments. The investing and speculating banks thus evolved into a receptacle which converted every conceivable type of funds into capital: the universal bank saw the light. Contrary to received notions this was not a fundamental prerequisite for industrialisation in Germany but a form of banking not in evidence until after 1870. As late as 1900 the certified amount of savings and deposit accounts with all German loan banks came to just less than 1,000 million Marks.

The big German banks often exerted a direct influence on the business decisions of industrial firms: they were centres of 'business decision making'. Their representatives sat on numerous boards of directors but not usually because of their holdings of shares. In 1912 only one of the seven big banks held shares and industrial debentures in excess of three per cent of its assets. Nevertheless in that year the Deutsche Bank had a seat on the boards of 159 firms and was thus represented on that committee which decided long term business policies and especially determined plans for investment.

With the discovery that the transfer of payments could be useful for the business of investment banks too, there emerged, later than in Britain, a large scale movement towards their amalgamation which lasted from about the end of the century until 1914. By its end all decisions concerning the German market for credit had become much more centralised. This reduced the securities exchange to just a tool of the big banks, a clearing house where they concluded deals not settled internally. It is not really surprising if, as a market for securities, Berlin remained much inferior to London, Paris or Brussels.

In mid-century the banks had still unloaded most of the risks of credit transformation on lenders in the form of variations in the prices of shares and on borrowers as uncertainty regarding the source of further credits should the first ones expire. With the development of deposit banking at the end of the century, the banks increasingly accepted this kind of risk and earned the margin of interest themselves. They thereby converted their own capital from a disposable fund, important as the biggest source of current finance, into a form of collateral. They held an increasing amount in deposits until its share of the published balances had risen to 72 per cent in 1910.

Examinations of the economic development of Germany have gravitated mistakenly towards an almost exclusive preoccupation with the joint stock banks. Yet they were never responsible for more than 25 per cent of the total of bankers' credits. Other types of bank too provided major portions of the finance needed for investment. Germany since the end of the eighteenth century had possessed a competent credit institution which offered to the owners of manorial estates (Rittergüter) access to letters of credit which were guaranteed by the corporate liability of provincial or knightly associations. These and other forms of public land banks mainly served the rural demand for credit which was not covered by dealers in grain and cattle in such ways as advances on the harvest. The idea of employing corporate associations as a broadly-based backing and thus gaining easier access to credit was utilised by Raiffeisen in 1849–54 for the system of rural credit co-operatives and by Schulze-Delitzsch in 1850 for the organisation of industrial credit co-operatives. The development of the mortgage in Germany however needed a new impetus from outside in mid-century although the provincial associations seemed to have provided a suitable precursor. Misgivings existed against allowing old or new mortgage banks the right to issue mortgage debentures and these were only allayed after the success of the French Crédit Foncier. Governments were after all much exercised over their own sources of credit and would not want to tempt the public with too many competing opportunities for investment. From 1862 on, as the business of dealing in mortgage debentures became institutionalised, it expanded in Germany too: it acquired much importance for commercial and residential buildings in the towns. The net investment by these banks between 1880 and 1913 was about on a par with that of the loan banks.

As already explained, the joint stock loan banks concerned themselves at first predominantly with outgoing business and did not begin to supplement this with systematic soliciting for deposits until 1880. Savings banks had long given pride of place to dealing with long term deposits. Even in the eighteenth century a public savings bank had been founded in Hamburg in 1778 as a welfare institution; it was to offer absolute security of investment for those members of the population who were not competent to administer reserves of money on their own. In Germany these savings banks, as public institutions, always enjoyed some privileges; in return they were prescriptively obliged, especially after 1850, to restrict their investments to lending on the security of real property or for central and local government securities. They hardly took any direct part at all in big business; around 1840 their lending to craftsmen had been of some significance but this almost disappeared later; in 1910 it absorbed only 3·1 per cent of the investments made by all savings banks. They were not permitted to give their clients cheque accounts until shortly before the world war. Figure 14 which shows the development of net investment for every kind of bank, demonstrates the unexpected height of the savings banks' contribution.

Regulation of the currency was one of the more significant consequences of the empire's foundation in 1871. Until then seven different silver currencies had circulated, based on either Taler or Gulden; in 1871–5 they were replaced by one gold currency with a gold Mark of a third of a silver Taler as the unit. Silver coins remained in circulation as currency but were no longer freely minted. Until then Britain alone of the great trading nations had adopted the gold standard; that the German empire immediately followed it indicated the deliberately western orientation of its foreign trade policy. By a happy coincidence it also delivered the German economy from the problems due to arise from the silver crisis at the end of the nineteenth century.

There were thirty-three private and state banks with rights of issue; the Preussische Bank in Berlin was the most important of these and in 1875 it was converted into the 'Deutsche Reichsbank' which now assumed the role of bankers' bank for the whole of Germany. Unlike the Bank of England or the Banque de France, the Reichsbank was not furnished from the start either with a ceiling to its issues or with a rule enforcing complete cover for them, to act as a check on the note issue; instead it was obliged to cover one third of its issues, with the proviso that all issues which exceeded the cash cover by a stated amount would be liable to taxation. Together with the practice of discounting commercial bills which was much employed in Germany, these two regulations proved flexible enough to provide all the means of payment required; the average circulation of bills in 1913 amounted to 10,260 million Marks, of cash to 6,500 million Marks. From 1875 to 1913 bank and government notes accounted with some regularity for a third of the circulating cash. It is unfortunately not possible at present to discover the amount of money transferred by bankers' giro. Compared to Britain the turnover of cheque clearing houses was strikingly lower; the principal reason for this may have been the fact that from 1876

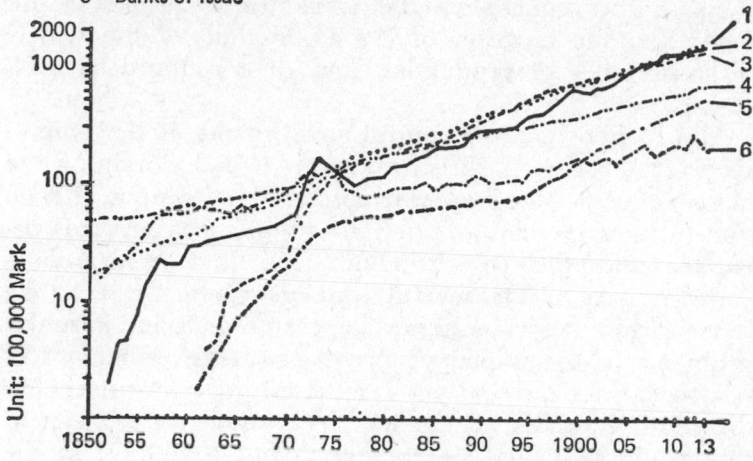

1 = Savings Banks
2 = Loan Banks without Issuing Rights
3 = Mortgage Banks
4 = Land Banks under the public law
5 = Credit Co-operatives
6 = Banks of Issue

FIGURE 14 *Financial strength of different types of Bank 1850-1913*

Reichsbank branches, established after all in every place of any importance, catered cheaply for the traffic in money. In addition a law regulating the use of cheques was not passed until 1908 and before then, payments made in anything but cash were of exceedingly dubious legal standing.

The Prussian authorities, the German imperial authorities and the central bank were all concentrated at Berlin: in their wake followed the centralisation of the money and capital markets which had hitherto been widely dispersed over the regions. After 1871 Berlin became the centre preferred by associations and other organisations. Its location between the two centres of heavy industry, the Ruhr and Upper Silesia, its reasonably convenient access to Hamburg as a North Sea port and to the agricultural region of the north-east, made of Berlin at one and the same time an administrative and an industrial centre. Both of them could take full advantage of the large concentration of intelligent workers here available. Not until 1871 did Germany acquire a capital city which could perform all these functions properly and effectively. Primarily all this had only been made possible by the major improvements in the transmission of news: this facilitated the creation of a web linking all the widely dispersed sites of production and of consumption to its centre.

Until after 1900 the central government of the empire received no share of direct taxation; it had to rely on the net revenues of the imperial posts and telegraphs and on some duties on consumption to supplement customs revenues and the constitutional (so-called 'matrikular') contributions of the several state governments. In 1913 indeed when it was immersed in rearmament and in major problems of social policy, the imperial government was responsible for only 36 per cent of all government expenditure in Germany. There was little about the tax system that could be called systematic, to put it mildly; in the several states around 1850 the composition of revenues differed widely. Saxony was the first country to introduce a progressive income tax in 1878; Prussia followed in 1891 and added a wealth tax in 1893; Bavaria, Württemberg and others delayed even longer.

Unquestionably Prussian commercial policies had, since 1818, been inclined on the whole towards liberalism. In 1862–6 Prussia or rather the customs union under Prussian pressure, concluded a series of commercial treaties with France which contained a most favoured nation clause. Thus they attached themselves to the free trade area created by the Cobden-Chevalier treaty of 1860. But the Prussian administration did not confine its application of liberal ideology to this field. It was vigorous, for instance, in promoting the freedom to practise any trade in Germany. In 1873 it was instrumental in the abolition of iron duties and in the halving of machinery duties. Support for this liberalism came from a bourgeoisie which benefited from economic prosperity and, even more, from the vested interests of the exporting Prussian estate owners.

Three developments of the 1870s made for a radical change in ideas. The first was the crisis from 1873 onward which seemingly marked the end of the first prosperous phase of industrial development and which raised the spectre of intensified competition due to falling prices, in national as well as international markets. Secondly corn and wool from overseas now began to compete noticeably on the German market too. Finally the socialist opposition was becoming more active. Bismarck responded with a scheme of elaborate cunning. He disavowed the erstwhile liberal forces and cleaned the administration of liberal officials. He welcomed the demand for agricultural protection which had just arisen and extended the welcome to industrial protection so as to secure the consent of industry. He implemented the proscription of socialist organisations in 1878 and pressed forward with the preparations for the introduction of a system of statutory insurance covering accident, sickness, disability and old age as from 1881. In the same year he finally restored some functions in public law to the craft gilds which had survived only as private associations since 1869. Each of these measures was opposed by some groups but all of them jointly made a package which 'loyal elements' could accept. The economic crisis laid bare the foundations of soi-disant liberalism in the Germano-Prussian state: a mere excrescence of the agrarian boom. In contrast to Britain the government was determined, once conditions had changed, to temper the wind for agriculture and hence for the economic base of the non-capitalist elements, the nobility and the peasantry. In 1880 Germany started on its road towards 'neo-mercantilism', towards 'state socialism' and, with its simultaneous colonial acquisitions, towards 'imperialism'. It must be borne in mind of course, in any evaluation of Germany's agrarian policies, that agriculture remained the occupation of almost 50 per cent of the employed population in 1880; the comparable figure had been 27 per cent when Britain repealed the corn laws. In some ways Germany remained imprisoned in its role as a late developer.

Appraisals of German 'state socialism' have differed

widely. The introduction of statutory sickness insurance in 1883, accident insurance in 1884 and old age insurance in 1889 contributed much to the social security of employees. As the scheme was in part financed by employers and government, it also effected some redistribution of incomes. Nevertheless the ideological context of these measures made them less than fully effective as a contribution to the emancipation of workers. Bismarck intended to immunise the workers with insurance against the temptations of socialist programmes and to make them dependent on the government. For a few years he did in fact manage to confound the opposition but the 'socialist laws', prohibiting the Social Democratic Party, failed to divide their forces as had been hoped and instead consolidated the opposition. The imperial authorities may have appeared progressive enough in providing collective safeguards against loss of income: they steadfastly refused any demand for intervention between employer and employee or to extend the protection of labour. In Britain much activity had meanwhile concentrated precisely on this subject; apart from some control over child and female employment, however, the protection of labour could not be improved by imperial legislation until after Bismarck's fall in 1890. In Germany unemployment benefit was at first organised by the trade unions; unlike Britain Germany did not resolve this problem by a system of statutory insurance before the first world war.

Class conflict did not make an appearance in Germany until fairly late; its characteristic political radicalism is the more remarkable. The programme of the Social Democratic Party, founded in 1863, contained some revolutionary clauses: probably these never really prevailed over the more pragmatic approach, certainly not with the socialist trade unions. But employers no less than employees conducted their conflicts quite evidently with much greater animosity than common in other western countries. On neither side were the official spokesmen prepared to accept each other in their mutual roles. True, the so-called Hirsch-Duncker Unions and the Christian Unions were less uncompromising in their rejection of the established order but they were numerically much inferior to the socialist trade unions. A German employer regarded himself as a patriarch, as the master in his own house in pre-industrial terms, with total responsibility for the whole social organism of his enterprise and generally well beyond this. This type of self-esteem made him particularly unyielding in any situation of conflict. For a long time employers refused any demand for the negotiation of wage agreements; strikes and even peaceable wage demands they interpreted as evidence of disobedience and ingratitude and hence of immorality. Undoubtedly though it was precisely the trade unions and the originally revolutionary workers' party which contributed signally to the pacification of labour: they converted an originally diffuse and anarchical opposition into a negotiable conflict of interests. Much of this may, in the end, be the result of the long continuation of economic growth; social disintegration was the immediate by-product of industrial revolution but growth was accompanied by a striking increase in income for the mass of the population. The risks entailed in a capitalist market economy seemed to be much greater but turned out to be, on the whole, less tragic for the individual. Finally the attitude of German workers at the start of the 1914 war proved their undoubted willingness to identify themselves with the nation at large, however one may want to assess this event against the background of a pacifist dreamworld.

BIBLIOGRAPHY

There is no recent comprehensive account of German economic history in the nineteenth century. Werner Sombart, *Die deutsche Volkswirtschaft im neunzehnten Jahrhundert und im Anfang des zwanzigsten Jahrhunderts*, fifth edn. (1921), is very readable and well organised but out of date. So too is the monograph by A. Sartorius von Waltershausen, *Deutsche Wirtschaftsgeschichte 1815–1914*, second edn. (1923), which contains more source material and is also more chauvinistic. More useful, with their emphasis on the study of comparative growth, are J. H. Clapham, *The economic development of France and Germany 1815–1914*, fourth edn. (1936) and reprints, and W. O. Henderson, *The industrial revolution on the Continent, Germany, France, Russia 1800–1914*, (1961), which is rather eclectically organised.

Th. Veblen, *Imperial Germany and the industrial revolution*, (1915, last edn. (1939), paperback (1966)), is more ambitious in attempting to combine political with economic history. Theodore S. Hamerow, *Restoration, revolution, reaction. Economics and politics in Germany 1815–71*, (1958), develops an interesting thesis but its economic history is defective in many details; this topic has been treated in greater depth in Helmut Böhme, *Deutschlands Weg zur Grossmacht. Studien zum Verhältnis von Wirtschaft und Staat während der Reichsgründungszeit*, (1966). Hans Rosenberg, *Grosse Depression und Bismarckzeit. Wirtschaftsablauf, Gesellschaft und Politik in Mitteleuropa*, (1967), unfortunately suffers too from overinterpretation of economic data.

W. Treue, 'Wirtschafts- und Sozialgeschichte Deutschlands im 19. Jahrhundert', in Bruno Gebhardt, *Handbuch der deutschen Geschichte* Vol. III, ed. Herbert Grundmann, eighth edn. (1960), pp. 315–413, can be referred to as a summary account, instead of the non-existent monograph on German economic history; it contains many bibliographical references but is rather weaker on scholarly economic analysis.

The best work at present available for the period until

1873 is perhaps a Marxist one, Hans Mottek, *Wirtschafts-geschichte Deutschlands. Ein Grundriss*, Vol. II, 'Von der Zeit der Französischen Revolution bis zur Zeit der Bismarckschen Reichsgründung', (1964). For the period since 1870 a liberal work, Gustav Stolper, Karl Häuser, Knut Borchardt, *The German economy. 1870 to the present*, (1967).

W. G. Hoffmann, Fr. Grumbach, H. Hesse, *Das Wachstum der deutschen Wirtschaft seit der Mitte des 19. Jahrhunderts*, (1965), is an outstanding collection of source material, fundamental for any study of more recent German economic history; the present work is to a large extent based on it. On more than 800 pages it contains chronological series, covering most of the aspects of economic development which are regarded as relevant for the study of economic history. It completes and replaces the well-known studies of Jacobs and Richter for price history, Wagenführ for the indexes of industrial production and Jostock for national income. The interpretation however is confined to an introduction of 170 pages. Arthur Spiethoff, *Die wirtschaftlichen Wechsellagen*, 2 vols., (1955), especially the second volume, giving the sources which had not been published before, remains at present essential.

Some fundamental problems of economic development in the mid-nineteenth century are discussed in H. Mottek, H. Blumberg, H. Wutzmer, W. Becker, *Studien zur Geschichte der industriellen Revolution*, (1965). H. Haushofer, *Die deutsche Landwirtschaft im technischen Zeitalter*, (1957), treats agriculture from an institutional point of view; for this studied quantitatively, cf. H. W. Graf Finck von Finckenstein, *Die Entwicklung der Landwirtschaft in Preussen und Deutschland 1800–1930*, (1960). There is no tolerably satisfactory history of foreign trade but there are some studies of foreign trade policies. The standard work on banking unfortunately remains J. Riesser, *Die deutschen Grossbanken und ihre Konzentration im Zusammenhang mit der Entwicklung der Gesamtwirtschaft in Deutschland*, fourth edn. (1912); the third edition was translated into English as *The great German banks and their concentration in connection with the economic development of Germany*, Washington D.C. (1911), by the National Monetary Commission. The earlier period is covered by Richard Tilly, 'Germany 1815–70,' in *Banking in the early stages of industrialisation*, ed. R. Cameron, (1967), pp. 151–82, with a bibliography. The standard work on financial history remains W. Gerloff, *Die Finanz- und Zollpolitik des Deutschen Reiches nebst ihren Beziehungen zu Landes-und Gemeindefinanzen von der Gründung des Norddeutschen Bundes bis zur Gegenwart*, (1913).

A history of working conditions which also deals comprehensively with more general problems in economic history is J. Kuczynski, *Die Geschichte der Lage der Arbeiter unter dem Kapitalismus*, especially vols. I–IV and VIII–XIV, (1961 f.f.). Kuczynski's accounts are occasionally partisan; they are completed and corrected above all in Ashok V. Desai, *Real wages in Germany 1871–1913*, (1968).

3. The Industrial Revolution in Great Britain

Phyllis Deane

CHARACTER AND ORIGINS

An industrial revolution is the term generally applied to the complex of economic changes which are involved in the transformation of a pre-industrial, traditional type of economy, characterised by low productivity and normally stagnant growth rates, to a modern industrialised stage of economic development, in which output per head and standards of living are relatively high, and economic growth is normally sustained. We can specify the nature of the transformation by saying that it is made up of a set of interrelated changes in (a) economic organisation, (b) technology and (c) industrial structure, associated with (as both cause and effect) a sustained growth of population and total output and (eventually if not immediately) of product per head.

The changes in economic organisation are of two main kinds: (i) a general, if gradual, shift from a family-based self-subsistent unit of production to the impersonal capitalistic form of enterprise producing for the market, with the aid of paid labour doing specialised jobs and operating with costly capital equipment, and (ii) the evolution of a national or international market for final goods, raw materials and factors of production, in which some of the most crucial and far-reaching decisions affecting both production and consumption are taken by specialist economic institutions (e.g. banks, corporate enterprise, trade unions, etc.). These are the organisational developments that underlie the massive shifts in the scale of economic activity and enterprise necessitated by sustained population growth and permitted by technical progress.

The changes in technology are largely the consequences of the application of scientific knowledge and a spirit of innovation to the processes of production and distribution.

They have generally been characterised by two main kinds of development: (i) the use of machines motivated by non-animal sources of power, and (ii) the replacement of old kinds of raw materials with new kinds which are either more efficient or less scarce (e.g. coal or iron instead of wood, cotton warp instead of flax, rubber instead of leather).

The changes in industrial structure have involved shifts in the disposition of economic resources from primary production to secondary and tertiary industry, from consumers' goods to producers' goods, from luxury trades to mass-production and from country to town.

The mechanism by which changes of this kind have led to modern economic growth is threefold: (i) by permitting a greater efficiency in the allocation of productive resources in land, labour or capital (including the employment of resources previously unemployed), (ii) by generating a continuous flow of improvements in the quality of the labour force (including the entrepreneurial element) through changes in economic motivations, skill, knowledge and energy level, and (iii) by generating a continuous flow of increases in the stock and quality of capital resources used in economic activity.

Each industrial revolution contains these essential ingredients then—these changes in economic organisation, technology, structure of economic activity—the mix and the relative significance of each ingredient varying with the historical circumstances in which it develops. There is nothing distinctive, however, about the ingredients themselves. What produces the revolution is their combination. What guarantees modern economic growth is their degree of development. Few of the changes which made up the industrial revolution that gathered momentum in England in the latter part of the eighteenth century, for example, were unprecedented changes. There had been capitalistic forms of production before. There was nothing new about production for distant markets or about a national or international credit link-up. There had been past successes in the application of science to productive processes—Watt's steam engine was not the first: Abraham Darby had smelted iron with coke in the early years of the eighteenth century: in agriculture 'what transformation could have been more decisive than the invention of the wheeled plough?'[1] The proportions of the labour force engaged in agricultural or rural occupations had been dropping in northwestern Europe for centuries. What distinguished the British experience in the latter part of the eighteenth century from all previous epochs, however, was that the changes concerned developed together, and on a scale that was sufficiently far-reaching and pervasive to set off a continuing and cumulative process of change and growth. It was the sheer scale and persistence of economic change that was new.

Partly because these changes have their roots in the distant past and partly because they belong to a continuous process of change reaching up to the present, it is difficult to attach the industrial revolution to a particular period of time. Yet if there is any meaning to the statement that a country must go through an industrial revolution before it can enjoy 'modern economic growth', we must be able to say something about when the long-term process of evolution developed revolutionary momentum and when the revolution was sufficiently advanced to generate continuous productivity growth. In terms of the proportion of national output produced for mass markets or by capitalist units of production some of today's developing countries (e.g. modern Zambia) are farther advanced than was England in, say, 1870—yet there is no doubt that England had by then gone through an industrial revolution and that modern Zambia has not. In terms of the technological frontiers reached by their most advanced producers, today's developing countries are far ahead of, say, early twentieth-century Britain. In terms of the share of agriculture in the national product or the percentage of labour force in agriculture, France in the last decade of the nineteenth century was probably no more advanced than Britain in the first decade, yet there is little doubt that the former had been through its industrial revolution by 1890 and that the latter

1. M. Bloch, *French Rural History*, p. 197.

had not by 1810.[2] In terms of average incomes per head Australia was richer than Britain in 1860 and Canada had a faster rate of growth between 1870 and 1900—yet neither Australia nor Canada could be said to have gone through an industrial revolution in the nineteenth century.

The question is whether an industrial revolution is a definite process to which we can assign a beginning and an end. Can we identify an industrial revolution in progress in the modern world? Can we date it, however roughly, in the historical record of today's industrialised countries. This is the question to which Professor Rostow was seeking an answer when he developed his concept of the 'take-off'.[3] Unfortunately this notion of a decade or two to which Rostow assigns the changes which transform the basic structure of the economy and the social and political structure of the society 'in such a way that a steady rate of growth can be thereafter regularly sustained',[4] turns out to have very little relation to the real world. In no case of successful industrialisation do we find a unique period of two or three decades, in which the objective and measurable characteristics of a 'take-off' (e.g. an acceleration in the rate of growth of national income, a sharp rise in the rate of productive investment, growth of a leading sector with sufficiently massive forward and backward linkages to affect significantly the national rate of economic growth) are conclusively confirmed by empirical evidence.

In effect, it is not useful to start with the assumption that sustained economic growth becomes inevitable and irreversible within the space of a few decades. There may be more than one great spurt in the process of industrialisation interspersed by periods of economic stagnation: or there may be only one relatively modest spurt followed by a gradual transformation stretching over several generations; or there

2. J. Marczewski, *Introduction à l'Histoire Quantitative* Tables 14 and 16, pp. 107-111.
3. W. W. Rostow, *The Stages of Economic Growth* p. 57: 'The take-off is defined as an industrial revolution tied directly to radical changes in methods of production having their decisive consequences over a relatively short period of time.'
4. *Ibid* pp. 8-9.

may be a significant spurt that subsides without ever leading to modern economic growth. What is interesting is to locate the critical changes or combinations of change and to try to explain why some come to a head slowly or rapidly or erratically.

As far as British experience is concerned, some writers, of whom Professor Nef is the leader, trace the British industrial revolution back to the late sixteenth and early seventeenth centuries. The period which Nef has picked out as one in which the pace of industrialisation first quickened decisively was the century 1540-1640—beginning with the dissolution of the monasteries and leading to an unprecedented industrial development during the latter half of Elizabeth's reign and the reign of James I. He finds evidence of an enormous expansion in coalmining and a variety of manufacturing industries, dating from the middle of the sixteenth century until the Civil War, and generating a pace of industrial growth almost as fast as that taking place in the period usually attributed to the first industrial revolution, i.e. between the mid-eighteenth century and the first Reform Act.[5] This upsurge, which was paralleled in a number of other contemporary European countries, was accompanied by a scientific revolution characterised by 'changes in the methods of scientific investigation in the direction of controlled experiments and accurate measurement' and by 'changes in the goals of industrial enterprise in the direction of quantity production'.[6] It had many of the characteristics, that is to say, of what we have chosen to define as an industrial revolution.

The difference, however, between this early period of industrialisation and the later period to which the industrial revolution is usually attributed was twofold: first that the earlier expansion was relatively slow in developing, that it affected a relatively limited area of the nation's industry, that it represented a relatively minor technological break-

---

5. J. U. Nef. 'The Progress of Technology and the Growth of Large-Scale Industry in Britain 1540-1640.' Reprinted in E. H. Carus Wilson, *Essays in Economic History*, Vol. I, p. 89.
6. J. U. Nef, *The Conquest of the Material World*, p. 220.

through; and second that it was unsupported by the expansion in agricultural output, in domestic communications and in international trade that characterised the second half of the eighteenth century. The difference, that is to say, was a difference partly of the sheer scale of the industrial developments concerned and partly of the wider range of economic opportunities opened up by organisational and technical change in branches of economic activity that lay outside the realm of industry proper—in agriculture, in road and canal transport and in overseas trade. These were the differences that permitted the industrial growth that gathered momentum in the eighteenth century, to break through the population barrier which had constituted the ultimate constraint on the growth of product per head in all preceding generations, and to survive the shock of a long and costly war.

There is room for debate concerning the date at which the industrial expansion began—whether it was in the 1740s or the 1760s or the 1780s for example: and there is also room for argument as to when the industrial revolution had become a self-perpetuating process—Rostow for example would presumably put it at 1802, the end of his 'take-off' period and others might put it at 1830, the beginning of the railway age. But, however these chronological controversies are resolved, there is no doubt that the English economy had been transformed out of all recognition between 1740 and 1840. Population had almost trebled and the total value of economic activity had probably more than quadrupled in a space of roughly three generations. Nothing of the kind had ever happened before either in this country or elsewhere.

The growth in population and output seems to date from the 1740s. There was nothing out of the way about the growth in population in the 1740s—Brownlee's estimates, for example, suggest that there was an increase of about $3\frac{1}{2}\%$ in the population of England and Wales between 1741 and 1751.[7] The significant break with the

7. J. Brownlee, 'History of Birth and Death Rates in England and Wales,' *Public Health*, 1916.

past was the fact that this rate of growth accelerated to about 7% in the 1750s and was maintained on the average of the 1760s and 1770s. This rate of population growth in the context of a pre-industrial economy would normally have resulted in a decline in product per head, as the number of people grew faster than national output. In fact, so far as we can judge from the available statistical evidence, output managed to keep pace with population. It was not primarily industrial output that made this possible however—it was agricultural output. In spite of a striking increase in the output of the export industries (which probably expanded by about three quarters between 1740 and 1770), it was the more modest increase of rather more than 10% in agricultural output that permitted the overall volume of economic activity to keep pace with population growth over this period.[8] The fundamental importance ascribed to agriculture in this context rests on its sheer size as compared with any other contemporary industry and its role as the source of raw materials to the bulk of manufacturing industry.

By 1770 then, the English economy had expanded significantly. The population of England and Wales had grown by nearly a fifth—adding more than a million people to under six million there in 1740. The evidence, such as it is, suggests that the agricultural industry began to grow—if not as fast as population not much more slowly. Expansion was achieved partly through a slow improvement of techniques by the more progressive farmers, but more by an extension of the cultivated acreage. There is no evidence that agricultural changes had yet reached revolutionary proportions except for a very few progressive farmers; though wherever farmers replaced the traditional third-year fallow with a fodder crop there must have been a noticeable improvement in overall productivity per acre. There was in any case an appreciable degree of slack in the economy to support a rising population, slack that showed itself in the shape of a corn export which was equivalent to

8. Phyllis Deane and W. A. Cole, *British Economic Growth* 1688-1959.

the subsistence requirements of more than a million people in the early 1750s.

The existence of a food surplus, plus the capacity of the agricultural industry to expand its output in response to rising demand, meant that population could grow without driving up food prices to levels that might generate explosive political and social discontent. It thus created a favourable climate for economic expansion. Something very similar—though for different reasons—was happening in Ireland, where the spread of potato cultivation was making it possible to support larger families on smaller acreages, and Irish population was probably rising at least as fast as English. This kind of enlargement of the production possibility frontier in agriculture was a familiar enough occurrence in the past historical record. There was no reason to suppose that it would continue to generate rising incomes once the productivity gains opened up by the new techniques had been grasped by the mass of farmers. Indeed if the innovations were too narrowly based—as was the case in Ireland where it induced heavy dependence on a single crop—the output gains built up gradually over two or three or more generations could vanish catastrophically in the space of a disastrous season or two, leaving starvation or emigration as the sole choices for a large fraction of the population.

If it was agricultural expansion that was mainly responsible for keeping total national output growing more or less in step with total population in the middle decades of the eighteenth century, and if agriculture's role in this expansion was permissive rather than initiating, are we to conclude that the upsurge which dates from the 1740s was no more than a once-and-for-all occurrence common enough in the experience of pre-industrial economies? If so then it is reasonable to take the view that the English industrial revolution effectively began in the 1780s and that the events of the preceding decades were important only in setting the stage for it.

Is there any evidence for the emergence of critical changes in economic organisation, technology or industrial structure *before* the 1770s? The statistical evidence suggests that overseas trade would be the place to look. For it is domestic exports, and particularly exports of manufactured goods, that make the spectacular leap forward in the middle decades of the century. The increase—estimated at about three quarters—in the output of the export industries between 1740 and 1770 was unprecedentedly large so far as we can judge from the available data for earlier periods, but the distinctive feature of this particular spurt was that it affected a wide range of domestic manufactures. English overseas trade had a long history of jerky expansion,[9] but until the eighteenth century these upsurges had depended primarily on the woollen trade and (in the later seventeenth century) on the re-export trade. It was in the middle decades of the eighteenth century that England emerged from the status of a one-crop exporter and began to sell a diversity of domestic manufactures to new markets in America, Africa, India and the Far East. By the early 1770s her export of manufactures to these areas had multiplied nearly eightfold compared with what it had been at the beginning of the century.[10]

So there were two reasons why the upsurge in overseas trade that took place in the middle decades of the eighteenth century opened up economic opportunities to English industry on a scale that was both beyond all previous experience and decisive in relation to future developments: (1) because of the wide range of domestic manufactures involved, and (2) because it represented the beginning of the world-wide multilateral system of trade which was to keep British exports expanding right up to 1914.

To a large extent, of course, the mid-eighteenth century expansion was dependent on political circumstances, and particularly on the fact that England was able to exclude the originally superior financial and commercial expertise of the Dutch from the growing North American market. Behind the protective barriers of the old colonial system,

9. Ralph Davis, English Foreign Trade 1700-1774, *Economic History Review*, December 1962, p. 293.
10. *Ibid.*, p. 291.

however, the English merchant community developed new commercial skills and organisational techniques which reduced the uncertainties and the costs of foreign trade. An elaborate degree of specialisation developed in the first half of the century. There was a long line of intermediaries—including ships' husbands, shipbrokers, underwriters, specialised agents and packers—through whom the provincial traders operating from inland towns could route their goods to markets at the other end of the world. 'Lloyd's it was said was better informed than Whitehall on what was happening abroad, on the prospects of war or peace and the disposition of foreign navies.'[11] By the 1740s London insurers were quoting lower rates than any other country and dealing with more of the international trade in this kind of service than any other country. Successful merchants graduated naturally from trading in commodities to specialising in banking and foreign exchange transactions and the growing expertise and renown of the London merchant community attracted to it a profitable commercial and financial braindrain from Europe.[12]

In consequence, when the War of Independence broke the English political control of the richest market in the New World, the interruption of trade with the American market was no more than temporary and the export upsurge resumed in the 1780s. And when Amsterdam was submerged by the Napoleonic invasion of the 1790s, London was ready to take its place as the centre of the world's money market.

Beginning in the 1740s then, we find evidence of a significant though far from spectacular rise in population, in agricultural output and in a wide range of exported manufactures—a rise which was temporarily retarded by the American War of Independence. The justification for treating this period from the 1740s to the early 1770s as part of the English industrial revolution, however, lies more in its organisational changes than in its technological or structural developments. There is little evidence of revolutionary

11. T. S. Ashton, *An Economic History of England: the 18th Century*, p. 133.
12. *Ibid.*, p. 140.

technological change before the 1770s and none of significant structural shifts. In agriculture there had probably been
a slow overall improvement in yields as best-practice techniques spread and a larger number of farmers adopted the
more flexible rotations, planted fodder crops on land that
would once have been left fallow and adopted the iron
plough in place of the wooden plough. But the evidence,
such as it is, suggests that the eighteenth-century rise in
agricultural output owed more to an increase in the sown
acreage than to an improvement in yields.[13]

Similarly for the other sectors of the economy, though
there were technological innovations developing and
spreading during the mid-century decades, it is doubtful
whether any of these innovations had more than a modest
impact even on the industry to which it belonged, still less
on a wider range of industries. The well-known early cotton
textile inventions for example—Kay's flying shuttle (introduced in the 1730s and adopted widely in the 1750s and
1760s) and Paul's carding machine (patented in 1748 and
spreading in the 1760s) were introduced into an industry
which accounted for less than half of 1 per cent of gross
national product. There were 17 coke furnaces in blast in
Britain in 1760 and a further 14 were built before the
American War broke out, but the bulk of the nation's iron
output was still produced with the aid of charcoal fuel.
More generalised perhaps were the effects of the early
canal construction boom of the 1760s and early 1770s,
which greatly reduced the costs of coal in certain towns; but
even these served a limited area and affected a limited
range of commodities.

The organisational developments of this period, on the
other hand—though it is not easy to assess their incidence
either in time or space—were more novel and pervasive in
their effects. The growing specialisation of commercial and
financial operations reduced much of the uncertainty of

13. J. D. Chambers and G. E. Mingay, *The Agricultural Revolution 1750-
1880*, p. 35. Part of the increase in the sown acreage was of course due
to planting with fodder crops fields that would have lain fallow under
earlier rotation systems.

producing for overseas markets to a calculable risk. Domestic trade was facilitated by developments in the internal system of credit. The mechanism of the inland bill of exchange permitted the development of a flexible nationwide chain of credit, linking a wide range of commercial transactors, large and small. The Bank of England had played a key role in Walpole's attempts to rationalise the government's finances in the 1720s and 1730s, and by the 1750s an investment in the Funds was one of the safest and most liquid forms of investment. According to Wilson the buying and selling of government stock had been reduced to a routine by 1750.[14] At the same time the balances held by the government's tax-collectors helped to strengthen the deposits at the disposal of the country banks and enabled them to lend more freely to merchants, farmers and industrialists in search of finance for expansion or improvement.

The changes in economic organisation which I have specified as being of the essence of an industrial revolution, in that they permitted the massive shifts in the scale of economic activity necessitated by sustained population growth, were of two main kinds: (1) the change from the largely self-subsistent family unit of production to the capitalistic market-oriented forms of enterprise employing specialised labour and costly capital equipment, and (ii) the evolution of a national or international market served by specialist economic institutions. How far had the English economy gone in these directions by 1770?

It is clear first of all that it had already made considerable progress along this path *before* the beginning of the eighteenth century. When Gregory King drew up his table of the income and expenditure of English families at the end of the century the class of 'cottagers and paupers' (among which the self-subsistence farmers must have been) accounted for less than a quarter of the total population and under 6% of national income.[15] When Patrick Colqu-

14. Charles Wilson, *England's Apprenticeship 1603-1763*, p. 325.
15. George E. Barnett (Ed.) *Two Tracts by Gregory King* (Baltimore, 1936).

houn compiled a similar table at the beginning of the nineteenth century he did not trouble to distinguish a cottager class at all, from which one may presume that the subsistence farmer was of negligible importance in the English economy.[16]

In industry too, things had moved quite far towards capitalistic forms of enterprise before the beginning of the eighteenth century. There had been an expansion in the share of the traditionally capital-intensive industries like mining and metal manufacturing. There had been a centuries-old movement towards capitalistic control of the textile industries as the independent handicraft system of manufacture, organised at the level of the individual family, gave way to the 'putting out' system whereby the merchant supplied the working materials and intermediate products and marketed the final goods. Wherever this occurred— and it was already general practice in the textile industries in the later seventeenth century—it meant that the crucial price-making decisions in relation to both inputs and outputs were made at the impersonal level of the capitalistic enterprise, though the technological decisions relating to the process of production continued to remain within the control of the individual or the family.

Nor did the widening of the market to national and international proportions begin in the eighteenth century: though it is in this respect that the developments attributable to the period between circa 1740 and circa 1770 seem to have been crucial. The marked improvements in the internal system of communications (roads, rivers and canals), the extension of the international market to almost the whole range of English manufactures and the development of specialised commercial and financial institutions were all significant characteristics of this period. The data do not exist that would permit a conclusive assessment of

16. Patrick Colquhoun, *Treatise on Indigence* (1806), Colquhoun's estimates and those of King are discussed in Phyllis Deane, The Implications of Early National Income Estimates for the Measurement of Long-term Growth in the United Kingdom, *Economic Development and Cultural Change*, 1955.

the effect of these developments on the rate of expansion of total national product; but it is reasonable to suppose that they were important. True the organisational changes which developed in the English economy during the middle decades of the eighteenth century were evolutionary in character rather than revolutionary. They were not sudden changes based on unprecedented or unparalleled institutional innovations. On the other hand, the fact that they developed to this pitch, and at this rate, in England and in no other country, does help to explain the timing and location of the first industrial revolution. They helped to create an environment that was conducive to technical progress. The fact that the market for manufactures was widening faster than the labour force was growing, was a stimulus to labour-saving inventions, while the development of specialist commercial and financial institutions provided the capital and the enterprise necessary to transform invention into innovation.

Thus, while there were other countries in western Europe in the eighteenth century—France and Holland in particular—which were operating at similar levels of productivity, were experiencing a like acceleration in the rate of population growth and had access to the same kind of scientific and technological knowhow, it was in England that the major innovations of the industrial revolution took shape and spread most rapidly and effectively in the last few decades of the eighteenth century.

THE ACCELERATION OF TECHNICAL PROGRESS

The critical changes that developed in the English economy before 1770 and that helped to set off the industrial revolution, or at least to set the stage for it, were thus largely organisational changes. They had their major impact in the growth of domestic and international trade and were closely associated with definite though undramatic changes in the scale of economic activity. These changes in scale were a consequence partly of the increase in overseas trade and partly of the increase in home trade that came with the growth of population and particularly of urban population. In short the English economy was expanding strongly in the middle decades of the eighteenth century and was developing new institutions to facilitate this expansion. It was also beginning to show increasing evidence of technological change.

The American war checked the expansion in overseas trade and slowed down the rate of population growth. Significantly, however, it did not interrupt the process of technical change which had begun to show up in the later years of the period that started in the 1740s and ended in the 1770s. Judging by the patent statistics the pace of technical progress accelerated sharply in the last decade or so of this period. In the 1760s the number of English patents sealed in a single decade exceeded 200 for the first time. Once before it had exceeded 100 in the course of a decade—that was in the booming 1690s when it reached 102. But the boom of the 1690s flared and died. In the 1770s the number of patents sealed went on rising, to reach almost 300, and it continued to rise so that it was over 910 in the first decade of the nineteenth century and 2,453 in the 1830s. A flow of new inventions had been set in motion in the 1760s that was never again put into reverse.

Of course the patent series is in no sense a measure of the rate of innovation. It is significant only as an indicator of the emergence of a fundamental change of trend. The timing and violence of the upward shift in the series in the 1760s and its gathering momentum in ensuing decades is some indication of the changing character and importance of invention in the English economy. Amongst the patents taken out in the 1760s and the 1770s were Arkwright's water frame, Hargreaves' spinning jenny, Crompton's mule and Watt's steam engine. In the following decade Cartwright's power loom and Cort's iron puddling process were patented. This was a remarkable collection of innovations with dramatic immediate consequences for the cotton and iron industries and important long-term consequences for manufacturing industry and transport generally.

The immediate consequences were most spectacular for the cotton industry. The spinning jenny was the first wholly successful improvement on the age-old device of the spindle. In its early forms, when still a cottage hand-machine, it had multiplied many times the amount of yarn that could be produced daily by a single pair of hands. Within a few years it had developed as far as substantial items of power-driven machinery based on large factories. Some of the jennies in existence at the end of the century held over a hundred spindles. Arkwright's water frame produced cotton strong enough to serve as warp and so made it possible to create essentially a new product, certainly new to mass markets—a British cotton cloth that was not a linen mixture. Crompton's mule combined the principles of frame and jenny to make this new cloth so much smoother and finer that it became a direct competitor with the silk and linen industries in a way the old coarse cotton industry could never have hoped to be. The first powered spinning mills were of necessity set up in rural areas where water power was available. Watt's steam engine (first applied to spinning in 1785) de-centralised the sources of power and made it possible to set up powered mills near markets and ports in urban locations that were not dependent on the seasonal flow of river water to provide the daily driving force for the machinery.

The resulting steep fall in costs and rise in demand enabled the cotton industry to expand from a very minor industry into the largest single British industry within roughly a generation. In the early 1770s the total net value added by the cotton industry to the national income probably did not much exceed, if at all, half a million pounds.[17] When Arthur Young calculated the English national income circa 1770 he did not bother to make an estimate for cotton.[18] But before the end of the century its

17. For estimates of net value added in cotton textiles 1760-1817 see Deane and Cole, *British Economic Growth*, p. 185.
18. Arthur Young, *Political Arithmetic*, Part II, London, 1779.

contribution to national income had multiplied more than tenfold and during the first decade of the nineteenth century the new industry was adding more to the nation's annual income than the woollen industry, the staple British industry of the eighteenth century. Nor was the woollen industry in decline. It shared (though to a much lesser extent) in the textile inventions and it supplied an expanding market at home and abroad. Between the early 1770s and the first decade of the nineteenth century the value that it added to national product is estimated to have expanded by nearly 60%—which was rather faster than the growth in population.[19]

The other industry that was transformed by the innovations of the second half of the eighteenth century was the iron industry. In previous decades technological change had crept through the iron industry at the snail's pace characteristic of a pre-industrial economy. Abraham Darby had smelted iron with coal in the first decade of the century but the process was far from common even in the 1760s. Charcoal was still the principal fuel used in the iron industry in the 1770s and its cost was rising as the woods were steadily depleted. It was not until the steam engine made it possible to get up a strong enough blast to keep coke burning fast that coal could be used as the main fuel in the smelting process: and it was Cort's invention of puddling (in a reverberatory furnace heated by coal) and rolling by steam power, that made it possible to use coal in the next stage of the process producing bar iron and hence to escape from its long dependence on imported bar iron. These innovations came in the 1780s and the break-through for the iron industry was almost as dramatic—though not as sustained—as for the cotton industry. Between 1788 and 1806 the output of British pig iron quadrupled and before another decade had passed Britain was a net exporter of bar iron.

This small group of seminal innovations—and there is no real doubt which of almost a thousand inventions

19. Phyllis Deane, Output of the British Woollen Industry in the Eighteenth Century, *Journal of Economic History*, 1957.

patented in the 1760s, 1770s and 1780s, really *were* crucial—together initiated a pace and a degree of technological advance that was beyond all previous experience. Once successfully proved they each—with the notable exception of the power loom—spread quickly through the industry concerned and generated relatively massive increases in output. The interesting question is why? Why did they appear at this particular period of time? Why did they have such a significant impact on the output of the affected industries?

Part of the explanation for the quickening of the pace of innovation in the 1760s and early 1770s must have been the state of business expectations. Markets had been expanding at home and abroad since the 1740s. There was every prospect of continued expansion. Both for institutional reasons and because recent experience had bred a sense of security, entrepreneurs were more ready to discount the risks of innovation. It would have been surprising if a proportion of the cumulating surplus generated by three decades of trading prosperity had not found its way into the manufacturing industries whose products were the merchants' main stock in trade. With markets expanding, interest rates low, and wage rates tending to rise, there was a positive incentive to search for and to adopt innovations which saved labour—particularly skilled labour.

In the cotton industry, for example, there was an obvious bottleneck in the supply of yarn due to a shortage of skilled spinners. It was an old problem which had been intensified in recent decades by the diffusion of innovations in other sectors of the industry—Kay's flying shuttle, for example and Paul's carding machine. The Society of Arts had recognised the problem by offering a prize in 1761 for the invention of a spinning machine. The jenny eased the shortage by multiplying the hourly product of the skilled spinner and the water-frame made it possible to substitute unskilled labour—particularly young people and children—for the experienced spinners who had had to supply the yarn for the warp.[20] The mule also saved hands, but because

20. S. J. Chapman, *The Lancashire Cotton Industry*, p. 53.

it was a heavier machine it permitted the substitution of male for female labour. The power loom further increased the possibility of substituting capital for skilled labour but, like all the steam-driven machines, it set up a strong demand for engineering skills in repair and maintenance as well as for coal fuel.

Thus the effect of this cluster of innovations on the supply conditions of the cotton industry was threefold—it eliminated a bottleneck, it increased efficiency by saving labour and it eased the possibilities of substitution both between capital and labour and between different kinds of labour (skilled) and unskilled, male and female, adult and child). On the demand side it produced an immensely improved commodity in a price range that made it saleable in a mass market and it opened up possibilities for continuing improvements in quality. It is not difficult to see why the spinning inventions spread rapidly and generated massive increases in output.

If the power loom took hold less rapidly than the spinning machines, it was no doubt because the labour shortage was less acute in weaving than in spinning, and also because the quality changes belonged more to the spinning branch than to the weaving branch of the industry. It was in the spinning mills that the spectacular cost-reductions were made. The continued relative shortage of labour in spinning in the second half of the eighteenth century may have been partly due to the changing composition of the labour force. Spinning was traditionally a woman's occupation carried on in the intervals that could be snatched from domestic duties. Weaving was a man's occupation. A rise in population that was largely due to a high birth rate and a falling infantile mortality rate meant both that women had less time to spare for spinning and that male heads of families needed to find additional ways of supplementing the family income. Hand looms could be bought at no very great cost or could be rented. Possession of or access to a hand loom provided its user with a form of insurance against underemployment in other occupations, and while there were relatively few alternative industrial opportunities for employment there were always enough hand looms in existence to supply the normal needs of an expanding trade. It was only in years of boom or when special fancy weaves were in high fashion that there were labour shortages in the weaving trade.

The existence of a mass market for its products both at home and abroad gave the cotton industry virtually unlimited scope for increasing its sales. This was one reason for the sheer scale of its expansion in the last three decades of the eighteenth century. The other was that, technically speaking, it was not really a new industry. The textile manufacture had been the staple British industry for centuries and the skills and techniques employed in cotton were basically the same as in the other textiles—wool, linen and silk. From the outset there was a merchant-capitalist system set up to carry the raw material to cottage workshops and take the cloth through the processing stages to market: there were domestic workers ready to buy or hire jennies and looms and capable of learning directly from relatives and neighbours how to operate them: there were importers with agents in raw cotton producing areas: and there were exporters specialising in textiles. As sales grew and profits piled up there was no lack of entrepreneurs with the financial resources and the technical and commercial knowhow to reap economies of scale by setting up spinning mills and factory villages. Meanwhile, the demand for cotton being part of the demand for textiles generally, was highly elastic so that as cost and prices fell sales soared.

Technological change in the iron industry assumed a different form. In the first place, it was not so much labour that was the crucial bottleneck as fuel and power. True, the fact that the industry was dependent on wood and water was forcing it more and more into outlying locations where available labour was limited; but labour supply seems to have been a factor of secondary importance. What mattered was that British ores, though plentiful, were generally of a quality that produced unreliable steel and that her blast furnace costs were high and rising as a result of the steady depletion of woodlands accessible to iron mines. The peak of the British charcoal iron industry was probably reached in the second quarter of the seventeenth century when the output of pig iron is estimated to have been in the region of 26,000 tons per annum; thereafter the industry stagnated or declined as the rising cost of charcoal rendered it uneconomic in one district after another.

The other main limiting factor to growth in the iron industry was a deficiency of technical knowledge. Because the immediate constraint lay on the side of natural resources rather than on the side of labour, technical advance in the iron industry took the form of improvements in processes rather than of labour-saving machinery. Essentially it was a problem of converting iron ore into cast or wrought iron or steel in such a way as to eliminate the impurities that made it brittle and to avoid running up prohibitively high costs of fuel. Different kinds of ore and different final products raised different problems. The only way of improving the basic process at existing levels of scientific knowledge was by repetitive trial and error. Such experiments were costly and could only be conducted by the wealthier ironmasters. Even for them, success depended partly on the composition of the ores used in the experiment, partly on the skills of the experimenter, and partly on luck—all factors which tended to be unique to a particular location.

In consequence, such technical advance as did take place in the first three quarters of the century spread slowly and had relatively little impact on the overall rate of growth of the industry. Although the Darbys of Coalbrookdale were producing iron with coke from the beginning of the century, they used the process mainly for the production of domestic hardware and it was not sufficiently cheap or satisfactory to warrant extension to many other uses. Later it was found that re-melting the coke-produced iron improved its quality and made it usable for a wider range of products, but there was still no great reduction in cost. Although Benjamin Huntsman had devised a method of producing cast steel by the crucible process in the early 1740s it was neither a cheap nor an easy process to imitate and it too spread slowly. As late as 1787 there were only 11 firms producing cast steel in

Sheffield; the rest depended for their material on imported Swedish bar iron. In 1760 when the Carron iron company set up its big coke blast furnace there were probably not more than 17 coke furnaces in blast in Britain.

No doubt the gradual improvement in practice at the coke-smelting furnaces, the scale economies permitted by the steady increase in the size of the typical coke furnace (there were inescapable limits to the size of a furnace fired by a fuel as friable as charcoal) and the steady depletion of accessible woodlands would have ensured the eventual domination of the coke blast furnace. A decisive change, however, took place in 1776 when John Wilkinson applied Watt's steam engine at his Shropshire factory and thus adopted an innovation which it was open to all substantial iron masters troubled by shortage of charcoal or power to adopt forthwith. This effectively broke the fuel and power bottleneck in the production of pig iron for castings and made it possible appreciably to reduce costs of production— not only because of the fuel and scale economies already associated with the coke-smelting technique but also because the steam engine permitted continuous production irrespective of weather. It also gave the iron master an unprecedented locational flexibility by freeing him from the need to stick close to fast-flowing water. The next stage was to convert the coke-smelted pig iron into a material which could be turned into wrought iron. The immediate success of Cort's puddling process was due largely to the fact that he combined the puddling and rolling processes, so gaining important additional economies. Although the puddled iron was inferior in quality to charcoal it was a great deal cheaper and was reliable enough for the great majority of industrial and domestic uses.

These developments spelt the end of the charcoal iron industry and removed the fuel and power constraint on the expansion of iron output. As costs fell, iron replaced wood and other metals like copper in a steadily widening range of uses. It was used for bridges, for building joists, for river barges, for ploughs, for water pipes, for boilers, and for machines; and because it had such wide possibilities of substitution, demand proved highly elastic in these early stages. The use of coke fuel and steam power made it possible to build much larger blast furnaces and to integrate the various iron manufacturing processes in a single vast unit of production, thus earning economies of scale.

In sum, the answer to the question what enabled the iron industry to quadruple its output in roughly two decades? is that it was due, on the supply side, to the marked fall in fuel and labour costs that resulted from the general use of coal and steam power in producing both pig and bar iron, and also to the increasing economies of scale permitted by the new integrated systems of production. On the demand side the answer lies partly in the wide range of industrial and domestic uses that were open to cheap iron and partly in the abnormal demand for armaments in the French wars. Foreign demand also grew as prices fell and British iron exports almost doubled between 1788 and 1806, in spite of the hindrances that war and the continental blockade put in the way of overseas trade.

There was no other British industry that broke all past productivity records as dramatically as cotton and iron did in the last two or three decades of the eighteenth century. To be sure, there was independent evidence of important technical progress elsewhere in the economy at the same period. The acceleration of enclosures for example, hastened the adoption of more progressive methods of farming: the two canal booms appreciably reduced transport cost for the industries the new waterways served: the steam engine was usable and was used in other industries besides cotton and iron: there were significant innovations in associated industries, e.g. in branches of the chemical industry stimulated by the tremendous expansion in the needs of the textile processing industries. Nevertheless it is principally on the experience of two industries—cotton and iron—that rests the justification for dating the beginnings of modern economic growth from the late eighteenth century. What was it about the handful of innovations we have discussed in this connection—a mere fraction of the total number of inventions or technical improvements attributable to the period—that was so decisive in relation to the future progress of the English economy?

It is the broader, long-term implications of these innovations that we are seeking to identify here. Their short-term consequences in terms of the rapid expansion of the industries immediately concerned and in terms of their sales to or purchases from other sectors of the economy are easy enough to recognise if not actually to measure. In arguing that they differed from previous innovations not merely in the *scale* of their impact on output and productivity, but also in triggering off a continuous process of productivity growth, we are making claims that are not so easily justified.

There are three characteristics of a technology which together determine its productivity potential: its efficiency in terms of the volume of inputs required to produce a given output; its access to economies of scale; its flexibility, i.e. its ability to substitute relatively abundant factors of production for relatively scarce factors when cost conditions change. The effect of the innovations introduced into the eighteenth-century cotton and iron industries and particularly of the steam engine was to start a process of technology change which was favourable to productivity growth in each of these three respects—efficiency, economies of scale, flexibility.

Efficiency. The implications for a continuous improvement in efficiency are not difficult to trace. The cotton machinery saved labour and improved the quality of the product. It was a kind moreover which lent itself to continuous improvement in design so that, as each machine wore out, its replacement embodied improvements that saved more scarce labour resources or permitted further quality improvements. The ironmaking processes saved fuel and labour and were also susceptible to continuous improvement, bringing with it a gradual but unmistakable reduction in waste, apart altogether from the periodic breakthrough made possible by basically new technical discoveries. The steam engine had virtually unlimited possibilities from the outset. Beginning as a device to pump water from coal mines, it was used for similar purposes, and with similar cost advantages, in copper, tin and iron mines. It provided an infinitely extensible source of power—saving labour and extending the capacity of capital equipment—for any manufacturing industry that could finance heavy fixed capital. Even in the absence of any further fundamental break-through in cotton machinery or iron-making processes or in the basic design of the steam engine, there was scope here for an infinite stream of improvements so long as output expanded and plant was replaced.

Of course, there are few new machines or new processes whose efficiency cannot be improved by relatively superficial modifications. What was historically unique about this particular set of innovations was the fact that their adoption involved (sooner or later) a structural transformation of the industry concerned from a domestic base to a factory base. This meant a crucial change in the nature of the decision to innovate. Once the productive process came fully under the control of the professional capitalist-entrepreneur, with his profit-maximising tendencies, the probability that opportunities for profitable innovation would be rapidly recognised, and taken, became very much higher than in situations where the crucial decisions were taken by the individual craftsman. It is the change in the character of the decision to innovate that explains more than anything else the rapid and continuous spread of technical change in the late eighteenth and nineteenth centuries by contrast with all previous periods. It is also relevant that the new cotton machines were in principle applicable to the other textile industries and that the new iron-making processes were in principle applicable to other metal manufacturing industries.

More important still perhaps, because the innovations in ironmaking—like the steam engine which gave them their impetus—represented technical progress in the capital goods industry they had implications for industrial productivity reaching far beyond the industries immediately concerned. These were the decisive changes which turned the iron industry into the father of all producers' goods industries, for until it could turn out cheap malleable iron, its output went as much to domestic uses and armaments as to industrial uses. The cheapening of producers' durables, the lengthening of their working lives and the possibility of fashioning cheap precision tools of almost infinite complexity, which these innovations opened up, had a very special impact on the process of industrialisation. By reducing the price of new capital goods it stimulated more new investment, thus increasing the rate at which new machine-based techniques were diffused through the economy. The developments in the iron industry represented the heart and core of the new machine technology. This is where the modern industrial economy was born. It is hard to imagine for example that the cotton industry (or indeed any other manufacturing industry) could have progressed at the rate or to the extent that it did without the prior innovations in iron making.

Economies of scale. The second novel and productivity-biased aspect of the new technologies which emerged at the end of the eighteenth century was the fact that they did more than save capital and labour and natural resources. They opened up altogether new possibilities for economies of scale, increasing returns per unit of input or output. Some of these economies of scale arose outside the individual firm and affected the industry or the economy as a whole. Thus, developments in ancillary industries (transport, banking, commerce, coal mining, etc.) stimulated primarily by expansion in the cotton and iron industries, brought cost advantages to and stimulated growth in a wide range of other industries. Some were internal economies reflected for example in the increasing returns obtainable from larger blast furnaces or larger cotton factories or machines, or more integrated operations. They begin to emerge significantly at this stage in English economic development because they are associated with rapid industrial growth and production for mass markets and they take a variety of forms. But whatever their form they were to generate a continuous stream of additions in industrial product per

head over and above the additions arising out of technical
advance.

Flexibility. Finally, the third respect in which the end-
eighteenth-century innovations in the cotton and iron
industry contributed to a sustained subsequent increase in
product per head stemmed from the fact that they made it
easier for producers to substitute one factor of production
for another. Sustained economic growth demands a continuous process of change in the disposition of economic resources: it calls for easy mobility of factors between uses
and an entrepreneurial readiness to re-combine them constantly in the most economical proportions—given their
prices and the prevailing technology. Obviously of course
the new machines and processes, and the steam engine in
particular, opened up extensive possibilities for substituting
capital for labour which would enable the profit-maximising entrepreneur to select and adapt new techniques in
relation to the relative prices of the accessible factors of
production. In some cases they permitted the substitution
of raw materials for capital. Peter Temin has shown for the
U.S.A. that 'capital costs formed a greater part of the total
costs for water power than for steam power and the choice
between the two at any location was affected by the interest
rate'.[21] It is reasonable to suppose that similar considerations affected English entrepreneurs making the choice
between water and steam power in the early stages of the
industrial revolution. The new machines and processes also
opened up possibilities of replacing one kind of labour in
relatively short supply with another kind of labour in more
abundant supply—skilled labour by unskilled labour, men
by women, adults by children, for example: or substituting
an abundant natural resource (coal) for a scarce natural
resource (wood). Indeed the most important feature of the
new processes and machines was not so much that they were
labour-saving rather than capital-saving (often they were
on balance labour-using when seen in the broad macro-

21. Peter Temin, 'Steam and Water Power in the Early 19th Century,'
Journal of Economic History, June 1966.

economic context rather than in the context of the innovating industry), but that they made it easier to reallocate factors of production and natural resources in more profitable ways.

Most important of all perhaps they broke down traditional barriers to change in the organisation and sequence of industrial activity. In a pre-industrial economy, dependent on fixed sources of power, like water, or on traditional handicraft systems, skills and techniques tend to be highly specific to particular industries and even localities. Often there is rigid specialisation of economic activity by sex and a rigid sequence of productive operations from raw material to final product. Technological frontiers tend to be narrow and impassable. The new machines and processes broke down these rigidities. It is significant, for example, that they emerged first in a small industry—cotton—which was too unimportant to have a strong vested interest in the persistence of traditional techniques. They also permitted new kinds of specialisation and skill to develop which were transferable between industries, carrying their technological advances with them. The metal-using industries provide the clearest example of the kind of technical convergence which emerged when the steam engine released the industrial economy from its dependence on fixed sources of power. In the refining, smelting, founding and machining sections of these industries there is a long line of common processes which permit innovations developed in one industry to be adopted readily in a number of other industries. Similarly the nineteenth-century machine tool industry (for whose development the innovations in the iron industry were an indispensable prerequisite) is another example of a case where technical advances devised in response to the pressures arising within one industry were easily adapted to the different needs of other industries. In these circumstances sustained economic growth became dependent not so much on a steady succession of major technological discoveries or inventions, but on a self-perpetuating stream of often very minor adaptations of past technical advances.

STRUCTURAL CHANGE

There are two main kinds of structural change involved in an industrial revolution: shifts in the activity structure of the economy from primary to secondary and tertiary forms of production, and shifts in the allocation of final output between consumption and capital goods.

CHANGES IN INDUSTRIAL STRUCTURE

Typically an industrial revolution involves a movement of labour and capital from the agriculture, forestry and fishing group of industries to the manufacturing, transport and trade sectors. If labour force and capital stock are growing fast enough there may be no need for agriculture to decline absolutely as industry grows. The shift of resources may be made simply by moving most of the surplus labour and wealth generated in the rural areas of the economy to non-agricultural activities. One thing is certain, however. An under-developed country is one in which a relatively high proportion of the population is engaged in agricultural occupations. A developed country is one which the proportion has dropped to fairly low levels.

The English economy had already begun to move in this direction before the end of the seventeenth century. It appears from Gregory King's estimates of the way the families of England and Wales got their incomes that not more than about two-thirds of them were primarily dependent on agriculture for their livelihood at the end of the seventeenth century. At this period there were no English towns outside London with more than 30,000 inhabitants and only three (Norwich, Bristol and Birmingham) with more than 10,000. In Scotland there was Edinburgh with 35,000 people and Glasgow which was roughly the same size as Birmingham. By the middle of the eighteenth century the towns had probably grown slightly faster than population but it is unlikely that more than about 16% of the British were living in towns: at the beginning of the nineteenth century the proportion had risen to 25%.

In a community where agriculture is of such overriding importance as a means of earning a living it is inevitable that its productivity levels and the changes in its fortunes should be a major determinant of national economic growth and change. For Britain the state of the harvest had a major impact on national economic prosperity until well into the nineteenth century. In the eighteenth century a good harvest was significant not only because it meant an increased rate of return to human effort for a majority of the population, but also because it entailed a redistribution of incomes in favour of the industrial sectors. When harvests were abundant, agricultural labourers stood to gain through increased employment incomes, thicker gleanings and lower prices for their essential food purchases. So that the short run effect of a good harvest tended to be to raise the wages of labour, to increase the purchasing power of all the lowest income groups (who had very little to spare for other things when the price of food was high) and to increase the profits of industrialists who relied on agricultural raw materials.

The long run effects of a sequence of good harvests may have been more complex than this, however. For the demand for foodstuffs tends to be inelastic, so that if their prices go down, people do not consume correspondingly more and total expenditure on food tends to shrink. A succession of good harvests with a stationary population may well have had such a depressing effect on agricultural profits, as to offset the stimulus to the industrial sector produced by lower costs and higher real wages. In the more expansive environment of the second half of the eighteenth century, however, population growth was pressing up agricultural prices and profits, agricultural investment was stimulated and incomes increased in both the agricultural and the industrial sectors.

Growth in the agricultural sector was thus closely associated both in time and in terms of cause and effect with growth in the rest of the economy. When population and overseas trade began to rise in the 1740s the demand for food expanded, food prices rose and agricultural investment was stimulated. This showed up in the acceleration of enclosures beginning in the 1760s. Private enclosures had been going on for centuries. By 1700 they had freed about half of the arable land of England from the grip of the customary open-field techniques. When corn prices began to rise in the second half of the century, increasing the incentive of the small farmers to resist dispossession, would-be enclosers had to find ways of enforcing compliance and between 1761 and 1792 nearly half a million acres were enclosed by Act of Parliament. In the French and Napoleonic wars, stimulated by war-time demand and (after 1801) facilitated by a stream-lining of the parliamentary procedure, a further million or so acres were enclosed. By then the job was nearly done, a mere fraction of the English land was still in open fields and in the period 1816-45 only a further 200,000 acres needed to be enclosed.

The traditional interpretation of the contribution of the enclosures to the industrial revolution was that they depopulated the villages by driving out the subsistence cottagers, who could no longer support themselves in the rural areas when their rights of pasture and common were removed, and by enabling the larger farmers to adopt labour-saving improvements on their consolidated holdings. This view however does not stand up to empirical test. There is no evidence, for example, that the rural areas subject to enclosure were the areas which lost population. Indeed the evidence, such as it is, supports the view that where enclosure stimulated agricultural development it encouraged the growth of new agricultural communities. In so far as technological change did take place in agriculture it tended to be labour-intensive rather than labour-saving. The enclosed farms called for more winter labour in hedging and ditching than did the open fields: the turnip and green fodder crops were labour-intensive: so too was the mixed farming which permitted year-round maintenance of milking herd or fat stock.[22]

In effect then, it was not the depopulation of the villages

22. See Chambers, (Enclosure and Labour Supply in the Industrial Revolution), *Economic History Review*, 1953.

by enclosure which provided the expanding industrial and commercial sectors with their labour supply, but the growth of population in general. In absolute terms the numbers engaged in the agricultural industry went on increasing until the middle of the nineteenth century. In relative terms on the other hand the population engaged in agricultural occupations was falling slowly in the eighteenth century, more rapidly after the end of the Napoleonic wars and very rapidly in the second half of the nineteenth century. In 1811 probably about a third (perhaps more) of the British labour force was engaged in the agriculture, forestry, fishing group of industries: by 1831 the proportion had fallen to about a quarter and by 1851 to rather more than a fifth.[23] This shift in the occupational distribution of the labour force was echoed in a shift of population from the country to the towns. In the first two decades of the century the small towns and rural areas were growing almost as fast as the total population of England and Wales. Then the rate of urbanisation accelerated. In the 1820s and 1830s the movement to the towns was considerable; it reached its peak in the 1840s when it was inflated by the Irish exodus and nearly three quarters of a million people were added to the English towns and colliery districts. It continued strongly through the next three decades and slackened only at the end of the century.

There are two sets of reasons why an industrial revolution, bringing with it the transition to sustained economic growth, involves a change in the balance of productive resources from agricultural to non-agricultural activities. One set stems from the side of supply and the other from the side of demand. On the side of supply the crucial difference is that agricultural output is normally subject to diminishing returns while manufacturing output and mechanical transport is normally subject to increasing returns. This is due partly to the fact that agriculture requires extensive land resources as well as labour and capital and that there is an absolute shortage of cultivable land: and it is due partly to the fact that the technological changes associated with

23. Estimates from Deane and Cole, *op. cit.*

modern economic growth have generally been more applicable to manufacturing industry and mechanical transport than to agriculture. The use of fixed capital equipment requiring renewal in whole or in part at relatively short intervals gives scope for continuous improvements in productivity, each replacement being an improvement on its predecessor. The application of science to the productive process also tends to stimulate further developments along similar lines. Once this kind of technological progress had started on any scale it had a tendency to perpetuate itself and to generate a continous improvement in productivity. As far as agriculture was concerned, however, certainly in the British case, the nineteenth century was well advanced and the industrial revolution effectively complete before farmers generally began to adopt either mechanical implements or the scientifically-based improvements in crop rotations or stock breeding methods and artificial fertilisers. Even then the scale of the developments along these lines were very modest compared with what was going on in manufacturing industry. The result was that the value of agricultural output grew little faster than the value of inputs into the industry, whereas in most manufacturing industries output grew appreciably faster than the corresponding inputs.

On the side of demand the main limiting factor to the rate of growth of agricultural output has been the fact that as average incomes grow the proportion that is spent on food and raw materials tends to fall, i.e. the demand for agricultural products grows more slowly than the demand for industries producing manufactures and services. Consequently an economy in which a high proportion of gross national product is earned in the agricultural sector is subject to a special constraint on the rate at which the demand for its products is likely to grow. To escape this constraint it is necessary to shift productive resources into manufacturing where demand is more elastic and tends to rise faster than the rise in average incomes. Moreover in so far as technical progress tends to be embodied in new investments, a slow rate of investment, which is a natural result of a slow growth in demand, will involve a correspondingly lower rate of improvement in productivity each year in agriculture as compared with manufacturing industry.

CHANGES IN THE DISPOSITION OF NATIONAL PRODUCT

The other kind of structural change that is associated with an industrial revolution is the shift in the disposition of final product. One of the principal reasons why an industrial economy enables its residents to achieve higher standards of living and productivity than are possible in a pre-industrial economy is that the members of its labour force have a larger stock of capital to assist their productive activities. By implication, the national rate of capital formation (i.e. the proportion of national income put into saving or the proportion of national output taken out in capital goods) tends to be higher in an industrialised economy than in a pre-industrial economy.

One can divide real capital into two main types—fixed capital on the one hand and stocks of goods (inventories) and work in progress on the other. Not only does the industrial economy adopt completely different sorts of fixed capital (machinery, engines, railways, etc.) from that available in a pre-industrial economy, it uses the traditional kinds of capital (buildings, livestock, inventories) in different proportions. From the point of view of producers operating in a pre-industrial framework of economic activity the real capital assets that are of prime importance are: buildings, land, standing crops, livestock and stocks of commodities awaiting sale or consumption. The tenant farmer's capital is tied up in his crops and his livestock: he can rent his land and his farm buildings. His implements are generally too primitive to be classified as capital. The operator in a domestic industry may own his loom or his spinning wheel and his house, but these items are unimportant in relation to the value of the raw materials that he processes, and the value of the goods he makes each year. The trader's stock lies partly in warehouses, ships and wagons and pack horses, but most of his capital is tied up in the goods that are carried in these things. A man setting up in business in a pre-industrial economy requires above all circulating capital to provide him with a stock in trade.

Transformation of the British economy from a pre-industrial to an industrial form then meant that the nation had to acquire a different set of capital assets, and to get into the habit of putting substantially more of its total incomes into capital rather than consumption goods, into saving rather than consuming. It is conventional, for example, to describe a pre-industrial economy as being one in which the normal rate of capital formation (i.e. the ratio of capital formation to national capital) is 5% or 6% and an industrialised economy as one in which the normal rate of capital formation is over 10% or 12%. This is a convenient rule of thumb which fits the British case fairly well.

There are two major questions that arise about this particular transformation. One is When? and the other is How?

The Timing of the Change in the Investment Ratio

To get the process into some kind of time perspective we ought to be able to measure the rate of capital formation at different periods on the journey from the pre-industrial to industrial state and to measure the proportions spent on different kinds of capital assets. Unfortunately the statistics are inadequate, especially for the early stages of the industrial revolution and before. All we can really hope to do in the present state of research is to get an impression of the relative orders of magnitude involved at the different stages of the development process.

Gregory King's estimates made at the end of the seventeenth century constitute a convenient starting point. At that stage land was the most important form of national capital, but in analysing the relation between capital and growth it is usual to focus on the *reproducible* capital stock of the nation and to leave land out of account.[24] King's

24. Actually in an economy which has not reached the limit of its cultivable area one can increase land, and extension of the cultivable

estimates divide the nation's reproducible capital stock into 3 categories: buildings which accounted for about 48%; trader's stocks of foods or raw materials and equipment, plus military stores and equipment, which together accounted for about 29%; and livestock which accounted for about 22%. In addition he calculated the value of consumers' 'capital'—gold, silver, jewellery, furniture, clothing, etc.—which he estimated to be nearly as valuable as the fixed assets and stocks of goods used in industry.[25] In effect a large part of the savings potential of the pre-industrial community went into unproductive kinds of capital investment. An important aspect of the process of transformation to a growing industrial economy was that it involved a shift of capital from unproductive to productive uses.

In peace time therefore the pre-industrial British economy normally generated a surplus which was available for saving and King's estimates suggest that something like 6% of the national income was annually put into some form of productive capital. The individual who wanted to increase his wealth found that he could do so by putting it into agricultural land and livestock, in new buildings and in trading and industrial stocks. In peace time the most productive outlets in terms of income-yielding potential were trade and industry: but their dependence on overseas trade made these investments peculiarly vulnerable to the recurrent disasters of war.[26] Even within the country the problems of protecting stocks of goods against such villains as thieves and highwaymen, and such misfortunes as fire, were considerable, so that a cautious man would put the bulk of his savings into buildings and land. These were not likely to bring him in a high income, but they were less subject to disaster. At this stage, that is at the end of the seventeenth

land resources of the nation was an important factor in eighteenth-century British economic growth.

25. See Phyllis Deane and W. A. Cole, *British Economic Growth* for detailed discussion of King's estimates.

26. See Deane, 'Capital Formation in Britain before the Railway Age' *Economic Development and Cultural Change*, April 1961, p. 354.

century, only a gambler would lend to government.

A comparable estimate of the national capital made at the end of the eighteenth century by the Reverend Henry Beeke suggests that buildings (including government property) accounted for about a third of the national reproducible capital around 1798, farm capital for about 19%, and industrial commercial and financial capital for about 46%.[27] The rise in the importance of industrial and commercial capital in relation to say, buildings, or farm capital compared with King's figures, is significant. By this time it included more machinery and producers' equipment, but mechanical aids of any kind were still subordinate in importance to producers' and traders' stocks of goods. Beeke did not attempt to calculate the rate of capital formation as opposed to the level of the capital stock, so if we want to judge how much this had changed since King's day we must look at the evidence on the kinds of changes in physical capital that had taken place during the eighteenth century, and the extent to which this would require increased saving.

There is little evidence of growth either in national incomes or of capital formation in the first half of the eighteenth century, but the second half saw considerable economic changes. Agricultural enclosures, for example, must have involved substantial capital expenditures on fencing and ditching and reclamation of waste lands. There was almost certainly an improvement in the quality and probably in the number of livestock. On the other hand there was hardly any farm machinery yet. The growth of cities involved construction of new buildings, and the improvements in the road and canal systems were another important new form of capital formation. The merchant shipping fleet was expanding in response to the growth of overseas trade. In the cotton and iron industries technological change meant the building of new factories and blast furnaces, and the installation of new kinds of equipment—spinning jennies, looms, steam engines for example. So there is evidence

27. H. Beeke, *Observations on the produce of the income tax and its proportion to the whole income of Great Britain* (1800).

for an appreciable expansion in the nation's stock of fixed capital in the second half of the eighteenth century, and for a particularly marked expansion in industrial and commercial capital. Some forms of capital accumulation required very large outlays. The inland navigation system alone must have absorbed £8 or £9 millions between 1750 and 1800.

On the other hand it must be remembered that population and national income were also growing unprecedentedly fast at this time, and that the sectors in which output was growing very rapidly were generally sectors in which capital was growing rapidly. So that if we think not so much in terms of the *absolute* level of capital formation but of its *relative* level—that is of capital formation as a percentage of national income, there is much less evidence for an appreciable rise in the level before 1800.

The same is true of the first twenty or thirty years of the nineteenth century. Investments in buildings and agricultural enclosures and ships continued to expand strongly. In place of the abnormally heavy investment in canals which characterised the 1790s we find an abnormally heavy rate of investment in docks and harbours. Investments in new docks and harbours have been estimated to amount to more than £18 millions in the first two decades of the century. In the second and third decades the big cities began to light their streets with gas and the textile factories found that gas lighting permitted them to run their machines continuously with day and night shifts for labour.

Again, however, the evidence is that output and income expanded as fast as, or nearly as fast as, capital expenditures in most cases. Moreover some of the innovations taking place in the latter part of the eighteenth and early nineteenth centuries were actually such as to economise in capital. The improvements in roads and canals, for example, while they involved substantial construction expenditures, had the effect of reducing the stocks of goods that merchants and industrialists had to hold and the amount of goods en route. When coal could be moved throughout the year along the canals, for example, it was less necessary for coal-using producers to store large stocks against the winter months when ships were penned in their harbours or the coal carts were bogged down on the muddy roads. When ships and other vehicles travelled faster there were relatively fewer goods held up in the pipe line. Similarly, when factories installed gas, machines that would have lain idle all night produced double the output for every pound that was sunk in fixed capital equipment. Capital-saving innovations in effect permitted a higher rate of return to be earned for a smaller capital outlay.

In sum, then, if we put together all the evidence we can find about the new investments which were associated with the period 1750-1830, and if we compare the amounts involved with the increase in total national income which certainly took place over this period, they suggest that the increase in the *rate* of capital formation was relatively small. It is in the 1830s that we find convincing evidence of an upward shift in the national rate of investment.

The 1830s was the decade when the railway age effectively began. The latest estimates[28] suggest that by then the expenditure in gross domestic fixed capital formation was taking between 4 and 5% of gross national product and net foreign investment about 1% of gross national product. If we make an allowance of up to 2% for annual additions to stocks and works in progress (it is unlikely to have been more than this on the average) it puts the average for the decade up to nearly 8%. The 1840s was the decade when the railway age got into top gear, taking gross domestic fixed capital formation up to between 6 and 7% of gross national product, while foreign investment became a little less important (falling below 1% of gross national product). These are decade averages. For particular years in the 1830s and 1840s the rate of capital formation was sometimes higher than this. For example, in the year 1847 when the second railway mania moved into what turned out to be the all-time climax of railway building in Britain, gross domestic

28. For the estimates in this paragraph see Phyllis Deane, New estimates of gross national product for the United Kingdom, 1830-1914, *Review of Income and Wealth*, June 1968.

fixed capital formation constituted about 10% of gross national product (compared with the decade average for the 1840s for only about $6\frac{1}{2}$%) and foreign investment dried up altogether—indicating presumably that the economy had reached its ceiling in respect of the funds it was then capable of raising for investment.

So the answer then to our question 'when?' is that the *rate* of capital formation expressed as a percentage of gross national product grew very slowly indeed over the period to 1820s, and that it when shifted from roughly 7% to roughly 10% in the space of two decades: this was largely the result of the railway construction boom but also owed a good deal to other factors like the growth of cities and the investments in power machinery in textile factories and iron works. It is worth noting that the level of investment had not yet reached its nineteenth-century peak. That came in the 1870s, actually in the decade 1869-78, when gross domestic fixed capital formation and foreign investment together accounted for over 11% of gross national product, so if we again allow 2% for additions to stocks and work in progress, it brings the total proportion of the national resources devoted to investment to over 13%. This is a conclusion which goes against the view that an industrial revolution cannot get under way without an appreciable increase in the rate of investment. The fact is that an important phase of the English industrial revolution preceded the railway age and that technological change in textiles and iron—the two leading industries of the industrial revolution—was not appreciably more capital-intensive than capital-extensive. In other words the rise in investment in cotton and iron was matched almost simultaneously by a corresponding rise in output. If there was a period when the rate of capital formation shifted up at all sharply, it was in the railway age, i.e. in the period between 1830 and 1850. This was when the community built up its basic overhead capital, its essential infrastructure. But even by 1850 the British economy had not reached its peak rates of investment for the nineteenth century.

The second question that calls for an answer is how? How did a poor community that was conditioned to putting aside 5 or 6% of its national output into productive investment manage to transform itself into a community which set aside an annual 10% or more for the purchase of capital assets? For this was what had to be done to build up the basic capital necessary to support a continuously growing industrial economy.

It had to do three related things in fact. It had to save more. It had to put more of its savings into productive channels (instead of allowing it to lie idle in useless hoards of gold and silver and consumers' stocks or unused bank balances). And it had to change the character of its investments—to tie up a larger proportion of its savings in the kind of assets that did not yield an immediate return in consumers' satisfactions (as did housing or country estates) and that were focused on profits (long-term profits) rather than immediate consumption; it had to buy more of the kind of capital assets that were not readily realisable, i.e. machinery and construction projects, rather than stocks of commodities bought in anticipation for a quick sale.

Increasing its rate of saving was probably the least of this country's problems. It had already by the middle of the eighteenth century some degree of economic surplus. The poor were spending their surplus on gin in the 1730s and 1740s, and on white bread, beer and tea later in the century. The rich spent theirs on port and overeating, but also on country houses and game preserves, and on lending to government. For by the second half of the eighteenth century government had reformed its finances and was among the most creditworthy borrowers in the economy. The rich had the true surplus of course. A century of successful trading overseas had built up a comfortable merchants' surplus of accumulated profits. The returned nabobs from India and the planters from the West Indies brought sizeable fortunes with them. However undesirable it might have been socially, the fact that incomes were very unequally distributed in mid-eighteenth-century England had its economic advantages. For it added to the investible surplus of the community. If this surplus had gone to the poor it would have been difficult to get it out of current consumption and into capital formation. The key to economic growth lay in diverting a genuine economic surplus in the hands of the rich from unproductive capital formation into productive capital formation.

To some extent the necessary diversion of funds happened naturally, as when the wealthy landowners started to use part of their fortunes to experiment with new crop rotations, new agricultural machinery and new strains of livestock, or to consolidate their estates into more economical units, or to enclose wastes and commons and put them under crops or livestock. They were attracted to do so in part by the sheer interest of innovation and in part by the rising price of food which was associated with increasing population, and growing urbanisation. Of course not all rich landowners were wealthy enough or enthusiastic enough to experiment with agricultural techniques on a large scale, and still fewer were in a position to spend a quarter of a million pounds on transport capital as the Duke of Bridgewater did when building his canal. But many of them had a direct interest in seeing that their tenant farmers (the source of their rent incomes) followed the latest developments in agriculture, or that the coal and iron mines on their estates were kept clear of water by effective pumping machinery and were connected to town markets by a good system of all-weather communications. Hence some of the nation's agricultural surplus flowed naturally into experiments in agricultural technique, or in steam pumping machinery, or in helping to finance canals and river navigation schemes. Similarly, prosperous merchants had a direct interest in encouraging investment in the manufacturing innovations that might supply them with cheap goods to sell abroad or might offer them an expanding market for raw materials obtainable in foreign markets. They were accordingly often ready to let innovating industrialists have raw cotton, say, or imported bar iron, on credit—until such time as the things that were made from them were ready for market. Thus, given that the prospects of innovation were good (because there was a rising demand for British products), there was a sufficiently direct relationship between the people who were earning profits in Britain's two major eighteenth century economic activities—agriculture and commerce—on the one hand, and manufacturing activity on the other, for funds to flow quite naturally from the sectors of the economy in which profits were accumulating into the sectors which were in a position to reduce costs, i.e. into the innovating sectors.

Often, indeed, in the relatively unspecialised eighteenth-century economy the funds moved quite easily from one industry to another because the prosperous entrepreneur tended to be actively engaged in more than one industry. Wilkinson the iron master had agricultural estates in which he experimented with new agricultural techniques. James Watt was part owner of a Scottish pottery works. And there were a great many minor entrepreneurs like Peter Stubbs whose career in the second half of the eighteenth century has been described by Ashton and who was innkeeper, maltster, brewer, corn merchant and file maker at one and the same time. The effect of course was to render the capital market more perfect than it would otherwise have been, for the individual active investor laid out his resources over a variety of forms of economic activity, strongly influenced in his allocation of funds by the rates of return obtainable in different alternative uses.

In addition, eighteenth-century entrepreneurs were accustomed to depend heavily on their friends and relatives for their capital. In case after case we find that the innovators fell back on their own resources and the resources of their immediate family and friends. The success of an enterprise was heavily dependent on the individual talent of its master and it was only his friends and his business associates —people who knew him and his market well—who could afford to lend him capital. This ready mobility of capital through personal contact was possible largely because the initiation of industrial enterprise required relatively small amounts of capital. Robert Owen, for example, started as a draper's assistant, borrowed £100 from his brother and went into partnership with a mechanic who made looms. That was in 1789. By 1809 he was able to buy out his partners in the New Lanark mills for £84,000 in cash.[29] Until late into the nineteenth century by far the bulk of British investment was financed by the plough-back of profits into the industries that generated them.

As the economy expanded, however, two things happened. On the one hand the need for large chunks of capital beyond the ability of a single individual and his personal contacts to provide, became more common and more urgent. And on the other hand the growth of incomes meant that an economic surplus was being generated by individuals who either did not wish to participate as active investors, or who had reached the limits of profitable capital accumulation in their own line of activity. If the national rate of investment was to be expanded in these circumstances, it was necessary to find some way of channelling the surplus of savers who had no personal wish to create fixed capital of their own, into the control of investors whose urge to create new fixed capital ran far beyond their personal capacity to raise funds.

This was largely an institutional problem. The obvious way of channelling the savings of the non-participant investor into productive investment was to set up a joint-stock company to which a large number of small capitalists could subscribe. If each individual subscriber's liability could be limited to the extent of his original share in the project then his risks were known in advance, and his willingness to contribute was limited only by his readiness to stake what might be a relatively small sum on the wisdom of the company's promoters. The danger was however that this could put a relatively large aggregate sum in the hands of a group of wild but plausible men who would run up even larger debts which they had no hope of repaying. In 1720 this danger had culminated in a national disaster through the mushroom growth of a host of speculative

29. E. Hobsbawn, *The Age of Revolution*, p. 36.

ventures promoted as joint-stock companies, many of them quite sound and promising ventures, but some wild to the degree of lunacy. The failure of the lunatic fringe destroyed confidence in the more reputable schemes. In the ensuing stock exchange crash many investors lost their savings and government passed the Bubble Act which specifically forbade the formation of joint-stock companies unless authorised by special Act of Parliament. Thenceforth an investor who took a share in a project not so authorised, was as fully liable for the debts incurred as if he were himself incurring them—so that none would lend on these terms unless he was himself active in the making of the firm's decisions, or unless he knew the managers so well that he felt safe in assuming unlimited liability for their debts.

There were some sectors, however, where the project was too expensive to be financed by a small group of investors, and where a number of substantial citizens were sufficiently interested in its success to be willing to subscribe. In these cases it was worthwhile going through the tedious and often lengthy business of getting a special Act of Parliament passed to permit a joint-stock company to be set up with limited liability. This procedure was often used to finance roadbuilding projects or new bridges or river navigation improvements. Numerous Turnpike Trusts were authorised by Act of Parliament and in the second half of the century the formation of joint-stock companies to build canals became common. Canals required large outlays of capital which—with the notable exception of the Duke of Bridgewater's pioneer venture—it was beyond the capacity of all but the most exceptional individuals to provide out of their own resources. Most of this capital was obtained by making use of the joint-stock form of company authorised by Act of Parliament. The new navigations, that is to say, were largely the products of corporate enterprise, initiated by local businessmen and landowners and supported by local bankers and city corporations. These were substantial voices in the community. Later, particularly during the canal mania of the 1790s, the geographical basis of the capital raised for the canal companies spread beyond the immediate region each canal was to serve, and many small savers without a direct interest in the result of the project were persuaded to invest in canal shares. This was a vital development in the institutions of capitalism for it meant that the channels were being cut which would link the resources of the small saver, the non-participant investor, with the great enterprises that individual capitalists found too massive for their personal budgets. When, in the 1830s and 1840s, much larger sums were required to finance the railways some of the institutional lessons had been already learned and the joint-stock company again performed the function of tapping the savings of the non-participant investors and channelling them into productive enterprise.

Until the Limited Liability Acts of the 1850s, however, the legal restrictions on joint-stock company operation meant that this form of institution was legally confined to a severely limited field. It could only be set up on the basis of a specific Act of Parliament and this required promoters of standing in the community as well as backers with the ready cash necessary to meet all the expenses of piloting a Bill through Parliament. It was not the only form of corporate enterprise that existed in the eighteenth century, however. In some enterprises where considerable amounts of capital were required—in insurance, building, the brass industry, the West Riding fulling industry for example— the Equitable Trust appeared: this involved the insertion in the original deed of settlement of a clause making each shareholder liable only to the extent of his original investment and so permitted a form of limited liability without going through the expensive process of obtaining parliamentary sanction.[30] Evidence of this kind of device appeared at the end of the eighteenth century and the beginning of the nineteenth century. It shows that where conditions were ripe for the establishment of the corporate form of economic organisation, entrepreneurs were quite capable of evading the strict letter of the law and suggests

30. R. S. Neale, 'An Equitable Trust in the Building Industry in 1794', *Business History*, July 1965.

that the effects of the Bubble Act were not so restrictive as has sometimes been imagined.

Nevertheless corporate enterprise was far from being typical. For the most part the capital was obtained by personal contact between investors and savers, and by ploughing back the profits of industry either into the industries in which they were earned or into some closely related industry. It was only when financing the massive social overhead capital embodied in giant transport and urbanisation projects that it proved necessary to draw on the small individual savings which were being generated by an expanding economy. Later, when the major part of this essential infrastructure had been laid down, the small savers and the non-participant investors in general had to turn to the foreign loan market to find the paper assets which were comparable to canal and railway shares in their general acceptability and hence liquidity.

THE EMERGENCE OF THE CAPITALIST INDUSTRY STATE

If we now take a broad retrospective view of the development of the English industrial revolution we can trace its beginnings from the 1740s under the stimulus of three interdependent factors—the development of international markets (particularly the markets outside Europe), the abnormal sequence of good harvests stretching from the late 1710s to the 1750s and the growth of population beginning in the 1740s. At this stage in the story—from the 1740s through the 1760s—there is little to distinguish the expansion then taking place from many another upturn in the rate of expansion of a pre-industrial economy.

Then, beginning in the 1770s, we find evidence of an acceleration in the process of industrialisation which seems to have stemmed largely from an unprecedented and internationally unparalleled spate of innovations which revolutionised two British industries—cotton and iron—in less than a generation. Overseas trade continued to grow—at a rate of growth alternately depressed and stimulated by wars and their aftermath—and gained a new momentum from the competitive advantages that technological change gave to the affected industries. Population continued to grow and to stimulate the investment in agriculture and transport which was a condition of further population growth. By the end of the century an essentially new British industry (cotton) had developed major proportions and an old one (iron) had escaped from a tightening natural resource restraint.

Whether the die was now cast and the economy had passed beyond the point of no return on the way to full industrialisation and modern economic growth it is difficult to say. The process of change was complicated by a major war. There seems little doubt that the first phase of the French and Napoleonic wars, by severely reducing the competitive power of Britain's major European competitors, gave this country a permanent trading advantage in world markets. Probably also the hindrance which was placed in the way of the free flow of technical knowledge between Britain and Europe helped this country to maintain her technological lead for several decades longer than it would otherwise have done. So that although the continental blockade which characterised the second phase of the Napoleonic wars effectively restrained the further expansion of British overseas trade, the economic gains that had been made in the last two decades of the eighteenth century were not lost and Britain emerged from the great wars with a clear lead over the rest of the world in terms both of overall productivity and industrial technology.

Essentially, however, Great Britain was still a preindustrial economy in which the state of the harvest was the most significant determinant of the change in national income between one year and the next. Possibly it was merely a matter of time before the balance between manufacturing industry and agriculture would have shifted finally in favour of the former and a fully fledged industrial state, in which growth was the normal condition, would have emerged as a natural matter of course. The next major discontinuity in the process of development however coincided with the coming of the steam railways and, in the event, it was this that ensured the completion of industrialisation. For many of the countries which have passed through an industrial revolution, the coming of the railways constituted an essential part of the crucial break-through. The striking feature of the British case is that the decisive revolution in transport conditions—decisive in the sense that it permitted a substantial expansion in population and trade—occurred in other forms of transport, notably canals and roads; and that the coming of the railway coincides with a relatively late stage in the process of transformation from a pre-industrial to an industrial economy.

THE COMING OF THE RAILWAYS

It took a whole generation after Robert Trevithick put his steam engine to the task of pulling 25 ton loads along his railroad near Merthyr Tydfil in 1804 for the steam locomotive effectively to displace the horse and to get out of the experimental into the commercially viable stage of development. When the first line designed for steam traction was opened in 1825, in the form of the 27 mile long stretch of the Stockton-Darlington line, there were already nearly 200 miles of iron railroad authorised by Parliament to go beyond the bounds of a private estate and probably several hundred more running through the private estates attached to individual coalfields. Although the opening of the Stockton-Darlington line is generally regarded as marking the beginning of the railway era it is only in terms of hindsight that we can so describe it. Horsedrawn coaches continued to be used for passenger traffic on this line for some years yet and contemporaries remained dubious of the steam locomotive until well into the 1830s. The first clear commercial success was the Liverpool and Manchester line opened in 1830.

The fact is that the railways were expensive in both time and money, first to initiate (parliamentary sanction had to be obtained and the capital raised) then to build (each line in these early ventures encountered unpredictable construction problems and traffic opportunities), and finally to operate. It took time for the traffic to develop and for the equipment to be used to capacity. In this atmosphere of uncertainty and with so little past experience to learn from it is even surprising that so much capital was raised in the first railway mania which blew up into a financial crisis in 1836-37. In the event, the joint optimism of a multitude of over-enthusiastic investors resulted in many more miles of railway line being projected than the economy could conveniently digest at the hoped-for rate. A financial crisis was inevitable when the disappointed speculators tried to sell their shares and to liquidate their investments in a hurry. It was also inevitable that the pendulum of business optimism should then swing the other way, that when some of the less sound projects were discontinued through lack of finance, there should be a psychological stampede of the opposite kind and a marked disinclination to put any new projects in hand. Existing companies found it difficult either to raise loans to complete their lines or to extend their existing overdrafts.

Nevertheless if the financiers and the speculators were in a state of confusion and catastrophe, the physical consequences of the railways boom were unmistakable; the promotions of 1836-37 had added something over a thousand miles to the British railway network. By June 1843 there were nearly 2,000 miles of steam railways in operation in the United Kingdom. By then a new wave of construction was beginning to gather momentum and this, by 1848, had resulted in a completed total of 5,000 miles of railway which included all the main arteries of the modern British railway system. In 1847 which was the peak year of this massive investment boom, more than 300,000 men were employed in constructing or operating the railways, on which total expenditure was equivalent to between 8 and 9% of gross national product and not far short of the total declared value of the U.K. domestic exports. It was accompanied by another burst of irrational speculation, another 'mania' and a reaction so violent that the raising of the Bank Rate to 8% was inadequate to curb the panic outflow of gold without a suspension of the Bank Charter Act. It was the sheer scale of the railway investment boom of the 1840s that makes it so significant a feature of the industrial revolution in Britain. If it is true that the critical difference between an underdeveloped and a developed country is that the former normally saves 5% of its national product and the latter 12% or more, then it was in the 1840s that Britain crossed the threshold in this sense. Never before and seldom again, at least until after the second world war, did she put such a large proportion of her national product into laying down fixed capital equipment within her own borders.

In all, the consequences of the coming of the railways were so large and pervasive that it is difficult to get them into clear mutual perspective. As with the eighteenth-century developments in road and canal transport, there were direct and immediate gains to the economy in the shape of cost reductions, of greater speed, safety and reliability of travel and carriage, of extensions in the area of the market and of accessible natural resources. There was a further and much larger increase in the sheer scale of the traffic that could be moved about the country. There were massive demands for funds, so large indeed, that it is reasonable to regard the railways as having appreciably enlarged the nation's capacity to save. But there were in addition a number of ways in which the impact of the railways was different, at least in scale if not in principle, from the impact of the earlier transport revolution.

(i) First, like the canals they directly lowered transport costs and widened the market. But they also changed the character of the goods being carried beyond the purely local market. This was particularly important for perishables. Until the railways came, London (like the other big cities) depended for its vegetables and dairy produce on its immediate countryside. The quality was indifferent and the conditions under which live animals were kept in the London mews and courts were a menace to the health as well as to the amenities of the metropolis. Most of London's meat requirements were met by animals which were walked to market, for it was not practicable to slaughter the meat at point of production and send it a long slow journey by road wagon or canal. But when railways came it was possible to send live animals, dead meat, dairy products, vegetables and a variety of other foodstuffs from the countryside to the large towns with a minimum of wastage and a great saving of cost. Consequently as workers' incomes rose in the second half of the nineteenth century there was a marked improvement in the quality and variety of their normal diet.

(ii) Secondly, even more than the canals the railways were an important prerequisite to a further enlargement of the export sector. The growth of British overseas trade reached its peak in the mid-nineteenth century decades, immediately after the provision of the railways, and although its *rate* of growth slowed down later in the century, in absolute terms the volume and value of goods passing in and out of the country expanded strongly right up to the first world war. The era of the great specialisation when Britain supplied the bulk of the manufactured goods entering into world trade and imported cheap food in bulk from the virgin territories of the New World could not have taken place without the close net-work of railways leading to and from the ports.

(iii) Thirdly, and this is what makes the railway such a potentially significant factor in economic development, it had important linkages with the other key industries of an industrialising economy. The construction and operation of the railways set up a heavy demand for iron, coal and bricks—all commodities which Britain had ample resources to supply and all commodities which were basic to the process of industrialisation. An expanded demand for these commodities stimulated the industries producing them, encouraged innovation, and made possible important economies of scale in supplying producers' goods which could benefit a wide area of the economy. The coal, iron and building industries did not grow out of the railways in this country but they were carried forward to a totally different scale of operations by the railway age.

(iv) Fourthly the railway had a variety of important institutional consequences for the expanding industrial economy. The sums spent on it, the labour force engaged, dwarfed all previous operations and the capital sunk in these enterprises represented the development of economic empires which it required a new type of entrepreneur to rule. A new generation of constructional engineers grew out of the construction boom and business tycoons operating on the grand scale grew out of the vast capital transactions. They got their education in the hard school of practical experience. In the 1830s, when every new railway line was a new trail blazed, the great pioneer engineers who took the crucial decisions were distinguished by their ingenuity, energy and practical skill. In the 1840s it was the turn of the business tycoons, men who had the organisational skills needed to plan transport systems, link railways with canals, amalgamate competing companies and transform many short lines into long efficient channels of continuous communication. This stage of development required a new kind of contractor able to take advantage of the enormous flexibility and scale of operations opened up by the new form of transport. The canal system had been limited by the fact that canals could go only where there was a water supply. The roads were limited by the fact that they were constructed and controlled by a multitude of local authorities and turnpike trusts who lacked either the power or incentive or vision to set up the large units of control that the railway contractors were able to develop. The railways offered virtually unlimited scope for men of vision and enterprise.

(v) They also had important consequences for other forms of transport. A crucial difference between the railways and the canals was that from their early stages the railways were seen as a public utility rather than a private monopoly. The canal companies enjoyed a natural monopoly which they did not hesitate to exploit to the full. While the iron masters agonised over the fact that their goods were going rusty on the long slow journey by canal, and the cotton merchants complained that their raw materials and finished goods went across the Atlantic quicker than they travelled between Liverpool and Manchester, and farmers saw their produce spoil en route, the canal owners went on raising their prices and squeezing the customer. Of course it was not always possible to avoid delays on the canals. When they were caused by frost or drought or sheer pressure of traffic, for example, they were inevitable. Nevertheless by the 1820s the canals had begun to yield diminishing returns to their users and to constitute a bottleneck to the potential expansion of trade in many areas. It was largely in response to this kind of bottleneck that the Liverpool-Manchester line, the first railway designed with the public interest rather than private profit in view, was set up. The effect of the construction of a railway on the adjacent canal was always immediate for the owners had to adjust their rates or succumb to competition. It had been estimated that canal rates fell by amounts which were a third or a half of what they had been able to charge before the railways were built.[31] By 1865 nearly a third of the nation's canals and navigations were directly under the control of the railway companies.

Road traffic was also forced into a new mould by the railways. Like the canal companies the owners of stage coaches had been quick to exploit their local monopolies. Except in those areas where there was competition between a number of coaches, fares were extortionate. A House of Commons Committee reported in 1844 that even where competition was effective, as it was on most of the main routes in and out of the big towns, the rate was just under 4½d per mile. By contrast the fares adopted by the leading railway companies ranged from about 3d a mile for first-class passengers to 1½d a mile for third-class passengers: and all classes of passengers enjoyed greater comfort and speed on the railways than they did on the coaches. Between Liverpool and Manchester, in effect, the railways more than halved both the cost and the time of travel and pro-

31. W. T. Jackman, *The Development of Transportation in Modern England*, p. 635.

vided an almost unlimited capacity for new traffic to grow into. From the very beginning the railway carriages carried twice as many passengers as had been used to travel by coach and reduced the costs and delays of goods traffic.

The immediate effect was to sweep away a lot of the coaches running along roads parallel to the railways and to multiply the traffic on connecting roads. The increase in vehicles licensed suggests that the net effect of the railways was to increase rather than to reduce the number of road vehicles. True, there were some cases in the early stages of the railway boom when the reduction in the revenues of the Turnpike Trusts made it increasingly difficult to get private entrepreneurs to maintain the roads effectively. On the other hand, although the system of Turnpike Trusts eventually disintegrated in the face of railway competition, it was true of the roads as it was of the vehicles travelling on them, that while competing roads suffered, feeder roads flourished. And so great was the traffic generated by the railway, and the rise in local land values associated by its spread, that the eventual effect of what the famous roadbuilder Sir James Macadam called in 1839 the 'calamity of the railways' was a widespread improvement in, rather than a deterioration of, the road system. The local authorities for example, found themselves getting rising rate incomes as local properties soared in value and were able easily to shoulder the burden of road maintenance as they matured in organisation and administrative experience.

Taken overall, however, the significance of the railways in the British case is not so much in the fact that they stimulated industrial growth—which they did, of course, both in their construction boom and in reducing production costs for other industries—but in that they provided the economy with a system of internal communications which immensely enlarged its productive horizon. This was capacity into which the expanding economy could grow, unhampered by effective constraints on the scale of its traffic flow, until well into the twentieth century. The main lines of the system were there by 1850. By 1867 more than 12,000 lines of railroad were open in Great Britain and they were

more than providing the resources for their own maintenance and extension in the sense that annual net working
receipts were henceforth more than enough to finance
annual gross investment in the railways.

Thus, by the middle of the nineteenth century, once the
essentials of a modern system of communications had been
laid down, the British economy was technologically free to
continue the process of spontaneous industrialisation as far
as its comparative advantage justified. That it would go on
growing in product and productivity over the long run was
by then certain. In what direction the industrial sector expanded, and how fast the economy grew, depended henceforth on other factors—in particular for example on the
interaction between the pattern of world demand and the
structure of British natural resources.

There is however, another kind of change which is of
crucial importance in transforming a pre-industrial traditional economy into an industrial economy experiencing
modern economic growth, *and* in determining the pace of
economic growth once the process is complete. That is a
change in the social context of economic activity. To
transform a traditional economy into an industrial economy
it is necessary for the majority of producers to adopt a
succession of new techniques of combining the factors of
production (land, labour and capital) and raw material
inputs in the business of earning a living. This involves the
development of new forms of social relationship, new social
institutions and new systems of value. It is the ability and the
outlook of the men who take the vital decisions about how
and what to produce and where to sell, and of the workers
who put these decisions into tangible form, which largely
determines the character of economic change and hence
the pace of economic growth. If the entrepreneurs are not
sufficiently ready to experiment, or to take risks, to reduce
their costs or to find new markets, if the craftsmen do not
have or are unwilling to acquire the necessary skills, or if the
labourers are undisciplined or unwilling or discontented,
then economic change may be hindered and growth retarded.

The division of labour associated with an industrial revolution involves two kinds of specialisation. First, a specialisation by trade or industry so that an individual tends to be attached to a particular industry or occupation rather than to be 'jack of all trades', and second a specialisation between labour and capital. The first kind of specialisation brings with it certain advantages for productivity, because a producer who can spend all his time in one activity is likely to produce more goods and services per unit of effort or time, both because he does not have to waste time switching from one task to another, and because he is likely to become more technically expert if he concentrates on a narrower range of operations. This kind of specialisation also involves some disadvantages in that the narrower the range of functions which an individual has to perform the more monotonous his job is likely to be. Not all highly specialised occupations are boring, but one effect of a high degree of specialisation is to increase the number of purely routine tasks in an economy. This has important implications for the attitude to work which could outweigh some of the productivity gains due to the greater technical efficiency of a specialised worker. As an economy becomes more industrialised moreover the disutility of labour tends to increase for most workers, partly because the social satisfactions of work diminish.

The second kind of specialisation involved in an industrial revolution is a specialisation as between labour and capital. This too implies a significant change in the attitude to work. The capitalist industry state falls into two sectors— in one of which are the owners (or hirers) of the nation's capital assets, the entrepreneurs who take the crucial economic decisions as to what shall be produced and what prices shall be charged, and in the other of which are the operatives by whose labour the goods and services are produced. The basic distinction between the capitalist and the labourer, the employer and the employees, is marked by the character of the return which each gets from his contribution to the process of production. The capitalists receive profits, i.e. a return determined by the relationship between prices, output and costs of production. The labourers receive employment incomes—a contractual payment settled by a process of bargaining with the employer, i.e. the capitalist or entrepreneur. Of course it is perfectly possible even in a fully industrialised society for one individual to figure in both sectors—for a self-employed man to labour on his own account, for an employed man to get a profit from ownership of capital. But the distinction between employer and employee is fundamental to an industrial economy, and most producers would fall quite clearly into one category or the other.

The change in the social conditions in which the average individual earned his living was one of the most radical of the many profound changes involved in the industrial revolution. No doubt by the second half of the eighteenth century there were more people than ever before getting the bulk of their livelihood through the receipt of incomes from employment—but it was not yet a majority of the population; and the traditional hostility towards being forced into the position of a proletarian labourer was still strong. So that when the first factories were set up employers found it difficult to acquire a stable labour force. 'To accept a merely wage status in the factories was a surrender of one's birthright, a loss of independence, security, liberty.'[32]

The attitudes to work and leisure which characterise the self-employed individual or the family worker are totally different from those which motivate the wage earner who gets none of the profits of his own labour. While domestic industry was the normal form of industrial organisation and most farm labourers had an arable plot of their own and rights of pasture on the common, the numbers of mere wage slaves were few. 'So long as industry was carried on mainly by small masters, each employing but one or two journeymen, the period of any energetic man's service as a hired wage earner cannot normally have exceeded a few years, and the industrious apprentice might reasonably

32. Christopher Hill, in *Socialism, Capitalism and Economic Growth*, ed. C. H. Feinstein, p. 350.

hope, if not always to marry his master's daughter, at least to set up in business for himself.'[33] In these conditions the journeyman labourer was apt to look at the economy through the same kind of spectacles as his employer, and there was no basic division of interest between the employer and the employee.

As the size of the proletariat grew, however, the interest of the worker began to diverge from that of his master and so naturally he began to form associations with other workers in the same trade with whom he had some community of interest. These associations constitute the origin of the trade union movement. Skilled workers set up most of the more permanent unions with a wide range of objectives in which mutual insurance against unemployment and sickness ranked generally higher than bargaining with employers on questions of wages or conditions of work. Unskilled workers, with neither the funds nor the education to set up effective continuing associations, found that organised rioting directed against an oppressive employer's property—machines, raw materials, buildings—constituted a useful weapon in defence of their industrial interests.[34]

In the traditional pre-industrial type of economy where industry is largely domestic industry, the relationship between employer and employee is as much an expression of a social relationship as of an economic one. Employer and employed recognised mutual responsibilities which ranged far beyond that involved in a mere contract of employment. In eighteenth-century England workers expected to get a fair day's wage in return for a fair day's work and when there was some dispute about what was 'fair' in this context they expected the Justices of the Peace to arbitrate by fixing wages. Many of the early factory owners accepted paternalistic responsibilities to their labour force without question. The early factories powered by water, for example, were situated in factory villages where the employer made it his duty to look after not only his workers but their

33. S. Webb, *History of Trade Unionism*, p. 6.
34. E. Hobsbawm, The Machine Breakers, *Past and Present*, February 1952.

families; and there were many later factory owners who provided such amenities as housing for their employees and education for their pauper children long before there was any formal legal obligation for them to do so.

As industry became more urbanised however and as the use of machinery gradually replaced skilled handicraft workers with semiskilled or unskilled labour, the labour force attached to each employer became less and less distinguishable from a general mass of labour for which no employer left any particular responsibility. At the same time the development of profit-maximising criteria for entrepreneurial behaviour, which was the distinguishing feature of the new industrial capitalism, involved deliberate depersonalisation of the relationship between the capitalist and the worker. The new political economy, for which Adam Smith and the classical economists who followed him provided the theory, started from the premise that, if each individual sets out to maximise his own return, the beneficent forces of competition will ensure that the majority become richer than they would otherwise be.

It took time for the rules of the new political economy to become second nature to the employing classes, and still longer for them to become acceptable to the workers. When in 1795 the Speenhamland magistrates undertook to supplement the worker's wage in proportion to the price of bread and the number of mouths he had to feed, they were in effect giving explicit social recognition to the individual's right to a minimum wage. This decision which was adopted in many other parishes in the last years of the eighteenth century was one of the last acts of the old paternalistic type of economy. The Speenhamland system however had largely fallen into disuse before the new Poor Law formally denied the worker's right to a subsistence income in 1834.

There were two reasons for the weak bargaining position in which the working classes found themselves when the Industrial Revolution gathered massive momentum in England in the 1820s, 1830s and 1840s. One was the fact that the labour force had not yet taken the form which would enable it to exert an organised power over the worker's side of the wage bargain. Until at least the middle of the nineteenth century the typical British working man was either a casual labourer on the roads, railways, building sites or docks, or an artisan or mechanic in a small workshop. Even in factory trades like textiles there were, until the 1840s, more people engaged as outworkers, casually employed in their own homes than there were minding machines on the factory floor; and the factory operatives themselves were largely women, juveniles and children—none of them groups which were easily organised in a trade dispute.

Another reason was the rate at which the labour force was growing. The population reached its peak rate of increase of 16 to 17% per decade in the period 1811-31. The urban population grew even faster as the surplus rural population fled from a chronically depressed agriculture; and having once joined the ranks of the urban proletariat the workers were grateful to toil all the hours the employer required, because unemployment, which meant complete destitution, was a constant possibility. In the 1840s the influx of Irish in flight from the potato famines brought in a labour reserve which had no lower limit to the wages it would accept or the conditions it would endure.

At the same time the employers, anxious to keep the machines running night and day so long as there was a demand for their products, kept men, women and children working 12-16 hours per day and per night so long as trade was prosperous. When it was depressed they had no hesitation in casting off labour for there would always be a workless queue at the factory gate whenever they wanted to start up the machines again. When they wanted higher output they drove their workers harder. When they needed to contract they reduced the labour force or put men on short time at starvation wages. Whether this was a very efficient way of using a labour force, even a labour force which was as abundant as the British was at this stage, is doubtful. These preposterously long working days or nights must have resulted in some reduction in the effectiveness of the labourers' efforts, some hours in which the extra work gave negative rather than positive results.

Yet one of the reasons for the unprecedented expansion of the British economy in the nineteenth century was its access to a cheap supply of labour. While industrial profits soared in the decades of the 1820s, 1830s and 1840s money wages fell or stagnated. The employers were free from the labour problems which had constrained their predecessors in the 1780s and 1790s when the labour force was feckless, undisciplined and riotous, when regular attendance at the factory was the most difficult thing in the world to enforce on a labour force brought up in the seasonal rhythms of a pre-industrial society, and when skilled engineers were increasingly scarce. Once the French war was over and the soldiers and sailors had been unloaded on to a free labour market, nineteenth-century British employers were never seriously bothered by labour shortages. By the 1830s workers in many areas could get poor relief only under the austere and socially intolerable conditions of the new Poor Law, which set out to make the condition of the pauper more unpleasant than that of the poorest of the independent poor. Then, with the labour force expanding at an unprecedented rate, with women and children and Irish refugees providing a reserve of cheap labour with no bargaining power whatever, with the workhouse standing between the destitute worker and starvation, it became easy to assemble anywhere in Britain the masses of unskilled workers required for such large scale, discontinuous, construction projects as were involved in the building of the railways. It is significant that 1847, the year of the greatest railway boom of all time, was the year after the Irish famine when the wage standards of the labour force were being depressed by a mass exodus of desperate refugees from Ireland. Even skilled labourers who were capable of organising themselves into permanent unions and who had some degree of monopoly in their skills to use as a bargaining weapon, had not yet learned to exploit their industrial power to the full. They were still generally more concerned to assure themselves a 'just' wage by customary standards and to prevent dilution of their own ranks which might increase their prospects of unemployment, than to bargain for wage levels as high as employers could meet.

In effect, it was a characteristic and unique feature of the English industrial revolution that it reached its climax in an economic system which was as near being the prototype of a free-market, labour-abundant economy as there has ever been. True, before the middle of the nineteenth century, some weight was being thrown into the scale on behalf of the most helpless of the members of the labouring classes—the women and children working in the factories and the mines. The duty of the state to protect young children had never really been denied. Not even the most convinced supporters of the new rules of political economy were prepared to argue that the terms on which young children were to labour in factories ought to be determined by 'free' agreement between employer and employee. But until a factory inspectorate was set up in 1833 to enforce the rules which the state took it upon itself to put into the statute book on their behalf, they continued to be exploited as fully as the employers chose. The factory inspectors were among the first of a new body of government officials whose job was to intervene purposefully in the operations of the market economy. But the process of industrialisation had been pushed to its limits in the nineteenth century before the economic decisions of the State affected more than marginally the terms on which the factors of production were marketed.

CONCLUSION

The capitalist industry state which emerged from the English industrial revolution had reached what was essentially its modern form well before the end of the nineteenth century. By 1880 the population of Great Britain had more than trebled in less than a century and four out of every five of these people were living in large towns; agriculture accounted for only about a tenth of the gross national product; and more than a third of the nation's expenditure went on imports, largely in purchasing essential foodstuffs and industrial raw materials. The share of agriculture in gross national product was to fall a little more; the structure of manufacturing output was to alter considerably; and the economy was to become a little less open, and its growth rate more erratic, as the spread of the industrial revolution in the rest of the world forced the original country to adopt more defensive commercial policies. But in its most characteristic aspects the economic system which had taken shape by the fourth quarter of the nineteenth century was still in existence at the middle of the twentieth century.

BIBLIOGRAPHY

The English industrial revolution was a complex process of economic and social change which deserves study from a variety of viewpoints. It has been the subject of a massive output of published works. This short list is designed to introduce the student to a small but varied sample of this literature as a starting point for further study in depth.

Ashton, T. S., *The Industrial Revolution*, 1948. A deservedly famous brief survey stressing the human factor in industrial change.

Blythell, Duncan, *The Handloom Weavers*, 1969. A monograph describing the experience of one group of workers deeply involved in the transition from the domestic system to the factory system.

Chambers, J. D. and Mingay, G. E., *The Agricultural Revolution, 1750-1850*, 1966. An authoritative account of the agrarian developments associated with the industrial revolution.

Deane, Phyllis, *The First Industrial Revolution*, 1967. An analysis of each of the main aspects of the industrial revolution discussed from the point of view of a development economist. It contains a lengthy bibliography arranged by subjects.

Engels, F., *The Condition of the Working Class in England*, 1844, translated and edited by W. O. Henderson and W. H. Chaloner. A vivid contemporary account of working class conditions which reflects the climate of opinion in which Marxism was born.

Hartwell, R. M. (ed.), *The Causes of the Industrial Revolution in England*, 1967. A collection of reprinted articles, covering a wide range of interpretation and debate, prefaced by an introductory essay reviewing the state of research on this theme.

Hobsbawm, E. J., *The Age of Revolution: Europe 1789-1848*, 1962. An impressionistic study of the joint consequences for European economic, political and social history in the first half of the nineteenth century, of the French Revolution in 1789 and the industrial revolution in Britain.

Landes, David S., *The Unbound Prometheus*, 1969. A masterly survey of the genesis of the industrial revolution and its spread to western Europe and the United States.

Mantoux, P., *The Industrial Revolution in the Eighteenth Century* (12th edition 1961), with an introduction by T. S. Ashton. A classic and readable study which is still one of the best of its kind.

Musson, A. E. (ed.), *Science, Technology and Economic Growth in the Eighteenth Century*, 1972. A collection of reprinted articles focused on the role of science in technical change during the Industrial Revolution, introduced by an editorial survey of the results of research on this question.

Nef, J., 'The Progress of Technology and the Growth of Large-Scale Industry in Britain, 1540-1640' *Economic History Review*, 1934. An article describing industrial developments in Tudor and Stuart times as having most of the essential characteristics of an industrial revolution.

Raistrick, A., *A Dynasty of Iron Founders*, 1951. A biographical study of the contribution of a famous Quaker family to the eighteenth-century transformation of the iron industry.

Rowe, J., *Cornwall in the Age of the Industrial Revolution*, 1953. A regional study of the process of economic change as it affected the inhabitants of a single English county.

Rostow, W. W., *The Stages of Economic Growth* (2nd edition, 1971). This book, sub-titled a 'non-Communist Manifesto' propounds a universal stage-theory of economic growth, with particular reference to the prospects of today's developing countries. In support of this theory one period in the English industrial revolution (1783-1802) is identified as the prototype of the crucial stage of 'take-off into sustained growth'.

Thompson, Edward, *The Making of the English Working Class*, 1963. A lively history of the working class movement in the period of the industrial revolution which illustrates an important aspect of the social background of the industrialisation process.

Ward, J. T., *The Factory Movement, 1830-1855*, 1962. A study of the agitation for the restriction of hours worked by industrial labour and the regulation of working conditions.

Wilson, Charles, 'The Entrepreneur in the Industrial Revolution in Britain', *History*, 1957. A discussion of the changing function and character of the innovating business men.

4. The Industrial Revolution in the Habsburg Monarchy, 1750-1914

N. T. Gross

INTRODUCTION

The House of Habsburg was one of the major powers in Europe until World War One. Its domain covered an area of over 250,000 square miles, and comprised one-seventh of Europe's population in 1800 and still *circa* one-eighth of it in 1914. At that time the Austro-Hungarian Monarchy, with 50 million inhabitants, was the third largest state in Europe by population, the second by area. The story of nineteenth century industrialisation in the Monarchy is therefore an integral part of the economic history of modern Europe, even though the political entity concerned no longer exists. But additional, general interest may well be ascribed to this story because of certain specific features. For one, most theories and models of the Industrial Revolution have given prominence to those economies which 'took off'; but spurt-like development was not the only type of growth-path along which Continental countries followed the lead of Britain. The study of economies like the Austrian that, though definitely not stagnant, underwent the process of modernising transformation at a slow and protracted pace, as if plodding painfully along while eyeing with constant apprehension its fellow stragglers and with envy the rapid industrialisers overtaking it, should broaden and generalise our understanding of the historical experience of modern economic growth.

Moreover, the Austrian case is unusual, and perhaps unique, in the interrelation and interdependence between political and economic developments. Generally, the process of industrialisation coincided quite clearly with political ascent and consolidation, as prominently exemplified by the history of Germany. Within the Habsburg Monarchy, however, while the features of political and economic events in Hungary evidently conformed to the general pattern, the

The maps on pages 230 and 231 and 234 and 235 are taken from *The Habsburg Monarchy* by A. J. P. Taylor and are reproduced by kind permission of Hamish Hamilton

Austrian part of the Monarchy obviously diverged from it.[1] Here economic growth and industrialisation, continuous if not rapid, took their course during and probably accelerated towards the end of the very century which witnessed the political decline and progressive disintegration of the state. The long-run decline of Habsburg from the status of a First Rank Power must have hampered economic growth at least because of the persistent costly efforts to halt or at least disguise the process. Additional effects, though much more difficult to trace (such as in the area of entrepreneurial confidence and expectations), may have been particularly strong from the 1840's to the 1860's, the decades of disastrous foreign affairs. Thus, the mobilisation during the Crimean War, by which the Monarchy gained nothing and lost much political good will, capsized government finances and forced the termination of state railroad construction. Furthermore, the major effort costlier even than war is a lost war; and the Monarchy lost two wars within the seven years 1859–1866, and with them one of its most important protected markets, the Lombardo-Venetian Kingdom. On the other hand it is, of course, highly probable that an inherently stronger economy and its more successful growth would have been able to support a more vigorous and effective foreign policy.

The interaction between economic and socio-political developments in domestic affairs is, in general, at least as important. In this respect, too, the history of Austria-Hungary presents very interesting peculiar characteristics. In its dynastic, 'supra-national' structure the Habsburg Monarchy was an anachronism in nineteenth century Europe, though not the only one. Even the reconstitution of the Empire into the Austro-Hungarian 'dual' state by the 1867 *Ausgleich*, which formalised the main internal division of

1. As customary in the literature on the Habsburg Monarchy, 'Austria' here refers to the Cisleithania part of the Empire, including chiefly the Alpine and Karst provinces (and Northern Italy, when applicable), Bohemia-Moravia, and Galicia-Bukovina. 'Hungary' refers to the Lands of the Hungarian Crown, or Transleithania, i.e. Hungary 'proper', Slovakia, Transylvania, and Croatia-Slovenia.

The Habsburg Monarchy 1815–1918

0   50   100   150
Miles

Mountains

Military Frontier

Cracow annexed 1846
Lombardy lost 1859
Venetia " 1866
Bosnia and
Hercegovina annexed 1908

J.F.Horrabin

long standing, was in fact based upon outdated non-national foundations. In any but the smallest countries regional differences in resource endowment, cultural levels, and transportation possibilities are of obvious importance; in the Monarchy, however, geography was also ethnography. At least eleven different nationalities inhabited the Habsburg domains, interwoven in patterns of varying intricacy, and their growing national consciousness and aggressiveness was a basic trend of our period. On the one hand their dis-integrating strife was both cause and effect in economic development. On the other hand, the preservation of the Empire became more and more a series of rear-guard battles fought on many sides at once against both domestic and foreign enemies, most of whom had in common the inspiration of nationalism.

The distinction between foreign and domestic affairs is, obviously, an arbitrary one. The same personalities and social forces forged policies in both directions, and the flows of causation and interactions were multi-directional. The composition of the Habsburg Monarchy and the diversity of its policy goals, which make its nineteenth century history so complicated, also pose the challenging task of trying to discern the patterns of those interactions at least in certain instances. The interests which supported the policy of minimal foreign trade well into the second half of the nineteenth century, for example, were co-responsible for the diplomatic failures *vis-à-vis* the evolution of the Prussian-led *Zollverein*. The obstacles to foreign trade, I would contend, were one of the reasons for the slow rate of technical progress and industrialisation. And the retarded pace of economic growth and transformation not only made a change in trade policy more and more difficult, but also generally contributed to the erosion of Austria's position as a European power. In the last quarter of the century, to take another example, the will and ability of the Hungarian government to pursue a policy of economic development were as much the result of converging economic, social, and nationalistic forces as was the inability of the Austrian government to follow a similar line consistently. At the same time the conflict of interests between its two 'halves' also strongly influenced the political and economic foreign relations of the Monarchy, in particular with its Balkan neighbours.

The various regions and nationalities were, nevertheless, not exclusively or even pre-eminently engaged in fighting each other, although their politicians and in particular their parliamentary representatives usually gave this impression. The study of inter-regional economic relations and ot the 'contributions' of different geographical and ethnical units to modern economic growth in the Monarchy should be as rewarding as similar studies in the cultural domain. Unfortunately, historical writings on the Monarchy have been heavily influenced by the conflicts between its nationalities, and especially by attempts to 'justify' its long existence and/or its eventual decomposition. This influence, combined with the clear-cut discontinuity in the history of the area and people concerned, may explain the almost complete absence ot studies in the social and economic history of the Monarchy as a whole. That much ot general interest and many fascinating problems are to be elucidated by such studies I have tried to indicate in the preceding paragraphs. That the lack of previous research makes a survey such as the present one not only very difficult but perforce deficient should be obvious. All one can hope for is, that such bold efforts will contribute to the literature not only by their few fortuitous merits but also by the challenge embodied in their shortcomings. There are indications in the most recent years, though, that the dormant field of Austro-Hungarian economic history is being discovered and slowly populated. In part this is the result of contemporary interest in 'common market' examples. More generally, the passage of time since 1918 has been conducive to a more detached, academic approach to the history of the Monarchy. This is evident, not least, in the work of our colleagues in Prague and Budapest, where interest in economic history is at present particularly strong for obvious reasons. At the same time it seems that the tendency to ascribe both interest and prestige to research in *modern*

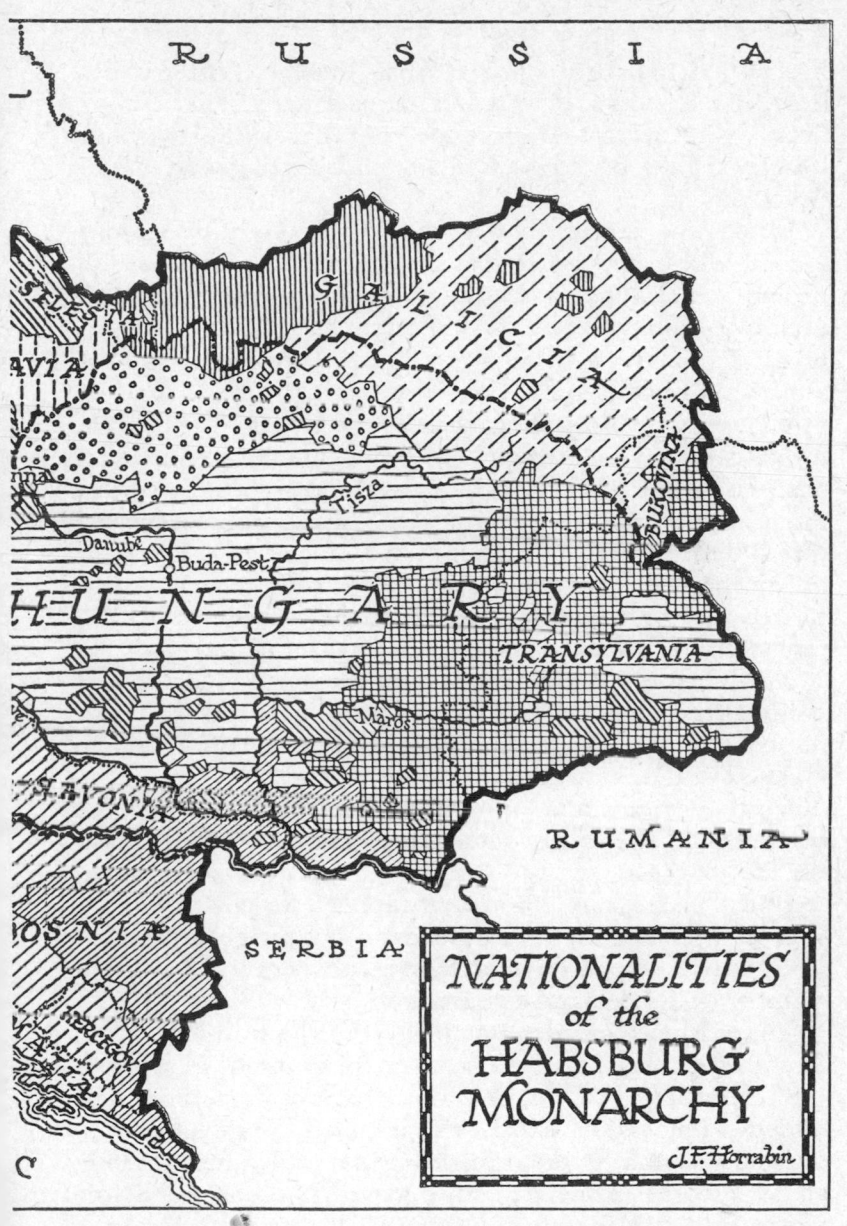

RUSSIA

GALICIA

BUKOVINA

Danube
Buda-Pest
Tisza

HUNGARY

TRANSYLVANIA

Maros

SLAVONIA

BOSNIA

SERBIA

RUMANIA

NATIONALITIES
of the
HABSBURG
MONARCHY

J.F. Horrabin

history has at last reached Central Europe. Last but not least, the concern of scholars in Germany, the United States, and other non-successor countries with Habsburg history should be considered an encouraging and useful development.

It may be permissible to round off this introductory section with a few reflections on the basic problem of the process which concerns us here. For this purpose it is most useful to think of industrialisation as resulting from a broad mobilisation of all the resources and energies at a society's disposal, achieving a discontinuous change in productivity levels and in their growth-path. Clearly the initial resource endowment, including human resources, is of crucial importance. With any given endowment, however, the process of transformation will be the more successful and rapid the fuller that 'mobilisation' of energies, i.e. their uni-purposeful channelling into economic development. Moreover, rapid growth in itself may then attract additional resources, from abroad and from 'non-gainful' pursuits.

This view evidently assumes the existence of social and political pressures towards modern economic growth. With respect to any follower country this is a safe assumption to make. The demonstration effects of successful industrialisation in Britain, and in other, earlier followers; the competition effects of factory products in domestic and export markets; as well as the growing importance of technical progress and industrial capacity for power politics, were all so strong, that the absence — not the occurrence — of imitative responses in a nineteenth century European country would demand explanation.

The existence of interests opposed to the transformation, on the other hand, can also be taken for granted. These were the institutions and forces which obstructed mobility and impeded innovation, which were inimical to rationalisation, to secularisation, to the primacy of material values. As long as the factors desiring economic change had only negligible power, industrialisation could not get under way. If, at the other extreme, social and political modernisation had already been in progress at the time that major economic stimuli and opportunities appeared, the combined impact of economic and non-economic forces in society could overcome the retarding factors and achieve the breakthrough to rapid growth. But in fact many societies did not conform to an 'all or nothing', stagnation or breakthrough, pattern. Where both sets of social forces manifested considerable vitality and persistence, the process of industrialisation was relatively slow and uneven. And the resulting social-economic framework, at any specific period, was full of contradictions and paradoxes. Such a case was the Habsburg Monarchy in the nineteenth century.

INITIAL CONDITIONS AND EARLY BEGINNINGS

The Habsburg Monarchy of the eighteenth and nineteenth centuries was composed of various geo-political blocks with quite different historical and cultural heritages. Moreover, its administrative subdivision only partly corresponded to economic data and ties. Ingenious attempts at presenting the Empire as a 'logical' economic entity built around the Danube river basin, though interesting exercises in *ex post* historical explanation, had to ignore fundamental geographical facts; and the same holds for each part of the 'dual' Monarchy. In particular, the provinces Galicia and Bukovina, annexed to the Empire in 1772-75, belonged to the 'Austrian' part, even though geographically they were in the east. Moreover, these two provinces as well as the Dalmatian Littoral lay beyond the mountain ranges which surrounded the bulk of the Habsburg domains, so that their economic ties were stronger with areas outside the Monarchy. At the other, western, extreme the small but economically active district of Vorarlberg was by nature part of the Swiss-Swabian textile region around Lake Constance, much more than it related to the majority of Austrian Alpine provinces. Without raising the vexed question of the Austro-Italian border, even to-day a matter of dispute, it is quite clear that Northern Italy, an area in which the extent of Habsburg rule varied from peace treaty to peace treaty, was in no meaningful sense an organic part of the Monarchy. No waterway led from Austria (nor from Hungary) to the Adriatic, and even after rail connection with Trieste was established (in 1854) this route was one of the most expensive for freight transportation. But even in the north the Empire had no indisputable natural boundary from the economic point of view. Although Moravia was orientated towards the Danube and especially towards the Vienna Basin, the same cannot be said for Bohemia. In spite of the mountain ranges which enclose this province in its characteristic rectangular shape, its waterway — the Moldau (Vltava)-Elbe rivers — leads to the North Sea. As a matter of fact the Elbe remained the chief link connecting Austria-Hungary with the Oceans, and Hamburg at least as important as Trieste for overseas imports and exports, until the very end of our period. It is therefore not surprising to find, that much of Bohemian economic activity was oriented to German markets and supplies. This tendency, in addition to its geographical basis, was reinforced by the ethnic and traditional connections between the Bohemian Germans and their neighbours beyond the border. Moreover, until most of Silesia was ceded to Prussia (finally in 1763) this had been the most developed Austrian province, the veritable jewel of the Bohemian Crown. Thus, many commercial and putting-out connections continued long after the political separation between Silesia and Bohemia, particularly in the textile industries.

We can generalise from these instances to say, that both geographic and historical factors combined to make the internal unity of the Austro-Hungarian Monarchy problematical. Over two-thirds of its area was covered by mountains and hills, and its most important river — the Danube — was unruly and in parts treacherous by nature. Transportation conditions were notoriously difficult, and later made railroad construction expensive. In addition to the ethnic diversity already referred to, the various provinces differed greatly in their general levels of economic and cultural development, as well as in their political heritage. Against these forces and traditions the policy of the Imperial government exerted itself to consolidate and unify, especially from the 1700's on. After laying the foundations of a centralised bureaucracy, Maria-Theresa and Joseph II (whose rule, partly overlapping as co-regency, lasted from 1740 to 1790) strove to achieve and buttress its supremacy over the institutions of seignorial, provincial, and ecclesiastical government. The Austrian version of 'enlightened' absolutism, also known as *Josephinismus*, remained the leading ideology of the Imperial bureaucracy at least until the 1860's, although it never succeeded in completely achieving its goals. In particular, the Magyar lords were on the whole quite effective in preserving many of their traditional privileges, including tax exemptions and the *de jure* legislative power of taxation, as well as a large degree of political autonomy in their rule over the Hungarian half of the Monarchy.

The administrative and legal reforms, in decreasing inter-regional differences and local powers of jurisdiction and law enforcement, definitely increased both mobility and security from the economic point of view. The wish to encourage economic development was certainly one of the principles that inspired many reforming measures, such as the decrees of religious toleration and civic emancipation (almost complete for non-Catholic Christians, partial for Jews). But economic development was viewed chiefly as a means for providing political aspirations with a sound foundation, more often than not understood in the narrow fiscal sense. To ascribe to the mercantilistic and paternalistic absolutism in Austria, or in any other country, the motives of a modern Welfare State is anachronistic. The interventionism of the later eighteenth century had yet to create the model of individual liberty and civic equality, by encroaching upon all institutional arrangements which interposed between the state and its subjects, before one could think of the need to limit such liberty and to counteract new types of inequality. The similarity between the concern of Maria-Theresa and her son with the improvement of education, with public health, or with population growth, and modern social legislation is therefore misleading. The conceptual framework as well as the social supports of the regime were entirely different.

For the economic unity and cohesion of the Monarchy the most important measures, after the currency reform of 1750 (source of the *Conventions*-florin in force until 1858, and of the famous Maria-Theresa thaler), were the tariff reforms. Most internal tariffs in the Austrian half of the Monarchy were abolished in 1775, in the Hungarian part in 1784; although the customs line between Austria and Hungary remained in force until 1851. In the years 1783-96 the two parts of Galicia and the province of Bukovina were joined to the Austrian unified customs area. Account had to be taken, however, of the geo-economic realities discussed above, and several areas were left outside the customs line of the Monarchy altogether: Tyrol and Vorarlberg (until 1825), the littoral provinces Istria and Dalmatia (until 1880), and a few free-trade cities of which the ports Trieste and Fiume (Rijeka) and the Galician border town Brody were the most important.

But for these exceptions, though, the entire Monarchy was enclosed by a common customs boundary, and by the so-called 'prohibitive' system. That was the Austrian name for an extreme form of mercantilist protectionist policy with respect to foreign trade. It consisted of import quotas, some of which were close to zero or outright import prohibitions; high duties on the permitted imports, at rates hoped to be forbiddingly high in effect; as well as high taxes or even prohibition on many primary export commodities. There were, of course, also measures aimed at encouraging exports of manufactures, and of those primary products (e.g. Galician grain) of which 'surplus' supplies were considered to be available. This foreign trade system was consistent with other aspects of Habsburg mercantilism, such as the ban on emigration and the encouragement of certain types of immigrants (see farther on), and with the general trend of considering population growth desirable which characterised that policy. Although the detailed measures of this system were varied periodically, it remained in effect, in its basic features, until mid-nineteenth century. The main concern of this Austrian version of mercantilism was not so much the balance of payments, as a kind of economic self-sufficiency. It was a 'Continental', inward-looking policy of development, and based on a very clear conception of regional complementary specialisation. The eastern provinces were destined to supply low-cost foodstuffs and raw materials to the western industrialising districts, and to serve correspondingly as their main markets for the products of crafts and factories.

Such division of labour was based, no doubt, on the existing structure of regional differences. Most fertile lands (though not the best-cultivated areas) were located in the lands of the Hungarian Crown and in Galicia, while the non-agricultural sector there was extremely small and retarded. Most centres of commerce and craftsmanship, on the other hand, were to be found in Bohemia, Moravia, and several of the Alpine provinces. To a major extent these were the results of natural endowment differences and of the previous historical fate of the various regions. And we know from theoretical analysis as well as from the historical experience of similar cases, that the mere joining together of these regions into a common customs area was likely to perpetuate and reinforce these structural differences, rather than levelling them out, through the operation of market mechanisms and in the absence of a consciously compensatory development policy.

The Imperial government, however, had no political interest in changing this structure, in diminishing the relative backwardness of the eastern provinces. Thus, on the contrary, all measures for the encouragement of industrial development (to be discussed in some detail farther on) were concentrated, in effect, in the western provinces. At the same time agricultural producers in the west, particularly in the Czech provinces, were afforded a degree of protection by the 'equalising' tax which was levied on Hungarian produce when crossing the internal customs line to the Austrian half of the Monarchy. As a result, the production of fine textiles, high grade iron and steel goods, and other manufacturing indigenous in western regions developed further; and was complemented by the growing output of foodstuffs (especially grain and livestock), raw wool and iron, but also coarse linen and woollens, in Hungary and Galicia.

Habsburg tariff policy was thus aimed both at the consolidation of the Empire and its relative economic isolation, as well as at consolidating and conserving the economic and cultural supremacy of the western, 'hereditary' Austro-Bohemian provinces. The historical concentration of the Monarchy's industry in a belt leading from Bohemia, through Moravia and the Vienna Basin, to Styria and Carinthia (with very few outlying enclaves) was effectively challenged only with the industrialisation policy of the autonomous Hungarian government from the 1880's on.

Moreover, the idea of Habsburg *Autarkie* was not a mere matter of choice, either, although rightfully pointing to the wealth and variety of the Empire's natural endowment. The small extent of foreign trade, though partly a result of policy, was a reflection of the basically underdeveloped stage of the commercial sector, relative to western Europe, of even the more developed parts of the Monarchy. This was the result of a combination of geographical and historical factors.[2] The poor transportation possibilities, already referred to above, obviously handicapped not only internal but also foreign trade. In addition, most Habsburg possessions were not advantageously situated within the network of European trade. Even in the late Middle Ages major trade routes had by-passed them; and their relative location deteriorated markedly in the early Modern Period, as the Continental economy became more and more Atlantic-oriented. While large sections of Germany, for instance, could take direct part in overseas trade, Austria (and Hungary even more so) remained dependent on inferior, indirect connections. Among historical developments which retarded the development of commercial capitalism in the Habsburg Monarchy, many scholars ascribe importance to the harm caused by the Counter-Reformation. The loss of

2. This discussion disregards, throughout, Austrian rule in the Southern Netherlands (1712–1797); and ignores, as too insignificant, recurring attempts at an Austrian overseas colonialism.

Silesia, a more recent setback, is of more certain relevance. If wholesale and foreign trade was crucial for the accumulation of capital and of entrepreneurial experience, and for the development of long-distance contacts, its small extent in the Austrian economy was particularly deplorable in the later eighteenth century, when foreign commerce — and especially trade with the Americas — fulfilled such a decisive role in stimulating industrial as well as agricultural production.

The weakness of the indigenous commercial sector found its expression in the relatively low degree of urban development, with an estimated 4·4 per cent of Austrian population in cities above 10,000 around 1800, and still a much lower proportion in Hungary. Even so, late-eighteenth century Austrian trade and banking was apparently heavily penetrated by foreign capital and enterprise: Germans, Swiss, Italians, and Greeks were prominent in domestic and foreign trade and connected activities. At the same time many industrial entrepreneurs were of the nobility. Not only because they had resources at their disposal, often under-employed manpower and natural wealth (in forests and mineral deposits) for which they saw new opportunities of gainful activity; but also because they had easier access to government subsidies, grants, and loans. Nevertheless, their pioneering role, in many cases undertaken at the Empress's instigation, was also indicative of the retardation of the bourgeoisie.

The policy of encouraging industrial development, begun by her father, Charles VI, was carried on by Maria-Theresa with special vigour in order to compensate for the loss of Silesia. In its principles and measures it corresponded to German *Kameralismus* even more closely than to French Colbertism. Aristocratic and middle-class *Fabrikanten* were aided by loans, tax exemptions, and the like, and if necessary excused military service and guaranteed freedom of worship. Many of them had been induced by the Court to go into such ventures, particularly a number of Bohemian lords; others had been enticed from Germany, the Netherlands, or Switzerland. Several of the larger firms were taken over by the government when they ran into too many deficits, but this practice was discontinued towards the end of the mercantilist period. For increasing the supply of industrial labour, at the various levels of skill and technical education, the Austrian government went to great lengths to attract craftsmen and technicians from abroad (including England, Italy, and Silesia), promising them not only high wages but also housing, exemption from conscription, and similar benefits. Furthermore, by means of instructors and special 'schools' improved techniques of spinning, weaving, and knitting or lacing were diffused in the rural areas. Most important, perhaps, were the exemptions granted to the new industrial establishments from the rules and supervision of the guilds. These 'privileges' were at first on a purely *ad hoc* basis, but slowly generalised to certain types of products and firms. As a matter of fact, well into the nineteenth century legal status, rather than size or technology, determined whether a firm was considered a 'factory' or a trade-shop. This was, however, general Continental practice; as was the confusion between manufactories, putting-out firms, and early factories (i.e. mechanised plants) in statistics and regulations.

It is hard to evaluate, and impossible to try and quantify, the impact of these measures (or of the importation of Merino sheep to Moravia) on the growth and directions of industrial output. In many cases a handful of experts or the encouragement of a loan must have been of strategic importance; in others the subsidised firms might have been established in any case, or constituted misplaced investments and a misallocation of effort. But it is highly probable that the chief influences of government policy on the development of industry were on the demand side. Some of these were direct effects, results of conscious measures, while others were indirect, incidental results of policy means aimed at non-economic goals.

First on the demand side are to be counted, no doubt, the effects of the policy of centralisation and consolidation of the Empire, which has been described above. At the same time that the supplies of foodstuffs and raw materials to manufacturing centres were increased, the market for industrial products was increased and unified significantly. This was achieved by the tariff, legal, and administrative reforms, as well as by highway construction during the eighteenth century (even in the mountains, where the cost deterrent was outweighed by political and military considerations), and by improvements in communications (from 1722 the mail was considered a state service in Austria). Second in importance were the various direct government demands, for war and peace, for the army, the Court, and even the bureaucracy (e.g. paper). Most larger establishments relied on the need of the Court and high society for luxury consumption (including import-substitutes, made possible by the protective system), or on the big army purveyors (which meant more standardised and large-scale production), as their mainstay. In this respect the numerous wars and chronic deficits of the Theresan-Josephine era (in 1762 the Austrian government pioneered in the issue of paper-money, the later notorious *Bankozettel*) stimulated production much more than they restrained it through cuts in subsidisation.

The result of all these developments, and of population growth which set in throughout the various Habsburg provinces during the eighteenth century, was a considerable growth of industrial production, both in old-established and in recently introduced branches. In the Alpine provinces excellent iron deposits had for long been the basis of extensive iron and steel manufacturing; first class steel products, such as cutlery and scythes, and sickles, were successful export items. In Vorarlberg (for export) and in the Vienna region textiles were prominent, with linen still strong and cotton (first introduced in 1724) gaining. In and around the capital luxury production was, of course, concentrated, among which silken and woollen fine fabrics were increasingly dominated by large-scale firms. The largest *Manufaktur* for woollens, in Linz (Upper Austria), was acquired by the state in 1754 and flourished until the 1780's. In Bohemia and Moravia, too, textiles were the most dynamic industry, whether in linen, wool, or cotton. Glass exports were still going strong, earthenware and porcelain production was developing. The vast majority of firms operated, in accord with the state of technology, by combining putting-out in rural areas with the employment of urban artisans for the more skilled and capital-intensive operations (whether on the firm's premises or also on a piece-work basis). A quantitative indication of this growth is provided by the reported doubling of sales from the western provinces to Galicia and the Hungarian lands during the last decade of the eighteenth century.

As in other parts of Continental Europe at that time, the connections and interdependence between agricultural and industrial production, as well as between them and population growth, were very close in late-eighteenth century Austria. Not only was a large portion of manufacturing carried out by rural domestic work, but a probably even higher part of mining and smelting was in effect a rural side-line. Other raw materials came from the fields and forests (including dyestuffs, and of course charcoal). Needless to say, carts and rafts were operated by peasants, and many a carter or village innkeeper branched out into commerce. Unskilled and semi-skilled rural labour, especially in the mountainous regions, was constantly shifting among mining, forestry, transportation, and agriculture, mainly in a seasonal pattern; and most of these day-labourers had tiny cultivated plots of their own. On the other hand, the rural dispersion of manufacturing provided demand for marketing of foodstuffs in the most outlying areas. Population growth, in part stimulated by additional employment opportunities, went to the larger extent into agriculture. Some innovations (such as the potato) and improvements spread, but mostly production was increased by land reclamation. A certain proportion of the additional population, however, became rural-industrial workers, some even without any land to tend. This was, again, mainly prevalent in the mountains, above all in the Bohemian and Moravian ones.

In this connection reference must be made to a so far here neglected aspect of the reform period, the peasant 'protection' policy of Maria-Theresa and the 'emancipation' decrees of Joseph II. Contemporaries were much impressed by the granting of personal freedom to all remaining serfs in the Habsburg domains, and this impression contributed substantially to the image of Austria as the most progressive government in Continental Europe on the eve of the French Revolution. But except on a part of the Crown Lands, the basic problems of tenure and of labour dues (called *Robot*, following the Slav provinces) were barely touched upon. The remnants of irksome personal servitudes, from feudal times, were abolished (at least *de jure*), and this resulted in the freedom to marry and to learn a craft, among others. But it is doubtful if effective mobility of the peasants actually ensued since a tenant who wanted to leave the land had to satisfy both his lord and the conscription authorities that he had no obligations outstanding. On the other hand, in conjunction with the phenomenon of population increase the granting of personal freedom to all peasant sons contributed to the occupational mobility of rural labour, and thus to the development of mining, industry, and even commerce. Moreover, the legal reforms (especially the penal code) and the growing power of the Imperial administration diminished the hold that the landlords had upon their peasants, by law and by force of their social and economic superiority.

The period of the Napoleonic wars exerted new pressures and disclosed new opportunities. Much of Europe's trade was dislocated; the enormous military demand for both goods and manpower produced shortages and inflation; not least England's technological revolution was making its impact on the Continent. In the face of these pressures and opportunities conditions over much of the Habsburg Empire were ripe for the introduction of factory-industry: capital, skills, and enterprise were available, and the institutional framework was reasonably favourable. The question of the long-run potential for a successful Industrial Revolution, though, was a more difficult one.

POLITICS AND ECONOMIC GROWTH IN THE NINETEENTH CENTURY

From the late 1790's until the fall of Napoleon, all over western and central Europe the preliminary spread of the Industrial Revolution became manifest, first of all in the rise of large mechanised cotton mills. In several centres, later on, the need for spinning and preparatory machinery gave the impetus for a domestic engineering industry. Bohemia, Moravia, and Lower Austria had their respectable share in this movement, isolated instances of which spread as far east as Hungary. As a matter of fact, one of the largest yarn mills on the Continent was probably in Pottendorf, near Vienna, significantly managed by an English mechanic. As elsewhere in Central Europe, the more vigorous and progressive firms in cotton and wool spinning survived the onset of peace and the slump of the 1820's; and even some textile machinery continued to be locally constructed, although it was much more expensive than in western Europe. Similarly among the lines claiming the distinction of having been the first railroad on the Continent the Habsburg Monarchy has a respectable candidate. The line Budweis-Linz really was the first Continental one of significant length, with 130 kilometres in 1832 (after seven years of construction), and 200 kilometres after its extension to the salt mines at Gmunden (in 1836).

Such auspicious beginnings notwithstanding, we do not find the Monarchy, or even its Austrian half by itself, among what may be termed the industrial nations at the end of the nineteenth century. Its share in world trade, and particularly in that of industrial products, was disproportionally small. In 1910 about 53 per cent of the economically active population of Austria was still engaged in agriculture, in Hungary as much as two-thirds. Domestic and foreign observers of the Austrian economy were well aware of its relative backwardness, of its slower rate of growth and industrialisation. This frustrating feeling became progressively more acute during the second half of the century; and it was so intense (and perhaps even exaggerated) because the most frequent comparison was with the German economic performance. Still, the estimated per capita national income, on the eve of the First World War, was in Austria only *circa* 60 per cent of the German, and less than 75 per cent of the French.

It is very tempting to put at least part of the blame for this apparently poor economic performance on political and social circumstances. At the same time the political historian will tend to attribute much indecision and failure to the weakness of the economy. This problem, with its danger of circular argumentation, has already been referred to in the introductory section above, at whose end the way out of the dilemma was also indicated. Clearly the argument is not circular of necessity; and just as comparative historical analysis poses the problem, a solution should be based on it, and such is the line of thought followed here. We have seen in the preceding section that the initial conditions for modern economic growth in the Monarchy, the combination of natural endowment and economic and social history, were not uniformly favourable at the end of the eighteenth century. In absolute levels of economic development, major sections of the Empire were extremely backward by West-European standards, while commercial capitalism was relatively retarded even in the more developed areas. In the course of the nineteenth century, as we shall see, the resources on which early Austrian industry had been based proved in several regions unfavourable for rapid growth under the new technological conditions. In particular, Hungary as well as the Alpine regions and the Vienna basin, the latter two traditional centres of industry, suffered from a quite severe lack of coal deposits, and of cokeable coal especially. In theory, such deficiencies in the prerequisites for rapid industrialisation could have been overcome by a concerted effort of private and government enterprise. Thus, e.g., coal could have been imported in even larger quantities than it was in fact, and existing resources could have been more rapidly opened up. But this would have required strong leadership, an effective fusion of policy goals, and a heavy emphasis on economic growth as a national objective. In this way the resources of private entrepreneurs as well as those mobilised by taxation, together with other administrative and fiscal means, could all be directed towards achieving a 'mix' of consistent political and economic goals, such as the unification and industrialisation of Germany.

In the actual historical circumstances of the Habsburg Monarchy, however, such a type of policy was impossible. The preservation of the Monarchy and of its dominant role in European power politics was the overriding policy goal of the Imperial government throughout the nineteenth century, although the struggle for achieving this goal became more and more frustrating and futile. Since the main supports of the Empire and its dynastic regime were the aristocracy (and the hierarchical principle in general), the Church, the army and bureaucracy, as well as the interests of the ruling social-ethnical classes in certain provinces — a policy of rapid modernisation and of promoting meritocratic social trends was out of the question. Moreover, although most Austrian governments in the second half of the century included promotion of industry in their policy-mix, each according to its fashion, none could pursue rapid industrialisation as a national objective. This, first of all, because no 'national' policy, in the strict sense, was to be envisioned. In Habsburg Austria nationalism was anathema, and the more so the stronger it became in the various provinces and in semi-autonomous Hungary (after 1867). Furthermore, since the German-speaking Austrian upper-middle classes were mostly convinced that the preservation of the Empire served their own economic and emotional objectives, they could not become the leaders of a strive for rapid transformation of the institutional framework. The most advanced bourgeoisie in the Monarchy thus became a partner of the supernational forces which held the Empire together, although these were mostly the very groups whose interests were endangered by capitalism in general and rapid industrialisation in particular. The result was a constant manoeuvring for compromises, which became so typical of Austrian domestic politics. The symbolic manifestation of this basic incompatibility of the economic and political goals of the Austrian-German bourgeoisie, led by the Viennese, was its persistent adherence to quasi-feudal social values (including in its consumption patterns). I have referred to these internal contradictions in the set of interests of both the Austrian government and the private entrepreneurial sector in the introductory section above, and we shall see them at work in the specific instances discussed throughout the present section.

On the whole, direct governmental influence on the course of economic developments was smaller in the nineteenth century than in eighteenth century Austria-Hungary. Still, it is important to point out that the progressiveness and leadership of the reform period was definitely lost by the well-known conservatism of the Metternich era. The reaction to Joseph's more extreme reforms had set in immediately with his death, in 1790, but only after the wars did the 'system' crystallise. In domestic as well as foreign policy the *Vormärz* regime, from 1815 to 1848, was determined to prevent another French Revolution anywhere in Europe. From this principle Francis I derived not only his opposition to the growth of industry (and with it of a proletariat) in his capital, Vienna, but his general reluctance to permit any change whatsoever. It was this rigid and suspicious attitude which prevented his granting the concession for a railway to the north. At least from the economic point of view, however, this is only half the story. Even though the system was intended as a rigidly conservative autocracy, its functioning was somewhat less rigid. Implementation was in the hands of the bureaucracy, whose ceremonious and ponderous ways, whose very excessive punctiliousness did not make for very effective administration. Moreover, just as Francis utilised procedural rules and intentional procrastination whenever they suited his aims, his officials could — if they would — try to use the same means for partly undermining, or at least mitigating, his policies. And indeed the higher ranks were permeated by relatively enlightened individuals. In their reading of

Josephinismus, one could adhere to the theory of economic liberalism, while concurrently denying political personal freedom. Much was done, therefore, to liberalise the rules of economic activity and to increase mobility of factors and property. All this, though, on a small-scale and often semi-official basis. Fundamental changes had to wait until the regime was under stronger attack.

Thus, while in the first half of the century a patchwork of modern industrial centres did grow up, this was still within a predominantly agrarian and artisan economy. Farmers and craftsmen, too, faced increasing inducement to produce for a wider market, but institutional and technological conservatism was strong among them. Perhaps the more so, because the islands of laissez-faire were also still surrounded by the sea of pre-capitalist traditions and relations.

In retrospect, one of the chief paradoxes of the *Vormärz* regime was its strict protectionist tariff policy. In intent it was based on historical continuity, and aimed at the promotion of Austrian industry. In effect, as most historians agree, it was a major factor in preventing faster industrial growth and innovation in this crucial period. This was recognised by a few officials, who prepared a reform programme in 1841–43, supported by Metternich, with the hope of thus paving the way for a fusion with the *Zollverein.* For this very reason the project was opposed by vested industrial interests, mainly those of the Vienna and Alpine centres (while in Bohemia supporters were numerous). In any case it is doubtful if both domestic conservatism and Prussian opposition could have been overcome. When in the 1850's the Austrian government was willing to overcome the opposition of group interests at home, political conditions in Germany were even much worse. Prussian leadership had become more consolidated, and her contention for exclusive predomination more self-conscious and revealed. The possibility of unifying Germany without — or even in opposition to — Austria was becoming dimly perceptible. Last not least, German nationalism had become much more articulate and influential, so that the multi-national composition of the Habsburg Monarchy was much more of an obstacle to its fusion with the *Zollverein* than it had been in the forties.

The peculiarities of doing business in such an institutional environment are perhaps best exemplified by the anecdotal story of the first Austrian railway, which has been mentioned above. The line was proposed, financed, and operated by private enterprise. Three banking houses with close Court connections founded the company, but the first 850,000 florins were subscribed by the public within one week (in March, 1825). Public opinion was much impressed by the vision of a link 'between the North and the Black Seas,' since the route connected the Moldau with the Danube. Soon, however, construction exceeded the original estimate both in cost and in time. The extension to Gmunden was conceived to ensure the profitability of the whole enterprise, Rothschild joined the original founders, and the additional *Privilegium* was obtained in 1832. The most crucial decision, however, had been taken already in 1828, when at the opening of the first section (65 kilometres) the initial budget of 1,000,000 florins was all but exhausted. The line, though intended for a horse-drawn train, had been built at first with a strong permanent way cautiously avoiding sharp curves. Now, however, specifications were revised to lower costs, and by doing so a future conversion to steam traction was consciously forgone. This was done against the counsel of Gerstner, the original concessionaire and the line's chief engineer until then, and at a time when the superiority of the locomotive had already been established. In France, as a matter of fact, steam traction was introduced in the very same year, on the Loire line. Was this a peculiar Austrian style of technical innovation, stressing short run appearances at the expense of growth potential? Was it an expression of despair from ever obtaining a steam railroad concession from the Imperial government? Or was it a rational decision, based on the confidence that government aid, in the form of tax exemption and the exclusive concession for salt transportation from Upper Austria to Bohemia, would guarantee monopoly profits even when the company's equipment was obsolete? In any case, the first Austrian railroad remained horse-drawn until the late 1860's, a living relic from a bygone era.

It is a moot question which of the Austrian industries would have prospered in the 1830's and 1840's under conditions of freer trade with other industrialising countries, and with Germany in particular. To most firms, no doubt, the protection of their market seemed preferable, and they viewed the low standard of living in the eastern provinces with indifference, counting (potential) consumers rather than purchasing power. The most we can criticise them for, in retrospect, is a too short time horizon. From the regime's viewpoint, the function of the tariff was to preserve Austrian superiority in the Empire, while satisfying the emerging industrial class to an extent sufficient for preserving domestic stability. And indeed the Austrian bourgeoisie made its peace with the *Vormärz* regime and with later 'conservative' governments. They preferred the security of political stability and a protected market, and probably also the glory of the Monarchy, to the hazards of parliamentarism, international trade, and autonomy to the non-German nationalities. It was this assignment of priority to the preservation of the Empire by the German-Austrian middle class which was a major factor in the outcome of the 1848–49 upheaval, as is well known. In the short run this preference helped to re-establish the absolute regime. In the longer run it found its expression in the relative absence of nationalist identification among the most developed ethnic group in the Monarchy.

Ironically, the 'neo-absolutist' regime which lasted from 1849 to 1860 (at least) entirely revised tariff policy, both by abolishing the interior Austro-Hungarian customs line and by leading the Monarchy as close to Free Trade as it ever was to come. The motives were primarily political, domestic and foreign, but a contributing factor was the belief of the leading bureaucrats in the virtues of economic liberalism. This at a time when, as a result of the defeat of the revolution and the reorganisation of government, the administration had become more self-confident and in many aspects more efficient. The breakthrough came with the new tariff of

1852, which did away with prohibitions and lowered rates considerably, and with the commercial treaty with Prussia of 1853. Further reductions came with the tariff of 1854, and in the late 1860's the Monarchy joined the round of commercial treaties which constituted the (short-lived) triumph of Free Trade ideology in Europe. By then, however, the political ambitions had been frustrated, and economic interests with respect to tariff policy were starting to shift in the face of new developments in world trade. With the tariff of 1878 the period of relatively low duties came to its end.

The most revolutionary act of the 1848 revolution, the Peasant Emancipation (which, perhaps out of deference to Joseph's decrees, was termed Land Emancipation: *Grundentlastung*), had to be retained and actually implemented by the neo-absolutist government. In essence this was one of the most sensible and just agrarian reforms in nineteenth century Europe, the more impressively so since the ruling classes had not been overthrown. The peasants were to retain all land held by them on the basis of feudal-type subjection (i.e. contractual tenancy was not affected), and were freed of all obligations towards their previous lords — payments in money, kind, and labour (*Robot*), as well as judicial and administrative subjection. The lords were to be compensated for loss of their income (not of their rights) along the following lines: *Robot* days were evaluated at one-third of wage labour; produce by tax assessment values; and one-third of total peasant dues was written off as the lord's expenses in carrying out his governmental functions. The yearly sums thus calculated were capitalised to a twentyfold amount. In Hungary the rules were different, and compensation was generally set at about one-third the market value of the land. All lords' compensation was paid out in 5 per cent bonds to be redeemed by lot within forty years. In Hungary and Galicia-Bukovina the burden of servicing and redeeming the bonds was carried by the central Imperial government. In the other Austrian provinces half of the sum was paid by the peasants, also over forty years, and half by the provincial (*Land*) government. In the Alpine provinces, where practically all servitudes had already been commuted into money payments, implementation of these arrangements was completed by 1854. In the Bohemian and eastern provinces the process was drawn out longer, and the fairness by which the determination of rights and dues and their assessment were carried through must have varied considerably from district to district.

As far as the reform went, its implications for economic growth were on the whole favourable. In the crucial aspect of retaining all rustical land the peasants in the Monarchy fared considerably better than their Prussian or Russian counterparts, and the same can be said of the burden and arrangements of redemption payments. The achievement of personal economic freedom was immediate; and this applied in most regions also to disposal of the land. In fact, later public discussion and some legislation was concerned with restricting the peasants' right to sell or fragmentate their holdings, and to the problems arising from rural indebtedness. In general Emancipation did not solve the problems of 'enclosure', i.e. the consolidation of holdings and the division and optimal utilisation of the commons. Neither legislation nor *de facto* settlements had solved the bulk of these questions in the Monarchy even after seventy more years; but it must be remembered that interests conflicted not only between lords and peasants, in this respect, but also between peasant owners and the landless proletariat. Socio-economic relations, in general, were at best left unchanged. The distribution of land and agricultural incomes remained unbalanced or polarised. The great lords retained sufficient economic basis for continuing their powerful political influence, and in many a case added to it by branching farther out into mining, industry, and even banking. In many provinces the political pattern was complicated by the national-ethnic aspects of class structure. While in Austria, when the peasantry was eventually granted the franchise, it proved itself no less a politically 'conservative' element than in France, for instance.

The incentives for increased production, and especially for improving agricultural techniques and organisation, had undeniable results, of which the growth and spread of sugar beet cultivation was symptomatic. This applies first of all to the owners of large estates, the previous domains, who predominated in Hungary and Bohemia but were to be found in all provinces. They were, on the one hand, faced with the need — so conducive to modernisation — to adjust to the loss of labour dues, and with new possibilities for obtaining credit on the strength of their redemption debentures on the other hand. The higher efficiency of free wage labour, particularly if combined with the partial substitution of capital and technological change for farm labour, proved itself throughout the Monarchy. If in the setting of new legal mobility less efficient farmers (both on domain and on peasant land) had to sell out, or too small units could not keep pace with the modernisers and were liquidated, this was not necessarily undesirable from the economic, as distinct from the social, viewpoint. Whether bought by big neighbours or by capital-endowed urban entrepreneurs, this land was certainly better utilised; even if a number of middlemen had made 'speculative' profits from the transfer. The incentives for growth and change were not, however, restricted to the large estates. Despite the obvious advantages of larger owners in obtaining information and evaluating it, the small peasant owners in the Monarchy were not necessarily inimical to market- and profit-oriented production. The strategic restraint was not the peasant's much exaggerated economic conservatism; but rather his actual ability to feel the impact of urban and foreign demand, dependent upon the size of these demands and upon communications, and to mobilise resources for his response. In this connection the concern towards the close of the century with peasant indebtedness is evidence not only of unsolved social problems but also of the extent to which smallholders raised mortgages on their land so as to have the means of developing it. The same is indicated by the spread of village credit co-operatives, mainly from the 1890's.

It was not only in the country that economic mobility presented a problem. In the towns, the *Gewerbefreiheit*, the right to choose one's occupation, was no less crucial: and its history reflects the transitory character of the liberal economic regime in Austria-Hungary. In spite of various advances towards institutional change, such as the revised mining law of 1854, it was only at the very end of the 'neo-absolutist' decade — in December, 1859 — that the Industrial Regulation decree could be pushed through. It did establish virtually full occupational freedom; but its rule was to be short. The government was soon driven to shifts to maintain the integrity of the Empire, among them a kind of extended protectionism. It was to appear as the protector of all groups and interests, as the balancing arbiter between agrarians and industrialists, upper and lower bourgeoisie, capitalists and proletarians. As the antagonism of nationalities became more embittered, and the 'great depression' made economic conflicts more acute, the regime staked its hope for survival on the lower middle class and even on the salaried and wage-earning masses. This led not only to a successive extension of the franchise by 'conservative' governments, in 1882, in 1897 and in 1907; but also to a new trend in legislation, from the 1880's on, which brought limiting amendments to the *Gewerbeordnung* together with various factory and insurance acts (after the German model). This corresponded to the attempts at balancing agrarian and industrial tariff protection. Paradoxically, the protection of the 'smallest' man by social insurance and the shielding of small business from crushing encroachment was coupled with a permissive, even encouraging attitude to the cartelisation of big business. As in Germany, cartels were considered desirable tools of law and order.

For the industrialist both tradition and self-interest suggested that the minimising of competition was the easiest way of maximising profits, just as protective tariffs offered immediate shelter against lack of resources and deficiencies of transport. Without minimising the role played by the banks, especially the joint-stock investment banks which had been introduced to Austria in the mid-fifties, in promoting mergers and cartels, the connection and mutual support between such organisations and the tariff has to be stressed. Industrial (and agricultural) trade associations were typically organised, to begin with, for the purpose of influencing tariff policy. Such associations, however, did not only provide a convenient setting for collusive agreements, but the very tariff protection which had been their original objective was now the soundest foundation for market-sharing and price supporting arrangements. Thus it is no accident that various forms of industrial organisation emerged already in the 1840's, and that towards the end of the century cartelisation in Austria-Hungary was more inclusive even than in Germany.

This is not the place for a detailed survey of Austrian fiscal and monetary policy in the nineteenth century, a period in which government had in any case much less economic weight than in the preceding or following century. An almost permanent characteristic of Austrian finances is manifest, though, the deficit budget. Theory and intentions notwithstanding, power politics and wars recurrently overthrew the most prudent budgetary planning. In addition to borrowing, more and more domestically as the century went on, the Austrian government had extensive recourse to the printing press, and for certain periods also to the sale of state property. The main era of chronic deficits lasted from 1848 to 1890. The Austrian florin was on a silver standard, but in practice (with legal recognition) irredeemable from 1848 until the establishment of a gold-standard currency (the crown) in 1892. During that period the Monarchy therefore had in effect a fluctuating exchange rate, as foreign currencies, bills, and securities could be traded freely. Since the extent of the deficit, and in particular of currency inflation, as well as the exchange rate varied considerably and unsystematically throughout the period, it is of course impossible to generalise about their influences. The rate of interest in the Monarchy was generally above that of Western Europe, but this was more indicative of its overall relative backwardness than of fiscal policy specifically. No doubt, though, the government deficit competed with investment projects for foreign and domestic loan funds. That a rise in the premium at which silver was bought increased exports and restrained imports is only partly correct even though the idea is prevalent in the literature; such a rise usually only counteracted the adverse effects of inflationary pressures on the balance of trade. On the expenditure side, the government demand for army supplies acted, of course, as a stimulant to various industries, mainly in the metal, engineering, and textile branches. This was particularly felt from the beginning of the twentieth century, when armament programmes were increasing rapidly all over Europe. In the last decades the Imperial government also increased its spending on infrastructure investments, mainly in transportation but also in irrigation and other land amelioration. In these areas, as in education and public buildings, the effects of which exceed their monetary dimensions by far, the central government also transferred income from the more to the less developed regions in the Monarchy.

Of particular import for industrial development in Austria-Hungary were the railways, as in other Continental countries. In this respect government policy underwent peculiar changes, which reflected many of the inner contradictions of the economy and its political system. The first important Austrian trunk lines, going north and south from Vienna, were started by private enterprise in the late 1830's. (Steam navigation had been started on the Danube already in 1830, and this important company remained in private hands all the time.) But an Imperial decree of 1841 reserved for the state, on principle, both the planning of the network and the construction, operation, and also acquisition of any specific line at will. The *Nordbahn* was continued by private capital, and from 1848 connected Vienna with the European network, via Prussian Silesia. But of 1070 kilometres in the Monarchy (including Northern Italy) that year, almost half had been constructed by the state. After 1850 operations were started by the government, too, and in 1854 *circa* 70 per cent of the lines were state railways. By then, however, it had become clear how heavy a burden the building and operating of railways was, and how far behind Germany and western countries Austria had fallen (in Hungary railways were still rudimentary in 1850). At the same time power-political demands were constantly increasing the deficit and raising the exchange premium. In the autumn of 1854 the policy was therefore reversed: a new concession law promised private ownership for 90 years, and a minimum-return guarantee; and several months later the government was authorised to sell its own lines. Until 1858 all state lines, including the just completed strategic *Südbahn*, were sold off; but the budget and currency were saved in vain — the war of 1859 upset them again. In any case it is clear that the great spurts in railway construction, in the later fifties and from 1867 to 1873, were carried out by private capital, although with the aid of government subsidisation (exempt rail imports and return-guarantees); while the state retained the basic planning function of determining the routes, not the least for their political and military usefulness. By 1875 there were 10,336 km. in Austria (after the loss of Italy) and 6,422 in Hungary. Now, however, both economic conditions and political ideas were different again, under the impact of the great depression. Until 1881 the Austrian government purchased private lines on the verge of bankruptcy, and from that year embarked on an official programme of nationalising the railways. The programme proceeded somewhat by jolts and jerks, as did state construction of additional lines, but long run progress was quite impressive. The largest purchases were in 1907–09, including the *Nordbahn*. When in 1913 the total Austrian network amounted to almost 23,000 km. 19,000 of them were state railroads. In Hungary a somewhat lower proportion of the total 22,000 km. were either state owned or state operated.

THE PHASES OF INDUSTRIAL GROWTH

It is not surprising to find that the rhythm of Austrian industrialisation corresponded by and large to the general European 'long swings' and business cycles. Thus, the first major impetus to modernisation and mechanisation of manufacturing came in the 1830's and lasted until *circa*

1846-47. The leading or at least most active sectors were the typical ones for the period — textiles and iron. These, in particular cotton and pig iron, were to remain the most important, best organised, and most protected branches of Austrian industry, and their growth remained geared predominantly to the domestic market of the Monarchy. Within 15 years to the peak of 1846, total 'exports' to Hungary from the Austrian provinces more than doubled, i.e. grew at a yearly average rate of 5 per cent. Another important market was the 'Kingdom' of Lombardy and Venetia, incorporated into the Empire's customs area in 1817 (and since statistically counted with 'Austria'). This North Italian market was an influential factor in the early revival of the textile industry during the 1820's, despite considerable competition by smuggling. (Reportedly, travelling salesmen of English and French firms in Northern Italy quoted prices including the risk-premium of the smugglers. Contemporaries were also of the opinion that many spinning factories at the Bohemian border were in fact only re-reeling English yarn; but it is impossible to evaluate the extent of such activities.) Several important firms from Germany and Switzerland established branches in Austria, so as not to lose their share in the North Italian market in cottons and woollens. The house of Schöller, of the leading 'captains' of Austrian industry throughout the century, was started that way.

The cotton industry of Lower Austria was based on eighteenth century developments, which had relied on the Viennese market on the one hand and on the advantageous situation of the area on the raw cotton supply routes from the Levant on the other. Spinning was mechanised during the blockade years, and benefited from the numerous small streams in the district south of the capital. This initial advantage in power supply later retarded the introduction of steam engines in this area. By the end of the 1830's cotton spinning in Lower Austria was practically all by machines, and mechanisation as well as the use of new chemicals was spreading vigorously in printing. The earlier spinning mills were parts of integrated firms which marketed only finished fabrics, but from 1801 on some of the largest were specialised firms. In Bohemia the cotton industry had its main centre in the north, around Liberec (Reichenberg), but the most important printing firms were in and about Prague. Spinning mills in Bohemia were on the average smaller than in Lower Austria, but started to use steam engines, at least as auxiliary motors, earlier. They were also more closely related to the other stages of fabric production. The leading cotton firms of Bohemia were built around a spinning or a printing plant, with a network of rural and urban putting-out for the weaving and finishing processes. The third cotton province of the Monarchy was small Vorarlberg, where during the *Vormärz* period local enterprise and capital slowly replaced the Swiss in the leading role. In total there were 435,000 cotton spindles in the Monarchy in 1828 (225,000 of these in Lower Austria, and 118,000 in Bohemia); almost 1,000,000 in 1841 (of which there were 388,000 in Lower Austria, 355,000 in Bohemia); and 1,346,000 in 1847. Austrian spinning was heavily concentrated on the coarser yarns, not the least because the tariff was per weight of yarn and thus afforded more protection to the lower counts. Weaving was practically all by hand, except in Vorarlberg, where 466 power looms (and almost ten times as many hand looms) were counted as early as 1841.

The wool processing industry in Austria developed rapidly in the 1830's and 1840's, and had its main centres in the districts of Vienna, Brno (the capital of Moravia), and Liberec. In the Moravian centre, in particular, it developed as a fashion industry, with two distinct seasons per year and a rapid turnover of patterns and designs. This character contributed strongly to the predominance of relatively small firms, who usually bought their yarn from spinning firms (or put the spinning out to them, even when they were mechanised), while keeping in close contact with the weaving and finishing either by putting-out or by having it done on the premises. Many of the Moravian designs called for mixed fabrics, i.e. using cotton and wool or other combinations. This fact frustrated the collectors of statistical data on the numerous hand looms, which could not be neatly classified according to the different textile branches. In general, Moravia was and remained the chief weaving province of the Monarchy, and supplied its services to, and bought yarn from, Bohemia and Lower Austria. Cloth and woollens were sent to Hungary, Galicia, Northern Italy, and abroad mainly to the Americas. Articles of the textile and clothing industries of Moravia and Vienna, which were closely interrelated, were exported to the Balkan and Levant countries, including specialised items for these areas (e.g. fezzes); although this export developed more in the second half of the century. Yarns were also imported in considerable quantities, especially the finer quantities, from England, Switzerland, and worsted also from Germany. In all discussions and lobbying with respect to tariffs the conflict of interests between the spinneries and weaving firms in Austria was prominent. The mechanisation of wool spinning in Austria did not lag much behind that of cotton spinning, and by the end of the 1830's it dominated the industry. Other processes, in preparation and finishing, began to be mechanised from the 1830's on, and the larger and more progressive firms and areas slowly, but surely, gained the lead in the industry. Weaving of all types of textiles, however, was still mostly carried out by hand (sometimes domestically, but more in small or even larger craft shops) throughout the century. In 1829 an Austrian treatise on technological progress (by Keess and Blumenbach) had already stated categorically that hand-weaving (of cotton) was a doomed craft in the Monarchy. In 1859 an official committee of inquiry found that machine-weaving of all sorts was still on a very small scale (especially in Lower Austria), even though progress had been made in recent years (particularly in northern Bohemia). While as late as 1902 Chapman expressed the view that 'Austria is one of the countries in which the battle between hand looms and power looms still continues'.

As in many other countries, linen remained the technologically backward, as well as the declining sector, of the textile industries in Austria-Hungary. The processing of flax (and hemp) fibres had been the original indigenous production of fabrics in almost all provinces of the Monarchy, and a flourishing export industry in several (largest of which, in output and exports, had been Silesia). Accordingly, this industry was strongly entrenched in the rural areas, and particularly in the mountain districts, both for local consumption and for the markets or merchant firms. When driven out of domestic and foreign markets by cotton fabrics, the linen industry lost many of its workers to this new sector, the transition being quite easy in most production stages. These were the domestic workers which suffered most from the Industrial Revolution, while trying to retain their (partial or full) livelihood from obsolete techniques. Since the British linen industry had mechanised earlier, even if lagging itself behind other textiles, Continental export centres (such as Bohemia) not only lost further export markets but also felt the competition of cheap and superior British yarns at home. As a result, some firms in Austria, especially in northern Bohemia, introduced mechanical flax spinning from the late 1830's, and this spread not insignificantly during the 1840's. Rural linen production was extensive also in Galicia and Hungary; otherwise these eastern provinces of the Monarchy remained practically without any textile industry whatsoever until the very end of the century.

The 1830's and 1840's also witnessed the development of coal mining in Austria-Hungary, from very small earlier beginnings. Anthracite and bituminous coal deposits were mainly in Moravia-Silesia and in Bohemia, with smaller isolated instances in Hungary and other provinces, while several provinces had lignite deposits of varying quality. Coal mining developed in close relation with the railroad network; many deposits were opened up only after a line provided the stimulus, while others (as in Ostrava or Pecs) were an important determinant in the planning of specific railway routes. In the Austrian half of the Monarchy bituminous coal production rose from *circa* 100,000 tons around 1830 to 540,000 tons in 1848-50 (per year), while lignite output rose from 80,000 tons to 340,000 tons (in the same years). Hungarian mining data for these years are unreliable; the trend was similar, but the quantities considerably smaller. Austrian coals remained generally more expensive than other fuels or power sources, particularly in the Alpine regions. This was attested not only by the persistent use of charcoal as industrial fuel (and of water power), but also by ingenious efforts to utilise the better distributed (though inferior) lignites, and even peat, in industry and for railway engines. The unfavourable price-quality ratio of Austrian bituminous coal in the international framework was highlighted by the increase in coal imports from a yearly average of 38,000 tons during 1846-49 to above 70,000 tons in 1850 and 1851, as a direct result of the connection of the *Nordbahn* to the Prussian-Silesian railroad. This increase was the more impressive since the northern Austrian railway itself passed through the relatively rich Ostrava coalfield, the most important of the Monarchy. Combining bituminous and lignite coals at their estimated heating power equivalents (i.e. taking lignites at half the quantitative value), and inferring their shares in foreign trade, I have estimated the growth of total coal consumption in Austria from 152,000 tons in 1831 to 746,000 tons in 1850, which implies an average yearly growth rate of 8·6 per cent.

Although the rate of growth of Austrian coal consumption in those years compares quite favourably with that in other countries in Western-Central Europe, not so the absolute quantities involved. Per capita coal consumption in the Austrian half of the Monarchy in 1850 was in the order of 43 kg., as compared with about 170 kg. in the *Zollverein*, 230 kg. in France, and close to 800 kg. in Belgium. On the other hand, per capita output of pig iron in Austria, also in 1850, was (at 8·8 kg.) much closer to the French figure (12·5 kg.) and higher than the German (7·3 kg.).

Output of pig iron increased less than that of coals; it only about doubled in twenty years, from 73,000 tons in 1828 to 154,000 in 1850 (including cast iron). The chronic ailments of the Austrian pig iron industry began to be evident during this period: the prevalence of small, conservative units in the Alps; the scarcity and disadvantageous location of cokeable coal; the vested interest of the owners of large estates, in the Czech and Hungarian lands, who viewed iron chiefly as a means for marketing more timber. Alpine pig iron, which accounted for about two-thirds of Austrian output during the second quarter of the century, was exclusively charcoal smelted until 1870. In the northern provinces the famous Vitkovice ironworks introduced coke smelting between 1836 and 1839, but remained the only firm to do so until 1854. This establishment was also the first in Austria to introduce puddling (in 1830) and the steam hammer (in 1844). It was closely associated with the interests (including the Austrian Rothschilds and the 'coal king' brothers Guttmann) owning the *Nordbahn*, and for long concentrated on supplying its needs. Other innovating firms, and those were few, also produced chiefly for the railways, in the face of duty exemptions on rails and rolling stock which the companies obtained as a form of government subsidy. In 1841 Austria had a total of 44 puddling furnaces, in twelve establishments, as compared with over 150 such furnaces in France as early as 1826. The foreign trade of the Monarchy in pig and bar iron remained on the whole quite small during the second quarter of the century, which reflected the prohibitive height of the tariff rather than the progress of domestic industry. In this respect the policy of the *Zollverein* provided an instructive contrast.

Relative factor costs in Austria particularly hampered the development of engineering, since this sector had to suffer from the deficiencies in both iron and coal production. Under these circumstances it is not surprising to find Austrian industry (as well as agriculture) late and slow in the introduction of steam power. Steam engines were expensive, whether imported or domestically produced, and then faced severe difficulties of fuel supply. As the development of coal mining, cheap iron production, rail transportation, and application of steam power are closely interrelated, their retardation in the Monarchy must have been mutually reinforcing. The investment in water wheels or even turbines was considerably lower, per capacity unit, and was therefore more profitable in the short run. But reliance on water power limited a firm's potential for growth and technological progress.

An official, and by all indications knowledgeable, survey of industry in the Monarchy for the year 1841 sets the total value of industrial output at 800 million florins, three-quarters of which were by the larger 'factories' and one-quarter by small firms and craft shops. The share of Hungary in this total was estimated at one eighth, but with respect to that part of the Monarchy the survey was less complete and self-confident. If we wish to look only at the product of 'big' industry in the Austrian provinces proper (i.e. excluding Hungary and Lombardy), and make a few adjustments (to exclude such items as raw silk and cheese, as well as flax and hemp goods produced for home consumption), we arrive at a total of 372 million florins. Of this 40·6 per cent were textiles, with the following sub-division (in millions of florins): 33·5 flax and hemp (for the market), 40·3 cotton, 63·0 wool, and 14·0 silk. Another 20·7 per cent of the total were the *Genussmittel* industries, i.e. tobacco, alcoholic beverages, and foodstuffs; while 13·4 per cent were metals and metal products. It must be remembered that *Gross-Industrie* at that time was defined by legal criteria, and definitely included the larger putting-out firms. Of the branches not specifically discussed above, leather and leather products was an important but backward industry; paper was just undergoing mechanisation and a change in the raw material basis; bricks and potteries were on the rise, and glass already declining somewhat; 'chemicals' were a mixed bag, and of uneven technological character.

The trend of the earlier 1840's continued after the slump and political disturbances of the end of the decade; and in general one can characterise the period from 1850 to 1873 as one of rapid industrial development by Austrian standards. This, although the world-wide slump of 1857 was distinctly felt in the Monarchy, and the early sixties witnessed a deflationary fiscal policy (in an attempt to restore the florin's convertibility). The booms of this period in Austria, therefore, were 1851–57 and 1867–73, the second starting later than in the rest of Europe because of fiscal policy. My estimates of coal consumption show an average yearly growth rate of 10·4 per cent for Austria during 1851–73, and of 11·5 for Hungary. These are the highest growth rates, by far, of coal consumption in the Monarchy for the whole century, characterising the period as that of most rapid economic modernisation. And indeed technological transformation proceeded in agriculture, mining, transportation, and industry at a vigorous pace. In part this was the continuation of the impact of early industrialising changes in the second quarter of the century, and in part the response to institutional and political changes (which have been discussed above). Purš, with a somewhat schematic approach, concluded that the 'industrial revolution' in the Czech provinces (the most industrialising section of the Monarchy) went through the phases of expansion and 'completion' during this period 1850–73, with mechanised technology and the factory system achieving predominance. He considers the depression of the seventies evidence that Bohemia-Moravia, and perhaps most of the Austrian part of the Monarchy, had reached the stage of industrial capitalism.[3] At the other extreme, März considers the depression which started in the seventies but continued in several respects in the eighties, too, to have been so severe and influential, that the booms of the third quarter of the century have to be viewed as 'false starts' only. März dates the 'take-off' in Austria in the last decade before the First World War; but he himself cites both 1904–12 and 1867–73 as the only periods in which the rate of Austrian economic growth was comparable with that of the more advanced countries.[4] As a matter of fact this kind of question can hardly be settled decisively: against the argument that the early spurt did not survive the 1873 depression one has to weigh the fact that the late, pre-World War one could never face a similar test. Moreover, I think it questionable whether

3. Jaroslav Purš, 'The Industrial Revolution in the Czech Lands,' *Historica*, II (Prague, 1960), 183–272.

4. Eduard März, 'Zur Genesis der Schumpeterschen Theorie der wirtschaftlichen Entwicklung,' in *On Political Economy and Econometrics* (Warsaw, 1965), esp. 370–71.

the concept of a single take-off or spurt is applicable to all countries, and in particular to Austria: though perhaps it is to Hungary.[5]

It is interesting to note, that during those twenty years of most rapid rise in coal consumption, constituting two decades of vigorous railway construction and important industrial investment, coal imports to Austria (from abroad and from Hungary) rarely reached 10 per cent of estimated coal consumption. These imports, furthermore, were partly offset by lignite exports. But this fact does only partly weaken the argument of deficient natural resources for industrialisation in Austria, since it does not detract from the relative backwardness of Austria by international comparison. Moreover, only the Czech provinces had 'sufficient' coal deposits for their given rate of growth, and even exported both lignites and 'black' coal (abroad and to other provinces). The Alpine centres of traditional industrial production, as well as the growing Vienna basin industry, undoubtedly suffered from lack of coal, and cokeable coal in particular, as we have already seen. Total Austrian domestic production of bituminous coal rose from 665,000 tons in 1851 to 4,487,000 tons in 1873, and lignite output from 356,000 tons in 1851 to 5,780,000 tons in 1873. In Hungary output rose from 61,500 tons of coal (100,000 tons lignite) in 1851 to 684,000 tons of coal (950,000 tons lignite) in 1873.

Austrian pig iron production rose from 160,000 tons in 1851 to 370,000 tons in 1873, which implies an average yearly growth rate of less than 4 per cent. In Hungary pig iron output increased from 43,400 tons in 1851 to 163,500 tons in 1873, i.e. at an average yearly rate of 6·25 per cent (but from a very low base). Although Austrian pig iron production more than doubled during those 22 years, this was less than the performance of other economies: France and England increased output about three-fold, while German output increased even much more rapidly (the statistics in the German case are not comparable for an

5. Cf. my article on 'Economic Growth and the Consumption of Coal in Austria and Hungary, 1831–1913,' *Journal of Economic History*, (December, 1971).

exact statement, because of boundary changes). A contemporary authority estimated the consumption of raw iron in the Monarchy as a whole to have been almost 200,000 tons in 1851 and 875,000 tons in 1873, which would imply a growth rate of almost 7 per cent per year.[6] While in the second quarter of the century, and even in 1851, domestic production somewhat exceeded raw iron consumption in the Monarchy, this relation started to change from 1852 on. Only in the mid-fifties, however, and then again from 1868 onward, did the import surplus of raw iron (and its estimated equivalents) reach significant dimensions. In the last boom years of this period, pig iron production in the Monarchy rose from 403,000 tons in 1870 to 534,500 tons in 1873, while consumption of raw iron rose from 760,000 tons to 875,000 tons respectively. In the early 1880's this type of difference, though in smaller proportion, began to reappear. The inability of domestic industry to supply the needed quantities of raw iron in boom years, in the third quarter of the century, was not the least a reflection of the persistent technological backwardness of Austro-Hungarian metallurgy. From the same source we learn that in 1883, when *circa* 90 per cent of world iron production was smelted with mineral fuel, more than half the output in the Monarchy was still charcoal smelted.

The share of Hungary in pig iron output was 17 per cent of the Monarchy's total in the thirties and forties, with small fluctuations around this average; rose to 25 per cent for the decade of the fifties, and to 32 per cent (by decade averages) in the sixties and seventies. In the Austrian half of the Monarchy, the chief producing provinces were Bohemia and Moravia-Silesia on the one hand, and Styria and Carinthia (plus some in Lower Austria) on the other hand. The northern group of provinces produced (again by decade averages) 31 per cent of the Austrian total in the 1830's, and 35–36 per cent in the next two decades. In the 1860's their output averaged 41 per cent of Austrian production of pig

6. Franz Kupelwieser, 'Die Entwicklung der Eisenproduktion in den letzten Decennien,' *Oesterr. Zeitschrift für Berg- und Hüottenwesen* (1886), p. 43.

iron, but this proportion fell again to 35 in the 1870's. Only from the early eighties did the share of the Czech provinces increase rapidly and consistently, due to the introduction of the Thomas process. Until 1870 all output of the southern group of provinces was smelted with charcoal. In Bohemia the first coke-using furnaces were started in 1854 in Kladno, but the method spread slowly only even there. Bessemer converters were first installed in the Vitkovice works in 1866 and in the Kladno complex in 1875. In evaluating developments in the Austrian iron industry during the spurt period of the third quarter we have to take into account that the major boom in Austrian railway construction, as well as other investments and innovations, took place during a regime of relatively free trade, so that important linkage effects were in effect diverted to foreign countries.

In the textile and other light industries mechanisation proceeded at an increasing pace during the years 1851–73, with a special impulse towards change in the wool and flax branches during the cotton famine years. The number of cotton spindles seems to have remained almost constant, in the Monarchy, between 1855 and 1875, around 1·5 million; of which Lower Austria and Bohemia had above half a million each. Power looms spread during the fifties and after 1866, in particular in the Liberec cotton and wool industry. In wool, factory production gained predominance over artisan output, and the Liberec district overtook the Brno centre in volume and technological progress. Another leading sector of Austrian light industries, the beet sugar refining, made spectacular progress during the 1867–73 boom, thanks to new mechanical and chemical techniques. In these years the area of beet cultivation was extended greatly, in particular in Bohemia and Moravia. This branch had important linkage effects both in agriculture and in the engineering industry. In Bohemia alone raw sugar consumption increased sevenfold between 1853 and 1872. During the seventies the share of the Monarchy in European beet sugar output rose from 20 to above 25 per cent. The growth of the sugar industry had an important political significance, too: the industries based on local agricultural materials provided the basis for the development of non-German-speaking enterprise and capital. In Bohemia and Moravia these were mainly the sugar and distilling branches, while in Hungary the steam-powered large flour mills fulfilled that function to begin with. In all these light industries, as also in brewing, new techniques and especially the use of steam power were spreading rapidly during the period under consideration.

Several of the developments so far outlined reached a degree of consolidation in the relatively meagre years following the *Krach* of 1873; while others were continued only from the early 1880's on, when industrial output began to revive significantly. In the last 30–35 years before the First War the economy of the Monarchy followed the general business cycle even more closely than before. As in many other countries, industrial growth experienced a spurt between 1904 and 1912, and government expenditure and investment probably played a more important role than previously. The lead of the northern (Czech) provinces in Austrian industrial output became strongly pronounced in this era, while in Hungary a nationalistic policy of industrial development became effective chiefly from the 1880's on. There can be no doubt of the importance of this policy for Hungary in the long run, particularly in view of the extremely low proportion of industrial production in the Hungarian national product at the beginning of that period. But on the other hand it seems clear that this policy diverted resources, domestic and foreign, from Austrian industry to Hungary, and thus prevented more rapid growth in Austria.

Total Austrian industrial product increased at an average annual rate of 3·6 per cent during 1880–1913, and by *circa* 4·5 per cent in Hungary. The major growth sectors continued to be textiles, metallurgy, and sugar; with the addition of engineering, and the new electro-technical and chemical industries. In the latter two, German enterprise, capital, and even more technology were of crucial importance for developments in both Austria and Hungary. Even in the leading industries, certain general deficiencies of Austrian industry as well as of the Monarchy's economy at large continued to be evident. High tariffs and cartelisation burdened the consumer, whose standard of living was lower than in Western Europe even in the more advanced provinces. Very large sections of the Monarchy remained very poor and correspondingly only in part integrated into the market economy. Provincial differences in tastes and customs persisted so that large-scale production was even more limited than by the size of the domestic market. In exports German products (as well as investments) competed more and more successfully and aggressively in such Austrian areas of interest as the Balkans and the Levant.

Main components of industrial output in Austria, 1841–1911 (per cent)

Sector	1841	1865	1880	1911
Textiles and clothing	41	41	34	24
Tobacco and foodstuffs	18	11	30	25
Glass, clay, etc.	15	6	7	8
Metals and products	14	16	13	20
Chemicals, fuel, power	2	2	4	10
Wood, leather, paper	10	24	10	14
	100	100	100	100

Based on industrial surveys of varying quality, from official sources, the above table compares the main components of Austrian industrial product (value added) in four bench-mark years. The table's most striking feature is the large share of consumer goods industries. As late as the 1880's the combined output of textiles, clothes, food, beverages, and tobacco still constituted close to two-thirds of all industrial value added. During 1841–80 the share of the industries which chiefly manufacture capital goods — bricks, glass, cement, machinery, vehicles, chemicals — actually showed a decline. Only by 1911 had the percentage of capital goods industries reached approximately the level of the textiles and foodstuffs group. The table also reflects several of the changes discussed above, such as the significant rise in the importance of food processing industries during the third quarter of the century. The rapid growth of paper production, and of other wood processing, on the other hand, was of particular import for the Alpine provinces. Other changes, such as the rapid growth of the chemicals and utilities groups from the 1890's, corresponded to general European developments. For 1902 we also have reliable data on Austrian industrial structure in terms of the labour force, from an industrial census for that year. These data include crafts and construction and are thus comparable with a similar German census for 1901-10. The share of textiles and clothing in the industrial labour force was 32 per cent in Austria and 28 per cent in Germany; while metals and their products employed 17 per cent in Austria and 20 per cent in Germany; and construction accounted for 13 per cent in Austria and 15 in Germany. These figures confirm our general impression, that Austrian industry did not succeed in catching up with German developments during the second half of the nineteenth century.

In conclusion, a few words about demographical developments may be in order. The average annual growth rate of population in the Austrian part of the Monarchy was 0·83 per cent from 1857 to 1910, as compared with a 1·09 per cent rate for Germany, for instance. In Hungary population grew at a higher rate during most decades after 1850 but slower in the 1850's and hardly at all in the 1870's. The Austrian crude birth rate fluctuated between 37 and 40 per thousand during all of the nineteenth century, but a falling trend is evident from the early seventies on. The Austrian birth rate was consistently higher than that of all countries farther north or west in Europe, and also higher than the Italian rate. In Hungary it was higher still. Provincial differences were, of course, quite considerable, reflecting economic and cultural factors. The Austro-Hungarian death rates varied within a range that was even more decidedly above that of western and north-western Europe. In Austria as late as 1866 total deaths exceeded the number of births for that year, while in Hungary population declined absolutely even later — between 1871 and 1875. In the Austrian half the death rate was in the range of

28·6 to 32·6 per thousand until 1890, but a falling trend is discernible from the early seventies again.

As a result of such high mortality rates, and of the proximity between their decline and the fall in the birth rate, the crude rate of population increase in the Monarchy remained low throughout the century. Population actually grew at an even lower rate, however, at least from the 1880's on, due to emigration. From 1871 to 1914 net emigration from Austria was *circa* 1·3 million, and from Hungary about the same number. The economic significance of these data is obvious: at a time when both technological and political conditions for large international migrations had become favourable, the relative economic backwardness of the Austro-Hungarian economy induced enterprising individuals to go abroad. Even though opportunities were provided by economic growth, it was not rapid enough in relation to the combined effects of domestic population increase and the demand (and glitter) of the faster growing economies. This interpretation is further supported by the seasonal emigration from Austria-Hungary, mainly to Germany, in the early part of the twentieth century (and perhaps even earlier). It is clear that emigration of such dimensions must have had, in its turn, effects on economic developments; and these were chiefly unfavourable: the impact on the age structure, and the drain of enterprising, vigorous, and in part skilled individuals. The fact that even the northern, most advanced, provinces of Austria were net emigration areas is particularly indicative of the unsolved tension between potentials and aspirations on the one hand, and the actual performance of the Austro-Hungarian economy (until the dissolution of the Monarchy) on the other hand.

BIBLIOGRAPHY

As already mentioned briefly in the text, the Habsburg Monarchy has so far been somewhat neglected in the literature of economic history. In most general textbooks on European economic history it is barely referred to. Its fate is better in monographic studies, such as Rondo Cameron's *France and the Economic Development of Europe* (Princeton, 1961). In general histories of the Monarchy, on the other hand, the economic sections may be good even if brief. Such are, e.g., C. A. Macartney, *The Habsburg Empire, 1790–1918* (London, 1968), and Erich Zöllner, *Geschichte Oesterreichs: Von den Anfängen bis zur Gegenwart* (Vienna, 1961).

Discussions of economic growth in Austria, following the modern approach, are (unfortunately for the general student) so far best in unpublished doctoral dissertations: Edward Marz [Eduard März], 'The Austrian Economy in Transition' (Harvard, 1948); Richard L. Rudolph, 'The Role of Financial Institutions in the Industrialisation of the Czech Crownlands, 1880–1914' (University of Wisconsin, 1968); and perhaps also my 'Industrialisation in Austria in the Nineteenth Century' (University of California, Berkeley, 1966). In any case I have relied on the latter two quite heavily here.

Great hopes are to be put in the forthcoming *History of the Habsburg Monarchy*, a collective enterprise to be published by the Austrian *Akademie der Wissenschaften* in German, and later also in English. The volume on economic developments is scheduled to appear in 1972. In particular one would hope that this work will not be subject to the distorted perspective from which all those books suffer that were planned to cover too long a period. No study, even if otherwise excellent, can do justice to the era of the Monarchy if the author wishes to continue its story up to the present. The discontinuity of the 1918 break-up is overriding: the Austrian Republic was a new entity. But when dealing with the 18th and 19th centuries, it makes no good sense to isolate the area of present-day Austria from the rest of Habsburg Austria. This is the main unsolved problem of Ferdinand Tremel, *Wirtschafts- und Sozialgeschichte Oesterreichs: Von den Anfängen bis 1955* (Vienna, 1969). It is also a drawback to the otherwise useful collection of articles (of uneven quality) in Hans Mayer (ed.), *Hundert Jahre Oesterreichischer Wirtschafts- entwicklung, 1848–1948* (Vienna, 1949), and of the concise but stimulating survey by Alois Brusatti, *Oesterreichische Wirtschaftspolitik vom Josephinismus zum Ständestaat* (Vienna, 1965).

Of more promise than fulfilment is the informative, but diffused and in parts anecdotal, volume by Heinrich Benedikt, *Die wirtschaftliche Entwicklung in der Franz-Joseph- Zeit* (Vienna-Munich, 1958).

On the eighteenth century recommended are: William E. Wright, *Serf, Seigneur, and Sovereign* (Minneapolis, 1966), although dealing mainly with Bohemia alone; and Friedrich Luetge (ed.) *Die wirtschaftliche Situation in Deutschland und Oesterreich um die Wende vom 18. zum 19. Jahrhundert* (Stuttgart, 1964); also the articles by Herman Freudenberger, 'The Woollen Goods Industry of the Habsburg Monarchy in the Eighteenth Century', *Journal of Economic History*, XX (1960), and 'State Intervention as an Obstacle to Economic Growth in the Habsburg Monarchy', *Journal of Economic History*, XXVII (1967). On the first half of the 19th century: Jerome Blum, *Noble Landowners and Agriculture in Austria, 1815–1848* (Baltimore, 1948), and his 'Transportation and Industry in Austria, 1815–1848', *Journal of Modern History*, XV (1943); also still valuable is Johann Slokar, *Geschichte der österr. Industrie und ihrer Förderung unter Kaiser Franz I* (Vienna, 1914). On the later part of the century — Eduard März, *Oesterreichische Industrie- und Bankpolitik in der Zeit Franz Josephs I* (Vienna, 1968).

Indispensable for the student of our topic are the translations of research done by our colleagues in Prague and Budapest, in the series *Historica* and *Studia Historica* published by the Academies of Sciences in Czechoslovakia and Hungary, respectively. Of particular importance is the recent volume 62 of the Hungarian series (published in 1970).

5. The Industrial Revolution in Italy 1830-1914
Luciano Cafagna

TWO KINDS OF OUTSIDE IMPETUS FOR NORTHERN ITALY'S ECONOMY BEFORE POLITICAL UNIFICATION (*c.* 1830–1860)

The influence of the industrial revolution on the predominantly agricultural economy of Italy's various regions before unification, during the first half of the nineteenth century, made itself felt in two important ways. Neither of them could yet be defined as the introduction of forms of modern industrialisation but they can nevertheless be regarded as its forerunners. The first, direct and palpable, concerned the development of trade exchanges with the rest of the world. It involved considerable expansion in a traditional export of primary products from certain northern regions of Italy, the export of silk, both raw and spun, for the spinning and weaving mills of France, Great Britain, Germany and Switzerland. The second, a matter of information and mental attitudes, concerns the various means by which the country was influenced or compelled to imitate those nations that had already embarked on industrial development.

The production of silk, a product of silkworm rearing and cultivation of the mulberry tree, was concentrated chiefly in North Italy, especially Piedmont and Lombardy. The explosion of industrial textile consumption in Western Europe and North America in the first decades after the Restoration[1] caused an increase in the demand not only for cotton and wool but also, if to a lesser degree, for silk. North Italy benefited particularly from this increased demand. For although European demand already tended to turn towards the East (first to Bengal, then, after the opium war, to China, concentrating in the last decades of the

[1]. i.e. the Restoration of the *status quo* after the Congress of Vienna.

nineteenth century on Japan), nevertheless a good deal of this demand could be satisfied within Europe itself, if only in those few privileged areas (in particular, North Italy and the South of France) which climatic conditions made suitable for silk production. These areas had traditionally, ever since the sixteenth century, fostered the development of mulberry plantations and of activities connected with the first transformation of the product of the silkworm, in other words the process of producing from the cocoon the filament of raw silk yarn (reeling) and the subsequent preparation of the filament silk for weaving (throwing). Much less progress had been made in weaving. This final phase in the cycle of silk textile production had become established on a considerably larger scale in France and also in other countries of Western Europe which relied chiefly on Italy for their supplies of raw or spun silk. Up to the middle of the eighteenth century techniques relating to these initial stages of silk textile production were more advanced in Italy than in the rest of Europe, even giving rise to one of the first notorious cases of industrial espionage.[2] Subsequently they remained at a standstill and were overtaken by the advances made in the rest of Western Europe. But between 1830 and 1850 the inducement of rising demand led to some modernisation of techniques, especially in the less elementary branch from the industrial point of view, that of throwing.

By about the middle of the nineteenth century there were in Piedmont and Lombardy together about 700–800 silk-throwing mills, mostly worked by water. At that time silk reeling and throwing gave employment to some 150,000, mainly peasants working seasonally (reeling went on for only one month of the year) in small mills scattered over the countryside and equipped with very simple machinery. But it is no exaggeration to say that these mills provided the first training in industrial labour for workers who were later used in other forms of production. It was also in connection with the sale of silk that capital-owning landowners

2. W. H. Chaloner, 'Sir Thomas Lombe (1685-1739) and the British Silk Industry', in *History Today*, vol. III, no. 11, Nov. 1953, pp. 778-785.

and merchant bankers first became interested on a large scale in an economic activity that was not purely agricultural. Moreover trade interests in silk-importing countries resulted in the influx into North Italy of Swiss and German businessmen who were to play an important part in turning Italy's first industrial efforts towards other directions. The development of silk production therefore contributed in several ways towards forming the external economies for a further industrial development. In this sense silk can be regarded as the first 'leading sector' for Italian economic development in the nineteenth century. For some hundred years, from the Restoration to the First World War, silk led the field in Italian exports, more or less regularly representing about a third of their total value.

As has been said, the final stage of silk production, weaving, was for a long time, and indeed up to the end of the nineteenth century, of considerably less importance, viewed quantitatively. The reason for this can easily be understood. Italy's economy, at this early stage, could only provide a large-scale response to the demand for a product for which she had a natural oligopoly and need face no competitors, a product for which trade lay with the foreign productive sector, not with the market of final consumers, which was controlled by the foreign industry. At the same time the Italian home market for finished goods could obviously not afford sufficient demand for a quality product like woven silk. Even the intermediary process of throwing (which provided the actual yarn) had a restricted and difficult development, confined in the eighteenth and early nineteenth centuries almost entirely to Piedmont, in virtue of a commercial policy which forbade the export of silk in its raw state. It must be emphasised that this mercantilism in fact went only halfway, lacking the courage and strength to extend as well to woven goods. Even this 'halfway' mercantilism was, however, abandoned around 1830.

The other branches of textile production—cotton, linen, and wool—were quantitatively much less important during the first half of the nineteenth century, though they were rather more industrial in character. Geographically, the cotton industry was concentrated in Piedmont and Lombardy, the linen industry in Lombardy alone, while wool manufacture was more widespread (in Piedmont, the Veneto, and Tuscany). The South, for its part, had a small nucleus of cotton production (Salerno) and of wool, both highly protected by customs duties. Except for flax and some wool, the raw materials used were not of domestic production. Indeed the greater part of finished goods consumed on the home market were imported, despite the customs protection they enjoyed. Many of the earliest small factories developed side by side with an import business, and were probably also used as cover for the importation of contraband finished goods, especially in the cotton trade. From about 1830 onwards cotton emerged as the most attractive commodity, after silk, for traders and for a small circle among the nobility who were prepared to interest themselves in non-agricultural economic activities. Italy's cotton industry, too, then began to experience the impetus of quite a number of immigrant Swiss or German businessmen who came, in particular, to Lombardy. '*The Golden Book* of industry and trade in Lombardy', wrote Nitti, 'abounded in guttural sounds and harsh terminations.'[3]

The productive phase of the textile sector which first began to assume industrial characteristics (i.e. concentration in small factories, use of centralised motive power and mechanical equipment) was that of spinning. Reference has already been made to the throwing and spinning of silk. In the other branches the greatest advances were in cotton and flax rather than in wool: wool was technically the most difficult to deal with, and also the individual regional markets (except for Piedmont, where supplies for the army could be counted on) afforded too restricted a demand.[4] Weaving, on the other hand, continued to be

3. F. S. Nitti, *L'Italia all'alba del secolo XX*, Turin — Rome, 1901; reprinted in *Scritti sulla questione meridionale*, vol. I, Bari, 1958, pp. 147ff.

4. Quazza, in *L'industria laniera e cotoniera in Piemonte dal 1831 al 1861*, Turin, 1961, observes (pp. 98–9) that 'the expansive capacity of cotton, regarded throughout Europe as the industry of tomorrow, the most profitable and the most susceptible of expansion, was seen to be greater

mainly of the nature of a handicraft, carried on for the most part in the peasants' own dwellings even though much of it was under the control of merchant-entrepreneurs. Prior to 1848 there were about sixty cotton-spinning mills in Piedmont and Lombardy, together with about 200,000 spindles. Thus the average number of spindles per mill was about 3,000–3,500, whereas in England at the same period the average was already around 10,000. A few mills were beginning to work on a larger scale: the Piedmontese *Manifattura di Annecy e Pont* had as many as 34,000 spindles. Productivity was very low: in Piedmont (1840–1843) the average was 28 spindles per worker, in Lombardy (1845) 31, whereas in England in those years the average was around 80.

A considerable part of the production was concentrated in larger and technically more modern mills. These mills strove to follow the rapid technological changes of other countries, but succeeded only partially and with several years' delay. The first mule-jennys of the early years of the century were followed, with a time-lag of 15–20 years as compared with other countries, by throstles around 1840; and semi-automatic mule-jennys came into use in Italy only in the years just before the unification, whereas in England self-acting machines had already appeared, a development that did not reach Italy till after 1860, five or six years after the Paris Exhibition of 1855 which launched them.

Thus it will be seen that the overall picture in the Italian textile industry was very restricted as compared with other countries: less than a thousand small factories for silk, cotton, flax and wool and of those only some fifteen of respectable size—surrounded by home-handicraft workers and seasonal work at the preparatory stage of silk-reeling. Nevertheless this small beginning, because of its concentration in particular areas, was already giving a new aspect to

---

than that of wool . . . The younger industry has the pre-eminence, because in it greater technical vitality is combined with greater economic convenience.'

certain agricultural regions situated at the outlets of the Alpine valleys.

Three basic conditions (over and above the natural factors favourable to silk) made this development possible: first, the availability of motive power, suited to small-scale factories, which was provided by the numerous streams coming down from the Alpine valleys; secondly, a good supply of cheap manpower recruited in an area of poor agriculture; and lastly the customs protection afforded by the tariffs adopted by the various Italian states after the Restoration. These conditions enabled Italy to produce goods of a rather coarse quality, destined for a poorer market, and so to compensate for the much lower productivity of her factories as compared with those of other countries.

We come now to the other type of influence exercised by the industrial revolution—what we described earlier as the 'informational' influence. The technological aspects of the industrial revolution aroused the interest of certain progressive intellectual circles and some more enterprising businessmen who were beginning to travel and study technical experiments in other countries. Propaganda about these innovations and about the need for up-to-date technical training appeared in various periodicals such as the *Annali Universali di statistica*, founded by Francesco Lampato with the collaboration of G. D. Romagnosi and Melchiorre Gioia (1818–1859), or the *Politecnico* of Carlo Cattaneo (1839–1844), both published in Milan. A small coterie of Italian businessmen aware of the need for modern techniques was also beginning to emerge, in addition to those of non-Italian origin. Societies and institutes arose to promote such knowledge, and schools for the instruction of qualified workers were founded in Milan and Turin. But all this took place in backward environments: even the technological publications were mainly concerned with agricultural techniques. Industrial circles were restricted and in general preferred to exploit the easy conditions afforded by low labour costs and customs protection. Innovations arrived late, and market conditions provided little stimulus to introduce them. Consequently the groups of intellectuals urging technical advance inveighed against protectionism and the exploitation of female and child labour. When men from these circles became councillors or—as in the case of Camillo Cavour in Piedmont after 1848—entered the Government, they worked for a more liberalising policy in trade which, by compelling the entrepreneurs to face competition for survival, would encourage innovation in the industrial sphere. This trend, furthered by favourable international conditions and by a policy of increased public expenditure, achieved positive results in Piedmont between 1848 and 1859.

Propaganda and action for the railways was the most important watchword of the movement for the modernisation of Italy on the model of the north-west European countries. The years of these first industrial beginnings in North Italy, between 1830 and 1860, were in fact the railway years for north-western Europe, where development of railways was combined with considerable developments in iron and steel and in engineering. In Italy the first railways were built quite early—the Naples–Portici line in 1830, and the Milan–Monza in 1832. But these were very short lines of small economic significance (in both cases they connected the capital with the King's palace!) and were not followed up for a long time by any further network. Before the unification of 1860 there was a good deal of talk about the lines to be constructed, but in general, except in Cavour's Piedmont, little was done. Inaction was blamed on the political division of the territory, and this was one of the important reasons contributing to a spread of unitary national consciousness. Up to the war of 1859–60 which led to the birth of Italy as a unified State, only 1,798 km. of railways had been built, of which 819 km. were in Piedmont and 522 km. in Lombardy and the Veneto.

Throughout this period no great impulse arose towards the development of iron and steel or engineering industries. Railways, retarded as they were, provided no such impulse; nor did the production of iron steamships, whose first sporadic manifestation in Italy was in 1855 (the *Sicilia* of 120 tons, built in the Orlando shipyards in Genoa); nor did the construction of machinery for other industries, for the limited demand for machines was met through purchases from other countries more technically advanced; nor, lastly, did any such impulse arise from military requirements since these, given the political division of the country, were on only a small scale. Nevertheless production for the limited military needs of the small individual Italian states constituted, together with agricultural equipment production, the basis of the modest iron industry existing in those regions of Italy where there were iron mines: chiefly Lombardy, followed by Tuscany, Piedmont (Val d'Aosta), and Calabria. In the main industrial countries the *direct* process of production of iron from the mineral (the *stuckofen* furnace, known in Italy as *catalano*) had by then been abandoned and in the first decades of the nineteenth century the *indirect* process had been generally adopted, whereby first the intermediary product of pig-iron was obtained from the mineral by means of casting in blast-furnaces. In England and other West European countries, however, the transition from the direct to the indirect process had been accompanied by the revolutionary substitution of coal instead of charcoal (which would have been impossible under the direct method); and this had drastically reduced fuel costs and led to concentration of works. In Italy, on the other hand, the lack of coalfields compelled producers to continue to use charcoal, thus seriously restricting the use of the possibilities offered by the new techniques. Iron works were therefore still dispersed among small separate factories each with its own small production. Blast-furnaces still used the puddling system (the Bessemer converter was invented only in 1856 and there were none at all in Italy at the time of the unification).

Nevertheless in the regions where some start had been made with railway construction before the unification (mainly Piedmont, as has been seen, and to a lesser degree Lombardy and, less still, around Naples), the first small-scale indications of a new machine industry were coming into existence. Genoa, Turin, and Milan, the towns of the future 'industrial triangle', witnessed the first signs of an activity which in the decades to come was to characterise their whole physiognomy as major industrial centres. For the time being, however, these were confined to repair workshops or at most assembly-shops for imported railway stock, such as the locomotives that emerged from the Ansaldo workshops in Genoa in 1855. But in general the first locomotives were imported ready-made from abroad, and domestic production's share in the great 'railway adventure' was modestly confined to supplying some of the wagons. This situation was to continue for a long time.

'THE FIRST COAT OF PAINT'. SLOW INDUSTRIAL
DEVELOPMENT UNDER THE FIRST FREE-TRADE
GOVERNMENTS (1860–1878)

The two most important economic ideals inspiring the men of the Risorgimento were, as has been said, the extension throughout Italy of that fundamental symbol of progress, railways, and free trade, which English economic literature had led them to regard as the principal propulsive factor of trade. These were the main directives of the economic policy of Italy's first governments as a unified state after 1860. Neither of them, however, gave any great impetus to the country's industrial development. Railway construction was speeded up, and between 1861 and 1876 reached a yearly average of 376 km. of new lines, as compared with 176 km. a year in the preceding decade;[5] but this had very little linkage effect on industrial activities. The demand for rails, engines, carriages and trucks, and iron for bridges continued to be supplied, with few insignificant exceptions, from abroad. It was administered by foreign concessionaire companies which had links with non-Italian firms and had no interest in undertaking or encouraging the far from easy venture of rapidly creating an Italian engineering industry

5. Construction of new lines averaged 290 km. a year in 1877–85, and 302 km. in 1886–1905. The years 1876, 1885, and 1905 marked changes in Italy's railway policy.

—to say nothing of an iron and steel industry, which would have involved facing up to the handicap of lack of domestic pit-coal. The only fractions of the demand on domestic resources to arise from railway construction were those relating to the least complicated technical aspects: the making of sleepers (which caused extensive deforestation of the mountainsides, leading to serious ecological damage particularly in the South) and processes connected with the construction of the tracks. This type of demand led, for example, to the first establishment of the cement industry, in Lombardy.

The other pivot of the early governments' economic policy, free trade, was born of a desire to intensify trade contacts with the rest of the world, and principally with the more advanced countries of Europe. Since Italy was a predominantly agricultural country (in the first twenty years after unification agriculture accounted for 57 per cent of the gross private national product), intensification of trade meant chiefly increasing exports of agricultural produce and imports of industrial goods. A free-trade policy therefore found favour among landowners and farmers producing goods for export (silk, oil, cheese etc.), who were considerably more numerous, stronger, and better represented in Parliament than the few industrialists concerned with cotton, wool, or iron. Protectionist trends received little backing in the country as long as agrarian interests were not seriously threatened by foreign competition—which came about only in the second half of the '70s, with the influx of cheap cereals from America—and as long as the modest efforts of domestic industries had not yet reached the point where the industrialists could adduce the argument of manpower employment to exercise pressure on the political authorities.

Italian industry made only slow progress up to about 1880. It profited chiefly from the greater scope afforded by a domestic market enlarged by the unification and somewhat invigorated by the increased public expenditure accompanying the establishment of the unified State. This came about very gradually, favoured by some unforeseen circumstances. The first of these was the Government's adoption of the *corso forzoso* (inconvertibility of banknotes),[6] made necessary by the heavy expenditure of the war of 1866 against Austria. The *corso forzoso*, by altering the rate of exchange, in effect operated like a devaluation of the lira, favouring Italian as compared with foreign products. The second was the economic boom following the Franco-Prussian war of 1870, the chief effect of which for Italian industry was a temporary reduction in the competitive pressure of foreign products on the national market. An exceptional and short-term situation such as this was seen as an opportunity for a qualitative change by many economic circles in North Italy: the first small group of industrial joint-stock companies came into being; and, especially in the sphere of textiles, some of the landed nobility were attracted towards employing capital in industry in the form of shares, while some banks began to be interested in industrial investments. The subsequent crisis of 1873 created great difficulties for these joint-stock companies and banks. But in general, though many banks went bankrupt, the industries that had become concentrated and strengthened financially kept on their feet, so that all in all it could be said that a step forward had been taken in the modernisation of the industrial sphere: concentration was tried out, and a search was begun for new forms of outside financing for industries.

While quite substantial progress between 1860 and 1880 can be established with some degree of precision in the spheres of railways and public works, it is much more difficult to determine the extent of industrial development during that period. The study of certain significant figures will show, however, that some moderate development did occur. The most striking progress was in textiles. Silk spinning in particular, underwent a minor revolution: spurred on by a crisis in the domestic supply of the raw material (due to a silkworm disease), the industry began to import some raw silk from abroad and definitely moved over to the final phase of the spinning process (i.e. throw-

6. Declaring the paper money of the banks of issue to be no longer convertible into gold or silver.

ing). The proportion of fully spun silk within total silk exports rose from 17 per cent in 1855 to 80 per cent in 1865. Estimated annual consumption of raw cotton by Italian spinning mills increased from around 100 quintals in 1860 to nearly 200 quintals a year in 1871–1875. The number of spindles in the cotton industry, reckoned at 400,000–450,000 in 1860–1861, reached 745,000 in 1876 (but, by way of comparison, it should be remembered that in England there were 33 million spindles by 1860). The increase in silk-spinning during this period was mainly concentrated in Lombardy, while that in cotton-spinning was in Piedmont, where also lay the main nucleus of wool production, especially at Biella. (Later on, however, though Piedmont continued to be the chief centre for wool, that for cotton moved over to Lombardy, presumably as a result of the exhaustion of a series of Lombard investments in the silk branch.) Perhaps even more important than the increases in productive capacity and production were the changes arising in the attitude of the industrialists themselves. They showed a greater readiness to assimilate technological advances, greater attention to the quality of production (which was still crude), and greater aggressiveness on the political plane: all this was indicative of a significant advance, though it did not become fully apparent until the subsequent period.

There were even fewer significant changes in the other industrial sectors. In the iron industry, the uneconomic production of pig-iron by means of charcoal-firing remained a problem; but Italian foundries in their manufacture replaced the archaic domestically-produced pig-iron by using instead imported pig-iron or scrap (which was becoming increasingly available on international markets at this time owing to the large-scale replacement on the railways of iron rails by steel). Consequently iron production increased around threefold between 1860 and 1880; but it was mainly an incomplete cycle of production (lacking the link of pig-iron production), and much of it was makeshift and of inferior quality (typical of the re-use of scrap). The component *steel*, which in these years was becoming the dominant characteristic of Western European metallurgical industry was, completely absent. The growth of the engineering branch remained modest, still confined to workshops carrying out marginal work for the railways or military commissions. Only small attempts were made to provide machinery for other industries, for example for the textile industry.

Nevertheless the front on which this modest progress took place was gradually expanding. Development affected a number of other branches as well as those of textiles and iron and machinery. First attempts at industrialisation were being made in the food industry: the first unit of a future big sugar-manufacturing complex opened in 1873; Francesco Cirio founded, in 1875, the jam and food preserves industry that was to become famous; and progress was made in the field of distilleries. Paper production rose from 240,000 quintals in 1862 to 600,000 in 1876. In 1872 G. B. Pirelli founded an industry, that of rubber, which was to have a remarkable future. First experiments were made in the production of chemical fertilisers (1875) and other chemical manufactures.

During these first twenty years, in short, there was a slow advance but no revolutionary development in the industrial field. The country's economic picture remained predominantly agricultural, and the exercise of an industrial activity still seemed like what the social scientists would term 'deviant behaviour'. Two factors, however, tended to diminish the isolation of these first industrial initiatives from their social environment. First, this limited development remained strictly concentrated within the country's north-western regions (which enjoyed the advantages of a more advanced agriculture and of proximity to the already industrialised European countries), and consequently their percentage weight within that area was higher than the national average within the country as a whole. Secondly, the three capitals of these regions—Milan, Genoa, and Turin—were acquiring the aspect of modern urban centres possessing considerable trade contacts with industrial countries: they were thus in a position to act as points of reference and bases for the industrialisation of their respective areas, not only through their factories, but also through their secondary schools and colleges (both Turin and Milan started polytechnics and technical schools during these years), their technical information publications, and the development of a financial and commercial milieu which was more prepared to support industrial initiatives. In Milan, in particular, the principal European firms producing machinery formed a commercial bridge-head towards the potential market they saw developing as a result of Italian industrialisation.

The years 1860 to 1880 can therefore be regarded as a prolongation—with no substantial break in continuity such as might have been expected from the political change—of the progress begun around 1830: a half-century in which, in the economic sphere of Italy's north-western regions, a 'first coat of paint' was applied, later to be embellished by the colours in which the future picture of industrialisation would be portrayed. In the 'seventies unmistakable signs of the growing importance of this infant industry could already be seen: in 1871–1873 a first industrial inquiry was carried out; in 1876 the first statistics of factories and employment in the principal sectors were compiled; and in 1878 the onset of the social problem in industry caused a first inquiry into strikes. Industrial activities received some undeniable benefits from Italy's political unification. But since economic policy remained anchored to the free-trade assumption of an international division of labour in which Italy occupied an eminently agricultural place, those benefits were strictly limited.

PROTECTIONIST TRENDS AND 'STIFLED' EXPANSION IN THE 1880's (1878–1889). CRISIS IN THE CENTURY'S LATTER YEARS (1889–1895).

Around 1880 however an important change occurred with the adoption of a different line in economic policy. Protectionist customs tariffs were introduced, at first, in 1878, on a small scale, and later, in 1887, more extensively. The

State intervened with direct support for the iron and engineering industries, instituting privilege quotas for Italian machinery in orders for railway supplies (the Baccarini law of 1882), giving assistance to national ship-yards (law of 1885), and promoting the development of a full-cycle iron and steel works at Terni (1886) to supply the merchant marine. An impetus was given to building developments in the big cities. In those years, too, the first provisions for social legislation were launched. Moreover in those years one of the main handicaps for the develop-ment of Italian industry lost much of its earlier weight: the reduction in freight-charges brought down the price of imported coal, which fell from an annual average of 370 lire a ton in 1871–1880 to 260 lire in 1881–1890 (the maxi-mum price was 500 lire in 1872–1873, the minimum 230 lire in 1886–1888). Coal imports therefore rose considerably: in 1877–1878 they were around 1,300,000 tons, but from then onwards they increased progressively to reach over 4 million tons at the end of the next decade.

At the same time a larger amount of private capital became available for non-agricultural investments. The international crisis and the ending of the *corso forzoso* com-bined to produce this situation. The agrarian crisis which developed around 1876 with the increased import of North American cereals made investment in land and farming less attractive. It also removed the hostility of agricultural circles towards tariff protection, thus leading to the forma-tion of an industrial-agricultural bloc of interests in favour of higher tariffs. Lastly, it created greater availability of manpower and brought down food costs to a low level. The ending of the *corso forzoso* in 1880 produced, in turn, a new influx of foreign capital, especially from France.

These new conditions at first had only limited effects on manufacturing activities. This was firstly because the new capital available tended to go into urban investments (building and public services such as lighting, transport, etc.) rather than into the manufacturing industries; and the same was true of labour which, when it left the country-side, went mainly into building in the towns. Secondly, the measures to encourage and support national industry (protectionism, State commissions) came up against an extremely unfavourable economic situation just when they were beginning to bear fruit: the years between 1889 and 1896 were the darkest years of the great depression in the international sphere and bore especially heavily on the Italian economy. The Italian banking system was wellnigh shattered by the effects of a paralysing crisis in the building industry, in which it was deeply involved. Consequently the promising impetus which seemed to have been given to the manufacturing industries, both through the new economic policies and through urban development (which produced a derivative demand for industrial goods such as building materials, wood, iron, and machinery for public services), received a severe check in almost all branches of industry.

The greatest and least impeded beneficiary of the new impetuses given to industry was the branch that had already established itself to a certain extent, in other words textiles, and especially cotton. Unlike other branches, the cotton industry had a practically uninterrupted rate of development and experienced no noticeable effects from the crisis around 1890. The main factors in this development—apart from those traditional factors that had favoured the birth of the industry—were the effects of tariff protection, the existence of channels of finance independent of the central nucleus of the banking system, and the enterprise shown in foreign markets by its businessmen. Tariff protection finally guaranteed the home market for the cotton industry, and as a result of urbanisation this was an expanding market. Consequently in this already established branch of industry the tariff of 1878 had an immediate effect, whereas in other branches such as iron and steel it proved, in the short run, insufficient to make up an already sizeable gap. The existence of a source of autonomous financing arose from the fact that a network of smaller banks had gradually developed on a local basis, often in the form of co-operatives, in the textile areas. These banks, it is important to note, remained largely immune from the crisis which between 1888 and 1894 hit the bigger banks, which were deeply involved in building speculation. Exports developed especially to Latin America, in the wake of the vast wave of emigration from Italy which began in those years. It then became apparent that in the cotton industry in a particular area of North Italy the most substantial nucleus of medium-scale entrepreneurship in the country had been developing. Though still tentative and unstable, this nucleus had from the outset certain definite characteristics which persisted right down to our own times, extending gradually to other branches of medium-scale business. The chief characteristic was its enterprise in placing surplus products in marginal areas of distant markets; but at the same time those outlets often proved difficult to maintain and the tendency was then to replace them as new opportunities arose. There was a general propensity to attach more importance to the commercial aspects of a business than to the technological or organisational sides, and much individualism still persisted, coupled with unwillingness for businesses to merge. And where this type of entrepreneurship prevailed, concentration was resisted, the family firm stood out against the formation of joint-stock companies, and self-financing was preferred to recourse to the capital market.

Some statistics demonstrate this situation. In 1876 the cotton industry had 627 factories with 52,000 workers; in 1900 there were 727 factories with 135,000 workers (it must of course be taken into account that in those 25 years the factories had gradually absorbed the work of the isolated handicraftsmen, especially in weaving). Of these 727 concerns, only 18 were shareholding companies. Nevertheless the average size of factories grew larger. The 745,000 spindles of 1876 had become 2,100,000 in 1900. Looms, numbering 26,800 in 1876, had in 1900 reached 78,306 of which 60,722 were mechanical. The value of cotton manufactures, estimated at 51 million lire in 1876, rose, despite the intervening fall in prices, to 304 million. Productivity consequently showed a considerable increase, from a production value of 940 lire per worker to 2,250 lire. The share of Italian cotton in world cotton production also increased:

in 1880 Italy consumed 1–1·25 per cent of the world's cotton, whereas in 1900–1901 she consumed 3·51 per cent. Production, however, still consisted mainly of crude-quality manufactures.

The second beneficiary of the new climate was at this stage, strange to say, the engineering industry rather than iron and steel. Here, however, the impetus was due less to customs tariffs than to other factors: the first large railway commissions given to national industry, orders arising from the formation of urban and suburban tramway networks in the main cities of the North (Milan and Turin), and finally the acquisition of a share in the market for machinery for the developing textile industry (especially for boilers, which became essential when medium-scale concerns expanded and moved over to steam-driven machinery). Shipbuilding was unable for the time being to take advantage of the provisions in its favour. It should be emphasised that these developments in the machine industry in general concerned less complicated types of work (for example, supplying industry's demand for boilers or turbines rather than for machine tools) or the assemblage of imported parts. The greater importance we have attached here to developments in the engineering industry rather than in iron and steel refers, of course, to the qualitative more than the quantitative aspects.

A new phase in metallurgical production, however, was just beginning to open up, based on the final abandonment of the traditional method of production (using charcoal for pig-iron) or the intermediary method (using scrap) and on the beginnings of steel production. This started at Terni and at Genoa in 1887 and seemed to show such promising growth up to 1889 that hopes were entertained of reaching and surpassing in quantity the national production of iron and even the amount of steel imported. But this process was halted by the economic crisis. The high point of steel production of 1889 was not reached again until 1904.

THE MOST IMPORTANT YEARS OF INDUSTRIAL DEVELOPMENT

STATISTICAL DATA OF A 'SPURT'

Not until after the end of the great depression can Italian industrialisation be said to have made a real spurt—though it remains to be seen whether it was a large or a small-scale affair. We shall discuss this point in the conclusion. The years from 1897 to 1913 undoubtedly witnessed a much greater increase than ever before in industrial production. The quantitative estimates available in this connection differ. According to the official valuations of the Italian Statistical Institute (ISTAT), manufacturing production on the eve of the First World War was about double that of before the great depression (the average level of manufacturing production in 1886–1890 was the same as that of 1896)[7]; according to an estimate of Gerschenkron, on the other hand, production over that period increased two-and-a-half times (he, however, maintains that between 1886 and 1896 there was a slight increase in manufacturing production despite the depression). According to the ISTAT valuation, the annual rate of increase in industrial production between 1896 and 1913 was 4.3 per cent, whereas Gerschenkron puts it at 5.4 per cent. Both indices register a greater increase in 1896–1908 than in 1908–1913. According to ISTAT, the share of industrial activities in the national product of the private sector rose over the period from a fifth to about a fourth.

A comparison of the censuses of 1901 and 1911 for population over the age of ten brings out a number of facts which, when analysed, demonstrate the transformation that took place during the crucial first decade of the new century.[8] The male population employed in manufacturing

---

7. This doubling is confirmed in Giorgio Fuà's review of the ISTAT estimates (v. bibliography).

8. Population over the age of ten is taken as a basis because work by children of under 15 was quite widespread at that time. The industrial

increased by about 400,000, absorbing 54 per cent of the total increase in male population over ten years of age. Female population employed in industry and handicrafts showed no significant net increase; but a study of the changes occurring in the various sectors shows that while 98,000 fewer women were employed in textiles—demonstrating the decline in work done at home in this sector, another indication of the industrial development—165,000 more women were employed in other branches; this meant a higher proportionate rate of increase than in the case of men (25 per cent as against 20 per cent). The figures for increase in employment in the various individual sectors show that the biggest increases occurred in the sectors that can be described as industrial in a modern sense, and the distribution between the sectors tends to become less concentrated and more diffused. This is a sign of the development of a more widely industrial society.

According to ISTAT's estimates, capital formation as a whole (dwellings, public works, plant and equipment) in the first decade of the twentieth century was 60 per cent higher (at constant prices) than in 1881–1890. But if capital investment in plant and equipment (whether in industry or in other sectors) is taken separately, it will be seen that capital formation increased more rapidly, being 114 per cent higher in 1901–1910 than in 1881–1890. The share of plant and equipment in total gross fixed investments, which was 54 per cent in 1881–1890, rose to 72 per cent in 1901–1910. With regard to industrial investments, confirmation of this trend, if only partial and indicative, should be looked for in direct findings of the time concerning mechanisation of manufacturing production. Between 1903 and 1911—years in which surveys of industrial activity were carried out—motor-power installed in manufacturing industries doubled, rising from 580,000 to 1,170,000 HP. Installation of electric motors was on a particularly large scale; they were used in converting a considerable part of

---

census of 1911 gives 228,000 such child-workers out of a total of 1,814,000 workers in industry.

the hydraulic power hitherto used directly in many industries, especially the textile industry. There was also quite a considerable increase in gas-driven motors, used especially for cereal-grinding and in the metallurgical branch. The efforts for greater mechanisation brought a considerable increase during these years in the importation of machinery and industrial equipment. Coal imports also increased from 30,904,000 quintals a year in 1881–1890 to 56,340,000 quintals in 1901–1905 and 91,944,000 in 1906–1913. Total motor power consumption (coal, electricity, and hydrocarbides), expressed in calorific power,[9] rose from an annual average of 25,286 milliard calories in 1881–1890 to an annual average of 48,748 milliard in 1901–1905 and 83,116 milliard in 1906–1913. The overall value of both equipment imports and energy consumption increased three-fold between 1888–1890 (the last years of the expansion of the 'eighties) and 1913, the eve of the First World War. These figures, it must be remembered, include uses both in industry and in transport. The latter is known to have absorbed about a quarter of total energy consumption just before the First World War, and its share was probably about the same in the preceding period. It may be concluded that the graph of these figures reflects pretty accurately the advance in the uses in the industrial sector, which strengthens the plausibility of Gerschenkron's figures for industrial production.

Thus during this period there was a breakdown of resistance to industrial development such as had not been possible when the movement towards expansion first began around 1880. It must be emphasised that the success of these efforts in the years now under consideration arose from the fact that, aided by the favourable international situation, the new trends in economic policy could at last take effect, and fuller scope could be given to that reserve of new attitudes and modernising tendencies which had been developing during the preceding period, and which till then had been partially paralysed by a serious recession. The reasons for the failure to succeed of the expansionist

9. Equivalent used: 1 kwh = 1 kg. coal = 7,000 calories.

movement in the 'eighties—unlike what happened in other countries such as Russia, in a similar situation of international economic depression—are largely to be attributed, as has been said, to the fact that non-agricultural investments during those years turned in the direction of urban development rather than industry (the building boom contained within itself an imminent prospect of crisis). The estimates of the formation of fixed capital in fact confirm that in the decade 1881–1890 the share allocated to housing and public works was equal to that for plant and equipment, whereas in the period 1897–1913 the proportion altered considerably, to a level of 1 : 3 in favour of plant and equipment.

INDUSTRIALISATION AGAINST A BACKGROUND OF BALANCED FOREIGN ACCOUNTS

Italian industrialisation in the years 1897–1913 did not—and this is a fact to be emphasised—involve any drastic change-over from consumption to investment in the use of resources. During this period per capita consumption increased considerably, though naturally at a lower rate than investment.

An effort towards industrialisation involves strong pressure on consumption when the use of productive factors (labour and capital) has to be diverted from the production of consumer goods (for instance food) to that of capital goods, or when a part of the consumer goods produced has to be diverted from the home market to be exported in exchange for imports of capital goods, or, again, when importation of the consumer goods needed to build up domestic stocks of some commodities is reduced to make way for importation of capital goods. In such cases the reduced availability of consumer goods on the home market causes their prices to rise more steeply than the increase in nominal wages, thus producing a fall in real wages, that is to say, a distribution of the income produced that is more unfavourable than before to incomes derived from labour. This picture, however, in no way corresponds to what happened in Italy between 1897 and 1913.

The average availability of foodstuffs per inhabitant, expressed in calories, underwent a sharp increase at the beginning of the period under consideration; it then remained constant for about ten years, to increase again in the last years (1911–1913). This was made possible, in the first place, because although part of the labour force moved over from agriculture into industry, agricultural and livestock production increased considerably during the period in question. The demand for some types of goods most in request (cereals, meat) increased at a greater rate than domestic supplies, and consequently foodstuff imports increased; but the export of certain other foodstuffs (cheese, citrus fruits, dried fruit) also increased considerably, and consequently the agriculture and foodstuffs section of the balance of trade (a section which had usually shown a credit balance in the past), managed to remain equalised for several years and only went into deficit towards the end of the period. And it was only in the last years of the period that the share of foodstuffs in total imports (a share which had fallen in the previous years, despite the absolute increase) went up considerably.

The increase in consumption was general, affecting other commodities as well as foodstuffs. The rate of expansion of consumption as a whole was only a little lower than that of the national income and was 2·5–3 times greater than the rate of expansion of the population. The greater part of non-foodstuff consumption was connected with the new way of life arising from increasing urbanisation, the main items being housing and clothing. The increase was unequally distributed, the main beneficiaries being no doubt the urban middle classes, whose importance was growing. But there were also considerable improvements in some of the richer agricultural regions of the North.

The pressure of rising demand soon made itself felt, and food prices went up, though without serious effects until the later years. For many years, indeed, the prices of foodstuffs most in popular demand (bread, *pasta*, rice, wine, sugar) actually fell, while prices, of the more luxury-type commodities (meat, butter, eggs) rose more steeply and continuously. But the workers, both in industry and in agriculture, showed a combative spirit and combined in strong organisations, thus managing to secure considerable increases in real wages, which in industry had risen by about 25 per cent by the eve of the First World War in comparison with the beginning of the expansion (at the end of the century). Naturally these wages still remained very low if compared with those of already industrialised countries; there were also significant differences between sector and sector, region and region, and big and small concerns as well as between men and women workers.

The fact that the increased demand for foodstuffs kept pace with the development of agriculture and the production of food helped to keep a favourable balance of payments during the expansion period and to ensure a significant expansion of consumption. But there were two other important factors. The development of export industries made it possible to contain within certain limits the unavoidable deficit caused by industrialisation which called for the supply of energy, raw and semi-finished materials and machinery. And invisible earnings—freights, tourism, and emigrants' remittances also sustained the balance of payments.

The principal exporting industry was that of textiles, silk, in particular, touching the highest levels in both production and export during this period. In 1907 the value of silk exports began to fall, and there was talk of a crisis in this branch, but just before the war its credit value within the balance of trade was nevertheless higher than in the years before the expansion period. The value of silk exports continued to represent between a third and a quarter of total exports, and this share fell only slightly when subtracting imports in the sector, which also increased owing to the fact that Milan had now taken the place of Lyons as the principal European market. Exports of the cotton industry also developed considerably, accounting in some years for a tenth of total exports. The balance of trade in cotton (which included both raw material imports and domestic consumption) was practically equalised. This meant that increased domestic consumption of cotton textiles was compensated in the balance of trade by exports. This estimate can also be applied to domestic consumption of textiles as a whole when we consider that the deficit in the balance for wool was in turn compensated by high net exports of those other traditional exports, hemp and flax.

But the marginal phenomenon (in an economic sense) which contributed decisively towards a favourable balance of trade at this time was migration. Italian emigration, especially overseas, assumed important dimensions during these years. It had begun to increase sharply towards the end of the 1880s. But in the decade 1901–1910 it reached an annual average of 600,000 persons. The majority of the emigrant workers sent part of their earnings home to their families or brought back savings if they returned home themselves. Calculations for the period 1901–1913 show that, against a commercial deficit of 10,230 million lire, invisible items showed a credit of 12,291 million, over a third of which came from tourism and over a half from emigrants' remittances. Emigrants' savings constituted a peculiarly Italian form of workers' contribution to industrialisation and gave rise to a phenomenon which Marx might have included among those forming the picture of 'primitive accumulation'.

These three advantageous circumstances—an expanding agricultural production, development of the export industries, and an increase in the invisible sector of the balance of trade, due largely to emigrants' remittances—enabled the effort towards industrialisation to go ahead in these years despite the meagre participation of foreign capital, and to be conducted against a background of balanced foreign accounts, without serious tensions in the prices system, and therefore, despite protectionism, with a balanced expansion of internal consumption. Some imbalances did occur in the course of this effort but they came from other sources.

A 'TWO-SIDED' INDUSTRIALISATION: ONE SIDE LOOKING TOWARDS THE PAST

Since the decisive impact of Italian industrialisation occurred after the end of the great depression, it follows that its development took place within the framework of the European Industrial Revolution's 'second wind'[10], in which the 'technological climacteric' of the great depression was overcome through the development of new forms of production.

The basic technological features of the 'second wind' were the large-scale use of new materials (steel and new chemical products), the introduction of new sources of energy, and a remarkable development in the machine industry. That development covered a great many different sides, the most important being expansion of the assemblage industries, multiplication of machine tools endowed with the new capabilities made possible by the use of steel, and the birth of the automobile industry.

Italy's industrialisation effort during this period presents a curious duality, for while it profited from the acquisitions of the first phase of the Industrial Revolution, it adopted only partially the new productions and technological assets brought by the revolution's 'second wind'. This two-sided character of Italian industrialisation at the beginning of the new century provides the reasons for the limitations of this 'spurt' and for many of the difficulties which impeded the development of the country's economy in the subsequent twenty years between the two world wars. For the market prospects of many traditional forms of production (such as textiles), on which industrial efforts had been concentrated during the years 1896–1913, began to decline, while the success of the new forms of production had not yet become fully established.

The textile industry was the chief representative of that

10. For the significance of this term see D. S. Landes, 'Technological Change and Development in Western Europe, 1750–1914', in *The Cambridge Economic History*, vol. VI, Cambridge, 1965.

aspect of Italian industrialisation which still aimed to profit from the results of the first wave of the Industrial Revolution. Italy's greatest industrial development at this time still lay in the textile branch, where the fundamental silk and cotton industries reached their full maturity. In fact the textile industry more than any other could rely on a considerable amount of means and equipment and of entrepreneurial skill. Its rate of increase appeared lower than that of other branches during the years of expansion, for the obvious reason that the point of departure was higher. But the importance of the textile industry can be clearly seen when we recall that it was the country's sole big exporting industry, accounting for some 40 per cent of the total value of the credit side of Italy's trade balance in the years preceding the First World War, and for nearly 60 per cent of its non-alimentary exports. It continued to be the main source of employment for workers in the manufacturing branch, accounting for about a third of such workers in the 1911 census. Even up to the eve of the war, in 1913, according to ISTAT estimates the added value of the textile industry represented 20 per cent of the total product of the manufacturing industries.

Textile progress in these years can be summarised in the following terms: complete conquest of the domestic market; accentuation of its character as an exporting industry; industrial development of weaving—which till then had been mainly organised under the 'putting-out' system—as well as of spinning; and mechanisation and electrification of both spinning and weaving.

Italy's export of silk, which since before the unification had represented about a third of the value of Italian exports, slightly reduced its percentage share during the period 1896–1915, but this slight fall occurred within an increased total value of exports. The quality of the silks exported improved considerably.

Cotton's trade balance, confined to manufactured goods, at the turn of the century moved from deficit to credit, and Italy became an exporting country for cotton goods. The cotton balance as a whole remained in deficit, however, taking into account the fact that net imports of raw material were used chiefly for production for the home market. Flax and hemp production for export also continued to increase. Less progress was made in wool exports; though their value went up, it remained below that of imports, although here too the export/import relationship improved.

The development of industrial weaving within the various branches of the textile industry had remained somewhat limited throughout the whole of the earlier phase, during which the main developments were, as has been seen, in spinning. In the silk branch, in 1876 there were only 250 mechanical looms and 12,000 hand-looms; in 1890 the figures were 2,500 and 12,000 and even in 1898 there were only 3,000 mechanical looms as compared with the 12,000 hand-looms. But by 1912 the proportion was reversed, with 15,000 mechanical looms to 5,000 hand looms. Exports of woven silk as a percentage of total silk exports moved from 6 per cent in 1885 to 17 per cent in 1913, at a time of exceptional expansion of silk exports as a whole. Particularly remarkable was the increase in exports of Italian silk textiles to England, where they had conquered positions held in the past by silks from Lyons. The radical change that had taken place in the industrial attitude of the silk-weavers is illustrated by the efforts made in investment: production by hand-loom involved virtually no capital investment, for a hand-loom cost only about 200 lire and was capable of a product worth some 3,000 lire a year. The average price of a mechanical loom, on the other hand, was 6,000 lire, and its annual production of woven silk was worth between 8,000 and 9,000 lire. The increase in investment in mechanisation of silk-weaving between 1898 and 1912 can therefore be estimated at 72 million lire of that period.

In the cotton industry there were 65,000 mechanical looms in 1896; by 1912 these had risen to 115,000, thus reaching an increase of 59,000 units. There were then still 30,000 hand-looms. The automatic Northrop machine was still practically unknown; it came into use only after the war. Cotton exports, unlike those of silk, had from the first consisted mainly of woven rather than spun goods, being for a different market: the Italian silk industry had in fact, as we have seen, come to birth as an industry supplying semi-finished goods for the industry of industrial countries, whereas the export side of the Italian cotton industry was originally based on supplying the consumer market of non-industrial or partly-industrial countries. Consequently the development in cotton exports was the reverse of that in silk: it was only *after* advances had been made in the export of woven cotton that considerable quantities of spun yarn also began to be exported to countries where cotton-weaving factories were beginning to develop, in some cases with Italian capital. In 1895 Italy exported woven cotton goods to a value of 21 million lire and spun yarn to a value of 2 million. In 1913 exports of woven goods had increased ten-fold, reaching a value of 210 million, while those of spun yarn had increased twenty-fold, reaching 39 million. The trend was rather different in the flax and hemp industry, which had started as an export industry in Italy with characteristics similar to those of silk, in other words as a supplier to foreign industry of semi-finished goods, based on local raw materials. This predominant characteristic was maintained, if to a lesser degree: in 1895 the value of exports of spun yarn was 13 million lire, of woven goods 4 million; in 1913 spun yarn reached a value of 23 million and woven goods 17 million.

Progress was more difficult in the wool branch, where the problem was to achieve a better quality product, which called for greater technical efficiency than in the other textile branches. Because of these greater technical difficulties, the trade balance for woollen manufactures, unlike cotton, had not yet as was said earlier, reached a credit position by the First World War, though it came near to doing so. Domestic production in 1913 covered 319,000 quintals, or 91 per cent, of the estimated 350,000 quintals of domestic consumption. (The percentage in value was lower, however, because dependence on imports concerned the more costly combing wools.) But the woollen industry remained weak on the export side: in 1913 woven and mixed woollen goods were exported to a value of 31 million lire, while the value of imports was 54 million. The inferior quality of most Italian woollen goods can be seen from the fact that the value per kg. of woven woollen exports was 10.80 lire, whereas that of imports was 18.15 lire. But the home market had been conquered for wool too, except for the finer combing wools. Developments in mechanical weaving, which had made this success possible, can be summed up in the transition from 6,507 mechanical looms in 1894 to an estimated 12,000 in 1915.

The development of weaving—which represents the greatest innovation in the story of Italy's textile industry in these years—came about on the basis of a striking expansion in the number of spinning-mills. Silk-spinning (reeling and throwing) was an exception in this respect, for its increase in production was effected mainly through a more intensive use of its existing productive capacity, involving no great investment and virtually no increase in manpower; but the organisation of labour and its distribution throughout the year improved, as also did its productivity.

Considerable investment occurred, on the other hand, in cotton-spinning. The 1,910,000 spindles of 1898 had risen by 1914 to 4,620,000. In the first years of the twentieth century Italy's rate of increase in the number of cotton-spindles was the highest in the world. Cotton-spinning benefited greatly from the new source of hydroelectric power. The ring spindle was much more widely used in Italy than the self-acting spindle: in 1913 there were 3.5 million ring spindles as compared with 1.1 million self-actings. The preference was typical of the newer cotton-producing countries such as the United States, Japan, and India, whereas the reverse was true of Great Britain.[11] The use of ring spindles, which gave a third higher production than the self-actings, made it possible to achieve a considerable

11. Cf. R. E. Tyson, 'The Cotton Industry', in D. H. Alcroft ed., *The Development of British Industry and Foreign Competition (1875–1914)*, London, 1968, pp. 121ff.

increase in production with a reduced labour-force (thereby reducing the loss that regulations on night work caused to entrepreneurs) and to speed up production in general.

The main technical effort of the woollen industry, aided by tariff protection, consisted at this time in promoting the production of the finer and more costly combing wools in preference to the traditional carding wools. This effort chiefly affected spinning, whereas weaving suffered from it in a sense because with customs duties the cost of combins wools went up; consequently the wool balance continued to be in deficit as far as the finer and more costly combins goods were concerned. However the number of combing-spindles rose more rapidly than that of carding-spindles, and combing-machines began to be used, the most frequent type being the French rectilinear machine, with a lower hourly productivity than the circulating type of machine used in England.

It is worth noting, as an instance of the two-sided character of Italian industrialisation during this period, that in the textile industry as a whole the stage of manufacture represented by dyeing remained backward. Dyeing was linked with advances in chemicals and was therefore more orientated towards the 'second wind' stage. Despite the advances made in this field, most of the raw silk exported by Italy was not dyed, and much of the silk that needed to be dyed had to be temporarily exported to France, Switzerland or Germany for treatment. There was a similar situation in the cotton industry with regard to both mercerisation and dyeing, which were largely done in Germany.

According to ISTAT's estimates, the textile industry, together with the foodstuffs industries and other agricultural-manufacturing industries, in 1913 still represented 60 per cent of the total added value of the manufacturing industries. About 60 per cent of the 1.5 million workers registered in the manufacturing industries (1911 census) were also employed in that group, which could be considered the traditional side of the Italian industrial edifice and was still the most important from the quantitative angle. The group developed considerably during this period, not only in the textile branch but also in the branches of timber and foodstuffs industries. This development was particularly marked in certain foodstuffs sectors such as sugar (which was favoured by protectionism), alcoholic drinks (beer, liquor distilleries), sweets (especially chocolate), food preserves, and macaroni, sectors which had big export trade, especially to reception countries for Italian emigrants. Modern mechanisation and concentration began to develop in other important—and hitherto dispersed—industries, such as cereal-milling and olive-crushing.

PARTICIPATION IN THE 'SECOND WIND' OF THE INDUSTRIAL REVOLUTION

The aspect of Italy's industrial development in 1896–1914 which was more definitely orientated towards the Industrial Revolution's 'second wind' was undoubtedly the birth of a hydroelectrical industry. A large part of the capital set free by the nationalisation of the railways in 1905 was directed towards this branch of investment. Nor was it fortuitous that the big commercial banks, formed through German initiative after the banking crisis of the 1890s, turned their interest in this direction. These big banks evolved a positive strategy of intervention in relation to this particular opportunity for investment, resting as it did on the solid foundation of a patrimony of natural resources to be exploited in the big Alpine river basins. This strategy, according to many contemporary commentators, combined Italian industrial development with the export interests of German industry, first for electrical machinery, then for machinery in general, and finally for all kinds of industrial products, and it therefore tended in a certain sense to give Italian industrialisation a 'complementary' character. But it was nevertheless a project to be actively pursued, a sort of planning operation in a milieu that was not particularly rich in capital and initiatives. It did not edge out other plans, for no such other plans existed, and it therefore represented a positive way of promoting industrialisation.

Between 1895 (the year in which a law favouring the transport of power from a distance came into force) and 1914, a vast amount of capital was invested in electrical constructions. The value of the installations reached 1,000–1,200 million lire, a figure equal to around 4 per cent of all fixed investments in plant and equipment during that period. By 1914 these generating plants were producing a power of 1,150,000 kw. (of which 850,000 kw. was hydroelectric), with an annual production of 2,575 million kwh. This tremendous development had a great psychological effect in Italian economic circles, giving a sense of release from the industrial impotence to which many still believed Italy was doomed because of her lack of energy resources. People made the satisfactory discovery that hydroelectrical production alone could replace around 2 million tons a year of coal imports, or about a fifth of all the coal imported. It was not much, but on the eve of the war there were a great many hydroelectrical resources still to be exploited.

It must also be emphasised that the major part of the new hydroelectrical production was destined for industry. The textile industry absorbed the highest proportion, followed by the machine industry. Iron and steel's consumption was not very high (though in those years it was more widely believed than was later to prove technically justified that electro-metallurgy would have a great future), whereas that of the chemical industry was by comparison quite large—this was, in fact, one of the chief potential fields for industrial consumption of electric energy. Taken as a whole, the industrial census of 1911 shows that at that date half the power of the motors installed in the manufacturing industry was electric.

The other great 'new' industry to be born in this period was that of steel. In 1895 Italy's production of steel accounted for about a quarter of her total iron-and-steel production, which still consisted chiefly of iron. But the level of production was low, little more than 200,000 tons;

and the steel industry itself was still virtually non-existent. By the eve of the First World War, however, Italy had achieved some steel production, though it was still comparatively modest: 933,000 tons in 1913 (and 427,00 tons of pig-iron). Iron production at that date was only 193,000 tons. Thus Italy's economy seemed to have entered—with the aid of tariff protection—on the age of steel, viewed at least from the point of view of production in her iron-and-steel industry. The reality was unfortunately less satisfactory. First and foremost, unlike what happened in the other 'new' industry, electricity, the price of the existence of the iron-and-steel industry was really paid by the user sectors that were not protected, and chiefly by part of the machine industry. It must be borne in mind that the steel age is the era not only of its production but also, and more particularly, of its utilisation. Italy's industrialisation effort could realise to a certain extent the first condition; it was less able to realise the second.

Moreover, the course embarked on by the Italian steel industry was not calculated to help it to recover from its original disadvantage of low productivity in a nascent industry. Such recovery would in any case have been difficult given Italy's great drawback, her lack of low-grade anthracite deposits. The basic technological choice was the decision to adopt the Martin furnace in preference to the Thomas convector. This was the same choice that had been made by the steel industry in England, while it differed from the methods adopted in France and Germany. Now, as is well known, the Thomas process permitted quicker and therefore more economical production, despite the higher cost of the plant; but at the same time the Thomas process, because of its greater speed, called for greater skill and technical care and in general gave a less homogeneous product, less adaptable (in particular, less suitable for use in sheet form) and leaving more slag. A characteristic of the Martin process, on the other hand, was that it afforded the possibility of using scrap, in the proportion of fifty-fifty with pig-iron, in the production of steel. Moreover the Martin process was more fungible. Lastly, it allowed for greater elasticity in production and was thus better suited to the uncertainties of the market in which Italian production operated.

The reasons for Italy's iron-and-steel industry's choice of the Martin process, thus differing from that of other continental countries, were various and complex. They were to some extent the same that had prompted that choice in England, where the importance of the shipbuilding industry, with its demand for iron and steel plates, had played a part; but the context in Italy was different: there the birth of the iron-and-steel industry was closely connected with commissions for the navy and with the protection accorded to the shipbuilding industry. Secondly, this choice was influenced by the preceding structure of the Italian metallurgical industry with its high consumption of scrap and its reluctance to embark on the continuous process of manufacture, including the whole cycle of working the mineral. In the early stages, in other words, there was a shortage of pig-iron production, which would have afforded the advantage of large-scale vertical economies deriving from the thermic unity of production: steel production consequently started with the use of scrap and imported pig-iron, and this conditioned its subsequent development. Thirdly, various centrifugal forces pushed in the direction of a production divided into several units, and this both limited the advantages of large-scale economies and also impeded capital-intensive investment (the Thomas plant called for an investment at least ten times higher, and for a minimum size five or six times greater, than the Martin plant). Italy's iron-and-steel works were scattered in various different places: some in Liguria, connected with the naval shipyards; others in Lombardy which derived from the old iron industry of the valleys and were developed by an environment that was the most industrially advanced part of Italy; in Umbria there was the isolated works at Terni, established through government initiative; the vicinity of iron ore in the isle of Elba led to the location of pig-iron production in Tuscany; and, lastly, the first laws of 1904 providing incentives to establish industries in the backward South resulted in the establishment of a new iron-and-steel works near Naples. The results of this dispersed development, coupled with the serious disadvantage of having to import the necessary coal, meant that the Italian iron-and-steel industry led a very difficult life right up to the time of the reorganisation following the Second World War. The Italian industrial structure was endowed with the component of steel, but it had it in the form of a weak joint, in constant need of care and assistance.

The truer protagonist of the steel age, the machine industry, had an even more difficult progress. It is, in fact, relatively easier to further the birth of a metallurgical industry—by means of tariff protection and assured outlets (commissions for railways and naval shipyards)—than of a machine industry. The machine industry has a great variety of production; in order to specialise it needs vast industrial markets; it often needs to be in a position to compete on international markets in order to achieve sufficient dimensions; and, lastly, it needs a large number of skilled workers, who are difficult to come by in the early stages of an effort towards industrialisation. Despite the protection accorded to the naval shipyards, not even this branch of heavy engineering production succeeded in dominating the home market. England continued to be the chief supplier of merchant vessels for the Italian shipowners, who still preferred to rely on the old and well-tried capability of British shipyards. In 1913, against a national production of 536,000 tons, 1,495,000 tons of shipping was still imported, 893,000 tons of which came from England. The position was even more unfavourable in relation to ships' engines: 45,000 HP of national production, as against 146,000 HP of foreign production, of which 92,000 HP was British. National industry did, on the other hand, succeed eventually in securing the monopoly for railway construction material, as a result of the nationalisation of the railways in 1905. Even in this case circumstances were not particularly favourable for the Italian industry; in the three years following the passage of the railways into State

hands, some 38 per cent of the largest and most urgent
commissions had to be given to foreign industry, because
during the last period of private management urgent requirements of rolling stock had accumulated to such an
extent that the national industry alone could not cover
them. This was the last unhappy chapter of that history
of lost opportunities that the railways represented in Italian
industry.

Henceforth, however, neither shipbuilding nor railway
construction constituted the sinews of modern engineering.
The modern machine industry was *par excellence* an industry
for creating 'new' goods, whether producer goods (such as
electric motors, internal combustion engines, machine tools
for mass production, agricultural machinery, office machines,
sewing machines, etc.) or consumer goods destined to
change the way of life, such as bicycles or motor-cars. On
the whole Italian industry did not participate at this stage
in the field of 'new' investment goods except for some
occasional rare and promising initiative such as that of
typewriters, production of which was started by Camillo
Olivetti at Ivrea in 1911, or of typographical machines.
A breach was opened up, however, in the field of 'new'
consumer goods by the bicycle and motor-cycle industries,
and above all by the automobile industry. This last was
probably one of the most brilliant and effective examples of
Italian industry's participation in the new international
industrial movement of those years, and, more generally,
it was of great importance in opening the way for the rise
of a modern machine industry in Italy by stimulating inventions in this field, creating a skilled labour force, and
promoting the rise of collateral types of production (among
which must be mentioned the aluminium industry). In the
years immediately before the First World War some 20,000
motor vehicles a year were registered in Italy, only 3–
4,000 of which were imported; this meant that the domestic
market was controlled by national production. Naturally
it was still a very limited market, for the automobile was
then a luxury in a society like that of Italy, still a long way
from the mass consumption age. Production reflected this

characteristic of the market: it consisted chiefly of large cars, built by methods that still savoured of handicrafts, very different from the methods that were already gaining ground in the United States, where mass production, with an extensive development of cast and stamped parts, had begun. Because of this characteristic of Italian automobile production, there were at first too many isolated initiatives in this field; it was not until after a crisis arose in 1907 that a process of concentration began.

To complete the picture of the share of Italy's industrialisation movement in the 'second wind' during the years before the First World War, something must be said about developments in the chemical industry. This was one of the 'new' sectors in which development followed more routine lines: here there was no outburst of enthusiasm such as accompanied the early hydroelectrical advances, no rapid growth such as protection and commissions encouraged in steel, not even daring ventures such as men like Agnelli or Olivetti were attempting in some particular branch of the machine industry. The Italian chemical industry took practically no part in the two fields which had been opened up in that sector by the discoveries of the second half of the nineteenth century—the production of alkalies (used in the textile, soap, and paper-making industries) according to the new (Soda Solvay) methods, and the synthesis of organic components, which found its widest applications in the field of colouring materials, explosives, pharmaceutics, and photography, opening up the way—with artificial silk —to man-made fibres. Italy's absence from the more advanced sectors of chemical developments was due partly to her shortage of experienced scientists and technicians in this field, partly to the lack of those carboniferous products which formed the basis for the second of those developments.

The Italian chemical industry at the beginning of the twentieth century was concerned chiefly with fertilisers for agriculture, especially superphosphates, whose productive increase is shown in terms of production of sulphuric acid.

This rose from 139,000 tons in 1898 to 645,000 tons in 1913. Italian production of superphosphates covered 95 per cent of domestic consumption.

From 1905 onwards nitrogenous fertilisers were also produced, especially through the related production of calcium carbide, calcium cyanide, and ammonium sulphate. Production of these nitrogenous fertilisers, however, was both small as compared with that of more advanced countries and quite insufficient for the growing demands of Italian agriculture, which had to procure much of its supplies from abroad: in 1913, domestic production accounted for 134,000 quintals of ammonium sulphate, while 217,000 quintals were imported. Potassium fertilisers were little used at that time, and were all imported.

THE AGENTS OF THE SPURT: THE STATE, ENTREPRENEURSHIP, THE COMMERCIAL BANK

It would be a mistake to underestimate the fact that the Italian industrial development of the years 1896–1913 occurred within a favourable international economic climate, in the upper trend of what Kondratieff calls a 'long wave'. This appears the more significant when we recall the important part played in its growth by the export trade, both in agricultural and in industrial goods (especially textiles), a result of the rising trend of international demand. It is more difficult to estimate the effect of the movement of international prices, bearing in mind the big increases in imports made necessary by the growing dynamism of Italian industrial production. The terms of trade showed a tendency to worsen. Clearly, however, protectionism counteracted (at the expense of the home market, which nevertheless continued to expand) many of the negative effects both of falling and of rising international prices. Industrial investments were able to benefit overall from the fall in prices of imported machinery. The substitution of internal sources of energy (electricity) for imported sources (coal) enabled many industries to escape the effects of the periodical increases in coal prices. But it must be added that in the years of greatest expansion (1902–1905) the price of imported coal remained low.

Such was the international framework. But the favourable international situation does not suffice to explain Italy's industrial expansion at the beginning of the century. As was mentioned in the previous chapter, a strongly protectionist tariff was in force in Italy from 1887 (only slightly mitigated by the trade treaties concluded in the following years with various countries), but the crisis of the 1890s had impeded the effects of this measure. Its effects, however, became apparent as soon as the international economy emerged from the depression and optimism returned to business circles. State action for the promotion of industrial development was not, moreover, confined to tariff protection. Domestic industry received other forms of aid, the most important being orders for the railways, which had been nationalised in 1905, navigation bounties, and building awards for ships produced in Italian shipyards. This legislation in favour of the shipbuilding industry also went back to the 1880s (1885) but it had had no immediate effect because of the depression (which in this field had shown itself in a heavy fall in freight rates). These measures of support for heavy engineering went some way towards compensating for the greater burdens which that sector had had to sustain through tariff protection for the metallurgical industry. All the rest of the engineering industry, however, derived no benefit from such compensation, and this caused disputes, the echo of which still reaches us today from many historians who speak of the damage caused to the engineering industry by a largely metallurgical protectionism. It must however be emphasised that the more technologically efficient parts of the engineering industry—those concerned with machine tools for the industries or for electro-engineering—suffered less from the high cost of materials than from the shortage of skilled labour and from the still limited size of the market for industrial capital goods. A tariff protection of the engineering industry which was working for the other industrial activities, on the other hand, would probably have damaged the other industries' possibilities of securing equipment more than it would have helped the engineering industry itself.

The protection assured by the State to many industrial activities—metallurgy and heavy engineering, the textile industry and the food industry—was a very important factor in the spurt of these years. The State, however, itself played no part in entrepreneurial or financing activities, and its furtherance of industrial development did not take those forms (as it was later to do, after the First World War). Private entrepreneurs and certain financial operators therefore played a very important part in the development of industry.

There were quite a number of such capable private entrepreneurs: this can be seen from the fact that industrialisation at this time was carried on in numerous smaller factories rather than in large-scale concerns. Except for the iron-and-steel industry and one or two other concerns, the majority of factories were of small or medium scale. This was true of the textile sector and also of the more difficult engineering sector, which was not yet widely established but which, as has been seen, embarked on some promising ventures (automobiles, typewriters, typographical machines). The same can be said of the chemical industry. All this limited the advantages of concentration, but at the same time such diffusion meant that there was a more widely spread readiness for economic ventures which is one of the most difficult factors in industrial development. It could probably not have been overcome but for the fact that in the more advanced regions of the 'triangle' there was a long-standing tradition of small concerns, especially in the textile field, many of which had been strengthened, as was said earlier, by the influx at various times of foreign entrepreneurs who had imparted their methods. The Italians' capacity for entrepreneurship may not seem to have amounted to much when compared with that of English or German businessmen, and when account is taken of the support given by protectionism and the low wages paid. Their chief defect lay in factory organisation, but they showed a certain initiative in foreign markets and afforded some examples of technical ingenuity. There were some early instances of Italian businessmen who proved capable of embarking on the process of concentration or merging in sectors where dispersion had hitherto been the general rule (e.g. the automobile and chemical industries).

The activities of private industrial entrepreneurs in certain sectors found special support, both financial and otherwise, in the commercial banks. After the banking crisis which, beginning in 1889, had led in 1893 to the failure of the principal Italian banks, the void thus created in the banking system had been promptly filled through the initiative of German bankers, who had promoted the establishment of two new credit institutes, the Banca Commerciale Italiana and the Credito Italiano. These institutes operated after the German model of deposit and investment banks, becoming deeply involved in financing the birth and development of industrial undertakings in Italy. These banks, grasping the great possibilities of the hydro-electrical industry and also profiting by the conditions created by protectionism in certain fields (especially iron and steel), did not confine themselves to direct financing but also helped the concerns to form shareholding companies and to concentrate and reach agreements among themselves when this seemed advantageous. They also intervened in the running of the enterprise and gave technical assistance. It is interesting to note, in confirmation of the entrepreneurial activity of these banks, that they operated principally in the *new* sectors of Italian industry, almost completely neglecting the more traditional sectors such as the textile industry.[12]

And it was chiefly in the new industries that concentration and the formation of shareholding companies developed. According to the industrial census of 1911, the sectors in which share companies were most widespread were production and distribution of energy, mining, metallurgy, and

12. This emerges clearly in a dissertation by Jon Sheldon Cohen, *Finance and Industrialisation in Italy 1894–1914* (University of California), which the author kindly allowed the present writer to see.

chemicals. Formation of shareholding companies was on only a limited scale in the textile sector, especially in the more traditional branches such as the silk industry. But on the whole the progress of industrial share capital was remarkable: between 1896 and 1914 it increased around ninefold.

The spurt made by Italian industry in the years 1896–1913 was thus the result of a *combination* of different factors, none of which can claim an exclusive or predominant role in it. Some of these factors were traditional (such as private entrepreneurship), others were of the kind that operated especially in historic cases of retarded industrialisation such as that of Germany (the mixed deposit and investment bank). Even the State's protectionist policy (which was the only outstanding manifestation of State support for the industrial development) is not a particular characteristic of *late-joiners* countries. It was adopted by virtually all the countries that became industrialised during the nineteenth century, with the exception of Great Britain, whose industrial revolution had begun in the eighteenth century, and who, in any case, had had protectionist precedents in the mercantilist era.

CONCLUSION

In the formation of industrial Italy it is difficult to pinpoint any real 'big spurt'. Even the chief supporter of this theory, Gerschenkron, appears somewhat embarrassed at mentioning that the growth rates of Italian industrial production, even in the years of greatest development, do not approach the much higher rates achieved by other countries at similar stages.[13]

This impression seems to be confirmed when a comparison is made between the absolute levels of Italian industrial production and those of other industrial countries before and

13. Gerschenkron, *Economic Backwardness in Historical Perspective*, Cambridge, Mass., 1962, p. 78, mentions the cases of Sweden (12% per annum in 1888–96), Japan (8.5% per annum in 1907–13), and Russia (8% per annum in the last decade of the nineteenth century).

after the period 1896–1913. For example, the ratio between Italian iron and steel production and that of other European countries (U.K., Germany, France, Belgium) in 1889 was 1: 11.7: 10: 4: 2.4. In 1913 the ratio was 1: 8: 17: 4.6: 2.5.[14] As can be seen, except in relation to the United Kingdom, the ratio had worsened to Italy's disadvantage, rather than improved. The same phenomenon is evident from a comparison of the respective 'apparent consumption' of basic metallurgical products. Italy's relative share of the world seems to improve, however, in the textile sector: cotton spindles and looms installed in Italy, which in 1895 were respectively 1–1.85 and 2.48 per cent, had risen by 1913 to 4.11 and 5.07 per cent.[15] This may be regarded as a further confirmation of what we have called the two-sided character of Italian industrialisation in these years.

The percentage of the total population which was employed in industry in Italy remained not only well below that of other already highly industrialised countries such as Great Britain and Germany, but also below that of industrialised countries with a large agricultural population, such as France.[16]

The reasons for the lack of 'violent' growth in Italy *in a single period* (seeming to suggest, rather, a development by successive spurts of limited duration, some of them before, some after the spurt of 1896–1913) are probably to be sought in two directions: on the one hand, in the *composite* character of the agents of development, none of which really operated with great force and which therefore did not cause a great concentration of effort in any one par-

14. I. Svennilson, *Growth and Stagnation in the European Economy*, Geneva, U.N. Economic Commission for Europe, 1954, p. 261.

15. R. Tremelloni, *L'industria tessile italiana*, Turin, 1937, p. 142.

16. On the basis of data given in I. Svennilson, *op. cit.*, pp. 47 and 236, the percentage of the population employed in mining and manufacturing industries in the various countries on the eve of the First World War was as follows: Great Britain 12.9% (1907/1910), Germany 10.1% (1907/1910), France 7.7% (1901/1900), Belgium 10.1% (1910/1910), Switzerland 12.0% (1910/1910), Italy 4.7% (1911/1911). The years in brackets indicate respectively the year of the datum relating to population and the year of the datum relating to workers in industry.

ticular period; and, on the other hand, in the territorially restricted area in which this development took place. This generated a growth characterised in the middle period by certain factors of equilibrium (in the foreign trade accounts, in the relation between investment and consumption), but with the prospect, on a more long-term view, of growing imbalances. These imbalances showed themselves clearly after the First World War. Some important assets in the foreign accounts were then drastically reduced (notably emigrants' remittances); the most traditional component of the Italian industrial structure, and its largest exporter, the textile industry, entered upon a climacteric period; and the technological and territorial limitations of the pre-ceding development exploded to produce a serious excess of productive capacity in the heavy industries, which found themselves faced with a territorially restricted domestic market (owing to the lack of economic progress in the southern regions) and endowed with a still largely archaic industrial structure.

The extent of the territorial concentration of Italy's industrial development in one particular area can be clearly seen from the relevant statistics. In 1911, the date of the first serious industrial census, 58.06 per cent of workers in industrial concerns employing more than ten persons were located in the three north-western regions in which 21.6 per cent of the population lived (the percentage falls to the still very high figure of 49.16 if we take into account concerns employing less than ten persons, in other words mainly handicraft workshops). Those three regions ac-counted for 48.89 per cent of all mechanised horse-power. In effect, more than half of the country's real industrial potential (factories and workers) was concentrated in an area inhabited by 9,412,000 persons, an area in which the relation between population and industrial potential was therefore about twice as high as the national average in that respect. Unfortunately no regional breakdown of the industrial product of that date is available. But it is obvious that the productivity of the Italian industrial apparatus concentrated in the three north-western regions was very much higher than in the rest of the country. If it was possible, therefore, to compare the product, and not merely the number of factories and workers, the degree of territorial concentration would be seen to be much higher, as also would be the difference in relation to the national average.

If we consider in isolation the industrialisation indices of the 'little country' composed of the three north-western regions, the difference in relation to the level of industrialisation of Central and Western Europe appears much less than if such a comparison is made in regard to Italy as a whole. In those three regions taken alone, in 1911 the percentage of the population employed in secondary activities was 9.6 per cent, as against 3 per cent in the rest of Italy (the national average was 4.7 per cent). In the three regions of the 'triangle', in short, the proportion is not very different from that found in the smaller central-western European countries such as Belgium or Switzerland.

To a certain extent, the process of industrialisation of the three north-western regions of Italy was conducted like that of an autonomous small country. Italy's political unity at the beginning of the twentieth century was still a very recent fact, which had not fully impinged upon the great differences of economic and social structure, mentality and customs which had grown up in the past. It is important, therefore, to emphasise that Italian dualism was not formed during the period of industrialisation—that period did not *create* differentiation in a previously homogeneous economic fabric, but merely intensified a profound differentiation that already existed. As an Italian economist, Saraceno, has said, administrative unification was not accompanied by a process of economic unification: the two Italys in fact continued to proceed separately along their earlier paths and each to maintain on its own account its prevailing economic relations with the rest of the world. This was especially true of the northern regions, where foreign trade, financial relations, and the exchange of entrepreneurial and technical experience with other countries had a strong influence on all economic activities, whereas relations with the southern regions remained extremely limited. This coincides remarkably with Kuznets' view that 'foreign trade has a greater importance in the economic activity of small nations than of large ones'. If we take into account the fact that the one great economic operation to include the whole of the national territory in the first fifty years of United Italy's history—the railways —was, as was mentioned earlier, of little importance for industry, we find further support for insisting on the analogy with the 'small country'.

Nevertheless the fact that the small industrial northern area formed part of a country of wider dimensions was not without influence on its own possibilities of development. In the first place, the level of public expenditure capable of providing an impulse to industrial production, especially of a military nature, was certainly higher than would have been possible for a small country. In the second place, although the basic domestic market for manufactured consumer goods was situated in the wealthier regions, the urban centres, at least, in the rest of Italy undoubtedly provided an appreciable share of that market. These factors may perhaps not be considered decisive. But there is a third factor that must not be under-estimated: the balance of the foreign accounts, within the framework of which, as has been seen, the effort for industrialisation of the new country's early years developed, received a decisive contribution from emigrants' remittances, and the majority of those emigrants were poor peasants from the southern regions. Thus one of the characteristic features of Italian dualism—the extreme poverty of the South— played a part as an organic component in the structure of the development process that went on between 1896 and 1913.

BIBLIOGRAPHY

The most important data are to be found in Istituto Centrale Di Statistica (ISTAT), *Sommario di statistiche storiche italiane 1861-1955*, Rome, 1958. A later edition (*Sommario di statistiche storiche dell'Italia 1861–1965*, Rome 1958) summarises the data for the period 1861–1920 in ten-yearly averages, and is therefore less useful to the historian. An official reconstruction of the historical progress of the national income and its components is given in ISTAT, 'Indagine statistica sullo sviluppo del reddito nazionale dell'Italia dal 1861–1956', in *Annali di statistica*, 1957, series VIII, vol. 9. This reconstruction has been critically reviewed and subjected to rectification by G. Fuà, *Notes on Italian Ecomomic Growth 1861–1964*, Milan, Giuffrè, 1965, who summarises the results of a team inquiry conducted on behalf of the Social Science Research Council of New York with a contribution from the Ford Foundation. This inquiry is now in course of publication (*Lo sviluppo economico in Italia. Storia dell'economia italiana negli ultimi cento anni*, edited by G. Fuà, Milan, Franco Angeli). For the historical development of industrial production, see A. Gerschenkron, *Economic Backwardness in Historical Perspective*, Cambridge, Mass., 1962, which gives a critical consideration of earlier writings on the subject.

A full history of Italy's economy after the Unification was begun by a historian of great experience, Gino Luzzatto, but he died before being able to complete it. Only the first volume has been published, *L'Economia italiana dal 1861 al 1914* (vol. I—1861–1894), Milan, Banca Commerciale Italiana, 1963. A general history is Shepherd B. Clough's *The Economic History of Italy*, Columbia University Press, 1964. A still irreplaceable work is E. Corbino, *Annali della economia italiana (1861–1915)*, 5 vols., Città di Castello, 1931–1938, which gives a full history of economic events and, more especially, of economic policy.

There are several general histories of Italian industry. The latest is by B. Caizzi, *Storia dell'industria italiana dal*

XVIII secolo ai nostri giorni, Milan, UTET, 1965, especially useful for the period before the political unification of 1861.

A brief outline which can form the basis for further reading is R. Romeo's *Breve storia della grande industria in Italia*, Bologna, 1963 (2nd edition, enlarged). Still useful for its definition of the outstanding characteristics of the industrialisation process is the first attempt at a general history in this field, R. Morandi's *Storia della grande industria in Italia*, Bari, Laterza, 1931 (frequently republished in recent years by Einaudi, Turin). Full and detailed information about the individual industrial concerns is given in A. Fossati, *Lavoro e produzione in Italia dalla metà del secolo XVIII alla seconda guerra mondiale*, Turin, Giappichelli, 1951. Useful works are the two volumes edited by the Confederazione Generale Dell'Industria Italiana, *L'industria italiana*, Rome, 1929, and *L'industria italiana alla metà del secolo XX*, Rome, 1953, which contain much historical information about various branches of industry including the less important ones. A work that can be regarded as a prelude to these volumes is the full survey done by a scholar of industrial problems during the First World War, P. Lanino, *La nuova Italia industriale*, Rome, L'italiana, 1916–1917, 4 vols.

A. Caracciolo (ed.), *La formazione dell'Italia industriale*, Bari, Laterza, 1969 (new edition), brings together some of the most recent critical contributions on the history of economic development and the formation of modern industry in Italy (Spaventa, Gerschenkron, Romeo, Dal Pane, Fenoaltea, Cafagna, Eckaus, Tosi, Zangheri). For a fuller range of Italian discussion of these problems see also E. Serni, *Capitalismo e mercato nazionale in Italia*, Rome, Editori Riuniti, 1966; R. Romeg, *Risorgimento e capitalismo*, Bari, Laterza, 1959; P. Saraceno, *L'Italia verso la piena occupazione*, Milan, Feltrinelli, 1963; M. Komani, 'L'unificazione economica', in *La formazione dello stato unitario*, Milan, Vita e Pensiero, 1963; G. Are, *Il problema dello sviluppo industriale nella età della Destra*, Pisa, Nistri-Lischi, 1965. Important contributions by various authors on particular aspects are to be found in *L'economia italiana dal 1861 al 1961*, Milan, Giuffrè, 1961 (Biblioteca della rivista *Economia e Storia*).

There are not many historical studies on the individual branches of industry. The textile industry has been the most fully covered, in the following volumes: R. Tremelloni, *L'industria tessile italiana. Come e sorta e come è oggi*, Turin, Einaudi, 1937; G. Quazza, *Industria laniera e cotoniera in Piemonte, 1831–1861*, Turin, Museo Nazionale del Risorgimento, 1961; V. Castronovo, *L'industria laniera in Piemonte nel secolo XIX*, Turin, ILTE, 1964, and *L'industria cotoniera Piemonte nel secolo XIX*, Turin, ILTE, 1965. Both the last two works are published in the important *Archivio Economico dell'Unificazione Italiana*, under the auspices of the IRI (Istituto per la Ricostruzione Italiana) and directed by C. M. Cipolla, which collects together numerous studies on particular aspects (prices, wages, production, foreign trade) and which was the first to initiate quantitative investigation of the period before Italy's political unification. For the iron and steel industry, still to be consulted is G. Scagnetti, *La siderurgia in Italia*, Rome, 1923. Few works exist about the engineering industry; among them see especially the recent volume by L. De Rosa, *Iniziativa e capitale straniero nell' industria metalmeccanica del Mezzogiorno, 1840–1904*, Naples, Giannini, 1968. A good geographical and historical study on an important agricultural-industrial product, sugar, is L. Gambi, 'Geografia delle piante da zucchero in Italia', in *Memorie di geografia economica*, 1955, A.VII, vol. XII.

A full selected bibliography including minor publications is G. Mori, 'La storia dell'industria italiana contemporanea nei saggi, nelle ricerche e nelle pubblicazioni giubilari di questa dopoguerra', in Istituto G. G. Feltrinelli, *Annali* 1959, a.II.

6. The Industrial Revolution in the Low Countries 1700-1914

Jan Dhondt and Marinette Bruwier

INTRODUCTION

The Low Countries, i.e. modern Belgium, Holland and Luxemburg, underwent profound political changes during the period 1750-1850. Originally they were made up of three distinct states: the Republic of the United Provinces corresponding to the modern Netherlands (31,000 sq. km.), the Southern or Austrian Provinces (28,000 sq. km.) and the principality of Liège (5,700 sq. km.). In 1797, the Austrian Provinces and the principality of Liège — under French occupation since the war against Austria — were officially annexed by France under the treaty of Campo Formio. Holland, too, fell under the influence of France, first as the Batavian Republic, and then as the Kingdom of Holland under Napoleon's brother Louis Bonaparte. From 1810 onwards it was increasingly treated as part of the French Empire.

After the collapse of the Empire, the whole area discussed here was formed into the Kingdom of the Netherlands, under the House of Orange. However this union proved unsatisfactory for economical as well as religious reasons. In 1830, the Southern Provinces seceded and Belgium became a separate kingdom.

Despite their ancient ties, the Northern and Southern Netherlands were always keen competitors, with the North concentrating on commerce and the South on industry. Thus at the time of the Industrial Revolution the North lacked both coal and iron — no really important industries were set up there before the middle of the nineteenth century. The South, on the other hand, was rich in coal and fairly well provided with iron, and, moreover, had an old industrial tradition, with the result that the Industrial Revolution took root there more quickly and more firmly than anywhere else on the Continent.

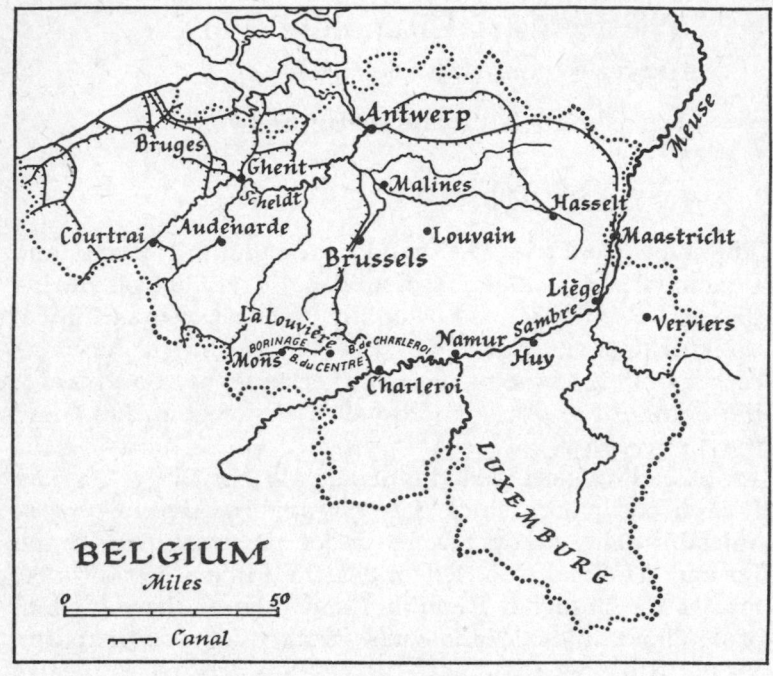

BELGIUM

Brussels and Antwerp, today the two largest Belgian cities, used to be of considerably lesser importance. To begin with they lacked industries — Antwerp at the lower end of the Scheldt estuary was primarily a port and a commercial centre. In the sixteenth century, when the North was split off from the South, Holland was given maritime control over the river Scheldt, which it closed completely under the treaty of Munster (1648). Antwerp now ceased to be a port and, relying on the immense capital accumulated during its period of great prosperity, turned itself into a leading financial centre. Then, towards the end of the eighteenth century when Antwerp was under French rule, the Scheldt was reopened, and the city expended all its vast energy on the redevelopment of the port. These are the reasons why the Industrial Revolution by-passed Antwerp.

Brussels, formerly an important textile centre, ceased to be an industrial city at the end of the Middle Ages. In the sixteenth century it became the capital of the Netherlands and as such a city of civil servants, of officials, and the luxury trade. In the nineteenth century the big financial houses, such as the Société Générale and the Bank of Belgium, naturally had their headquarters in the capital, and it was from here that they gained control over the most important industries, and especially over coal and iron. Thus the capital, by the end of the Industrial Revolution and through the activities of its great financial houses, had come to dominate industry without having any industry of its own.

COAL AND IRON

Rich coal seams running from Northern France to the Ruhr cross Belgium from west to east. With the exception of the Limburg seams which were not exploited until the twentieth century, the Belgian coal-producing area is completely confined to the Walloon (French-speaking) part and has largely moulded its economic development. There are four traditional coal 'basins', namely: the Borinage or 'Couchant de Mons' in Western Hainaut; Charleroi, in Eastern Hainaut; the 'Centre', between the Borinage and Charleroi; and Liège Province. These basins yield iron as well as coal, the ferrous deposits being not far from the coalfields. Until 1860, Belgium was self-sufficient as far as iron for her industries was concerned.

Coal and iron were two crucial factors in the development of heavy industry during the time of the Industrial Revolution, though not the only ones. Motive power was another. The Walloon area was fortunate in this respect as well — its sharp contours, especially in the east from Charleroi to Luxemburg, are crossed by swiftly flowing streams which provided the power for a host of water mills.

Rivers, of course, not only supply power, but also serve as important means of communication and transport, and at no time was this more true than at the beginning of the

Industrial Revolution. Belgium is crossed from south to north by two rivers: the Scheldt in the west and the Meuse in the east, each constituting a major axis that divides Belgium into two large sectors (perpendicular to the political division of the country) — the Flemish North and the Walloon South — with the Meuse basin and its tributaries forming one unit of communications and the Scheldt basin another. Hainaut is part of both, the Charleroi district being dependent on the Meuse and the Borinage on the Scheldt. The result was that the two regions had quite separate economic contacts and outlets. A related problem was that of East-West communications, which in turn was connected to the problem of the economic relations with the Brussels-Antwerp axis, i.e. the (financial) capital and the chief port. Traditions played their part, too, with different skills and economic activities being deployed or developed by the leading families of the different regions. We shall be returning to this point; in the meantime, we shall merely point out that the Borinage and Liège have the oldest coal-mining industries in Europe — going back to the thirteenth century, while the metal industries are traditional to the Meuse basin, where their roots go back into prehistory. In more recent times nail manufacturing was widespread throughout the region, while Luxemburg and the Sambre and Meuse valleys produced a great deal of pig iron by charcoal refining.

COAL

What was the impact of the Industrial Revolution on this area? It seems that there were two distinct pressure points: coal in the west, and the metal industry in the east. And curiously enough, the impetus in the latter did not come from within the industry, but from developments in textiles.

MINE PUMPS

Between the coal seams of the east (Liège) and the west (Borinage) there was a difference that proved to be important: while the pumping out of water posed few problems in the east, where the water could be drained from the mines into the lower-lying valleys through simple pipes, the Borinage was not nearly so fortunate. This explains why Liège Province, despite an ancient tradition of metalworking and despite the fact that some of the first Newcomen engines on the Continent were constructed in and exported from the Province in 1720, used no more than four Newcomen engines itself in 1760, a figure which rose only to ten in 1812. In the Borinage, by contrast, the use of Newcomen engines developed rapidly. The first appeared at Paturages in about 1737, but was quickly discarded when that particular model proved to be unworkable. After this, however, the use of this type of engine spread quickly throughout the entire region. In Charleroi the steam engine appeared even earlier (1727, at Lodelinsart) but its use spread much more slowly (a total of 13 during the years 1725-1815).

The Watt engine, too, made very slow headway. A single-acting model was set up in 1785 at Jemappes, but maintenance proved so difficult that, in 1818, it was replaced by a Newcomen pump. In 1838 more than 90% of all pumps in the Borinage were still of the Newcomen type. At about this time, however, the older types of 'fire-pump' began to be replaced with new engines developed by local specialists.

As regards Liège, it was not until 1820-30 that the use of the steam engine really began to spread. In 1839, 31 steam engines producing between them 3,223 h.p. were used for pumping water, in addition to the five hand pumps and 63 underground drainage systems in existence. The steam engines were mostly of the Watt type, though still based on the reciprocating and not on the rotary principle. It was only towards the middle of the century that this model was replaced by the direct-acting engine.

COAL MINING

So much for pumping. As far as coal mining itself was con-

cerned, steam engines first appeared in the Borinage under
French rule. Even then they numbered no more than three
or four altogether, mostly constructed by Perier in Paris.
They became more common from 1814 onwards, when the
Boulton-Watt system was increasingly adopted (nine models
were in use in the Borinage by 1823). There was disagree-
ment as to the value of the Edwards system.

The years 1820-30 brought a flood of steam-driven coal-
winding machines: by 1829, 82 pits in the Borinage were
using steam and only 55 were worked by horse power.

In the Charleroi region the process of transformation, in
coal-winding as it was soon to be in pumping, was more
gradual: eight steam engines for 128 pits in 1830, roughly
one new engine per year from 1830 to 1835, then a rush:
five in 1836, another five in 1837, and seventeen in 1838, by
which time a total of 48 engines was in use. Hand-winches
— there were still 91 of them — were no longer used for
work at any great depth. For all that, 59 winding-engines
were still worked by horses.

The spread of steam engines in the Liège coal-mining
industry was slower still — in 1812 the total number of
steam engines used for water pumping and coal-winding
was only twelve. In 1810, the first steam engine, a Watt-
Perier, for winding-up coal, was erected by Orban. By 1815,
Cockerill was building double-acting Watt rotary engines,
working first at low pressure and then at medium and high
pressures. From 1820 on, these techniques began to spread
through the Liège region which, by 1839, was using 59
steam engines in coal-mining, producing a total of 1,303 h.p.
Twenty-nine hand-winches and five horse-driven winches
also continued to be used.

FINANCE

The introduction of steam engines for pumping and coal-
winding raised a host of new problems, chief among them
the technical and financial organisation of what had become
exceedingly large industrial enterprises. Formerly most Belgian coal fields from Liège to the Borinage were worked

co-operatively by the miners, but this was only possible while mining operations were confined to the surface or very shallow depths. By 1700, in the Borinage at any rate, the average depth of the shafts was 70 metres, and there were cases of mines 167 metres in depth. No wonder therefore that, in the eighteenth century, the social nature of mining operations became radically changed. Henceforth they were increasingly run under the direction of nobles, high officials, and above all, coal merchants from the towns — some of whom were French or of French origin. In the Charleroi region they included iron masters interested in procuring a regular supply of coal. These new groups obtained mining concessions from the local landowners, often in perpetuity.

The new associates introduced new equipment, and began to combine their several concessions in order to rationalise the work. This trend was given a great impetus when Belgium was annexed by France: by French law the state alone had the right to grant concessions, and the state favoured large associations. One result was the introduction of new machinery; another was a marked increase in production.

PRODUCTION AND MARKETS

In the Borinage, production rose from some tens of thousands of tons in the middle of the eighteenth century to 750,000 tons in 1806 and to approximately two million tons in 1846. At that time, the Centre was producing 600,000 tons, Charleroi 1,200,000 tons and Liège 1,300,000. The Liège figure was four times what it had been in 1812; the Charleroi figure doubled between 1835 and 1841. Productivity also increased: in the Borinage, where it took 92 men and 19 horses to produce 100 tons of coal in 1820, 40 men and three horses did the same job just six years later.

In Liège the annual production per worker increased from about 55 tons in 1812, to 85 tons in 1835 and to 95 tons in 1847. At the same time shafts were sunk deeper and deeper. In the Borinage, the average working depth in about 1700 was 70 metres; the lowest recorded depth was 167 metres. In 1829 the *average* was 167 metres and the lowest depth 297 metres. In Liège, again, the average depth was 100 metres in the eighteenth century; in 1839 the corresponding figure was 151 metres, and the lowest depth was 510 metres.

How did the newly-won coal reach its markets?

The Borinage is situated on the Haine, a tributary of the Scheldt, and it was along these two rivers that coal first left the Borinage mines, chiefly for Flanders and Northern France. When a new road system was constructed in the eighteenth century (Mons-Brussels; Mons-Ath; Mons-Valenciennes) it became possible to carry coal to the entire western half of the Austrian Netherlands. The owners of the Borinage mines, who had a powerful voice in the Hainaut Provincial Estates, were able, for a time, to sabotage the construction of a similar road system between the Centre and Brussels.

However, the Borinage itself found its mining outlets blocked by political developments; in particular, as France spread northwards, the coal routes even into the rest of Belgium crossed the frontiers several times, with all the problems that entailed.

There were other obstacles as well, chief among them competition for the North French market from the Anzin mines, and for Flanders from the English. Even in the lime kilns of Tournai (Hainaut Province), Belgian coal was ousted by foreign imports.

These obstacles were, however, removed by the French annexation of the Low Countries and the continental blockade. New canals were built (Mons-Condé; Pomeroeul-Antoing), and while local glass works and forges created an increased home demand for coal, so the French needs grew as well. From about 1800 to 1835, the Borinage remained France's chief coal supplier (even when Belgium and France were separate), accounting for 75% of all French consumption and edging out English coal from Flanders. Borinage coal even reached as far as the French Departement du Nord and the Pas de Calais. Under the name of *flénu*, Borinage coal was highly prized in Paris and Rouen, particularly by the gas-works.

In the Borinage itself, however, there was no industrial outlet for local coal. Much the same was true of the 'Centre' where the position was, if anything, worse, for lack of suitable roads. This situation was remedied by the construction of a highway to Brussels and of a canal from Charleroi to Brussels. As a result, the 'Centre' became the major supplier of coal for Brussels and central Belgium. In any case, the growth of the glass and metal industries in the early nineteenth century created a considerable local demand for coal.

Charleroi, as well as being very close to Mons, lies on the Sambre and is therefore part of the Meuse river system. However, the French frontier is nearby and this presented an obstacle to the free flow of coal. Moreover, the Sambre and Meuse valleys with their forges and great demand for coal belonged to the Principality of Liège before the French Revolution, and this posed further customs problems. For that very reason Charleroi had to seek an outlet to the North, which it obtained by the construction of a road to Brussels.

At the beginning of the nineteenth century an east-west road (Mons-Binche-Charleroi) was opened to link Charleroi with the Scheldt, and so gave access to the markets of Northern France. In addition a canal was built linking Charleroi with Brussels and Antwerp. Navigation on the Sambre was improved which facilitated access to Paris via Oise. At the same time, a powerful metal and glass industry developed in Charleroi (as in the 'Centre') with an increase in local consumption of coal.

Turning now to Liège, we find that Liège soft coal was ideal for the manufacture of coke, and since Liège lies on a large river linking France to Holland, there were no transportation problems here. For all that, coal consumption was chiefly local. This situation became even more marked by the development of a big metal industry in the area.

On the whole, the technical and commercial aspect of

coal-mining varied from region to region. The true coal belt is in the Borinage, and it was here that the new methods (especially 'fire-pumps') could be used very early and on a large scale, thanks to the financial support of local coal merchants. It was in the Borinage that a marked increase in coal production could be observed as early as the second half of the eighteenth century, and it was the Borinage that ear-marked the greater part of its coal production for distant markets.

The other three coal-mining areas developed at a different rate. Here progress was intimately linked to the expansion of the metal industry, and as the latter was late to enter the Industrial Revolution, so coal mining lagged behind the Borinage as well.

It should also be noted that, as early as about 1835, the Borinage coal industry fell more completely under the control of the big Brussels banks than did the rest.

IRON

Two parts of modern Belgium had an iron industry that went back to well before the end of the eighteenth century. These were Liège and Charleroi which, as a result of the Industrial Revolution, became the two great modern centres of the Belgian metal industry. (The 'Centre' became one too, but only after 1850.) This does not mean that there was a direct link between the old and the new industry, nor that the two areas developed in identical ways.

In Liège, the old metal industry was located in the nearby Ardennes, some 25 miles outside the city, where swiftly-flowing rivers provided the motive power needed. Cast iron was produced with charcoal as fuel and was hammered into a solid bloom of malleable metal. Gradually the works moved closer to the city and specialised in the manufacture of guns and cannonballs. Then came a third phase, immediately prior to the Industrial Revolution: local cast-iron production ground almost completely to a halt; as the finished product was increasingly imported from Luxemburg, and the Sambre and Meuse valleys. In Liège, the imported cast iron was cut into rods for the manufacture of nails, or beaten into sheets. Both industries declined during the eighteenth century and their decline was not even halted by the construction of steam engines. Here, as elsewhere, vain efforts were made to use soft coal as a reducing agent.

CHARLEROI

Charleroi, like Liège, was not originally the centre of the iron industry which was concentrated in the nearby Sambre and Meuse valleys. There were few blast furnaces but many forges, foundries and plate works in which the use of coal was already widespread in the eighteenth century. As a result these factories moved progressively nearer the coal deposits around Charleroi, where a nail industry had been established for a very long time. In 1783, Charleroi had a horse-powered foundry. In about 1803-4 the English method was first used: that is, new forge-bellows, allowing an increase in the height of the furnaces. In 1807 Paul Huart-Chapel, one of the great names in the Belgian Industrial Revolution, invented a reverberatory furnace for melting down scrap iron. In 1812, Georges Gautier-Puissant, a French officer resident in Charleroi, built a modern rolling-mill at Acoz, but no one else in the region followed his example. In the Liège region, on the other hand, cylindrical rolling-mills rapidly replaced the foundries closed by the ruin of the nail industry. Twenty-five such mills were installed between 1800 and 1815, most of them small enterprises built by the owners of the old foundries as replacements, and like the latter powered by water.

A modern metal industry developed in the Charleroi region side by side with the old, under the impetus of several pioneers and with relatively few technical contributions from outside. In the Liège region, by contrast, there was a clear break between the old and the new manufacturers. Here the Industrial Revolution led to concentration on a single product: spinning machines for the wool industry in

Verviers. James Cockerill, an Englishman, played the principal role in this development.

In the Charleroi region the most important names were Paul Huart-Chapel (born 1770) and François Isidore Dupont (born 1784). Special mention must also be made of the technical expertise and advice of Thomas Bonehill (1796-1858), who arrived from Britain in 1824.

Huart-Chapel, who founded and managed several metal factories, was principally an inventor. His reverberatory mill, built in 1808, has already been mentioned. In 1821 he set up a puddling furnace to convert pig into wrought iron. In 1822-23 he established at Marcinelle-aux-Hauchis a factory comprising several puddling furnaces, a foundry and a hammer driven by a 30 h.p. steam engine (Boulton and Watt system). He developed the process of coal-smelting, and in 1824 was given leave to build the first coke blast furnace in the Charleroi area. It was fired in 1827. In 1822, Huart-Chapel had received a large government subsidy (44,000 florins) and he was, moreover, backed by Fontaine Spitaels of Mons, a banker who had made his fortune out of Borinage coal. Huart-Chapel himself married the daughter of an important local iron master, and his brother-in-law was his chief associate.

François Isidore Dupont was the son of a peasant. An enthusiastic mechanic, he constructed a windmill when he was still a boy. Later, he built up a fortune from the nail business and in 1809 opened a traditional forge at Feluy. In 1821 he substituted a factory with rolling mills, an English furnace and a high pressure steam engine (Wolff system). In 1829 he decided to build a coke blast furnace — another had been installed a year earlier at the Hourpes factory, which had been using steam engines since 1820, as well as smelting iron ore. This factory, the most important during the Dutch period, was too far from the coal mines and hence ran into trouble. Bonehill probably assisted in its development. He was certainly technical adviser to Baron de Cartier d'Yves of Bouffioulx, and to Ferdinand Puissant, members of two old iron 'dynasties' who decided to modernise their factories in 1826. Another, Hoyoux, improved his rolling mill at Acoz by the addition of a blast furnace capable of running on coke or wood, six reverberatory mills and a puddling furnace. That year, Baron de Cartier started to convert his old plateworks at Bouffioulx into a blast furnace using coke or wood. Ferdinand Puissant, with the help of Bonehill, set up new factories at Marchienne au Pont.

Two other large concerns were also established in 1829: one at Couillet where Fontaine Spitaels' 'House of Commerce' set up four blast furnaces and two hundred coke furnaces; the other at Chatelineau built by Leon Willmar and his brother Pierre who was an officer in the engineers. The Willmar company had links with John Cockerill (brother of James) and with Gustave Pastor, particularly through the iron-mining concession at Chatelet.

These two companies were rapidly absorbed into larger ones but it is interesting to note the original breadth of vision of their founders, at a time when the superiority of coke blast furnaces was by no means generally recognised. Thus during the industrial building boom of 1829-1830, de Cartier and Edmond Puissant still set up one charcoal furnace each at Couillet and Goegnies respectively. Moreover, even the owners of the blast furnaces in Monceau-Imbrechies near Chimay, in the heart of the traditional metal industry, employed a number of British technicians — Roger of London, Bridger and Waller of Canterbury, and Thomas of Dublin — to build a furnace that could run on charcoal or coal according to choice in order to produce different qualities of cast iron. In the event, this particular furnace was barely used, but the mere fact that it was built in the first place is clear proof of the vitality of the old methods. In 1831, five of the nine blast furnaces in the region had to be closed for lack of custom. The refineries were not so badly hit by the slump, and in 1833 10,515,000 kg. of cast iron was produced either by coke or by charcoal, the first type at a lower price.

LIMITED COMPANIES

More than anything else it was the emergence of limited companies that made possible the rise of powerful industrial groups in the Charleroi Basin. François Isidore Dupont (died 1838), his son Emile (died 1875) and the de Dorlodots of Acoz were among the few to succeed in financing really modern concerns by private means.

Local industrialists began early on to band together into companies. In 1829, Huart-Chapel, with the help of Montois Fontaine-Spitaels, the bankers and themselves owners of blast furnaces, founded the first big company in the area. In 1835, at the initiative of the *Société de Commerce*, a branch of the Brussels *Société Générale*, this company became a limited company known as *Société Anonyme hauts Fourneaux, usines et charbonnage de Marcinelle et Couillet*. Its interests included blast furnaces, rolling mills, workshops and iron and coal mines. By 1841 this large combine with its eight blast furnaces was one of the most important European iron producers. This was just one example, the first of many. Although some large concerns remained in the hands of their founders, from 1836 most metallurgical concerns in Charleroi passed into the control of the large Brussels banks, chief among them the *Société Générale* which advanced the necessary cash against a controlling interest.

What was the yield from these enterprises? For the blast furnaces of Couillet, Richtenberger, the Brussels agent of James de Rothschild, mentioned the figures of 10% in 1838 and 14% in 1846.

How far were the shares really open to public subscription? Their nominal value was at least 500 francs, often 1000 francs and in some cases, 10,000 francs. Such limited companies as *La Providence*, Hourpes, which comprised several collieries, started with ten or even twenty shareholders, but as late as 1841, when the *Société des Laminoirs et usines de Zône* was liquidated, most of the 27 shareholders mentioned by name were men intimately associated with the economic life of the region. Similarly, most of the newly-formed companies were run by the same bankers from Mons and Charleroi, the same old-established iron masters, glass makers, coal-mine owners and people with such names as Huart-Chapel, Champiaux-Chapel, the Puissants, Drion, Houtart, de Dorlodot, Endebien.

THE RISE IN PRODUCTION

The year 1835, which saw the formation of the first limited company, also saw a pronounced changeover to coke blast furnaces. Although only nine of the existing fourteen blast furnaces were working, the Chamber of Commerce announced plans for the opening of a further fifteen. Certainly many of them remained inactive during these years of change, but there was a marked rise in unit production: one blast furnace increased its output from 10 to 18 tons of cast iron of equal quality, or to 20-22 tons of slightly lower quality. For the whole region the production of cast iron increased from 31,436 tons in 1835 to 52,628 tons in 1840, 60,085 tons in 1845, and 118,575 tons in 1847, i.e. on the eve of the 1848 crisis and during the period of maximum expansion.

While charcoal furnaces still provided 6,300 tons of cast iron in 1836, this figure fell to 1,407 tons in 1845 but rose again slightly to 3,297 in 1847. By 1851, the last such furnace had closed down in Hainaut. In 1847, the total production was 9,112 tons of cast iron, 32,637 tons of malleable iron, and 2,034 tons of hammered ironwork and rod-iron.

LIÈGE AND VERVIERS

At Liège, the course of development was rather different. Several miles to the north of that city lay Verviers, an important centre of the woollen industry. This industry was organised in workshops, each with several dozen workers engaged on such tasks as scouring, washing, teazing, carding, fulling, napping, cropping, dyeing, etc. Spinning and weaving, however, were done at home by highly skilled craftsmen.

As the eighteenth century drew to a close, the industry at Verviers became very adventurous technically, and adopted a host of improvements in different spheres of cloth preparation and finishing. One of the chief innovations, no doubt, was the introduction of the new teazer or willey, which served to open and clean wool before scribbling and carding. But the turning point came in 1799 with the arrival of William Cockerill (1759-1832, father of John and James), an English expert on the latest spinning techniques. With the help of a local manufacturer, J. F. Simonis, Cockerill opened a workshop for the construction of spinning machines. Simonis, for his part, was to be the sole user of these machines, an arrangement that would have restricted Cockerill's output. He accordingly encouraged his son-in-law, J. Hodson, another English mechanic, to start a workshop of his own. As a result, most cloth factories in Verviers were able to equip themselves with the latest in spinning machines. James Cockerill, himself, was finally released from his obligations by his initial backers.

There was a strong and natural tendency for firms to combine into larger units; thus while there were 150 independent firms in 1789, that figure had shrunk to 50 by 1850. The firms of Biolley and Simonis, which were the first to be interested in Cockerill's inventions, became by far the biggest in the area during the course of the nineteenth century, accounting for about a third of the entire cloth production. In conclusion it should be said that the modernisation of the cloth industry was at first limited to spinning alone.

THE GROWTH OF IRON PRODUCTION IN LIÈGE

The success of Cockerill and Hodson encouraged many others; in less than twenty years, ten new carding factories and twenty machine building shops were set up near the textile centres of Verviers, Hodiment, Ensival, Spa, Eupen and also at Liège. The founders of these factories were not the old iron masters but textile merchants and mechanics. the latter led by William Cockerill, who, with the modest fortune he had made in Verviers, founded a metal factory at Liège which rapidly became the most important in the region—with 2000 workers it employed more than twice as many men as all the older metal factories put together. To begin with, however, Cockerill's financial resources were rather slender. He started his factory in 1807, and in 1809, when he tried to acquire a larger building, it took him nearly a year to get together the purchase price of some 50,000 francs. In 1809, he employed a mere 240 workers including 100 children, but by 1812 he was employing 2000 workers, and his annual turnover was some 2,500,000 francs. Cockerill was then concentrating almost exclusively on the building of machines. He was not yet using steam engines, and he was not active in other spheres. Meanwhile other metallurgical enterprises were opening up in Liège. Nicholas Delloye, born at Huy in 1755, who had invested heavily in *biens nationaux*[1] came to metal from the paper industry. By 1812, he had acquired six rolling mills and a large tin shop. In 1812, his production was worth 1½ million francs, compared with Cockerill's 2½ million. The third largest metal firm in the region was that of Depauw-Van Hasselt, an iron master from Limburg. It comprised one blast furnace and two rolling mills, and production in 1812 was worth 500,000 francs. But it was Cockerill's concern that took the first step on the road to industrial revolution. Thus, in 1813, it was the first to turn its attention towards the construction of steam engines (Watt system). However, the resulting technical revolution was not so much the work of the first generation: it was not William Cockerill, for example, who played the leading part in these changes but his son John, who, moreover, transferred the factory from Liège to Seraing in 1817. This was also the period when such important new names as Henri Joseph Orban (1779-1846) made themselves known. The son of a Luxemburg businessman and iron master, Orban was at first interested in the coal industry, and in fact was the first to use a steam engine to wind up coal in the Liège district

[1] Property, mostly ecclesiastical, confiscated and sold off by the French revolutionary government.

(1810). In 1821 he entered the metal industry when he bought up the firm of Depauw-Van Hasselt.

However, the reign of captains of industry in the Liège district was brief. Soon afterwards, high finance came to the fore (in Liège it was the Bank of Belgium, founded in 1835, rather than the *Société Générale*) and launched several limited companies that absorbed the chief concerns of the day. Between 1835 and 1837, four large companies were thus founded: Les Vennes, Saint Leonard, Charbonnages et Haut Fourneaux d'Ougrée, and Fabrique de Fer d'Ougrée, with a total registered capital of four million francs. In 1842, the Cockerills were in serious financial difficulties and their businesses, too, were turned into a limited company. All these companies — and there were many others set up at the same time — followed a trend that was characteristic of the Charleroi region as well: the formation of vertical trusts comprising coal mines, blast furnaces, foundries, rolling mills and engineering workshops. By about 1850, Cockerill's had become the largest of all, owning six of the eighteen blast furnaces in the province, employing 4,200 workers—a good third of the total labour force in the Liège metal industry. The reader may also be interested in the following technical details:

In 1845, the Liège metal industry used 37 steam engines. This figure increased to 98 in 1855 and to 123 in 1859. However the old-fashioned paddlewheel had not yet been completely discarded, and there were still 105 in use in 1845, 72 in 1855 and 71 in 1859. Coke blast furnaces appeared in Seraing in 1829 and in Grivegnée in 1835. There were five of them by 1837, fifteen in 1839. These furnaces had five times the output of charcoal furnaces, and helped to turn Liège into an important cast iron region which it was not in the eighteenth century. The oldest puddling furnace on record was installed by Orban in 1821, and there were 68 in 1850. The coke furnace was introduced by Cockerill in 1836 and so was the use of hot air in blast furnaces (1837). Orban built the first rolling mill to produce iron bars in 1837, and his example was immediately followed by Cockerill. De Cartier was the first manufacturer in Liège to use rolling-mill rolls; Francotte opened a wire works in 1838.

THE GHENT TEXTILE INDUSTRY

Flanders, formerly a leading woollen centre, turned its attention to linen at the beginning of the eighteenth century. The linen itself was produced in the countryside, and sold in the market towns of which Ghent was the most important. There the cloth was bought for export, chiefly to Spain whence it was mainly re-exported to Latin America. In the middle of the eighteenth century the same merchants began to show a keen interest in coloured, printed cottons. This was true not only in Ghent but in other large market towns as well as, for instance, in Antwerp; however, it was in Ghent that printed cottons were most widely manufactured, bought and sold. The work was not mechanised, but carried out in large workshops. The industry grew rapidly from about 1780 onwards, and this had a double effect on the cotton industry. To begin with the Ghent cotton printing passed out of the hands of general cloth merchants into those of specialised manufacturers. Secondly, these began to make vast profits, so much so that, at the turn of the century, the chief financiers and the majority of the founders of new mechanised enterprises were printed cotton manufacturers. The development of the printed cotton industry was briefly checked by political events at the end of the eighteenth century: the Belgian uprising against Austria; the war with France; and the annexation of the Netherlands by France. Ultimately, however, the industry profited from free access to the large French Empire.

For all that, it was not a printed cotton manufacturer but a local merchant who started the Industrial Revolution in Ghent. Lievin Bauwens came from a family of wine merchants and traders in colonial produce who were also important tanners. It was in the family tannery that Lievin Bauwens first introduced some of the new techniques he had learned in England. On one of his frequent visits to that country he must have conceived the plan of bringing to the Continent a complete spinning plant with mule jennies, steam engines and English workers. The project was implemented despite the grave problems resulting from the war between France and England, from the English ban on the 'export' of mechanical information, and from the Flemish peasant uprising against the French. Some machine parts were confiscated by English customs, which forced Bauwens to 're-invent' them. He did this with so much success that his machines won first prize at the Paris Industrial Exhibition of 1801. The Flemish uprising forced him to set up his first spinning mill at Passy, near Paris; in 1801 he established his second at Ghent, and in 1803 his third at Tronchiennes, near Ghent. These factories were equipped with mule jennies and were steam driven. At first, Bauwens' was the only machine shop to turn out mule jennies and this explains why they were fairly uncommon in Belgian spinning plants. Nevertheless there were quite a few continuous spinning machines, probably built in Rouen.

Soon afterwards, several other big spinning factories were opened as well, most of them steam-powered. At about the same time, steam was also being introduced into the Ghent paper and chemical industries. In 1806, 70,000 spindles were operating in Ghent (the 1808 yarn production was 472,000 kilos). All these factories were dependent on Bauwens for their machines, and he supplied them only to his relatives or to industrialists who had entered into special partnership agreements with him.

In 1803-1804, the Lousbergs, a family of leading industrialists, founded at Renaix, not far from Ghent, a combined spinning, weaving, and cotton-printing factory. The Lousbergs used power looms for weaving, and Bauwens jennies for spinning, together with continuous machines. But their enterprise foundered and no one else followed their example.

In 1806, conditions in the cotton industry were radically changed by the Continental Blockade. Unbleached cotton fabrics for printing and raw cotton for spinning disappeared from the market (which was, moreover, artificially boosted by speculative stock piling and disorganised by the arrival

of smuggled yarn from England). The result was a tremendous increase in small mechanised spinning concerns
run by speculators, so much so that the cloth needed for
printing was increasingly being manufactured in Belgium,
the weaving being done by home industries, helped by the
spread of the flying shuttle which Bauwens had introduced
several years earlier. Many spinning shops began to in-
corporate rural weaving establishments and sometimes did
their own printing. Bauwens was no longer the sole builder
of mule jennies; his business had become a vertical trust
comprising construction, spinning, weaving, colour printing
and bleaching establishments. All this took place in a highly
unstable economic setting, rent by numerous crises, of
which that of 1810-1811 was the most serious with numerous bankruptcies including the Lousbergs', and with
Bauwens crippled by debts. However, after each crisis production rose to new heights. Thus while 288,000 kg. of
thread was spun in the first quarter of 1810, the disaster
of 1811 was offset by an output of 273,000 kg. during the
second quarter of 1812. Towards the end of 1813, however,
political events — the end of the Napoleonic Empire and
of the Blockade, the union of Belgium and Holland, and
the free flow of English products — led to the collapse of
the Ghent cotton industry. Stagnation lasted until 1823.
From that date, and especially from 1825 onwards, the
Ghent cotton industry found a new outlet: the Dutch Indies
opened up by William I of the Netherlands, who, *inter alia*,
established a special company to buy Ghent cotton goods
and to sell them directly in the Dutch Indies. But the Ghent
cotton manufacturers did not wait passively for Dutch aid.
From 1819 onwards they made tremendous efforts at
technical modernisation. It was at this time that steam
power became predominant — during the French period
the cotton industry had used a mere half-dozen steam
engines. Between 1809 and 1819 no new ones were installed,
but in 1819-1820 alone, six new steam engines were brought
in and by 1830 there were fifty of them. Nor was this the
only development. In 1821 power looms began to appear,
some made in Ghent by English mechanics, some smuggled

in from England, but the majority soon afterwards constructed in Ghent itself by 'Phoenix', a firm that became famous throughout Europe. By 1840 cotton weaving was completely mechanised in Ghent. From 1830-1838 the number of power looms in Ghent increased from 700 to 2,900. This was not as much as could have been expected but Ghent was never more than a secondary centre of the weaving industry — here spinning predominated, with 283,000 spindles in 1830.

One word more about linen. As we have already stated, in the eighteenth century Flanders was a large centre for the rural linen industry, exporting cloth to Spain and South America. This commerce was severely disrupted by the Continental Blockade, with the result that the cotton trade gained the upper hand. However, the linen industry was so firmly implanted in Flanders, and moreover, had the advantage of being based on indigenous raw material, that several attempts were made to save it by mechanisation. But though Lievin Bauwens and several others tried from about 1800 onwards to develop mechanical methods of spinning flax, none of their attempts proved truly successful. In the end, it was decided to import flax-spinning machines from England. These machines were used to equip two huge factories — the 'Lys' and the 'Ghent' — founded in 1838. Each had 10,000 spindles, and they were run as limited companies with a capital of 4 million francs each, much of it subscribed by Brussels bankers. Although the latter were thus present at the very birth of the Belgian linen industry, it was not until decades later that they penetrated the old family cotton businesses and not until after the First World War that they controlled them.

SUMMARY AND CONCLUSION

The acceleration in the pace of the Industrial Revolution during the last three-quarters of the eighteenth century in the Southern Provinces and Liège was due to technical inventions, as well as to political developments. In particular, the Austrian government helped to protect local manufacturers against competition from England and Holland Financial factors were also involved; thus agricultural prosperity led to the accumulation of large capital sums. From at least the middle of the eighteenth century Flemish merchants, nobles and coal merchants proved most anxious to invest their capital in various sectors of industry, the more so as the population increase in the middle of the eighteenth century led to a great increase in demand. All this may be summed up as follows:

a) there was an increase in the number of mining companies in the Borinage and Charleroi, and a large number of merchants and rich nobles were attracted to the area;

b) the rise in Flanders of a centralised Flemish cotton printing industry caused the replacement in Ghent of the capitalist-at-large by the manufacturer;

c) there was a marked increase in production; the quantity of coal exported via the Haine river increased from 16,000 tons in 1764 to 100,000 tons at the end of the century;

d) exceptionally high profits were made in certain new industries, such as printed cotton and coal mining by means of steam pumps (Borinage and Charleroi).

All this went hand in hand with a new invention: Newcomen's 'fire' engine. It was put to wide use very early on: in 1721 in the Liège area, in 1725 in the Charleroi region, in 1734-40 in the Borinage. However its subsequent career was rather chequered: it took root very quickly in the Borinage (39 engines installed by 1790) and very slowly in the Liège region (less than 10 by 1812). Liège historians have attributed this to the difference between the contours of Liège (hills) and those of the Borinage (valley floors). This has certainly played some small part but it would seem that in the eighteenth century the Borinage was a hive of industry while Liège was not. Its metal industry also declined. In fact it was the use of the Newcomen engine (and not the Watt engine which was never popular in the Borinage as a pumping device) that was responsible for the difference. In particular, the introduction of the Newcomen engine led to the formation of large companies and made their owners even richer. During this period the metal industry was stagnating, and it was only in 1800-1815 that water-powered rolling mills were set up in the Liège and Charleroi regions. As for the production of cast iron, it continued to be based on antiquated methods throughout the eighteenth century.

The peak of the Belgian Industrial Revolution is often placed during the French period (1794-1814), and this is largely true for Ghent cotton and Verviers wool. In Ghent alone 70,000 spindles run on steam power were introduced within six to seven years. There were 283,000 spindles in operation in 1830. In Verviers mechanical wool spinning was introduced in about 1800, and grew apace although steam engines were still few and far between as late as 1840. At Ghent too it was only in about 1820 that steam engines were put to general use in industry. In the cotton, as in the wool industry, mechanical weaving techniques came very much later (in Ghent, as in Verviers the use of the flying shuttle spread only with the advent of mechanical spinning): in about 1830-1840 in the Ghent cotton industry, and in about 1860 in the Verviers wool industry. Mechanical linen spinning remained of minor importance until about 1838.

The French period was much less important for the coal and metal industries than it was for the textile industry. There were however three factors that encouraged growth: 1) French mining laws favoured large enterprises; 2) the market extended over the whole of the French Empire, and 3) the provisioning of the army created a large demand and produced a great deal of capital ready for new investments. For all that, the Belgian coal industry made little progress and though the metal giants of the next few decades — Cockerill, Huart-Chapel, and Orban — made some headway, they could show no spectacular gains — except for Cockerill who built spinning machines for the Verviers wool industry.

There is little doubt that, for the coal and iron industries, the years 1820-1830 were of decisive importance technically. Steam engines for winding up coal first made their appearance in about 1810 and became dominant in 1820-1830. The use of steam pumps spread even more rapidly. Productivity and production increased markedly (the Borinage increased its coal output from 750,000 tons in 1806 to 2 million tons in 1846). At about the same time, steam engines also conquered the Ghent textile industry.

But it was chiefly in the metal industry that the years 1820-1830 proved of paramount importance. From 1829 onwards, puddling furnaces and coke blast furnaces spread rapidly in the Liège area, and from 1824 in the Charleroi area, while steam engines were used throughout the industry.

Production of cast iron rose very steeply in the Charleroi basin (11,500 tons in 1833; 31,000 tons in 1835; 118,000 tons in 1847).

Let us now look briefly at the social and economic background and the outlook of the men who ushered in this revolution.

In the Ghent and Verviers textile industry they were largely the old capitalists, men who had grown rich in the pre-mechanical age. At Verviers it was the eighteenth century textile manufacturers who mechanised the wool industry; at Ghent the cotton printers. A generation later, however, things changed: while the woollen cloth manufacturers remained prominent at Verviers, in Ghent it was foreign technicians that made their mark in cotton printing. In coal and iron, however, the lead came mainly from bankers, coal merchants and local industrialists in the Borinage, and from the old iron masters and glass makers in Charleroi. In Liège, coal mining was developed partly by Verviers wool manufacturers and in a few cases by such simple workers as Henri Bury, but the real innovations, in coal no less than metal, were the work of skilled technicians and inventors, some with family connections in the metal world, but all with a love for technology. This was true of Paul Huart-Chapel and of Georges Gautier-Puissant, both of whom were related to old industrialists. François Isidore Dupont was an exception in that he was a son of a peasant.

At Liège, Cockerill, too, was a self-made man. The Delloyes, Orbans and Lamarches on the other hand, had family connections in the metal industry. As for the outlook of these new industrialists, all of them, as we said, had a keen desire for technical progress, often coupled with a personal taste for mechanics.

The Bauwens, the Lousbergs in the Ghent textile industry, the Huart-Chapels, the Duponts in the Charleroi metal industry, and finally the Cockerills, were of course real inventors, but all the other big industrialists between 1800 and 1840 we have mentioned (and many we have omitted), were all of them amateur innovators, to say the very least. Beyond that, they were all great visionaries, if anything too much so. The Bauwens and Lousbergs tasted failure. John Cockerill just scraped through. Many of the leading industries were taken over by the *Société Générale* or the Bank of Belgium, because they were ruined by debt, and this despite the highly profitable nature of the industrial activities in which they were engaged. Hence it is true to say that, although they were impressive builders of industrial empires, the men in charge were obviously bad administrators. They had yet another trait in common: they were not only advanced in their technical outlook but also in political ideas. Bauwens in Ghent, like Delloye at Huy, for instance, was a declared republican.

Where did they obtain the necessary funds? There were certainly many sources. There was, for example, the nobility which readily financed Ghent textiles; there were the big landowners and the 'rentiers', who often invested their capital through the banks. Finally there was the capital of the old, eighteenth-century commercial and industrial dynasties; the merchants of Ghent, the iron masters of Hainaut and Namur, and the wool merchants of Verviers.

In addition, the Industrial Revolution was financed through speculation in *beins nationaux* — most captains of industry at the time were large-scale investors — and through the vast profits that accrued from provisioning the Republican army. (The Bauwens, for instance, were among the foremost army suppliers.) Yet another source of finance was the big profit made during the period preceding the Industrial Revolution proper, when cotton printing and 'fire' engines in coal mining and other innovations yielded quick returns. The early story of James Cockerill is typical in this respect.

Moreover, the State intervened — sometimes on a large scale — under the French régime and then, more systematically, under the Dutch.

And then in the final phase of the Industrial Revolution the banks stepped in directly, and so did countless citizens who bought shares in the public companies formed with the support of the *Société Générale* and the Bank of Belgium. There was also foreign capital, supplied by the Rothschilds among others.

All this resulted in a complete transformation of the Belgian economy, so much so that by 1840, Belgium had become one of the foremost industrial nations on the Continent.

It was also in Belgium that the first and relatively densest railway network was inaugurated—soon after the plans for this network were published during the first days of national independence (1830). At about the same time, it was also decided that Belgium should have a strong free trade movement, which, in fact, became firmly entrenched after 1861.

THE NORTHERN NETHERLANDS

While the provinces making up present-day Belgium had been devoted to industry ever since the Middle Ages, the provinces of the present-day Netherlands had been traditionally given over to shipping and commerce. Thus, in 1803, it was calculated that Dutch manufacturing industries paid out no more than a million florins in wages each year. During the same period, the number of firms that really merited the title of 'industrial' was limited to a rifle factory with 140 workers at Culemborg (Kuilenburg); Voombergh's cloth business in Amsterdam (250 workers in 1805); a glass works at Leerdam with some 50 workers; and fourteen sugar-beet refineries (which appeared with the Continental

HOLLAND

Miles

0 — 50

⚊ Canal

Blockade and died again when it was lifted), several of which employed from 40 to 80 workers. And that was all — the naval dockyards of Dordrecht that formerly employed 120-150 now employed a mere dozen. Moreover the textile industry, which had flourished in the eighteenth century, was a predominantly rural affair, and as such completely decentralised. True, there were some textile shops employing up to 1,650 workers (the stocking factory in Amsterdam) but these were charitable concerns run by the municipality for philanthropic rather than economic ends.

Another indication of the extraordinary weakness of Dutch industry was the very belated and limited adoption of steam power: while the South installed a host of Newcomen and Watt engines in the early eighteenth century, the North contented itself with a small number of steam pumps (used in the polders from 1787), and the first steam engine to be used in industry was that installed in the Boon flour mill (Amsterdam) in 1797. A second was installed soon afterwards at Brill —but that was all.

In general, the eighteenth century, and especially the French period, was a time of economic decline in the North. The population of most of the towns declined spectacularly as well, since what 'industry' there was (except for textiles) was of course concentrated in urban areas. In economic changes, Holland lagged far behind the rest of Western Europe.

However, the French period had important political no less than economic repercussions on Dutch life. Thus a political evolution was begun in 1795 which led from the Batavian Republic to the Kingdom of Holland under Louis Napoleon, to annexation by the French in 1810, to independence under the House of Orange in 1813, and to union with present-day Belgium and Luxemburg from 1814 to 1830, when the Netherlands attained its present form. Holland did not regain her colonies until 1814, but the French period brought her unified institutions and a unified legal code, the abolition of internal customs and of the guild system, and a single and modernised fiscal system.

What was the situation in the different Dutch industries at the beginning of the Industrial Revolution?

Naturally enough, the rise of the Dutch metal industry paralleled that of the steamship, the first of which appeared in 1823 in Rotterdam. Soon afterwards a steam-engine repair shop was set up which later became a plant for the construction of steam engines (1825). In 1852 the 'Maatschappij voor Scheeps en Werktuigbouw Feyenoord' (today the Wilton Feyenoord Company of Schiedam) employed 650 workers. Similarly, Amsterdam witnessed the foundation of the Amsterdamse Stoomboot Maatschappij in 1825, the setting up in 1827 of a repair workshop which later became the Koninklijke Fabriek van Stoomwerktuigen, a factory for the manufacture of steam engines that is still in existence. In 1848 this factory employed some 800 workers.

Dutch metal-smelting works had a much older history — iron ore, wood and water power, were found together in Achterhoek, along the old Ijssel, and 'fire mills' first appeared in the seventeeth century. Foundries quickly sprang up nearby, producing stoves, pots, weights and other things. By 1850 further iron works had sprung up in Deventer, Keppel and other towns, employing some 65 to 145 workers each.

As for textiles, the old urban industry (wool at Haarlem, silk at Leyden) had practically disappeared, but a new rural industry had developed in Twente and in Northern Brabant, where local peasants did piece work for the town capitalists during the winter. This type of home industry spread across Holland in 1800-1825, and so did home brewing and tanning. In some of the smaller workshops the owner often worked side by side with his men.

In about 1819 the use of Hargreaves jennies and Crompton mules spread throughout Twente province. These were usually set up in special sheds where a dozen or so workers could tend them. At the same time, steam power was first introduced into the Dutch textile industry: in Leyden in 1818 in a weaving mill, in Eindhoven in 1820 in a weaving mill and cotton-spinning plant, in Tilburg in 1827 and in Almelo in 1830 in a cotton-spinning plant.

The revolution of 1830, by which Belgium and Holland were cut off from each other, had a number of industrial repercussions. Some Belgian firms, fearing exclusion from the East Indian market moved to the north. With the encouragement and financial support of the Dutch Government, the Belgian industrialist Wilson established a weaving, bleaching and cotton printing firm at Haarlem, which was the first entirely mechanised textile mill in Holland. Other Belgians followed his example, chief among them T.

Prévinaire, 'the father of the Dutch cotton industry', who set up shop in Haarlem in 1834 and quickly became the leading cotton manufacturer in Holland (with 600 workers as against Wilson's 381). In addition, Prévinaire employed 278 home weavers. His factory was equipped with a laboratory, by far the oldest in Holland, for the chemical study of colours, and his Andrinople red dye was famous. The Ghent cotton-spinning firm of Poelman-Fervaecke, with 677 workers in 1838, also moved to Haarlem, which thus became the Manchester of the Netherlands.

It was also as a result of the 1830 revolution and with the aim of replacing Belgian supplies to the Far East market, now closed to the Belgians, that a movement grew up in Twente and was to have spectacular social effects. At the urging of Thomas Ainsworth, an old colleague of Cockerill, it was decided to establish weaving schools in Twente where training could be given in the use of the flying shuttle. The results were remarkable—pauperism disappeared from Twente almost overnight. The first power looms were installed in 1846, and the first steam-powered loom in 1853. The factory system thus took root in the metal and textile industries first.

Special mention must also be made of Pierre Regout's factories in Maastricht. He, too, built his first shop in 1830, in the wake of the revolution, followed by a nail factory in 1834, a pottery in 1836 and cut glass factory in 1838, all of which were successful. In addition, he set up a less successful rifle factory and gas-works.

It should be added that diamond cutting and sugar refining were amongst the first Dutch enterprises to attain the size of modern industry; in the early nineteenth century, diamond cutting was still largely performed in small workshops, but in 1822 a factory was established in Amsterdam (where the whole diamond industry was concentrated) introducing first horse power and later steam power, which by then was already in wide use in sugar refining.

Not that there was a high degree of industrialisation in Holland in the first half of the nineteenth century. The number of steam engines in use in Holland in 1837 was 72 (producing a total of 1120 h.p.); by 1853 the figures had increased to 392 engines and 7193 h.p. respectively. Yet Belgium, in December 1838 could already boast 1049 engines producing a total of 25312 h.p.! In Holland, by contrast, it was not until about 1850 that industrial mechanisation really got under way.

In the textile industry, for example, six steam spinning machines were established in Twente during 1850-1861. This was a modest spurt, but the trend was temporarily checked by the American Civil War and the resulting cotton famine. For all that, there were 41,000 spindles in 1861, and 173,000 in 1873 with a marked concentration (7,500 per factory in 1894, 10,200 in 1872). By about 1860, hand spinning had almost totally disappeared.

As in so many other places, Twente introduced mechanised spinning well before mechanical weaving. The first experiments with power looms date from 1846 and power-weaving was started in 1853, and here, too, growth was most marked after 1860: there were 2,022 power looms in 10 factories in 1860 and 8,760 looms in 36 factories in 1870.

In 1848, the wool industry of Tilburg and the rest of Northern Brabant was still relatively unmechanised (a mere nine factories out of 58 had a steam engine) but by 1864, 32 out of 84 factories and by 1874 55 out of 142 factories, were steam-powered. This expansion was due to the development of flannel in 1851.

Helmond was the centre of the cotton industry of Northern Brabant, and here home industry reigned supreme until 1866, when a mere 214 workers were employed in factories and 2,400 worked at home. Between 1866 and 1876, home industry gradually ceded to factory work.

In the metal industry we find that steam first reached the Achterhoek foundries in about 1850. The use of iron for a host of new purposes (stoves for heating, rails, iron ships, replacement of copper utensils with iron ones, etc.) caused a considerable growth in the number of foundries (six in 1830, 50 in 1871). These employed between 15 and

50 workers each, and some were run as engineering work-shops.

A number of minor industries, too, may be counted among the fruits of the Industrial Revolution, particularly in so under-industrialised a country as Holland used to be. Thus the tobacco, footwear, sugar and starch industries advanced rapidly from handicraft to factory production. Again, while a single private firm with 200 workers produced gas for lighting purposes in 1825, by 1881 there were 31 municipal gas-works. During the same period, relatively large concerns appeared in other fields as well. Thus official statistics show that, in 1857, there were quite a number of master stonemasons employing 50 to 100 workers, glassworks with 40 to 60, a type foundry with 70 workers and a candle factory with 130. For all that, Dutch industry was very far from powerful even in the late nineteenth century. This becomes particularly clear when we look at the development of the railway. Thus while Holland had 170 km. of rails in 1850, Belgium had 861 km. The first Dutch railway link (Amsterdam-Haarlem) was opened in 1839, but other lines followed very slowly — the Dutch attached much more importance to waterways. Public credit, too, was slow to come to the aid of industry: public loans represented a total of 1,030 million florins in 1850, and the shares of commercial, industrial and banking companies 92 million florins. In 1856 the government still refused to approve the formation of limited liability companies — these were first authorised in 1863.

Except for the Dutch East Indies, where she maintained special privileges until 1850, Holland was an early champion of free trade, and in 1848, 1854 and again in 1862, enacted legislation to that effect despite strong protests from local industrialists. These measures remained in force until 1932.

BIBLIOGRAPHY

BELGIUM

Whereas the Dutch Industrial Revolution has recently been treated in a general study, no comparable work exists for Belgium. Hence a nineteenth-century text retains much of its value to this day.

Nathalis Briavoinne's *De l'industrie en Belgique, causes de décadence et de prospérité; la situation actuelle* (2 vols. 1839) is undoubtedly the most detailed work in print on the subject, and constitutes a mine of information. Briavoinne was a Frenchman, whose rather questionable activities forced him to seek refuge in Belgium in about 1830. He became a journalist, founded a Belgian press syndicate, and was the first to use the term 'industrial revolution'. Passionately interested in technology, he devoted several books (among which the one we have quoted is the most important) to the development of Belgian industry from the end of the eighteenth century to the 1830s. Though he wrote as a journalist, he collected a vast number of documents and, in particular, gathered data from his many business acquaintances. He was an extremely intelligent man with a keen grasp of reality. His main work reviews various industries one by one from a technical and commercial rather than financial point of view.

Among more recent studies, special mention must be made of R. Demoulin's *Guillaume Ier et la transformation économique des Provinces Belges, 1815-1830* (Liège 1938). A more recent article, J. Craeybeckx's *Les débuts de la révolution industrielle en Belgique et les statistiques de la fin de l'Empire* (Melanges G. Jacquemyns, Brussels 1968, pp. 115-144) deals more particularly with the preceding period. In addition, a Belgian team has recently begun to take an interest in the history of the industrial revolution in their country. This team includes P. Lebrun, E. Hélin, G. Hansotte, Mlle Bruwier and J. Dhondt. One of their earliest studies was 'La revoluzione industriale in Belgio, strutturazione et destrutturazione delle economie regionali', published in *Studi Storici*, II, 1961. Due to a printer's error, this work appeared under Lebrun's name alone, though it was, in fact, written by the whole team, which also hopes to publish a far more comprehensive study in the near future. The two members of the team responsible for the present short work would like to stress that as far as the Liège metal and coal industries are concerned, they have based themselves on unpublished texts by Hansotte and Hélin.

For publications dealing with specific regions or sectors of industry, the *Mémoires Statistiques* published by the local prefects during the reign of Napoleon and under the Empire merit special attention. These prefects were obliged to submit statistical tables or other local details of economic interest to their ministers. Such accounts became matters of routine and the results have been preserved in the Archives Nationales, Paris, Series F. In addition, most prefects also published at least one more detailed paper, and since most of these were written at a time (between 1800 and 1810) when the Industrial Revolution had barely begun, they are of the utmost importance. The most important for our subject are Thomassin's report on the Ourthe Département (published in 1879), Pérès' on the Sambre and Meuse Département (published in 1802), Garnier's on the Jemappes Département (first published in 1950 in the yearbooks of the Mons Archaeological Circle), and Faipoult's on the Escaut (Scheldt) Département (published in 1950 in the Proceedings of the Ghent Historical Society).

It was these and other papers that Minister Montalivet consulted when writing his *Exposé de la situation de l'Empire presenté au corps legislatif* (Paris 1813), a veritable statistical yearbook, giving detailed data for the various *départements* of the Empire, including modern Belgium (for critical evaluation, see Craeybeckx, *op. cit.*).

For the wool industry we have P. Lebrun's excellent *L'Industrie de la laine à Verviers pendant le 18e et la début du 19e siècle* (Liège 1948). For cotton, special mention must be made of J. Dhondt's 'L'industrie cotonnière grantoise à l'époque française' (*Revue d'histoire moderne et contemporaine,* 1955, pp. 233-279) and the many articles of Mme Coppejans-Desmet in the *Bulletin de la Commission Royale d'Histoire* (1960, 1962) and in the *Handelingen van de Maatschappij voor Geschiedenis van Gent* (1959, 1967, 1968).

Hainaut is dealt with in R. Darquenne's *Histoire économique du département de Jemappes* (Mons 1965), and in the following earlier works: G. Decamps' *Origine . . . industr. houillère . . . couchant de Mons* (Mem. Soc. Sci. Hainaut 1880 and 1889); G. Arnould's *Bassin houiller du couchant de Mons* (Mons 1877); J. Monhoyer's *Industrie houillère . . . Centre* (Mons 1873); A. Warzée's *Exposé . . . de l'industrie metallurgique dans le Hainault* (Mons 1861); and A. Toilliez's *Mémoire sur l'introduction des machines à vapeur* (Mons 1836). Mention must also be made of J. Plumet's 'La société du grand-conduit' (*Annales cercle archaeol. Mons* 1940); van den Eynde and Darquenne's 'Les débuts de la société de Mariement' (*Annales cercle archaeol. . . . La Louvière* 1966), and Revelard's 'La société de Haine St. Pierre' (*ibid* 1967).

For the metal industry (Hainaut and Liège), the reader is referred to A. Wibail: 'L'évolution économique de la sidérurgie belge de 1830 à 1913' (*Bull. Inst. Sci. Econ. Louvain* 1933, pp. 31-61); A. Warzée: 'Exposé historique de l'industrie du fer dans la province de Liège' (*Mem. Soc. Emulation Liège* 1860); A. Engelspach-Larivière: *Description du Luxembourg . . . richnesses minérales* (Brussels 1828); M. Deprez: 'Le mouvement des prix et des salaires dans la métallurgie namuroise au début du 19e siècle' (*Annales Soc. Archaeol. Namur* 1953). Metallurgy in Luxembourg is also the subject of a very important study, namely, M. Bourguignon's 'La sidérurgie, industrie commune des pays d'Entre Meuse et Rhin' (*Ancien Pays et Assemblées d'Etats,* Vol. 28, 1963). (The Luxemburg metal industry disappeared with the Industrial Revolution.)

For the Industrial Revolution in Liège, there exist numerous studies by Hansotte, a summary of which can be found in 'La révolution industrielle dans la métallurgie du bassin de Liège' (*Cahiers de Clio*, Brussels 1966).

For a history of Belgian banks — a subject that has been greatly neglected — the reader is referred to R. S. Chlepner: *La Banque en Belgique*, Vol. 1 (Brussels 1926), and more particularly to M. Lévy-Leboyer's recent *Les banques europeénnes et l'industrialisation internationale dans la première moitié du 19e siècle* (Paris 1964).

HOLLAND

We can be very brief·in dealing with Holland, and this for two reasons. To begin with the Industrial Revolution reached Holland fairly late in the day, and had a limited scope — there was an almost complete absence of heavy industry. Secondly, economic developments in Holland in 1795-1940 have been treated comprehensively in I. J. Brugman's excellent *Paardenkracht en Mensenmacht* (The Hague.1961) which has a 17-page bibliography, to which the reader is referred. In addition, the following works dealing with specific sectors, and most of them provided with good bibliographies, also deserve special mention: J. A. Boot, *De Twentsche Katoennijverheid 1830-73* (1935); A. J. Maenen, *Petrus Regout 1801-1878, een bijdrage tot de sociaal ekonomische geschiedenis van Maastricht* (1959); J. C. Westermann, *Grschiedenis van de ijzer en staalgieterij in Nederland* (1948); B. W. de Vries, *De nederlandse papiernijverheid in de 19e eeuw* (1957); and M. G. de Boer, *Leven en Bedrijf van Gerhard Moritz Roentgen* (1923).

An overall account of the industrial situation of Holland at the beginning of the nineteenth century can be found in Leonie van Nierop's 'Een enquète in 1800. Een bijdrage tot de ekonomische geschiedenis van de Bataafse Republiek' in *De Gids*, 1913 (especially pp. 304-322).

I. J. Brugmans has published statistical tables for the first half of the nineteenth century: 'Statistieken van de Nederlandse nijverheid uit de eerste helft van de 19e eeuw' (R. G. P. 2 vols. 1956). The 1850s are treated in 'Staat van de Nederlandsche fabrieken volgens de verslagen der gemeenten . . .' published by the Netherlands Society for the

Furtherance of Industry (Haarlem 1859), and the year 1871 in L. J. Brinkman's *Statistiek van de Fabrieks en Ambachtsnijverheid in Nederland* (1874).

It should finally be noted that important contributions to the history of Dutch industry can be found in a large number of commemorative publications issued on the anniversary of various industries or enterprises, no less than in the archives of some of the leading Dutch concerns.

Notes on the Authors

CLAUDE FOHLEN
was born in Mulhouse in France in 1922. He was Professor of History at the University of Besançon from 1955 to 1967, and since 1967 has been Professor at the Sorbonne. His publications include *L'industrie textile en France sous le Second Empire*, Paris, 1955; *L'Amerique anglo-saxonne*, Paris, 1965; *La France de l'Entre-deux-guerres*, Paris, 1966; and *Histoire du Travail*, Paris, 1960.

KNUT BORCHARDT
is Professor of Economic and Social History and Economics at the University of Munich and was formerly Dean of the Economics Department and Rector of the University of Mannheim. He is Editor of *Jahrbücher für Nationalökonomie und Statistik*, and among his publications are: *Europa – ein Modell für Entwicklungsländer?* (1967), and (with Stolper and Hauser) *Deutsche Wirtschaft seit 1870* (1964, 1966), English edition entitled *German Economy, 1870 to the Present* (Weidenfeld & Nicholson, 1967).

PHYLLIS DEANE
is a Lecturer in the Faculty of Economics and Politics and Fellow of Newnham College, Cambridge. Amongst her best known publications are *The First Industrial Revolution* (1965) and (with W. A. Cole) *British Economic Growth 1688–1959* (2nd ed. 1967).

N. T. GROSS
was born in Vienna in 1926 and has lived in Israel since 1939. He has an M.A. in Economics and History from the Hebrew University, Jerusalem, and a Ph.D. from the University of California at Berkeley. He is a Lecturer at the Hebrew University and in 1971/2 Visiting Lecturer at Harvard University. His publications include several articles

on the economic history of Austria in the nineteenth century and an introductory textbook on economics (in Hebrew).

LUCIANO CAFAGNA

was born in 1926. He was Assistant Professor at the Bocconi University of Milan and he researched at the Instituto G.G. Feltrinelli of Milan. He is presently Professor of Economic History at the University of Siena. He has published various papers on the problems of the Italian economic growth in the eighteenth and nineteenth centuries, including *La rivoluzione agraria in Lombardia, Origini del dualismo economico in Italia, L'industrializzazione italiana.* He also edited the anthology *Il Nord nella storia d'Italia.*

JAN DHONDT

was born in 1915 and studied at the University of Ghent where he obtained his Doctorate in 1938. In 1944 he became Professor of Modern History and was made Professor of Medieval History in 1962. From 1963 to 1966 he was Recteur (President) of the University of Lubumbashi in The Congo. He has published a number of books and articles on Carolingian history, the history of France and Flanders in the Middle Ages, and economic and social history of the nineteenth and twentieth centuries.

MARINETTE BRUWIER

was born in 1922 and studied at the University of Liège where she obtained her Doctorate in 1953. From 1948 to 1955 she was Assistant in Medieval History at Liège, and from 1958 to 1962 archivist and head of the historical service of the 'Credit Communal' Bank. She was Professor of Economic History at what became the 'Centre Universitaire du Hainaut' at Mons and was made a full professor in 1968. Her main publications have been on economic history of the middle ages and modern times, mostly of the Hainaut.